A BRITISH PROFESSION OF ARMS

CAMPAIGNS & COMMANDERS

GREGORY J. W. URWIN, SERIES EDITOR

A British Profession of Arms

The Politics of Command in the Late Victorian Army

Ian F. W. Beckett

University of Oklahoma Press | Norman

Library of Congress Cataloging-in-Publication Data

Name: Beckett, I. F. W. (Ian Frederick William), author.
Title: A British profession of arms : the politics of command in the late
    Victorian Army / Ian F. W. Beckett.
Description: Norman : University of Oklahoma Press, [2018] | Series:
    Campaigns and commanders ; volume 63 | Includes bibliographical references
    and index.
Identifiers: LCCN 2018010568 | ISBN 978-0-8061-6171-6 (hardcover : alk. paper)
Subjects: LCSH: Great Britain. Army—Officers—History. | Great Britain.
    Army—History. | Great Britain—Colonies—History, Military.
Classification: LCC UB415.G7 B43 2018 | DDC 355.3/3041094109034—dc23
LC record available at https://lccn.loc.gov/2018010568

A British Profession of Arms: The Politics of Command in the Late Victorian Army is Volume 63
in the Campaigns and Commanders series.

Interior layout and composition: Alcorn Publication Design

For
Rev. Arthur Taylor,
Head of History, Aylesbury Grammar School, 1962–92.
All aspiring historians should have such an inspiration.

Contents

Illustrations

Figures

Maps

Acknowledgments

Quotations from the Royal Archives appear by gracious permission of Her Majesty the Queen. Quotations from Crown copyright material in the National Archives appear by permission of Her Majesty's Stationery Office. I also wish to acknowledge my thanks to the following for their courtesy and kind permission in allowing me to consult and quote from archives in their possession and/or copyright: The Rt. Hon. the Earl of Dundonald, Viscount Gough, Earl Haig, Michael Maude Esq., Henry Parker Esq., Sir Richard Pole-Carew Bt., Sir Henry Rawlinson Bt., Earl St. Aldwyn, the Marquess of Salisbury; and the Hon. Mrs. Sue Tyser.

Similarly, thanks for allowing consultation and/or quotation from archives in their possession and/or copyright is due to the courtesy and kind permission of the Australian Defence Forces Academy Library; the Australian War Memorial; the Bodleian Library; the Trustees of the British Library; the Cadbury Research Library Special Collections of the University of Birmingham; the Syndics of Cambridge University Library; the Board of Trustees of the Chevening Estate; Cornwall County Record Office; Devon County Record Office; the David M. Rubenstein Rare Books and Manuscript Library of Duke University; Gloucestershire Archives; the Trustees of the Imperial War Museum; Kent History and Library Centre; the Campbell Collections (formerly the Killie Campbell Africana Library) of the University of KwaZulu-Natal; the KwaZulu-Natal Archives; the Trustees of the Liddell Hart Centre for Military Archives, King's College, London; Lincolnshire Archives; the Middle East Centre, St. Anthony's College, Oxford; the National Army Museum; the National Records of Scotland; the National Library of Ireland; the National Library of Scotland; the National Library of Wales; the National Trust; the National War Museum, Edinburgh; Queen Mary University Library; the Royal Artillery Museum; the Royal Engineers Museum; the Royal Pavilion Libraries and Museum (Hove Public Library); South Lanarkshire Council Museum; the Sudan Archive, Durham University; Suffolk Record Office; the Wellcome Library; Warwickshire County Record Office; and Wiltshire and Swindon Archives.

Particular thanks go to Pamela Clark, Allison Derrett, and Karen Lawson of the Royal Archives; Dr. Caroline Jackson; Dr. Alastair Massie of the National Army Museum; Emily-Ann Krige of the Campbell Collections; and Pam McFadden of Talana Museum.

This monograph has been a long time in its preparation and writing, and particular thanks are due to all the staff of the record repositories recorded above for their assistance over the years. In addition, I would like to thank the staff of the General Alfred M. Gray Marine Corps Research Center, USMC University, Quantico, Va., and the Templeman Library of the University of Kent for their help. I also owe a debt of gratitude to the many scholars who have been so generous with their time during my work on the late Victorian army, including Rodney Atwood, Stephen Badsey, Jeremy Black, Brian Bond, Tim Bowman, Christopher Brice, Steven Corvi, David French, Richard Goldsbrough, John Gooch, Ian Harvie, Tony Heathcote, Rob Johnson, Halik Kochanski, John Laband, Stephen Manning, Alastair Massie, Stephen Miller, Tim Moreman, Nick Perry, Gavin Rand, Edward Spiers, Peter Stanley, Roger Stearn, Hew Strachan, Keith Surridge, Bruce Vandervort, André Wessels, and Craig Wilcox.

I must also thank Professor Gregory Urwin of Temple University for accepting this volume for his series, and both Chuck Rankin and Adam Kane of the University of Oklahoma Press for their patience. Two anonymous reviewers made valuable suggestions. Thanks also go to Bob Fullilove for his expert copyediting and to Erin Greb for the maps.

Of course, none of the above can be held responsible for any errors of fact or interpretation on my part.

Abbreviations and Acronyms

AAG	assistant adjutant general
ADC	aide de camp
AG	adjutant general
AMS	assistant military secretary
AQMG	assistant quartermaster general
ASC	Army Service Corps
CB	Companion of the Order of the Bath
CGS	Chief of the General Staff
CIE	Companion of the Order of the Indian Empire
CIGS	Chief of the Imperial General Staff
CinC	commander in chief
CMG	Companion of the Order of St. Michael and St. George
CO	Colonial Office
CoS	chief of staff
CRA	commander, Royal Artillery
CRE	commander, Royal Engineers
CSI	Companion of the Order of the Star of India
DAAG	deputy assistant adjutant general
DAG	deputy adjutant general
DAGRA	deputy adjutant general, Royal Artillery
DAGRE	deputy adjutant general, Royal Engineers
DAQMG	deputy assistant quartermaster general
DG	director general
DGME	Director-General Military Education
DGO	Director General of the Ordnance
DMI	Director of Military Intelligence
DSO	Distinguished Service Order
EA	Egyptian Army

GCB	Knight Grand Cross of the Order of the Bath
GCIE	Knight Grand Commander of the Order of the Indian Empire
GCMG	Knight Grand Cross of the Order St. Michael and St. George
GCSI	Knight Grand Commander of the Order of the Star of India
GCVO	Knight Grand Cross of the Royal Victorian Order
GOC	general officer commanding
HRH	His or Her Royal Highness
HSH	His or Her Serene Highness
IG	inspector general
IGAF	inspector general of auxiliary forces
IGF	inspector general of fortifications
IO	India Office
KCB	Knight Commander of the Oder of the Bath
KCIE	Knight Commander of the Order of the Indian Empire
KCMG	Knight Commander of the Order of St. Michael and St. George
KCSI	Knight Commander of the Order of the Star of India
KCVO	Knight Commander of the Royal Victorian Order
KG	Knight of the Garter
KP	Knight of St. Patrick
KRRC	King's Royal Rifle Corps
KT	Knight of the Thistle
LOC	line of communication
MP	member of Parliament
MS	military secretary
OC	officer commanding
OFS	Orange Free State
PFF	Punjab Frontier Force
PS	private secretary
psc	passed Staff College
QMG	quartermaster general
RA	Royal Artillery
RE	Royal Engineers
RHA	Royal Horse Artillery

RMA	Royal Military Academy (Woolwich)
RMC	Royal Military College (Sandhurst)
SGO	surveyor general of the ordnance
VC	Victoria Cross
WO	War Office

A Note on Titles, Ranks, and Currency

The highest rank of hereditary peerage was that of duke followed in order of precedence by marquess, earl, viscount, and baron. Conventionally a baron was addressed as "Lord," but "Lord" was also routinely used to characterize those holding rank as marquess, earl, or viscount. The eldest son of a duke, marquess, or earl invariably carried a title in the next rank down from that of his father. Other sons carried courtesy titles including the honorific prefix "Lord" for the other sons of dukes and earls, or, as also in the case of all sons of viscounts and barons, the courtesy prefix of "The Honourable." A lesser hereditary title not conveying the rank of peer was that of baronet. As titled gentry, baronets took precedence over those holding other knighthoods although all were conventionally addressed as "Sir." Baronets also carried the abbreviation Bart., or Bt., after their surname.

Knighthoods—classed as Orders of Chivalry—were also ranked in precedence (with one exception) according to their date of origin. In order of precedence these were the Most Noble Order of the Garter (1344), the Most Honourable Order of the Bath (1725), the Most Exalted Order of the Star of India (1861), the Most Distinguished Order of St. Michael and St. George (1818), the Most Eminent Order of the Indian Empire (1878), and the Royal Victorian Order (1896). The Ancient and Most Noble Order of the Thistle (1637) and the Most Illustrious Order of St. Patrick (1783) pertained to Scotland and Ireland, respectively.

The Orders of the Garter, Thistle, and St. Patrick were restricted in numbers and were Knights Companion of the Order. The other orders were ranked internally in precedence as Knight Grand Cross or Knight Grand Commander, Knight Commander, and Companion or Commander depending on the order in question. All knights were addressed as "Sir."

In terms of gallantry awards, the Order of the Bath was extended to include a military division in 1815 with the CB intended originally to enable awards to be given to reward more junior officers for gallantry or distinguished service. Increasingly, it was awarded for distinguished service alone although it was the only such award open to officers until the institution of the Victoria Cross (VC) for all ranks in 1856. The Distinguished Service Order (DSO) was instituted in 1886 as an award for leadership for which the CB was not deemed appropriate, recipients having to be mentioned initially in dispatches. It was available for gallantry and distinguished service until becoming solely a gallantry award in 1917. Technically, the DSO was an "Order" and recipients were "Companions."

It should also be noted that a brigadier general held an appointment and not a rank.

All monetary values are rendered in contemporary predecimal values of pounds, shillings, and pence. Twelve pence (12d.) = one shilling (1s.). Twenty shillings = one pound (£1).

For those wishing to equate Victorian currency values to the present, the Bank of England's inflation rate calculator suggests £100 in 1870 would be worth £10,923 in 2016; £100 in 1880 would be worth £11,039 in 2016; £100 in 1890 would be worth £11,792 in 2016; and £100 in 1900 would be worth £11,279 in 2016, prices having dipped in value in 1899. (See also http://www.bankofeng land.co.uk/education/Pages/resources/inflationtools/calculator/default.aspx.)

A BRITISH PROFESSION OF ARMS

INTRODUCTION

In a television interview in 1985, Gen. Sir John Hackett remarked of the military profession, "You offer yourself to be slain. This is the essence of being a soldier. By becoming soldiers, men agree to die when we tell them to."[1] The statement echoed themes from Hackett's 1962 Lees Knowles Lectures, suggesting the essential differences between the "profession of arms" and civilian pursuits. Nonetheless, Hackett still defined the military as resembling other professions such as medicine and the law as "an occupation with a distinguishable corpus of specific technical knowledge and doctrine, a more or less exclusive group coherence, a complex of institutions peculiar to itself, an educational pattern adapted to its own specific needs, a career structure of its own and a distinct place in the society which has brought it forth."[2] According to the national census, those belonging to professional classes and occupations grew exponentially through the nineteenth century. In 1881 the largest single category of those regarded as among the professional classes was the clergy (21,700), followed by barristers and solicitors (17,400), physicians (15,200), and army and naval officers serving at home (15,000).[3] To give more specific detail of the size of the army's officer corps, in January 1870 there were 11,629 commissioned officers in the British army. In July 1872 there were 9,502, and in August 1878 the number had fallen to 7,909.[4] Between 1885 and 1906, a total of 16,472 officers were commissioned.[5] The army, therefore, represented a substantial profession by the turn of the twentieth century.

The British army has invariably been seen as standing apart from other professions and, frequently, from society as a whole. While the extent of military participation in Britain during the French Revolutionary and Napoleonic Wars was substantial, there was nothing that might really equate to a "nation in arms" outside the conscription imposed in the two world wars of the twentieth century and, arguably, the extension of national service to 1963. Certainly between 1815 and 1914 the army was unrepresentative of wider society. As the Royal Commission on Purchase put it in 1857, the middle classes, defined as a class between the clergy, the legal and medical professions, and higher merchants on the one hand and "work people" on the other, had "no place in the British army under the present system."[6] The army remained marginalized because of its scattered global deployment, and also because it was distanced from society by dependence on the unemployed and poor for rank-and-file recruits. That official definition of the difference between the middle class and the professional class in 1857, however, does illustrate that the army was readily equated with the higher professions, and it was clearly seen as a profession in the national census. Its officer corps largely shared a common social, educational, and cultural background not just with the landed aristocracy and gentry but also with the traditional higher professions of the church, law, and medicine. One ongoing research project at the Universities of Oxford and Northumbria includes fourteen serving army officers residing in its nine specified urban areas within a sample of one thousand professional men, in an attempt to establish whether the cohort as a whole represented a self-sustaining social group distinct from the rest of the middle class.[7]

Nonetheless, the army has been seen as an "oddity" in long preserving the vestiges of a vanished warrior tradition when the growth of professionalism required institutional change.[8] One classic analysis of the rise of professionalism in Britain and the United States specifically excluded the military as well as the clergy since they did not "transact their services on the market."[9] The "market model" has been challenged, and it can be argued that Church of England clergy confronted increased competition from nonconformist and other churches.[10] Army, clergy, and the civil service are a better fit for a "service" model, which would also include other professions, but with the distinction that the service provided by army, church, and government was arguably to the nation and wider society rather than the consumer even if, in the case of the clergy, that service was only offered in reality to those members of society who professed to be Anglican.[11]

The concept of military professionalism itself is problematic. Hackett's definition of professionalism is a modern one. In the eighteenth and nineteenth centuries, military professionalism was more understood in terms of identification with a particular occupation and a process of self-study.[12] Generally, professionalism might be regarded as the cultivation of particular skills and competence in a specialized area, requiring appropriate training. Yet modern models of military professionalism are narrowly interpreted from the perspective of civil-military relations. Equally, they have struggled to explain why Britain does not fit the proffered models of direct or indirect military influence over policymaking.[13] In particular, Samuel Huntington assumed an idealized vision of the professional soldier as an altruistic servant of the state governed by the military ethic. For Morris Janowitz at least, Huntington ignored the fact that long service regulars were committed to their own careers and were almost bound to become political animals as a result of lobbying in their own interests. As will be seen, so far as the late Victorian army is concerned, Janowitz's assumption of self-serving careerism is rather closer to reality than Huntington's. Indeed, there has been a tendency to ignore the wider collective values and attitudes that might characterize career soldiers. There has also been a tendency to interpret professionalism as a progressive process, which may or may not equate to reality. Thus, the "feudal/aristocratic" model advanced by Yorgos Kourvetaris and Betty Dobratz, while superficially fitting the evolution of the Victorian army and naval officer corps, ignores the possibility that they could be both aristocratic and professional.[14]

The question arising from Hackett's assumptions, therefore, is how far the following of the profession of arms might be seen as motivated, like any other profession, by considerations of material reward and career advancement. Soldiers were men like any others, and it would hardly be surprising if they did not have ambitions like other men. Notwithstanding the obvious boundaries between soldiers and civilians, what if we were to view the profession of arms simply as a profession like any other?

The late Victorian army did not stand far outside the pattern of other professions in nineteenth-century Britain. It has been suggested, for example, that "ritual culture" was one mark of an evolving sense of Victorian professionalism.[15] Uniforms and ceremonial and regimental customs were certainly just as distinguishing as any arcane procedures to be found in the universities, the law, or Parliament. On the other hand, while a public school education was equally relevant to all the established professions, further education at the universities of Oxford and Cambridge was far less common for those in the army, for a degree promised more fruitful employment elsewhere.

The rise of competitive examination, of which those for the Indian Civil Service and Home Civil Service (as recommended in 1853 and 1855, respectively) stand particularly representative, has also been seen as a mark of the "triumph" of professionalism.[16] It has been suggested that patronage and corruption, amateurism and inefficiency, and secrecy and lack of accountability were all supplanted between 1780 and 1880 by selection and promotion by merit, accountability, and professionalism.[17] It has also been argued that after 1890 an earlier class system gave way to a "professional society" structured around career hierarchies, "in which people find their place according to trained expertise and the service they provide rather than the possession or lack of inherited wealth or acquired capital."[18]

In reality, examination could still be circumvented by patronage and nomination, and it tested general (and classical) education rather than technical proficiencies. Examination was but one means of defining the specialist knowledge that established professional status. Other means were the introduction of standardization in training, increased centralized control and regulation, and the adoption of a conscious self-identity.[19] Such development typifies both market and service models of conscious professionalism, since all professions shared a certain service ideal whether motivated by the need to achieve legitimacy or otherwise. Of course, the army's status was already validated by its long-legalized monopoly on armed might and the warrior tradition.[20] As will be shown, examination played an increasing role in the army, and, following the abolition of the purchase system for commissions in infantry and cavalry in 1871, there was a struggle to achieve selection by merit in promotion and appointment. Yet, abolition did not guarantee the victory of merit over seniority. Moreover, patronage remained significant within all professions including the army, with the growth of central and especially local government providing many additional opportunities for its exercise.[21] Ironically, in view of the staunch defense of existing forms of military patronage, one argument advanced against both abolition of purchase and selection by merit was that they would increase favoritism, motivating military conservatives to prefer what has been described as the "deadening weight" of seniority.[22]

The continuing relevance of military patronage in varying forms, as recounted in this study, renders void the argument that patronage remained a feature only of the Church of England after 1871.[23] That the latter institution preserved patronage is not in doubt. While the parochial organization of the church hampered any logical promotion system, appointment to benefices depended variously on the favor of the Crown, Oxford and Cambridge colleges, public institutions and trusts, London livery companies, or purely private individuals. The number of benefices grew as the church sought to meet the challenge of the perceived spiritual needs of an expanding population by creating new parochial subdivisions, notably in urban areas. Many new benefices were in the gift of bishops, but those in the gift of individuals remained constant at around 50 percent of all appointments. Moreover, both livings, and also the right to nominate the person to fill the next vacancy could be readily purchased. Clergymen were barred from such purchases, but others could act on their behalf. In 1878 one in nine of all private livelihoods was in the hands of a patron-incumbent.[24] Episcopal influence was enhanced by the rise in the number of benefices, which created "a substantial degree of professional, diocesan-based promotion,"[25] but the appointment of bishops itself was highly politicized as it rested in the hands of the prime minister acting for the Crown.[26]

The example of the clergy has some bearing on the experience of the army's officer corps. In a purely commercial sense, consumer choice was the difference between success and failure in law and medicine.[27] But the opportunity for advancement in law and medicine also rested on the ability to attract clients through connections. While more opportunities opened in central and local government service, and for that matter were available in military and naval medicine, it was difficult to build a medical general practice without friends or funds.[28] Partnership with an older practitioner was the most favored route, especially within families. In the London-based elite of the medical profession, extending to hospital appointments, where nepotism was rife, family connection was particularly important.[29] Competence became more valued, but "Victorian medical and surgical elites continued to measure their colleagues and success by the standards of lay culture, social distinction, and other non-professional criteria."[30] Emerging professions were just as prone to the same patterns of activity. The network of engineers and contractors in metropolitan London operated on "a mixture of written and oral contracts established through professional competition, personal reputation, kinship, apprenticeship, and patronage."[31]

Comparison to the army can also be made with the Royal Navy, in which a selective compulsory retirement scheme introduced in 1870 was abandoned in 1874. Retirement on the grounds of age or nonactive appointment gradually prevailed, but, in theory, promotion from captain to rear admiral continued to be governed by seniority until after 1945. In practice, selection was increasingly exercised for active commands.[32] Yet naval appointments were heavily politicized and frequently a matter of political party management. So apparently radical a naval reformer as Adm. Sir John Fisher (Lord Fisher from 1909), the First Sea Lord from 1904 to 1911, actively believed that "favouritism is the secret of efficiency,"[33] albeit in the identification of talent or at least among those who supported his own views.[34] It has also been suggested that those opposed to the "informalisation" of naval tactics in the 1880s and 1890s shared common links in terms of service at the Torpedo School, HMS *Vernon*; service in the Royal Yacht Squadron or appointments as royal aides de camp; involvement in the Royal Geographical Society; or membership in the Freemasons.[35] Service in the Royal Yacht Squadron qualified officers for accelerated promotion, while flag lieutenants continued to benefit from the so-called haul-down promotions granted to admirals upon their leaving commands. In 1899 no less than twenty-five officers of flag rank on the active list had been flag lieutenants in their youth.[36] It has been argued there was increasing emphasis on specialist technical knowledge as well as general competence, but, while promotion and advancement were effectively by merit, "some men gained them more easily than others."[37]

The recognition of professional status was also very much a matter of prestige and its potential rewards. The Victorians were obsessed with honors. As Lord Curzon remarked on one occasion, the British imperial community had "an insatiable appetite . . . for titles and precedence."[38] In this regard, army officers shared that craving with other professions. It has been suggested that the emerging profession of civil engineers with its hierarchy of independent consulting engineers, assistant engineers, clerks, and pupils sought social gentility "with all the accoutrements of titles, estates, and the way of life to go with them."[39] Also striving for recognition were Victorian scientists, who lacked any standard for obtaining regular employment, and thus were constantly concerned with the issue of money.[40] Not all could hope to scale the heights of their profession, and progress could be slow without wealth or connection, but all would benefit from the association of interest that provided a "spectrum of social advancement."[41]

There is, then, much to suggest that the late Victorian army did not materially differ from other professions of the era. This study is an attempt to test that hypothesis through an examination of the internal dynamics of the officer corps, taking the analysis of the nature of Victorian military professionalism beyond the constraints of models of civil-military relations by probing the collective attitudes and values of those pursuing military careers. The historiography is not well developed in this regard. More general studies of Victorian professionalism have rarely touched on the army, and, where they do, attention has been limited. In keeping with his concern to document the growth of professionalism, W. J. Reader focused mostly on the abolition of purchase, while John Bourne's study of patronage devoted but two pages to the army.[42] Despite the wealth of specialist published studies on the late Victorian army, there has been little emphasis on officers' careers. Understandably, this is particularly true of general studies but, insofar as there has been any focus on officers, it has tended to concentrate on the abolition of purchase, the social composition of the officer corps, and the wider relationship between officers and society.[43] In part, this is a result of the almost complete absence of surviving papers of the military secretary, who controlled appointment and promotion, but also from the immensely time-consuming need to remedy that defect by delving into the voluminous correspondence of leading soldiers in order to reconstruct their ambitions and frustrations. In addition to surviving official papers, what soldiers told each other or confided only to their diaries or to their wives reveals a fascinatingly complex picture both of what was true and of what was believed.

The present volume is divided into two parts. In part 1, there is further discussion of the extent to which the army could be regarded as increasingly professional in terms of the dissemination of military knowledge with exploration of the quest for material reward, and for honors and awards. This is followed by analysis of the complex process of selection and appointment to command. A significant additional internal factor bearing on appointment was the rivalry between different factions—the "rings"—within the officer corps, but, beyond the army, there was the even greater interplay of external influences including political, public, and royal pressures, for the army did not exist in isolation from the society from which its members were recruited. Reference will be made to comparable factors at work in those other professions that have been subject to detailed study, although such studies have not often shed much light on the internal dynamics of progression, promotion, or appointment in the military profession.

The interaction of all these internal and external considerations is illustrated further in part 2 by reference to particular case studies. Those selected for more detailed investigation are the choice of commanders in chief in India and Britain, the Second Afghan War (1878–81), the Anglo-Zulu War (1879–80), and the South African War (1899–1902). In this way, an altogether wider survey of the nature of military professionalism in late Victorian Britain will emerge.

Given all those influences pertaining to command, it was not surprising that, when Fredrick, Earl Roberts was about to come home from South Africa in 1900 to succeed Garnet, Viscount Wolseley as CinC at the War Office, the secretary of state for war, the Marquess of Lansdowne, warned him of the difficulties of the position: "There are so many cross currents. So many cliques to reckon with. So many people to keep in good humour. The Court, Parliament, Society, the Army itself, with all its subdivisions."[44] What follows bears out Lansdowne's warning. The late Victorian army was a profession with all that that implied.

PART I

CONTEXTS

CHAPTER 1

THE PROFESSION OF ARMS

In beginning to assess the similarity of the military profession to others in the late Victorian period, it will first be necessary to explore the nature of professionalism in the army, before passing, in turn, to the matter of ambition, the seemingly pressing concern with monetary rewards, and the pursuit of honors and awards.

Professionalism

How far the late Victorian officer corps developed as a professional body in terms of the dissemination of military knowledge can be debated. Despite its being seen as dominated by the aristocracy, the army had not come under pressure from civilian reformers in the first half of the nineteenth century, other than in demands for further economies. With the exception of periodic interest in flogging, there was no real concern about conditions under which soldiers served.[1]

While progress should not be exaggerated, that did not mean the army went unreformed. There was more practical education for artillery and engineer cadets at RMA Woolwich. By the 1850s there were competitive entrance examinations for Woolwich and RMC Sandhurst, and promotion examinations for those up to the rank of captain, albeit undemanding ones. It was not intended this would open up the army to the "great industrial class," but it was hoped it would encourage greater professionalism among those who would continue to officer the army.[2] There was nothing to suggest that widening the officer corps' social basis would increase its ability.[3]

There is an almost Whiggish sense in which historians have found a growth of British military professionalism from the "swordsmen" of the seventeenth century onward.[4] Often it was a case of a minority struggling against amateur gentlemanly ideals. But then it has to be borne in mind that British officers were not separated from the interests, lifestyles, and accepted norms and values of their wider social class—that of the landed. Social relationships were more important than professional ones, and the supposed separateness of military life has been exaggerated.[5] It has been suggested that officers of the Royal Navy had a special interest in maintaining their particular status in the face of the general rise of professional society. Given the impact of technology on naval affairs, they were confronted by the demand for scientific and technical expertise at a time when traditional landed society was under sustained social, economic, and political pressure.[6] Soldiers were not challenged in the same way. Nor does there appear to have been any crisis of identity among army officers relating to the wider impact on landed society of the agricultural depression of the 1870s to 1890s, the expansion of the electorate, and the emergence of new elective regulatory bodies in local administration.

While examples of resistance to change are hardly absent from earlier periods, the late Victorian period is often particularly characterized in such terms. There are well-known stories of officers more interested in sport than war, and of character rather than intellect being the mark of suitability for commissioning. Character was shaped by an idealized contemporary vision rather than universal or timeless values. It was not contingent on the outcome of actions but on demonstrable qualities irrespective of success or failure.[7] Character was one of the marks of the gentleman on whom the church, the bar, the higher ranks of the civil service, and the magistracy were all equally dependent.

When the soldier-adventurer Fred Burnaby, later killed at Abu Klea in the Sudan in January 1885, tried to interest fellow officers of the Royal Horse Guards in useful military pursuits, he received the reply, "We don't come here to soldier."[8] Similarly, colleagues in the Guards sought to dissuade the Hon. Paul Methuen from going to Staff College, which would make him a "military bookman."[9] Going in for the Staff College examination in 1878, Douglas Dawson of the Second Coldstream discovered it would interfere with Ascot. His commanding officer remarked, "My dear boy, if you will go in for this sort of thing, you must expect to have to do with people who don't understand the ordinary pursuits of a gentleman."[10] According to Count Edward "Glick" Gleichen, Staff College students were seen as a "set of shirkers who left their regiments with a view to an idle two years at the College, to be followed by loafing and well-paid jobs in the plums of the profession."[11] Famously, Frederick Maurice, professor of military art and history at the Staff College from 1885 to 1892, wrote in 1872 that "the British army officer hates . . . literary work even in the form of writing letters."[12]

On the face of it, there is much apparently substantiating the image, not least the struggle of the Staff College for recognition and its graduates for employment. From a point in 1870 when twenty candidates were admitted annually to the two-year course, the entry number rose to twenty-four in 1884 and to thirty-two in 1886. No infantry or cavalry regiment could provide more than one student in any year, and there could be only four artillery and two engineer officers (admitted only after 1872) per intake. In 1886, artillerymen qualified for the first seven places with the result that some failed candidates were admitted and successful ones excluded.[13]

In any case, there were real difficulties militating against the development of an intellectual community with the army still widely dispersed across the globe, and with customary divisions between arms and regiments. There was a sense in which there was a "parochial professionalism centred on the regiment and the demands of imperial campaigning."[14] There were also economic and political limitations. The army was perceived as less important than the Royal Navy. Britain was first and foremost a global maritime power, whose naval mastery depended on maintaining a technological lead over its immediate rivals. Naval supremacy required an ever-more costly investment in evolving technology.

Nonetheless, the army's officer corps was not one of unremitting intellectual bleakness.[15] By the end of the nineteenth century, publishers were offering military series. There had been military journals much earlier: the *United Services Journal* (later the *United Service Magazine*; 1827), the *Naval and Military Gazette* (1833), the *United Service Gazette* (1833), and the *Journal of the United Service Institution* (1857). The Royal Engineers Institution published its first proceedings in 1837, and the Royal Artillery Institution in 1857. Membership of the latter reached over 1,700 by 1890.[16] Military journals bear comparison to publications of learned societies such as those for zoology (1826), biology (1836), and chemistry (1841).[17]

It is difficult admittedly to assess how far military publications were read or disseminated. Books consumed or written by officers might merely represent a consensus view, or be a synthesis of foreign treatises, lacking all originality.[18] A distinctly "Continentalist" school of thought has been identified that had little relevance to frequent employment in colonial warfare.[19] The rather more practical requirements of actual campaigning found a much more distinctive British voice in the theory of "small wars," of which the supreme example was Charles Callwell.[20] The great strategic debate within the British and Indian military establishments over how to fight a war against Russia, however, was conducted primarily through the circulation of official or unofficial memoranda by leading protagonists. Success by one school or another was measured not by publication but by successful lobbying for senior appointments.[21]

Irrespective of the sources of growing military professionalism, the empire could not have been expanded without soldiers harnessing advances in medicine, weaponry, and communications.[22] There are innumerable examples of new technologies such as the telegraph and the railway being applied to the army's colonial campaigns.[23] The reconquest of the Sudan certainly demonstrated the significance of modern artillery, magazine rifles, and machine guns.

Winston Churchill wrote that the battle of Omdurman (2 September 1898), in which some eleven thousand Mahdists were killed for the loss of just forty-eight British, Egyptian, and Sudanese troops, represented the "most signal triumph ever gained by the arms of science over barbarians."[24]

The Royal Engineers were constantly at the forefront of innovation in the science of fortification and submarine mining. Given the small number of civil engineers and scientists, the corps supplied engineering services to society at large. Ordnance survey, irrigation, dams, railway and road construction, prison and museum design all claimed their skills. Contributions to other scientific pursuits such as astronomy and archaeology were equally marked.[25]

Of course, technology was not always the answer to the problems encountered in colonial warfare.[26] Nor did technology count necessarily on the battlefield itself. Well-known lines from Belloc's *Modern Traveller*—"Whatever happens, we have got the Maxim Gun, and they have not"—need to be balanced by those equally familiar lines from Newbolt's *Vitae Lampada*: "The Gatling's jammed and the Colonel dead." The fabled square was indeed broken at Abu Klea, despite the presence of Gardner machine guns. Generally, however, it could not be said the army lagged much behind its Continental counterparts even if the challenge of the South African War demonstrated how much more needed to be achieved to shape a thoroughly modern army.

Ambition

It is hardly surprising if soldiers harbored ambitions of rising in their profession. Neatly encapsulating all professionals, Lord Salisbury once warned the viceroy, Lord Lytton, "If you believe the doctors, nothing is wholesome; if you believe the theologians, nothing is innocent; if you believe the soldiers, nothing is safe."[27] On another occasion, Salisbury told Lord Cromer that if soldiers "were allowed full scope, they would insist on the importance of garrisoning the moon in order to protect us from Mars."[28]

Oliver St. John, political officer at Kandahar, wrote to Alfred Lyall, the foreign secretary of the government of India, in January 1879 after the conclusion of the first phase of the Second Afghan War that Sir Donald Stewart deserved credit for keeping things quiet when his subordinates "are burning for a row, and egging him on to march somewhere in hopes of stirring up one, the more so that [Frederick] Roberts & [Thomas] Baker have fully indulged their warriors."[29] One of Garnet Wolseley's leading adherents, George Colley, successively MS and PS to Lytton, suggested the CinC in India, Sir Frederick Haines, envisaged "a great campaign on the Oxus and a peerage."[30]

Reflecting on the disaster befalling Lord Chelmsford at Isandlwana in Zululand in January 1879, Sir Charles Gough, commanding a brigade in Afghanistan, wrote:

> Is there not too much presumptuous pushing in the British Army? Men thrusting themselves forward on very superficial grounds and often accepted at their own valuation in trusting to *luck* to pull them through and gratified by public applause and decorations. Fortunate is the man whose progress upward is gained step by step and with experience upon experience. These are my moralizings on the downfall of Lord Chelmsford, but then the appointing authorities must seek for the *best man of the public service*—and they are to blame if inferior men are appointed—if when they fall foul as Lord Chelmsford they also fall foul on the authorities who appointed him![31]

Wolseley was certainly seen as ambitious, egotistical, and dictatorial.[32] Famously, Disraeli wrote to Queen Victoria in 1879, "It is quite true, that Wolseley is an egotist, & a braggart. So was Nelson."[33] Wolseley's great rival, Frederick Roberts, was characterized in September 1879 by a former friend as "one of the most self seeking men I have ever come across and would override everybody & anything that stood in the way of the attainment of his ends." Roberts "would do anything or say anything which he thought would be acceptable to the reigning powers."[34] Henry Hanna, a constant critic, accused Roberts of the most ruthless careerism.[35]

With expeditions in the offing, there was always the clamor to be chosen. On the eve of the Egyptian expedition in July 1882, Sir Daniel Lysons wrote a wonderfully nuanced letter to the CinC at Horse Guards, the queen's cousin George, Duke of Cambridge.[36] Lysons suggested volunteering services was "a conceited assumption of superiority over ones comrades and an expression of want of confidence in ones superiors." Yet, he was "always ready to do any thing and go any where at a moment's notice should my services be required."[37] In 1875 Lt. Gen. William Napier, the RMC governor, wrote to the MS to say he was not sure general officers should offer their services but that, in the event of a war, he would wish to be considered for a field command.[38] Wolseley had at least some admiration for the attempt by "that madman," retired Lt. Gen. William "Hellfire Jack" Olpherts VC, to join him on his way out to Zululand in May 1879 in the hope of employment. Wolseley had to get him removed from the steamer at Dartmouth.[39] In 1882 the highly eccentric Lt. Gen. Sir Henry Havelock-Allan VC turned up in Egypt and took part in the Highland Brigade's attack at Tel el Kebir allegedly armed only with a riding crop. As "mad as ever," Havelock-Allan wanted a recommendation for employment, which was impossible.[40]

In choosing the staff for the Indian expeditionary force for Egypt in 1882, Sir Donald Stewart deprecated the offer of Lt. Gen. the Hon. Sir Arthur Hardinge, CinC at Bombay, to serve under Wolseley. If circumstances arose unexpectedly in the field, then all would be well and good, he said, "but I cannot admire the spirit of the man who deliberately disregards his rank in the Army, and says he will serve under any body."[41] Cambridge warned Wolseley not to accept the services of any officers who went to Egypt without authorization.[42] He repeated the instruction for the Gordon relief expedition in 1884 with particular regard to Fred Burnaby: "What I object to is officers finding their own way out, having the means to do so, & then getting *themselves* appointed whereas quite as good men, who have not the means & possibly the *independence* to put themselves forward are doing their duties at home & are naturally much disheartened by seeing their fortunate comrade pushing themselves forward."[43] Burnaby slipped out of England suggesting he was going to the Cape, the War Office fearing he wanted to take part in any operations in Bechuanaland. Instead, Burnaby passed swiftly through Egypt to arrive at the front.

In 1895 during operations for the relief of Chitral, George Younghusband's attention was deliberately drawn away from the ranks of the King's Own Scottish Borderers by Sir Bindon Blood as Lt. Col. Philip "Micky" Doyne of the Fourth Dragoon Guards was serving in the ranks disguised as a private when supposedly on leave.[44] The number of officers trying to get to the Sudan in 1898 led Charles à Court (later Repington) to write cheerfully to Reginald Wingate, "please arrange to have 2 or 3 campaigns before the dervishes are extinguished in order to wipe off the most pressing claims."[45]

Younger officers could be forgiven for doing their utmost to go on service when their seniors were so ready to do so. Hugh "The King" McCalmont was a serial offender. McCalmont was wealthy enough to visit China at his own expense in 1876 to report on the political situation. He anticipated this might be useful experience in the event of any hostilities. McCalmont then used his leave to go to Constantinople "to watch how things were proceeding, and to try and get a footing out in these parts in advance of hostilities in due course supervening." McCalmont extracted a promise from the British military attaché to employ him in the event of a crisis. When war broke out between Russia and Turkey in April 1877, McCalmont was appointed an additional attaché.

McCalmont employed the same tactic in 1880, going to Afghanistan at his own expense despite his OC's initial opposition. He got attached to the brief expedition against the Marri. McCalmont's most blatant venture was to slip away from his command of the Fourth Dragoon Guards in Ireland without informing either the general officer commanding (GOC) of the Belfast Brigade or the GOC in Dublin to try to see action at Suakin. Then adjutant general,

Wolseley allowed McCalmont to go. McCalmont and Arthur Paget, whom he met up with at Brindisi, decided to bypass Cairo in case the GOC there, the Hon. Sir James Dormer, tried to stop them. They made it to Suakin but Sir Francis Grenfell only allowed them to observe his operation to clear the Mahdists away from the town. In 1898 McCalmont volunteered to go to the Sudan, a hopeless request given there was no place for a major general, not least one senior to the Egyptian Army's sirdar, Sir Herbert Kitchener.[46]

Another example of a young officer pushing for recognition was Winston Churchill. Churchill was desperate to get to the Sudan in December 1896, writing to his mother, "Two years in Egypt my dearest Mamma—with a campaign thrown in—would I think qualify me to be allowed to beat my sword into a paper cutter & my sabretache into an election address."[47] An appeal to Kitchener failed although Churchill was successful in joining Bindon Blood in the Malakand in 1897. That merely prompted another attempt to get to the Sudan. Kitchener knew his man. As told to Churchill, Kitchener remarked in August 1898, he "was not going to stay in the army—was only making a convenience of it; that he had disapproved of my coming in place of others whose professions were at stake & that E[velyn]. Wood had acted wrongly & had annoyed him by sending me. But that I was quite right to try my luck."[48]

Equally there was suspicion of those who attempted to get away when a campaign was likely to be prolonged. With the fall of Khartoum in January 1885 and the prospect of a renewed Sudan campaign in the autumn, Wolseley complained of "poor spirited creatures" wanting to go home.[49] When the Bechuanaland expedition of 1884–85 resulted in no hostilities, it was reported, "As is usually the case when there is no chance of war or glory [Sir Charles] Warren and all with him are in desperate fever to get away."[50]

Monetary Reward

Active service was an obvious route to career advancement, but, judged by the evidence of their private correspondence, it was also the case that many soldiers were obsessed with remuneration. An army career was certainly potentially far more expensive than a naval career, given that the financial bar for the latter was lowered by the earlier age—between thirteen and fifteen—at which naval cadets could be accepted for training.[51]

In January 1870 the annual pay of a lieutenant colonel was £310.5s.0d in a line infantry regiment, £326.10s.7d in the Royal Artillery and Engineers, £419.15s.0d in the cavalry of the line, £488.3s.9d in the Guards, and £522.5s.10 in the Household Cavalry. At the other end of the scale, lieutenants received annually £118.12.6d in infantry of the line, £124.14s.2d in the artillery and engineers, £133.16s.8d in the Guards, £164.5s.0d in the cavalry, and £188.11.8d in the Household Cavalry.[52] Between 1871–72 and 1901–2 base rates went entirely unchanged for captains. The basic pay of infantry majors actually went down over that period, while that of infantry lieutenant colonels went up marginally. Allowances remained flat.[53] As Sir Henry Brackenbury pointed out in 1868, officer's pay had remained effectively the same since 1806 while living costs had risen by 50 percent.[54] The general assumption was private income would supplement pay. Other professions including the law, architecture, and civil engineering equally required private means.[55]

The officer corps was not predominantly aristocratic, and landed society was never closed to those who acquired wealth and adopted its values. To be landed, however, did not necessarily equate to having wealth, particularly given the decline in land values as a result of the 1870s agricultural depression. In 1883 there were 137 peers serving in the army and 417 from what could be characterized as the "greater gentry," with estates of between three thousand and ten thousand acres, and an annual income in excess of £3,000.[56] There was likely to be concentrations of peers, heirs, and younger sons in more socially prestigious regiments: between 1850 and 1899, for example, 59 peers or peers' sons served in the Grenadier Guards alone.[57] But many younger sons of peers serving in the army would not inherit estates, while many peers and heirs who did serve spent only short periods in the army. Chelmsford was one of a number of landless peers, his father having been ennobled as Lord Chancellor.

There are varying figures for the social composition of the officer corps. Based on the definition provided by *Burke's Peerage and Landed Gentry*, for which two thousand acres was the minimum required for inclusion, Razzell postulated a division between aristocracy, landed gentry, and "middle class" officers. This produced 53 percent aristocracy and gentry in 1830, 50 percent in 1875, and 41 percent in 1912.[58] Otley's figures, based on cadet admissions registers for the RMC and RMA, suggested that in 1880 the fathers of 25.5 percent of those at Sandhurst and 12.8 percent of those at Woolwich were gentlemen, and 45.8 percent and 53 percent, respectively, military professionals. Sandhurst and Woolwich, however, supplied only 55 percent of army officers between 1885 and 1906.[59]

More reliable figures are those calculated by Spiers through a variety of biographical sources for all colonels and general officers in 1854, 1868, 1899, and 1914. Among general officers, the percentage of those from the peerage and baronetage declined from 17 percent in 1854 to 12 percent by 1899; the percentage of gentry rose from 29 percent to 39 percent. Sons of military and naval officers were steady at 18 percent in 1854 and 19 percent in 1899, while those whose fathers were clergymen and professionals rose marginally from their very low base.[60] Fairly similar patterns have been observed for the clerical and medical professions.[61]

Abolition of the purchase system on 20 July 1871, by which many infantry and cavalry officers had previously obtained their commissions, did not materially change the officer corps' social composition. Abolition advantaged younger sons and the sons of those on fixed incomes, such as army officers and clergymen, with the onset of the agricultural depression.[62] After abolition, moreover, the CinC remained able to impose social qualifications on candidates for commission in addition to educational requirements. "Fitness" was also determined by regiments.[63] The army became more dependent on the products of the English public school, whose values were seen as a guarantee of social acceptability. Of those regular officers who served in the South African War, 62 percent had been educated at public schools, with 41 percent from the top ten schools, and 11 percent from Eton alone.[64] In passing it should be noted that promotion from the ranks was and remained possible, but its incidence declined markedly through the nineteenth century from 22.9 percent of all commissions in the period 1830–39 to 2.0 percent by 1896–1900, although there had been a few variations in between. Few so promoted rose beyond the rank of captain, and most were confined to the appointment of quartermaster or (in the cavalry) riding master. The difficulty of the lack of pecuniary means was constant, and social prejudice was extended not just by fellow officers but also by the other ranks, who tended to want "gentlemen" as their officers.[65] Sir Luke O'Connor, the army's first recipient of the VC, and Sir Hector Macdonald both became major generals after battlefield promotions for gallantry in 1854 and 1880, respectively. Uniquely, Sir William Robertson, who enlisted in 1877 and was commissioned in 1888, reached the rank of field marshal. But these were exceptional cases.

Educational background, attendance at RMC and RMA, regimental camaraderie, and more informal leisure pursuits such as hunting and other field sports, racing, gentlemen's clubs, and masonic lodges all contributed to a shared ethos. Military clubs were particularly important. The principal clubs were the Guards Club (1810); the United Service Club, aka "The Senior" (1816); the Junior United Service Club, aka "The Junior" (1827); the Army and Navy Club, aka "The Rag" (1837); the Naval and Military Club, aka "The In and Out" (1862); and the Cavalry Club (1890). They often had long waiting lists, with many candidates withdrawing prior to the eventual ballot for admission.

Participation in these informal networks beyond the mess most necessitated a private income. Entering the Scots Guards in 1882, Francis Fletcher Vane was advised by his father that £300 per annum would suffice, but this amount proved wholly inadequate. The advent in "society" of "Transatlantic millionaires and South African lucky adventurers" affected everything, "and amongst other things brought up the cost of living in Her Majesty's Guards."[66] Gleichen entered the Grenadier Guards a year earlier. His private allowance of £360 p.a. also proved inadequate. While he neither gambled nor hunted, and lived at home when in London, Gleichen was still often £200 overdrawn.[67] Hubert Gough's annual allowance from his father when he joined the Sixteenth Lancers in 1889 of £360 per annum was again not enough. Gough even gave up smoking and drank the cheapest claret.[68]

Norman Stewart, son of Sir Donald Stewart, found the recognized establishment for an officer's servants, some shared with colleagues, consumed half his pay even in India.[69] Ian Hamilton barely got by in the Ninety-second Gordon Highlanders with £200 per annum, his mess bills averaging £270 a year.[70] In 1899 William Cairnes suggested the minimum needed in the Guards was £300 p.a. In the fashionable Tenth Hussars, whose honorary colonel was the Prince of Wales, £500 would barely suffice.[71] In the 1890s £300 per annum represented the average annual income of the salaried middle class, and £25 was a reasonable annual income for an agricultural laborer.[72] Given what a cavalry lieutenant colonel earned, a cavalry subaltern required a private income as great as his OC's salary.[73]

Notoriously, the case of two young officers of the Fourth Hussars bullied and forced out of the regiment for lack of means came before Parliament in June 1896: they had private incomes of £500 and £300, respectively.[74] Significantly, it was said one of them could not keep racehorses or hunters. In 1903 three Grenadier subalterns were threatened with flogging unless they competed in the brigade drag hunt. Participation in major military polo tournaments in India required a considerable outlay, with junior officers often buying expensive ponies, which cost even more to transport around the circuit. There was much support for the supposed military and manly virtues deriving from polo, but Roberts and Sir Evelyn Wood, ironically a noted rider to hounds, were adamant that polo was doing more harm than good.[75] Writing in The Times in January 1900, Lt. Col. Amelius Lockwood, former guardsman and long-standing MP for Epping, suggested too much was being spent on mess bills, hunting, horse racing, and polo. "C.O." responded that it was sport rather than mess bills doing the damage.[76]

The queen herself expressed concern in 1884 that officers of the Household Cavalry required an apparent private income of at least £1,000 per annum.[77] When commissioned in the Second Life Guards in 1880, Sir George "The Mite" Arthur had to spend £600 on his new uniforms and anticipated the two horses required would cost between £150 and £500 each depending on the quality of the animal and his own weight.[78] John Brocklehurst, from a wealthy silk-manufacturing family, received £1,000 per annum from his aunt to help maintain him in the Royal Horse Guards.[79]

Ostensibly investigating military education, the Akers-Douglas Committee, reporting in March 1902, judged that expenses in the cavalry required a private income of £400–700 and were a factor deterring applicants. The issue was significant when the army needed 800 new young officers annually and Sandhurst and Woolwich combined provided only 510.[80] The committee commented, "We may require from the candidates either money or brains; the supply is most unlikely to meet the demand if we endeavour to exact both." If chargers were provided by the government, uniform changes restricted, and interregimental polo tournaments and packs of hounds prohibited, an officer should be able to get by on a private income of £200 per annum, the committee estimated.[81] Lt. Col. the Hon. Richard Lawley of the fashionable Seventh Hussars saw no difficulties in securing sufficient candidates for his own regiment but admitted £600 was needed so that an officer "should not be the earthenware pot swimming with the iron one."[82] Two former cavalry OCs estimated requirements at £500–600 and £600–700, respectively.[83]

Reporting in July 1902, the Stanley Committee was specifically intended to inquire how commissions could be afforded by those of "moderate means." It calculated an initial outlay for an infantry officer of £200, and for a cavalry officer of between £600 and £1,000 depending on the regiment. Annual expenses would require a private income of £100–150 per annum for an infantry officer, and a minimum of £300 in the cavalry but with £600–700 being more likely.[84] Although the committee suggested ways expenses could be reduced, it did not recommend any increase in the pay rates as laid down in 1806, simply accepting the continued need for private means.[85]

By way of comparison, many curates earned no more than £90–120 per annum, and most clergymen in nonprivate benefices received perhaps £150 at a time when agricultural depression hit clerical incomes derived from tithes especially hard. In 1863 the Ecclesiastical Commission considered £300 the minimum required for an urban living and endeavored to bring clergymen up to this level. There was no comprehensive scheme for clerical pensions until the 1920s. Doctors with lucrative practices in London could easily top £1,000 yearly, but the average was perhaps £300–500. Those professionals operating in rural areas would earn far less.[86]

Inevitably, many officers lacked means. Col. Robert Home was so impoverished he spent evenings at a sewing machine to keep his children in clothes.[87] Henry Brackenbury recorded in his memoirs "how great are the difficulties of a military career to an officer who is not possessed of private means."[88] In 1883 when his promotion prospects appeared slight, Sir George White made inquiries about his likely pension, writing, "it is endless worry and mental wear & tear living up to & beyond your income."[89]

Wolseley himself is a case in point. His father, an impoverished major, died when Wolseley was seven. The family was left in straitened circumstances—Wolseley was the eldest of seven children—and his first commission was secured through nomination on the strength of his father's service. Wolseley advanced without purchase through courage and determination, fueled by having to assume the role of principal provider for his mother and two of his brothers, George and Fred. As Wolseley later wrote, "I was always full of cares. Even as a boy I never was happy, for I was always too ambitious & too squalidly poor to be the independent gentleman I felt I ought to be."[90] It did not help that Fred's various business ventures so often failed. Paul Methuen believed Fred had cost Wolseley £30,000 by 1897.[91]

In Natal in 1875 Wolseley's pay was fixed at £5,000 per annum for what was intended to be a six-month appointment as administrator, with his additional unattached pay, and £200 for his outfit.[92] His first month's expenditure entertaining various colonial officials and others he wished to influence to accept the proposed new colonial constitution was £1,400. As he told another brother, Richard, he was obliged to subscribe "to every dirty little race meeting and association in the country."[93] Appointment to the Council of India in 1876 was welcome not only because Wolseley believed it to be a stepping-stone to an Indian command but also because it paid £1,200 when he had been receiving £1,000 as IGAF.[94]

Contemplating potential future employment in January 1887, Wolseley noted the Aldershot command, with various allowances, was worth £2,528 and included house and garden. This was better than his current pay as AG of £2,700 without a house, which was costing him £800 a year. The Malta command would bring in £5,000 per annum and also included a furnished house.[95] Almost as soon as he arrived in the Irish command in 1890, when he had expected £4,300, Wolseley pointed out that due to recent adjustments the pay and allowances were less than those allowed his predecessor.[96]

When Malta again seemed a possibility in 1893, Wolseley wished to remain in Ireland, where the pay was slightly better and the entertainment costs were less; the post also left him available should Cambridge retire as CinC. Lady Wolseley also wanted a field marshal's baton for her husband as it would mean a few hundred pounds more, a fact to which she, as the one who paid the bills, was "by no means indifferent."[97] In 1895, with Wolseley now CinC, he calculated that, despite the annual salary of £4,500, he would be worse off than in Ireland since he would have to pay £1,000 a year for a London house. Moreover, the five-year tenure would conflict with the usual minimum rental term of seven years.[98]

When Lady Buller criticized Wolseley's manner in 1899, Sir Redvers Buller reminded her Wolseley was a self-made man and had endured "hard trials," whereas he had inherited his brother's wealth, which gave him a secure social position.[99] Equally, Buller sympathized with Thomas Baker when his local rank of major general in 1879 made him senior to Baker, for the latter was entirely dependent on his army career "while as for me I could leave it at any time."[100] Even Buller, who owned upwards of five thousand acres, suffered from the agricultural depression. In 1886, while serving as special commissioner for Kerry and Clare, he complained that the need to keep up a London house as well as one in Dublin was proving very expensive at a time when he felt the need to economize.[101]

Frederick Roberts also lacked wealth. The son of an East India Company general, Roberts spent nineteen years in mostly staff posts, before becoming acting quartermaster general (QMG) in India in 1874. Roberts had never commanded in the field until catapulted to prominence by his leadership of the Kurram Field Force in the first phase of the Second Afghan War: within nine years he was CinC in India. His lack of means was considered one reason why in 1881 he might prefer the Madras command to becoming QMG in the WO, the latter position worth a mere £1,500 per annum.[102] As Roberts wrote to the secretary of state for war, Hugh Childers, he had already made preparations to return to India, "which my very limited income is not well able to afford, and I have looked forward to the Madras Command as a means of, at least, recouping myself for this outlay, and of meeting other heavy expenses, which I would not have incurred, without such a prospect before me."[103]

In 1887 one of Roberts's protégés, George "Prettyboy" Pretyman, felt Roberts had not been properly rewarded for his command in the Third Burma War (1885–86) but noted Roberts was not anxious for a peerage unless there was a sufficient monetary grant to go with it.[104] With the prospect of a peerage raised anew in 1892, Roberts returned to what he felt had been the poor monetary reward offered with his baronetcy back in 1881, claiming his private means "are almost *nil.*"[105] A peerage would be of no use without more income, as he could not afford to live in London. Promotion to field marshal would likely rule him out of employment opportunities.[106]

It was rumored that Roberts had heavy debts not cleared even by his tenure as CinC in India between 1885 and 1893.[107] Roberts denied that he was dissatisfied with the Irish command, to which he succeeded in 1895, on the grounds of its expense. But he wrote after meeting Lansdowne in 1897, "I find it difficult to manage in Dublin, and another move would entail further expense and loss of property."[108]

Several other field marshals also lacked wealth. Donald Stewart had married when only a lieutenant, a circumstance noted by his biographer as "not on the lines of extreme prudence."[109] When Stewart felt he might be offered the Madras command in 1879, he noted, "the pay is only sufficient to keep a family going, and I do not wish to stay in India merely to live. I can do that at home." He felt, however, unable to refuse.[110] Robert, Lord Napier was judged so poor in 1885 that Cambridge advised the queen he should not be given the colonelcy of the Royal Horse Guards not only because he had been originally commissioned as a Bengal engineer but also because he could not afford the uniforms.[111]

Evelyn Wood was just as concerned by money. Returning from Natal, where he had been acting governor and high commissioner following the death of George Colley at Majuba in February 1881, Wood was offered the temporary governorship of the Isle of Man. The post had a salary of £1,800 plus a good house, and he was guaranteed it would not harm his future military prospects. However, he did not believe this sufficient.[112] Subsequently, Wood declined to stay on as sirdar in March 1885, claiming the post had cost him £1,600 of his capital as well as causing him to miss the chance of joining the Suakin expedition.[113] Moving to the Aldershot command in 1888, Wood reckoned the outlay on house and stables would be £3,000 more than it had been at either of his two previous commands, at Chatham and Colchester.[114]

Among general officers, both Sir Archibald Alison and his son-in-law, James Dormer, were constantly conscious of money. In July 1882 Alison was annoyed at the prospect of demotion to a brigade command when he had been acting in command of those troops hurriedly landed at Alexandria prior to the arrival of Wolseley's main force. Alison retained major general's rank when Wolseley arrived, but found his pay amounted to only £1,370 per annum, compared to the £1,700 he had earned as head of the WO Intelligence Department.[115] Unexpectedly, Alison was asked to command the army of occupation. Alison at once said he feared the expense.[116] As a local lieutenant general, Alison would earn £5.10.s a day, an increase of £3 a day on his major general's salary plus £2 per day table allowance. The promised allowance was not forthcoming after two months. Alison pointed out entertainment was liable to run at £700–800 per annum in excess of his allowances: "In command of the force here I feel I ought to entertain a good deal, it seems due to the large numbers of officers here and is the only means of making them acquainted with the European & official society in Cairo and of giving them an opportunity of meeting the many persons of note who are constantly passing through."[117] Wood by contrast was getting £4,000 for commanding just five thousand men in the reconstituted EA while Alison commanded thirteen thousand.

Joining Wolseley's staff on Cyprus in 1878, Dormer urged his wife to try to cut down on domestic expenses. With his allowances amounting to only £1 a day and mess bills and expenses running at 17s.6d a day, he feared he could not save much.[118] He accepted the post of AQMG at Malta, worth an additional 5s a day. By January 1879 he was still "screwing down to the utmost" in trying to send home £10 or £15 a month but found he simply could not live on his local pay.[119] Dormer believed it was as well he had not been asked to join Wolseley in Zululand in 1879, "as I literally could not afford it, & buying horses & outfit & starting a new campaign is so awfully expensive."[120] In early 1882, while serving as AQMG at Portsmouth, Dormer feared he might be offered a "white elephant" district command in England or Ireland that he could not afford.[121]

Chelmsford turned down Western District in 1880 "on account of limited private income."[122] In part, Frederick "Ben" Stephenson felt compelled to give up the Cairo command in June 1886 since he could not continue "without a drain upon my very modest private means which I can ill afford."[123] Cambridge and Secretary of State for War Campbell-Bannerman saw the value of retaining Stephenson in Cairo but could only contemplate adjusting his table allowance. This was duly doubled and backdated.[124]

There were some means of supplementing income. One was writing for the press, which might also bring an individual's name to notice. On half-pay for a time after the 1870 Red River expedition, Wolseley wished he could find more to write about for *Blackwood's Magazine* as it brought in £20 a month.[125] Frederick Maurice and Henry Brackenbury were also frequent contributors to *Blackwood's*. Apart from the £300 Brackenbury received from *Blackwood's* for his history of the Asante campaign, in 1877 he received four guineas per column for twenty-five columns of 1,100 words each from the *Illustrated London News*.[126] In 1878 Wolseley noted that his articles for the *Nineteenth Century* not only "keep my name before the public" but also paid twice as much as any other periodical.[127] Johnnie Gough, second son of Sir Charles Gough, was advised by his mother in 1889 that if he wished to "stand out a little from the common herd," he should offer his services as an artist to an illustrated periodical. This "would always ensure your going on service even if your Regiment was not going out."[128]

Reginald Wingate, director of the EA's intelligence department, was perpetually short of money. Wingate began writing for Reuter's in 1889 but then turned to authoring books, as he saw the popularity of campaign accounts. His first effort, *Mahdism and the Egyptian Sudan* (1891), was not a commercial success, but his editions of the memoirs of two of the Mahdi's captives, Father Josef

Ohrwalder's *Ten Years' Captivity in the Mahdi's Camp* (1892) and Rudolf Slatin's *Fire and Sword in the Sudan* (1896), were best sellers.[129] There were potential dangers, though, as the queen's PS Arthur Bigge wrote to her in August 1895 in reference to the frequent writing of Wolseley and Evelyn Wood: "It is a lucrative business but it takes a soldier out of his element into the world of letters."[130]

Quasi-military employment in the colonies was another option, although £4,000 per annum was certainly not sufficient to persuade Archibald Alison, George Greaves, or George Colley to stay as governor of the Gold Coast in 1874. The Colonial Secretary, Kimberley noted, "One & all replied—'not if we received £4000 a day!'"[131] There was also the prospect of finding employment in the reconstituted EA after 1882. The initial twenty-five officers selected had to speak French sufficiently to carry on correspondence, and be prepared to pass in colloquial Arabic within six months (a requirement later shortened to three months), but they could earn £450 per annum on an initial two-year contract.[132] All would enjoy a rank higher than in the British army, and command of a battalion would bring in an additional £750 yearly. As one of the first officers, Andrew Haggard, put it, service with the EA "was a distinct step in most instances on the road to fortune."[133]

Even in Egypt, military service could mean expense. In 1891 Archibald Hunter, then governor and commander at Tokar, was earning £1,000. This was £200 more than in his previous post as second in command of the Nile Frontier Force, and he also received a wound pension of £200 per annum. As Tokar was inland, however, supplies of all kinds were more expensive. His capital gave him £160 per annum, but £100 of that went to insurance. Additional expenditure on entertainment and equipment meant he was finding it hard to make ends meet and "for some time past I have been getting poorer & poorer in capital every year."[134] Promoted to major general at only forty in October 1896, Hunter needed to secure continued employment. Fearing he had little influence, he assessed, "I must perforce to remain on in this country where employment is assured to me. Had I ample means, the simplest thing to do would be to see this campaign to a close and then take a command in the United Kingdom or the Colonies & lead the humdrum life of a peacetime soldier, & marry & settle down."[135] Remaining in the Sudan also meant he felt he could not now marry his fiancée. All in all, he would have preferred not to have been promoted so early. His mood was not improved in November, by which time six months' campaigning had cost him £1,200 whereas he would normally only have expected to spend £600. Matters improved in February 1897 when his additional pay meant he was out of debt for the first time since 1884.

At the very end of the Victorian period, opportunities also appeared in the new Western African Frontier Force in 1897, the West African Regiment in

1898, and the King's African Rifles (KAR) in 1902. Conditions were not attractive compared to Egypt, however, and in the case of West Africa the susceptibility of younger and older men to disease led to a restriction on service to those aged between twenty-two and thirty-five. In order to attract candidates, pay was very generous. It was still difficult to find able candidates; Richard Meinertzhagen suggested in 1902 that KAR officers were "mainly regimental rejects and heavily in debt."[136]

Honors and Awards

If increased pay was one tangible reward for advancement in the military profession, honors and awards were also keenly pursued as a mark of success in the general competition for status.[137] Faced with an extensive list of military recommendations for honors in 1894, the colonial secretary, Lord Ripon, noted, "The demand for these things is as you know extraordinary and the task of selection difficult & disagreeable."[138] The services' weekly, *The Broad Arrow*, commented similarly in January 1880 that too large a number of decorations "discontents the unsuccessful and excites a morbid activity for the acquisition of honours which is inconsistent with the principle of their bestowal."[139]

An extreme example of the thirst for reward is afforded by Charles MacGregor actively seeking, first, the Victoria Cross and then, when this looked increasingly unlikely as he rose in rank, pursuing the KCB or the KCSI as an alternative route to prominence. Constantly thwarted, not least by his quarrels with superiors who might otherwise have recommended him for the VC, MacGregor resolved by 1864 that his best chance for advancement lay as a specialist on Central Asian affairs, which would make his services indispensable in the event of a major war. Not surprisingly, MacGregor was scornful of what he considered the "unmanly" and "unsoldierlike taunt" that "Russophobia" was driven by "KCB mania," a phrase used by Lytton but apparently originated by the former undersecretary at the India Office Mountstuart Grant Duff.[140] MacGregor's diary for the period from September 1879 to September 1880 contains two references to the possibility of still getting a VC alongside forty-eight references to his hopes of the KCB or KCSI, and seven references to the likelihood of a peerage. Like an actor approaching Oscar night, MacGregor had a penchant for rehearsing acceptance speeches in reply to imaginary toasts in his honor.[141]

MacGregor received the KCB in January 1881, becoming QMG in India with the local rank of major general. The rank, however, was not made substantive when MacGregor reached the end of his appointment in 1885. Passed over for a divisional command in favor of a junior colonel, he accepted command of the Punjab Frontier Force in November. Having reverted to colonel, he was earning less and holding an inferior rank than five years earlier.[142] MacGregor died of peritonitis in February 1887, less than a fortnight before receipt of the official news that he had finally been made a substantive major general.

MacGregor's case may have been unusual, but every campaign was replete with its list of honors and awards, which caused endless wrangling. Burgeoning honors reflected a wider trend in Victorian Britain, with new orders created such as the Order of the Star of India and the Order of the Indian Empire. In 1876, in view of the growth of the empire and of campaigning, Colonial Secretary Lord Carnarvon proposed to Cambridge that the Order of St. Michael and St. George, of which Cambridge was head, should be expanded. From 25 GCMGs, 60 KCMGs, and 100 CMGs, Carnarvon wanted 15 more GCMGs, 40 more KCMGs, and 50 more CMGs. Cambridge agreed.[143]

In 1880 there was an amendment to add auxiliary forces' officers to the Order of the Bath. At the time there was provision for 50 military and naval GCBs, 123 military and naval KCBs, and 690 military and naval CBs. It was suggested there should be 30 CBs for officers of the auxiliaries, with the number of CBs increased overall to 705, the deficit being made up by a reduction in the number of civil CBs.[144] In 1886, due to the number of small expeditions for which only the CB or a brevet was realistically available, it was proposed to increase provision again on the queen's birthday to 55 GCBs and 145 KCBs, but retaining 705 CBs.[145] Given the reluctance to increase brevet promotions, the question remained whether an additional class of the Bath or an additional award should be introduced. The queen felt a new decoration might interfere with the award of the VC. In any event, the Distinguished Service Order was introduced in September 1886.[146] In 1891 the secretary of state for war, Edward Stanhope, was concerned that with so many names being put forward for promotions in the Bath, its value would be diminished in the eyes of the public. He cited examples of officers who had seen no service for years.[147] Lord Randolph Churchill opined in 1886 that the GCB seemed to be reserved for those achieving immense slaughter for no national object.[148]

There was inflation not only of honors but also of brevets, by which officers were rewarded for distinguished service with an army rank superior to their regimental rank. While automatically junior to someone holding the equivalent substantive rank, brevet rank would enable an officer on occasion to exercise command over regimental seniors who did not hold a brevet. Local and temporary ranks were also conferred on many occasions, giving juniors superiority to nominal seniors.

Wolseley once remarked to the Hon. Neville Lyttelton that "small campaigns were very useful in their way, in that they gave the authorities opportunities for pushing on capable officers by brevet promotion for service in the field which it would have been difficult to ensure in any other way."[149] Significantly, Evelyn Wood told Wingate the rewards for the 1896 operations in the Sudan were not given out in proportion to the results achieved but "to bring forward men, not for what they had done, but for what we hope they may do, and to lift them out of the ruck, in order that the country might get value from them later."[150]

Redvers Buller, for example, was a brevet colonel in 1879 when still only a regimental captain. A yardstick did apply, however—those who were advanced had to be seen as sufficiently competent to undertake the duties of the rank to which they were promoted.[151] Testifying to the Elgin Commission, Maj. Gen. Sir Bruce Hamilton remarked that brevet promotion had created a false system of reward, giving some men perhaps eight years' advantage but discouraging others who then left the army as they did not see the prospect of advancing in rank. Yet he also suggested that brevets for active service were important when there were too few campaigns to go around.[152] This was clearly the case for Hamilton. Evelyn Wood said Hamilton had "jumped about 20 years in about two" through brevets for the Third Asante War and the Benin campaign.[153]

Gerald Graham's brevet colonelcy made him senior to fifty other colonels in the Royal Engineers.[154] When the sons of Hugh Childers and Sir John Adye received brevet majorities in 1885, they advanced over 340 artillery captains and 210 engineer captains, respectively. Wolseley wanted to advance them even further to brevet lieutenant colonelcies, but Cambridge declined until such time as they had reached their substantive majorities.[155] The advancement of Herbert Stewart, Buller, and Brackenbury to major general enabled them to leap over 575, 285, and 280 colonels, respectively.[156] Unsurprisingly, most senior witnesses before the Penzance Commission in 1875 believed brevets had been given out far too generously, although Cambridge suggested the Order of the Bath remained valued precisely because it was given more rarely.[157]

The Third China War in 1860 had seen the deployment of some 14,000 troops, and brought 29 brevets, but the Abyssinian campaign of 1867–68 with 12,500 troops saw 63 brevets and 30 honors. The Anglo-Zulu War with 17,000 troops committed resulted in 67 brevets and 42 honors; the Egyptian campaign in 1882 resulted in 135 brevets and 73 honors for 31,000 men deployed; and the Sudan and Suakin campaigns in 1884–85 combined, involving 22,000 men, saw 129 brevets and 48 honors.[158] For Asante in 1873–74, for which just 3,500 troops had been deployed, in addition to Wolseley's personal awards, there was one GCMG, one KCMG, five KCBs, twenty-six CBs, two promotions to brevet colonel, fourteen promotions to brevet lieutenant colonel, and twenty-four promotions to brevet major.[159]

The first phase of the Second Afghan War resulted in 244 officers being named in dispatches with an additional 29 in a supplementary list.[160] Frederick Haines's submissions for honors after the end of the war included thirteen KCBs and sixty-two CBs, as well as recommendations for a further seven KCBs in the future. He was told to reduce the number of KCBs by a quarter and the CBs by half.[161] Haines merely struck out the junior officers in each grade. Donald Stewart, who felt himself overrewarded with a KCB for such a short campaign, managed to persuade Haines to review the KCB list in terms of merit rather than seniority. Stewart had little interest in the KCB: "I suppose it is a pleasant thing to be a K.C.B., as people think so much of it, but it does not give me any very great delight, and few people know the difference between it and a K.C.S.I. or any other sort of knighthood."[162]

The CB list proved more difficult to prune since service records did "not always give an accurate estimate of the value [of] an officer's work during a campaign."[163] Subsequently, a supplementary list was sent in after Maiwand and the last phase of operations in 1880. A particular problem arose concerning potential rewards to officers of the Bombay Army because Maiwand had been a defeat. The Bombay government itself cut down a list of no fewer than eighty-one officers recommended by its CinC, Henry Warre.[164]

Comparisons were apt to be made. Roberts felt too many CBs had been given out for the Egyptian campaign in 1882 when he learned there were insufficient vacancies in the Order to accommodate his recommendations from Afghanistan.[165] Secretary of State W. H. Smith had not wanted a "golden shower" for men simply doing their duty.[166] The war correspondent Bennet Burleigh thought too few honors and brevets had been given for the first Suakin campaign in 1884, compared to those awarded for Wolseley's "much less hazardous and trying" campaign in Egypt in 1882.[167] Maj. Gen. Johnson Wilkinson, an Indian officer not at all hostile to Wolseley, recalled that "many of the gentlemen who happily returned unscathed from that pleasant Egyptian War had their manly bosoms covered with medals at the rate of about one a week, during the period they were engaged in the Egyptian campaign."[168]

While a similar number of KCBs and CBs were awarded for the Gordon relief expedition (20) and second Suakin expedition (25), there were far more brevets given for those on the former (71) compared to the latter (20). According to a letter to *The Times* by "Scrutator," Sir Gerald Graham had mentioned 170 names in his final dispatch, but this was cut to 60 by Wolseley, who then inserted his own recommendations of men not mentioned by Graham.[169]

Controversy over honors was also provoked by the Third Burma War. George White felt too little reward had been made for the Burma campaign, which had added 180,000 square miles to the empire: all would have valued a specific campaign medal rather than a bar to the India General Service Medal.[170] Roberts was also disappointed by the lack of honors for Burma, believing Wolseley lay behind it.[171] This may well have been true since Roberts's protégé, Reginald "Polly" Pole-Carew, reported Wolseley had influenced the MS, George Harman, who had taken the view there had been little action. The Prince of Wales, too, had been led to believe there had been only thirty-seven casualties in the campaign.[172] Roberts was required to cut the list of CBs to just seven.[173] Roberts, who felt keenly the difference in the number of awards for recent frontier actions in Egypt, wrote that "so long as Egyptian heroes can get decorations for a picnic lasting as many weeks you must not be surprised at my pressing the claims of those who have done what seems to me, more valuable work."[174]

As with the question of monetary reward, the honors sought and gained by Wolseley and Roberts provide instructive examples. In accepting the KCMG for the Red River expedition in 1870, Wolseley suggested that "being Sir Garnet is not much, but still it will put me in some mysterious way or another on a different footing with other colonels."[175] After Asante in 1874, he turned down a baronetcy, as well as refusing a GCB on the grounds that such an advance in the Order would offend more senior officers.[176] Wolseley accepted the KCB and promotion to GCMG. He suggested the liberality with which honors had been awarded after Napier's Abyssinian expedition in 1867–68 had unnecessarily inflated military expectations. Lest it be thought that Wolseley was entirely altruistic, he felt a baronetcy was only "a reward reserved for common people," specifying the Duke of Devonshire's "gardener," Sir Joseph Paxton.[177] Wolseley entertained some hopes he might get a peerage. This was not forthcoming, but he accepted a one-off sum of £25,000 in lieu of a smaller annual pension of £1,200.

Wolseley angled again for a peerage after the Anglo-Zulu War.[178] He wanted to consolidate his claim to the supreme command in India, stressing he had "now done a number of troublesome jobs for the present Ministry & that they certainly ought to give me what the party give to head clerks in public offices." He feared his lack of means might suggest he did not want a peerage, but he would "sooner be a very poor peer than a poor knight" although he also felt a pension with a peerage important to ensure his financial future.[179] He expected to be offered the GCB again but felt it had been devalued by being given to Chelmsford.[180]

Wolseley was then denied a peerage by the queen while he was QMG. The issue arose in March 1881 partly as a result of Childers's wish to compensate Wolseley for not being sent to avenge Colley's death at the hands of the

Boers at Majuba. Roberts was selected to go to Natal instead. Wolseley could not be spared from the WO because the government needed a strong voice in support of its further military reforms.[181] It was also intended that Wolseley would become AG. Gladstone duly recommended a peerage for "strong public reasons." The government needed additional support or military reform in the House of Lords following the death of the former CinC in India, Lord Sandhurst, in 1876. Older officers opposed reform, and the only younger military peer was Chelmsford, "whose political and general associations naturally place him at a distance from the Administration."[182]

The queen and Cambridge objected on the grounds of Wolseley's likelihood of commenting on matters solely the prerogative of the CinC. They would only accept the possibility of Wolseley being a peer if he was no longer QMG. For the queen, a peerage would be seen as a reward for supposedly treating Cambridge with contempt, "and it would be understood that the surest way to preferment is disloyalty to superiors if only some support is given to the political tenets of the Govt. of the day."[183] Cambridge was prepared to resign on the issue, but so was Childers. Gladstone argued, in turn, that there seemed to be an underlying argument that no soldier could be a peer and also either AG or QMG. Cambridge was also laying down a rule for himself that he would support government policy only if he agreed with it but would keep silent if he did not.[184] The queen's private secretary, Sir Henry Ponsonby, recognized the dangers of Cambridge being seen as the primary obstacle to Wolseley's peerage.[185] Gladstone threatened resignation at one point but then told Wolseley he could not resign in view of crises abroad—Czar Alexander II had just been assassinated—and in Ireland.[186]

A peerage for Wolseley was now impossible, but Cambridge was backing himself into a corner, not least when told he must set down his official objections to Wolseley as AG in writing.[187] To save face, Cambridge did not recommend Wolseley's appointment as AG but offered no objection to it.[188] Wolseley finally secured his peerage after his victory at Tel el Kebir in September 1882: as Cambridge pointedly wrote to him, "a Military Peerage as the result of a successful campaign is the highest honour a soldier can aspire to at the hands of his Sovereign."[189] In characteristic form, Wolseley angled for a viscountcy rather than a mere barony, which he said was available to "every whippersnapper of a diplomatist or party supporter."[190] Wolseley also wanted a pension attached. In lieu of a pension, he received a monetary grant, as did the naval commander, Sir Beauchamp Seymour, who was also made a peer. Roberts and Stewart had both accepted a £12,500 lump sum commutation rather than a £1,000 annuity for their services in Afghanistan.[191] Since Wolseley had already received £25,000 for Asante, there was some resistance to another lump sum.[192] A sum of £30,000 was eventually agreed to.

Comparison was made between Wolseley and Roberts following the Second Afghan War. There was public and political pressure for a worthy reward for Roberts after the march from Kabul to Kandahar following Maiwand in July 1880, but Gladstone and Hartington pointed out that Donald Stewart had been in overall command and would have carried the responsibility for failure. Consequently, both got the GCB. Roberts was promoted to substantive lieutenant general and received the Madras command, and Stewart initially became the military member on the Viceroy's Council.[193] As will be discussed in a later chapter, some characterized Roberts's march from Kabul to Kandahar as a "race for the peerage" in competition with a rival relief force led by Sir Robert Phayre. Neither received one.

Roberts was wont to point out that he was in sole command in his appointments for all but three months of the two years he was in Afghanistan, and had won four major actions in that time. He resented how the Liberals appeared to slight his achievements by lauding Stewart's earlier march from Kandahar to Kabul, given that he thought his own more significant in the context of the war. He noted Sir John Keane had received a peerage for the lesser Ghuznee campaign in 1839. With some justification, he felt targeted by the Liberals for having seemingly been allied "to their opponents as a political partisan."[194]

The Prince of Wales believed Roberts deserved a baronetcy given that Wolseley had been offered one after "that poor little six months campaign" in Asante.[195] Cambridge originally opposed promotion for Roberts and Stewart but was prepared to countenance a baronetcy for Roberts.[196] While doubting Stewart had been the equal of Roberts, the queen was prepared to approve baronetcies. Childers duly recommended both for baronetcies as well as Haines, although the latter declined it. Roberts, who was aware the queen had pressed for a baronetcy for him, accepted it on the condition he would receive a grant of not less than £20,000. Upon returning from South Africa, Roberts was annoyed to find the amount reduced to £12,500 but felt he could not refuse given the queen's earlier intervention.[197] Roberts was averse to too much publicity being given to his case. He did wish it questioned, however, whether Wolseley should have been given a proportionally larger sum, in lieu of a pension, than that offered himself and Stewart, especially as he had been compelled to accept the same as Stewart, who was nine years older.[198] In the end, Roberts received his peerage upon leaving India in 1892.

One other prestigious reward requires analysis, namely the VC, to which particular significance came to be attached. National anxiety at the performance of the army in the Crimean War and public outrage at the suffering of ordinary solders combined to awaken a new interest in the army. Announced in January 1856, the VC satisfied public pressure for the recognition of heroism. Heroism was a concept to which Victorian society was readily attracted, although its precise definition in terms of the VC evolved through refinements of the criteria in successive royal warrants.[199]

The initial rush of awards in the 1850s (296) slowed significantly in the 1860s (39) but began to rise again in the 1870s (48). Concerns that the awarding of too many might devalue the distinction led to a reduction in awards in the 1880s (21) and 1890s (27) prior to the South African War. Although the VC was open to all ranks, between 1856 and 1904 46 percent of all awards went to officers, who at most comprised 10–12 percent of the military and naval establishments.[200]

Perhaps inevitably, controversy frequently surrounded the award. The eleven VCs awarded for the defense of Rorke's Drift in January 1879 went some way toward deflecting the continuing attention paid to the disaster at Isandlwana, despite the fact that reportage of Rorke's Drift was actually eclipsed by the ongoing Isandlwana coverage.[201] Wolseley, himself fearless in action, doubted the situation had left the defenders with any other recourse but to fight for their lives: this tempered any gallantry.[202]

Wolseley had decided views on the claims being made for Lt. Neville Coghill and Lt. Teignmouth Melvill, the latter killed carrying the Queen's Color of the One/Twenty-fourth Foot from the field at Isandlwana.[203] Wolseley acidly noted that heroes had been made of two men "who taking advantage of their having horses bolted from the scene of action to save their lives" and that, indeed, "it is monstrous making heroes of those who saved or attempted to save their lives by bolting."[204] Posthumous awards, however, only became possible in 1907, when Melvill and Coghill were among those honored.

Even the rescuing of men from the Zulu at Hlobane in March 1879, for which two VCs were awarded, including one for Buller, was controversial when several other participants had also risked their lives. It has been claimed that all awards for Hlobane were confined to a "favoured circle" around Evelyn Wood and Buller.[205] Certainly awards in 1881 to two others for an action in the caves on the southern side of Hlobane—Lt. Henry Lysons and Pvt. Edmund Fowler—owed much to pressure on Wood from Lysons's father, Sir Daniel Lysons, then QMG, although the award had to await a change in the regulations in 1882.[206] There was more controversy over the three VCs awarded for an engagement on the White Mfolozi in July. One went to Lord William Beresford, who, it was believed, had got himself an appointment in Zululand "with the resolution of qualifying for the Victoria Cross."[207] Another candidate, Lt. Frederick Hutchinson, failed to get the VC despite a lengthy campaign by his father. Exasperated by what he saw as Hutchinson's presumption that the VC was his son's personal right, Buller, who had commanded the action, passed the whole correspondence to the MS, where the matter ended.[208] As a mere lieutenant colonel, Hutchinson Sr. did not have the clout of Lysons's father.

There was a tendency to assume the VC equated with suitability for high command. Yet, it is difficult to judge how far its officer recipients did positively benefit in terms of promotion and allocation of commands. Possibly, there was an absence of coincidence in the three VC holders in principal commands of the small Indian expeditionary force dispatched to Malta in 1878.[209] Indian higher campaign commands generally were replete with holders of the VC in this period. In the Second Afghan War, prominent commands were held by Sir Sam Browne VC, Sir Frederick Maude VC, John Tytler VC, Hugh Gough VC, Charles Gough VC, and Frederick Roberts VC. Two subsequent CinCs in India, Sir George White and Sir O'Moore Creagh, won the VC in Afghanistan. It might be concluded, therefore, that the VC was sufficiently useful to be desirable.

Given that so much effort was devoted to military advancement, it is perhaps unsurprising that failure often resulted in efforts at concealment. As will be seen in the later discussion of the Wolseley and Roberts "rings" of adherents, those outside the favored circle could be cast as scapegoats. Battles such as Isandlwana and Hlobane in the Anglo-Zulu War also afford examples of this tendency.

By 1899 many soldiers were increasingly professional in their outlook, but, like any other professionals, individual officers were also motivated by ambition and the pursuit of reward. As with other professions, military men operated within a particular system of promotion and selection that determined whether opportunities for advancement could be seized or otherwise obtained. To that system attention can now be turned.

CHAPTER 2

PROMOTION AND SELECTION

P atronage and clientage in the army were certainly just as pronounced and
the nature of such relationships just as complex as elsewhere in Victorian
society.[1] Military patronage in terms of appointments and rewards was vested
in the Crown. It was subject to a degree of regulation, not least issues of
seniority, and increasingly, by term limits on tenure. Professional competence
as the concept of selection by merit also became more significant as will be
seen. Nonetheless, appointments and rewards were still liable to the interference of private interests, and even selection could depend on opportunities for
advancement that might occur from active sponsorship. The working of internal and external factors in promotion and selection are the subject of this and
the next two chapters, beginning with the mechanics of career advancement.

Regulations

The abolition of purchase took effect on 1 November 1871. Not all commissions
in the infantry and cavalry had been purchased; the proportion varied. In the
thirty years prior to 1871, approximately one-third of commissions in the line
infantry were not purchased but only one-sixth in the Guards and cavalry.[2]
Purchase had never applied to the artillery or engineers.

Nominated or purchased first commissions had been taken up as vacancies occurred. Within regiments, seniority applied in terms of the opportunity
to purchase subsequent vacancies at the relevant rank, subject to qualifying
periods. While not immutable, regimental seniority had been sacrosanct. As
an anonymous contributor put it in the *Quarterly Review* in 1868, "Croesus
himself could not purchase a step over the head of his senior if that senior
was able and willing to purchase the step. This is the law and the regulation."[3]
Weeding out incompetents had also proved difficult, other than by the lapse
of appointments.[4]

Prior to abolition, officers could sell out at any time, retire on half-pay
after twenty-five years' service, or retire on full pay after thirty years' service.
In the thirty years prior to abolition, on average even with the ability to purchase, it generally took nine years for a lieutenant to reach the rank of captain,

another ten years for a captain to reach the rank of major, and four and a half years more for a major to reach the rank of lieutenant colonel.[5] Pensions were granted only for meritorious service. The capital value of the commission was lost upon death or upon promotion to general rank, although the CinC could direct it be sold for the benefit of dependents. While other officers had practical interest in the vacancies created by a fellow officer's death, the state had a pecuniary interest, the system being a kind of tontine "in which each member stakes his life against that of the others."[6] This continued to be the case with the disadvantage to those who would have been promoted freely previously that they lost any monetary benefit of the higher rank. The death toll of purchase officers in the Anglo-Zulu and Second Afghan Wars by June 1880 saved the exchequer £33,607.10s in terms of the sums those killed would have received if they had sold their commissions.[7] Cardwell had declined to make an exception for those officers serving in Asante in 1873.[8]

By virtue of abolition, the state was obliged to compensate officers for the loss of investment and to provide pensions, at an estimated cost over time of £8 million. The overall value of officers' investment in regulation and overregulation payments—not compensated—was calculated as £10.7 million.[9] In addition, the imbalance of senior and junior officers—an infantry battalion had one lieutenant colonel and two majors, compared to eleven captains and eighteen subalterns—implied drastic curtailment of promotion prospects without the possibility of sales.

A royal warrant on 30 October 1871 laid down inadequate arrangements to try to engineer the retirement of junior officers. All subsequent appointments to the rank of major or lieutenant colonel would be vacated after five years. It was estimated it would take seven years longer to become a captain at the age of thirty-five, with a majority likely at forty-nine, and a lieutenant colonelcy at fifty-three.[10] By 1875 there were already 360 more officers in the line infantry who had served beyond the average period for their rank than in 1871. By contrast, in the infantry between 1861 and 1871, a total of forty-nine lieutenant colonels, 133 majors, 1,051 captains, and 1,623 subalterns had sold out.[11]

In the artillery and engineers, where seniority applied, promotion was notoriously slow. In 1876 the Penzance Commission characterized the variety of expedients employed to ease the problem as a complex "combination of contrivances" such as temporary reorganizations, added pensions, and supernumerary lists of officers on full pay without duties.[12] To equalize the position, all artillery and engineer captains were made substantive majors in the army in 1871. This only created an imbalance in that many more infantry and cavalry captains would be retired on age grounds than those in the artillery and engineers.[13]

Abolition curtailed the influence of proprietary regimental colonels but not the power of regiments. Although still possible under the Regimental Exchanges Act of 1875, the kind of exchange between regiments that had been common prior to 1871 was much reduced. There were no less than 1,419 exchanges between 1861 and 1870 but just 130 between 1872 and 1873.[14] Most officers were confined to service in their own regiments, with seniority within those regiments playing a greater part in promotion than seniority in the army. Appearing before the Penzance Commission, Cambridge was adamant that promotion within regiments must be by seniority. The commission itself asserted that no promotion system would give satisfaction to regimental officers that "does not adopt seniority in the regiment as the basis of Regimental Promotion."[15] Within the individual regiment accelerated promotion was relatively rare and patronage relatively limited. The situation persisted after 1902.[16]

Remaining purchase officers had significant grievances. They complained they could not sell any commissions gained after 1 November 1871, and that the limitation of tenure of majors and lieutenant colonels to five years with officers then passing on half-pay deprived them of the ability to qualify for a half-pay pension after twenty-five years, or a full pension after thirty. Reporting in June 1874, the Officers' Memorial Commission recommended an extended compensation scheme and a further inquiry to examine whether the legislation should be amended.[17] That further inquiry, chaired by Lord Penzance, was established in November 1874 to examine promotion and retirement.

Reporting in August 1876, Penzance recognized the flow of promotion had slowed. On average, a captain would now spend seven years longer before being promoted to major, and a major ten years longer before being promoted to lieutenant colonel. The rank of major would now be attained at forty years of age and that of lieutenant colonel at fifty-three. Given that the greatest turnover between 1861 and 1871 had been of captains and subalterns—only 82 of the 2,756 officers who had sold out had been majors or lieutenant colonels—changes had to be made now that promotion depended on retirement or death.[18] The recommendations were complex. Any nonpurchase infantry officers, for example, should be allowed to retire from the army with a gratuity after eight years' service. So far as senior ranks were concerned, all lieutenant colonels should be promoted to colonel after five years and thereby made eligible for further promotion but any not promoted to major general by the age of fifty-five should be retired. All general officers should be required to retire at the age of seventy. If implemented, promotion of captains to major should come on average after seventeen years' service, that of majors to lieutenant colonel after eleven and a half years, and that of colonels to major general after fifteen and three-quarters years.[19]

The need for change was accepted in principle, and changes were implemented through a royal warrant in August 1877.[20] But rather than a fully graduated system, the warrant introduced a step system with the earliest opportunity to retire on a lump sum of £1,200 after twelve years. Again in terms of higher ranks, lieutenant colonels could retire on an annual pension of £250 at any time, on £300 after twenty-seven years, and on £365 after thirty years, but they would be retired compulsorily on half-pay after five years' tenure. General officers would retire at age seventy, the list to be reduced gradually from 275 to 200 general officers.[21] The critical rank for a decision on an individual's future was that of captain, with most retirements at that rank, much as the ranks of ensign to captain had seen the greatest turnover under the purchase system. By March 1881, of the 979 officers who had retired under the 1877 warrant, no fewer than 909 were captains.[22]

Further changes were made in 1881. For higher ranks, lieutenant colonels would retire at fifty on a pension of £365 per annum. Colonels could retire at any time on £420 per annum, and would be retired at fifty-five on £420. Major generals could retire at sixty on £680 per annum or at sixty-one on £650, but would be compulsorily retired on £700 at the age of sixty-two. Lieutenant generals would get a pension of £830 if they retired at sixty-five or £840 if at sixty-six, but would be retired compulsorily at sixty-seven on £850. Full generals could go at £900 at sixty-five or on £990 at sixty-six, and would be retired compulsorily at sixty-seven on £1,000 per annum. Retirement gratuities were to be £1,200 for officers after twelve years' service, while majors and lieutenant colonels would receive pensions of £200 and £250, respectively, if they retired at any time.[23]

A further tweaking of the system in December 1886 saw penalties introduced for retiring early, since the number of officers was now declining at a moment when the number of other ranks was increasing. Only subalterns could now retire after twelve years. Lieutenant colonels could retire on £250 after fifteen years, £300 after twenty-seven years, or £365 after thirty years, or on £420 if resigning battalion command; they must go at fifty-five or if unemployed for five years on £420. For colonels there was now compulsory retirement at fifty-seven, or if unemployed for five years, on £500. Major generals could retire at any time on £700 but must go compulsorily at sixty-two on the same rate; lieutenant generals could retire at any time up to the age of sixty-seven on £850, but would go compulsorily at that same age and same rate. Generals could go at £1,000 under the age of sixty-seven, but would also have to go at that same age and rate at the age of sixty-seven. The changes had relatively limited impact in that the time to attain the ranks of captain, major, and lieutenant colonel showed little variation between 1886 and 1898.[24]

In terms of British general officers, besides four field marshals, there were 368 in August 1871: 276 from the Guards, line and cavalry, 48 from the artillery and engineers, and another 44 former Indian artillery and engineers taken into the British establishment after the Indian Mutiny (1857–58). Of these 368 generals, 176 were on retired pay, 25 on half-pay, and 2 on special retired pay.[25] The Royal Warrant of 1870 specified a limit of 275 British generals (excepting artillery and engineers) and 73 for the Indian Staff Corps. By January 1877 there were 315 British general officers and 43 Indian, representing a surplus of 40 British generals and a deficiency of 30 Indians. Adding together the effective and retired lists, there were 332 general officers in 1870, 456 in 1880, and 440 in 1885.[26]

The 1877 warrant had foreseen reducing the number of active British generals to 200. Childers wanted a reduction to between 140 and 160. Effective from 1 July 1881, generals would still be retired at sixty-seven but also if unemployed for five years. It was resolved there would be no promotions for the time being with various vacancies to be absorbed, although this was slightly modified by royal warrant in 1887.[27]

By October 1885, a total of twenty-one generals and thirteen lieutenant generals from the infantry and cavalry had been retired as reaching the age of sixty-seven, although nine of the generals and four of the lieutenant generals would also have gone by reason of unemployment. A further three generals and three lieutenant generals had been retired from the engineers and artillery.[28] In 1889 Edward Stanhope reduced the active generals' list from 140 to 100 on the grounds of efficiency but allowed for 85 commands to ensure sufficient employment. The reduction raised a storm of protest from effectively retired general officers, who believed themselves slighted by removal from the active list.

In 1889 there were ten generals, thirty-five lieutenant generals, and ninety-five major generals. Under the scheme, intended to start on 1 January 1891, there would be a maximum of twenty lieutenant generals and seventy major generals. The intention would be that sixteen of the lieutenant generals and fifty-one of the major generals would be employed.[29] There was to be gradual reduction by absorbing vacancies and restricting promotions. All major and lieutenant generals would now be chosen by selection, the original intention also being to apply this to generals as well.[30]

The question of nonemployment and, in effect, a roster for employment as vacancies occurred became an issue as reductions were implemented since there was always a surplus of general officers over actual vacancies. By 1893 Wolseley and Buller were complaining there were major generals still on the establishment—albeit unemployed—entirely unfit for command when able men were being driven out by the age regulations. Buller suggested one such major general was in a lunatic asylum, and another was the victim of creeping paralysis.[31] Wolseley felt there was little point in still employing 116 general officers, as was then the case, when there were posts for only 68: it added "grotesqueness to our official wickedness."[32]

Campbell-Bannerman felt a temporary solution would be to speed up reduction to 48 major generals, all of whom would be fit for command. By 1895, the total of general officers was still 113, but, as the Undersecretary of State Brodrick pointed out, Campbell-Bannerman had allowed ten colonels to receive major general's pay by virtue of occupying posts formerly held by major generals. Consequently, only seventeen actual major general's posts had been eliminated in six and a half years.[33] Wolseley considered there were still four too many generals, four too many lieutenant generals, and twenty-two too many major generals.[34]

In the Indian army, where purchase had also not applied, promotion was even slower than at home. In 1891 calculations showed that officers of the Indian Staff Corps were serving eleven, twenty, and twenty-six years on average before promotion to captain, major, and lieutenant colonel, respectively.[35] The Indian Staff Corps itself presented a particular problem in terms of its complex structure. It was established in January 1861 separately for the Bengal, Bombay, and Madras presidencies as a consequence of the transfer of officers from the East India Company's service to the Crown. The company had long divided administration into three presidencies, each maintaining its own military establishment, and this remained the case until the 1890s so that the "British army in India" existed alongside the Bengal, Bombay, and Madras armies. Most existing, and all new, officers became part of the Staff Corps. While being promoted regimentally for the purposes of seniority, they were available for both civil and military appointments. It thereby guaranteed promotion, albeit by length of service, which led to large numbers of senior officers for whom suitable posts commensurate with their rank could not be found. The system's labyrinthine complexity and innumerable anomalies generated endless difficulties.[36] Those unable to obtain promotion or civil employment—the "general list" officers—tended to hang on as long as possible for a modest pension. In 1882 it was decreed that regimental commanders and their immediate successors could not hold command after seven years or upon reaching the age of fifty-five, after which command was restricted to seven years or until reaching fifty-two. The three branches of the Staff Corps were amalgamated in 1891 but then abolished in 1903 with all officers simply appointed to the Indian army.[37]

So far as general officers were concerned, it was intended that promotion to the rank of general in the British or Indian army should be on one list strictly according to seniority. In 1864 the British and Indian lists had been separated.

This gave an advantage to Indian officers in terms of promotion from colonel to major general as there were fewer Indian colonels. To correct this imbalance, all British line colonels promoted to major general had their appointments antedated to place them above all major generals emanating from the Staff Corps on a single list in 1871. In 1877 further tinkering separated the lists once more as a result of the Penzance Commission's recommendations. Indian officers complained that they had not been properly represented on the commission, and expressed resentment at the mandatory retirement age of seventy, and at the reduction of the establishment of Indian generals from ninety-five to seventy.[38]

With the change to retirement rules in 1881, it was decided that Indian divisional commands could be held by either lieutenant or major generals, while first-class district brigades could be held by either major generals or brigadier generals. By such means, more employment could be found for general officers on the active list.[39] Cambridge had championed all brigades being in the hands of substantive major generals and all divisions being in the hands of lieutenant generals, to reduce the number of brigades in the hands of younger men.[40] The number of districts varied only marginally over time, the difference being that first-class district commanders reported to presidency army headquarters while the second-class district commanders reported to divisional commanders. In 1875 there were six first-class and four second-class districts in Bengal; four first-class districts in Madras; and two first-class and four second-class districts in Bombay. Ten years later, Bengal now had one additional second-class district, while Madras and Bombay remained unchanged. The number of divisions remained constant, with six in Bengal, three in Madras, and three in Bombay.

Until 1888, colonels acting as brigadier generals vacated second-class district commands if promoted to major general, but it was then decided to allow them to retain such commands until they were fifty-five: in 1892 this was changed to fifty-seven.[41] In 1890 the WO favored converting all second-class districts to major general's commands, thereby increasing the number of major generals from eight to nineteen, but the Viceroy's Council resisted the idea of restricting the choice to existing major generals or those at the very top of the colonel's list as it would limit selection.[42]

It was thought that if all second-class districts became major general's commands, then Horse Guards would take all British appointments out of the hands of the CinC in India. That might lead to the use of second-class districts as effective dumping grounds for otherwise unemployed major generals. As Henry Brackenbury expressed it, "they will put men in to prevent their being retired for non-employment."[43] With the replacement of the presidency armies with a corps scheme in 1895, the government of India ruled anyone losing his presidential appointment should be given an equal place in the new structure. In the case of Bombay, Sir Charles Nairne was therefore overruled when he wished to appoint Col. George Sartorius to either the Aden command or the Deesa second-class district since he had to find places for the secretary of the Military Department, Maj. Gen. Charles Cuningham, and the AG, Col. George Hogg.[44]

Cambridge, who had become CinC in July 1856, was alone exempted from the five-year rule on tenure as a necessary concession for his acquiescence in the abolition of purchase.[45] In practice, however, commands were often extended with both Wolseley and Buller spending seven years as AG, and Roberts seven years as CinC in India. For others, there were invariably complications over the conflict between age and tenure. Understandably, the general limitation of command tenure to five years and compulsory retirement if unemployed for five years from 1881 meant a constant juggling to secure posts that might enable individuals either to remain in the service or to prolong careers beyond retirement age by securing a post taking them beyond that age. In 1893 Cambridge proposed unsuccessfully that the retirement age for major generals be raised to sixty-four, but only as a means of extending the tenure of some favored individuals.[46]

Archibald Alison, for example, hoped he would be rewarded for his services in Egypt in 1882 with the substantive rank of major general as this would bring an earlier promotion to lieutenant general than might otherwise be the case and, therefore, the chance of later retirement.[47] Subsequently, Alison believed Cambridge had said the rule on retiring at sixty-seven could be waived in special circumstances, as had been done apparently for Sir Henry Smyth at Malta in 1890. In 1891, therefore, Alison indicated he would like the India command.[48] Cambridge raised Alison's name but was told firmly by Campbell-Bannerman that it was not realistic.[49]

The queen regretted Sir Daniel Lysons was to be removed from the Aldershot command in 1883 on the grounds of age three years into his five years' tenure.[50] That same year, special provision was made to retain Sir Andrew Clarke as IGF as a temporary major general when he would be compelled otherwise to retire since his work on colonial defenses was deemed essential.[51] In 1884 Roberts applied for a waiver for Maj. Gen. Sir Charles Keyes to remain at Secunderabad until he received his promotion to lieutenant general rather than retiring at sixty-two as the new nizam had just succeeded there, and there was no other suitable candidate.[52] Charles Walker Robinson thanked Cambridge for his appointment to the Mauritius command as a major general in 1892 and for the interest the duke had shown in "my being saved from retirement next year."[53]

Timing was all-important. Maj. Gen. Henry Warre, commanding at Belfast in October 1874, wanted to leave Ireland on health grounds and seek a command in a warmer clime. He offered to resign whenever Cambridge could make suitable arrangements for a successor. The MS, Maj. Gen. Sir Alfred Horsford, commented in passing, "Entre nous I may say that as the Duke generally selects for Brigadier Colonels high up in the List[,] a good man may lose a chance by finding himself suddenly made a Major-General."[54] Warre remained unemployed until 1878 when he received the Bombay command. By then he was approaching the top of the list of lieutenant generals and was so close to promotion to general it jeopardized a full term.[55]

Sir James Hills (Hills-Johnes from 1882) VC, who retired in 1888, was seen as "the victim of rapid promotion—like many others."[56] He complained he had been promoted too early. Hills-Johnes was first on the list for major general in 1879, but no actual command vacancy would arise for two years.[57] Hills suspected jobbery but Donald Stewart gave him this assurance: "No doubt there is a feeling of jealousy regarding Bobs [Roberts] and yourself among some Simla people, but I should not think of that as it cannot influence those who will have to decide the question of commands when the time comes."[58] With Stewart's support, Hills-Johnes secured command of Stewart's former division in the reconstituted Kabul Field Force in May 1880.

Two years later, there was still no command available although the rule on retiring after five years' unemployment did not apply to officers moving to the unemployed list from service in India. Hills-Johnes tried to get to Egypt in 1882, but Wolseley indicated an artillery general had already been appointed and there could not be a second.[59] Hills-Johnes was duly promoted to lieutenant general in 1883 at the age of only fifty and was simply too senior for any command likely to become vacant in India.[60] He had been ruled out of contention for Madras because there could not be two old Bengal artillery hands in high commands at the same time (the other being Roberts). He remained unemployed in 1887 when there could be only one lieutenant general from the artillery branch in Bengal at any one time. Moreover, due to the intended reductions, any lieutenant general commanding a division could not be replaced by another lieutenant general. Still vainly hoping for an active command, a retired Hills-Johnes asked for even a reserve battalion in 1900, but, not unexpectedly, he was "too big a man" for such a junior appointment.[61]

Process

Prior to 1889, selection for higher command and staff was vested solely in the CinC acting through the MS at Horse Guards. The latter had also been regulated in 1871 as a five-year appointment. Fitzroy Somerset, later Lord Raglan, had held the post from 1827 to 1852, while the incumbent in 1871, the notoriously bad-tempered Sir William Forster, had been in the post for eleven years.

It remained a key appointment. Cambridge always wished to secure someone with whom he was comfortable and, wherever possible, to hold on to them. Cardwell suggested Wolseley as Forster's successor, but Cambridge dismissed the idea as "simply ridiculous," preferring Maj. Gen. Caledon Egerton or possibly Sir Charles Staveley.[62] Cardwell objected to Egerton, possibly because he was the brother of a Conservative MP.[63] Cardwell seemed to favor a senior officer, so Cambridge suggested Lt. Gen. Sir James Lindsay, but he was a guardsman with little knowledge of line officers.[64] One compromise suggested was Egerton as MS and Col. James Armstrong as AMS in order to create "the outside impression that there is an infusion of fresh blood" although the latter would soon be promoted to major general.[65] In mulling this over, Cambridge was prepared to consider Wolseley anew as AMS. In any event, the Egerton-Armstrong combination was accepted by Cardwell, albeit Armstrong was appointed as DAG rather than as AMS.

Egerton died in May 1874 and Lindsay succeeded him, only to die himself in August. This presented Cambridge with a problem. He concluded Maj. Gen. Sir Alfred Horsford would suit him best, as he had a good manner and was a "good deal known socially." Cambridge felt it impossible to appoint the long-serving AMS for India, Edwin Johnson, as an Indian officer, whereas Edmund Whitmore was too junior. Interestingly, Cambridge had previously thought Horsford "not enough of a man of business."[66]

Whitmore duly succeeded Horsford in 1880. Of Whitmore, the *Whitehall Review* remarked on 21 October 1880, "those who have attended his levees say they can scarcely bring themselves to believe that they have breathed the same atmosphere as during the late regime, so courteously are they received and so thoroughly does the Military Secretary inspire them with a sense of confidence in his professions of friendliness."[67] Whitmore proved so acceptable that Cambridge was desperate to get his tenure prolonged even though Whitmore himself was anxious to be relieved of his duties. Cambridge insisted he remain; as Whitmore recalled: "I am to be kept on by the week like a charwoman."[68] In pointing out that Whitmore wanted to retire, W. H. Smith urged Cambridge "to take the very disagreeable plunge as on the whole the course which will most conduce to your personal comfort and to the interests of the Service."

Forced to accept Whitmore's retirement, Cambridge opted for the DAG, Maj. Gen. George Harman, as his successor.[69]

Succeeding to the post in 1901, Ian Hamilton found the work of MS peculiarly repugnant, "consisting as it does principally of the opposing a constant non possumus to the aspirations of one's friends & comrades."[70] At times, it was clearly difficult. Sir Reginald Gipps told Wallscourt Waters during a particularly frosty interview in 1893, "One never knows anything here for certain: that door there may be opened, and I will be told that some appointment, made by His Royal Highness, has been cancelled. That's all I know; good afternoon."[71] On another occasion, Horsford did not keep Cambridge informed. In January 1877 Charles "Chinese" Gordon initially declined a telegraphed offer from the khedive to return to the Sudan as governor-general. He then accepted when told by Horsford through an intermediary (Eyre) that Cambridge wanted him to go. On taking his leave of Cambridge, to Gordon's astonishment, the duke asked why he was going: "I was in a fix, for I feared compromising Horsford & Eyre. The fact was that the Duke never had heard of the telegram & consequently had given no opinion on it, & Horsford had used his name in vain." Having looked at the telegram, Cambridge said Gordon should go.[72]

Generally, the MS put forward three names as vacancies occurred. Candidates were usually notified they were in the running to ascertain their willingness.[73] There was little redress once a decision had been made.[74] To turn down what was on offer carried some risk, and thus required careful consideration on the part of the individual lest he jeopardize his future employment opportunities. In January 1872 William Chamberlayne was offered the post of colonel on the staff in Mauritius, and was informed that to decline would not harm his future prospects. Nonetheless, Chamberlayne was wise enough to accept.[75] In February 1884 it was pointed out to Col. Alfred Templeman, who commanded the Stirling regimental district, that turning down the command at Taunton when he had specifically asked for one in southern England was foolish. Later that same year, Col. the Hon. George Villiers, who had spent the last five years as military attaché in Paris, was warned "not to lose the substance in clutching at the shadow" by leaving in the hope that he might receive a staff posting when indefinite regimental employment was a more likely consequence.[76]

A certain amount of negotiation, however, was possible. In December 1877 Evelyn Wood, then AQMG at Aldershot, juggled the relative merits of becoming commandant of the Staff College with command of the 90th Foot. The 90th was due for the Cape, which at the time seemed unlikely to result in any great opportunities of active service even though the Ninth Cape Frontier War had erupted. The 90th was then due for Malta, where there might be better prospects of participating in any war in Europe. Moreover, accepting the Staff

College post might lessen the chance of getting a brigade command although it would suit his family.[77] Wood chose his regiment. In 1886 Wood turned down offers of a division in India and posts at Dublin and York before getting GOC of Eastern District at Colchester.[78] While at Aldershot in 1890, Wood turned down being considered for Bombay as he enjoyed Aldershot, and had a potentially expensive lawsuit under way in England contesting his aunt's will in favor of his sister, Kitty O'Shea. He would only go if, by doing so, there was a real prospect of succeeding Roberts as CinC.[79]

It was always possible for an officer to bring himself to notice by appointment through the MS or by attending the regular levees of CinC and MS. These were intended to enable the CinC to see all officers either upon taking up or leaving a command or staff appointment, but also any officer who wished to have his case taken up. In any case, it was often advantageous to appear before Cambridge so as to be known to him.[80] The levees are noted rarely in memoirs and correspondence, and their significance has been overlooked. Under Cambridge's administration, "plain clothes" levees took place fortnightly in the afternoon. One of the few descriptions is by James Edmonds: "The old Duke used to appear at 3 P.M. in evening dress, wearing the ribbon of the garter, and go to a standing desk on which the Military Secretary would lay each officer's dossier; the officer, if he had a grievance, at any rate had his say."[81]

William Butler attended a levee with Cambridge on returning from Natal in 1875: "His Royal Highness was kind and gracious, said some nice things about bygone service, and a week or two later I was agreeably surprised to receive a letter from his military secretary asking if I would accept the position of deputy assistant quartermaster-general at headquarters."[82] Richard Harrison, who had been AQMG in the Sudan before resuming his former post as AQMG at Aldershot, went to one of Harman's levees in 1886 since his appointment was coming to a close. Harman told Harrison, an engineer, he must look to returning to service with the corps. Harrison doubted this would be possible as he had been so long on staff work. In any event, he spent six months on half-pay before being made CRE at Dover and, after only four months there, CRE at Aldershot.[83]

Issues raised at levees were certainly followed up.[84] In June 1890 Cambridge understood Maj. Gen. Lord William Seymour's appearance before him was merely a courtesy call. When Seymour indicated subsequently that he wanted employment, Cambridge undertook to interview him again. Subsequently, Cambridge was sufficiently angered by press speculation that Seymour would get the command of British forces in Egypt to deny it publicly at a dinner at Marlborough House. Seymour, however, was told this would not injure his prospects and that he would get command of the Dover District.[85]

Sir Frederick Maude VC recorded uniquely the details of several appearances at levees over the years in such detail it is instructive to follow his experience at length. Between November 1873 and May 1884, Maude attended twelve levees with either Cambridge or the MS. On his second meeting with Cambridge on 17 March 1874, he recorded:

> He said I looked very young [Maude was fifty-three]: asked me what service I had & how I stood for my rank. Said I looked very young for that service & perhaps had been badly wounded [while winning the VC in September 1855]. I said I hoped my looking so young would not prevent my being employed upon an opportunity offered, & that I felt my wound every day. He laughed & seemed to say he would take care of me.[86]

Promoted to major general, Maude attended another of Cambridge's levees on 24 July 1874: "Shook hands—he said, at last you are a general. I suppose you are tired of walking about. I said, yes indeed I am & I wish your RH would give me something but I know you have many to provide for. He said yes and how [I looked] very young. I said I am not so young as I look: he laughed & said you look very young. He shook hands & wrote something down."[87]

Following his command of the reserve division of the Peshawar Field Force in the first phase of the Second Afghan War, Maude became unemployed when his five years' tenure at Rawalpindi was up. In May 1882 he saw Cambridge but, on this occasion, "asked for nothing."[88] In June he saw Whitmore on the possibility of becoming governor of Sandhurst:

> He says it is given away to someone who has been there or something like that. Was nice, but I do not think will take much trouble about me. . . . Asked if I would like to get to foreign manoeuvres, but he supposed not, as it would cost expense. I told him I did not like to sail under false colours & that I was rather deaf but that if he could get me anything I could hold I should be glad, as my time would be up in 85 & I should have to leave as a L.G. *He said he would.*[89]

Nothing came of this. Two years later, Maude, now a senior lieutenant general, saw Whitmore on 2 May 1884: "He said there was nothing against me, but nothing vacant, that possibly something might any day throw up, & he would do what he could for me. I let him see I felt it very much being passed over by [Lt. Gen. Sir George] Willis [for the Southern District] & so long unemployed: VC, 3 campaigns. Said he had no power now; all nonsense. I think my visit may do good, though there is nothing going at present."[90] With other posts escaping him, Maude sought explanation. It was finally Whitmore who indicated the real problem was Maude's deafness, and Cambridge confirmed this at another levee in May 1885.[91] Maude still hoped for perhaps South Africa or Madras, but Harman raised the issue of deafness, which he feared would "prove a great obstacle in itself, which unfortunately must be taken into account in so important a position as the one you aspire to."[92]

The levees continued under Wolseley. One reference in Wolseley's correspondence in September 1884 suggests he had held levees as AG: "I took out with me a copy of the list of officers who had sent their names to the Military Secretary for employment in Egypt, also the list of those who attended my levee as Adj. General asking to come here."[93] Keen for field service, Edward May believed only senior officers attended levees, but he was advised this was not the case. Attending to Wolseley in 1897, May found him leaning on a standing desk at a window clearly expecting to hear of a grievance: "I told him I did not want anything except to go on active service. He was manifestly relieved and considerably astonished." Wolseley promised he would try to meet May's wishes, and they fell into a conversation about May's horse artillery battery and new guns that had not yet been delivered.[94] Wolseley told his wife in July 1898 that making all officers attend in uniform "chokes off many a chap who has no red coat with him in town." It was also a tiring process "standing a long time and hearing numerous grievances."[95]

In addition to formal appointments, men could go to the WO on the off chance of an opportunity.[96] It was also common to visit the WO when on home leave.[97] It was certainly always possible to make preferences known. In 1883 James Dormer wrote directly to Whitmore to ask if he could be considered as AMS at Horse Guards although he had little hope of securing the position as a junior major general.[98] While expressing a willingness to take any post offered in 1895, Edward "Curly" Hutton specifically mentioned the soon-to-be vacant command in Canada.[99]

The process after the abolition of purchase was characterized as "seniority tempered by selection."[100] Cambridge outlined what he understood by this in July 1871:

> It is intended, unless I am greatly mistaken, that, after purchase has been put an end to, the system shall be one of seniority tempered by selection. For example, if an officer is unfit to command a regiment he will not by course of promotion receive the command of one, and, on the other hand, eminent professional talent will be recognized and encouraged; but care will be taken, as I understand, to preserve the regimental system as far as possible, providing also that purchase does not revive under a new form.[101]

In effect, promotion should proceed by seniority unless an officer was manifestly incompetent. Salisbury referred to it as "stagnation tempered by jobbery."[102]

Wolseley had long favored selection, writing in June 1868 of the GOC in Canada, Gen. Sir Charles Wyndham, and the lieutenant governor of Ontario, Maj. Gen. Henry Stisted, as "drivelling idiots. . . . I cannot help feeling that our Army System is rotten when it permits of such men ever rising to command anything."[103] As he also wrote in 1872,

> With us it is not the best men that are selected for commands, but those who possess what is termed "the best claims." The vested interests of officers have still great weight at the Horse Guards; and as long that it is considered that all vacant positons of importance must be given to the seniors, so long shall we suffer as an army and as a nation. Nine times out of ten the most important appointments are bestowed upon men as a reward for long, and perhaps, meritorious, service.[104]

In May 1885 Cambridge complained about Wolseley's wider comments on the selection of regimental commanders after his conclusions from viewing their performance during the Sudan campaign reached the secretary of state for war in a public dispatch rather than by being sent to him alone and in confidence.[105] Wolseley replied that Cambridge's opposition to selection was well known:

> I believe in selection. I see it worked in the Navy. It is indeed—nowadays—a most rare thing to find a Captain Commanding an ironclad who is unfit for his position. If it can be worked in the Navy and as regards all New Commissioned Officers in regiments, my contention is that it can be similarly worked generally in the Army, and I am indeed sorry to find that Your Royal Highness is displeased at my holding those views and at my venturing to put them into such a shape as to oblige the War Minister to consider them.[106]

Cambridge was not always consistent. According to the secretary of state, Gathorne Hardy, recording in October 1874, Cambridge "warns a man that he will not promote him & calls for his retirement & then suddenly puts his name forward for the step, with a reason which is untenable as it existed when he first threatened."[107] But on seniority, Cambridge never wavered. As he wrote to Roberts in March 1887, "I find [seniority] always answered better than simply to select what may be a better man if by so doing I hurt the feelings and prospects of deserving officers."[108] Wolseley complained in 1878 that

> HRH [Cambridge] won't employ the young rising men and amongst the old ones he has scarcely any choice, a few can walk—none could run upstairs, and the others are as feeble in body as they are behind the age in all that relates

to their profession. When will the time arrive when the clique of clerks who sell appointments and the idle Military Secretary sort of fellow, who is supposed to advise the CinC on such matters, will be driven from the War Office, and men selected for the high positons in the army irrespective of their age because they are the best capable of doing Her Majesty good service[?].[109]

So far as Cambridge was concerned, seniority remained sacrosanct. Childers wanted Evelyn Wood appointed to substantive major general as a reward for his services in South Africa in 1881, suggesting it would be a particularly suitable instance of selection. Cambridge countered it would be a "strong thing" when there were 140 colonels senior to Wood.[110] Of selection, Cambridge had written in July 1881, "The difficulties are I believe *insurmountable* without jobbery which I for one detest & it must end I think by seniority with *rejection* and even this we find on experience very awkward."[111] In November 1881 Cambridge similarly wrote that selection "to my mind can only lead to jobbery & injustice, though I quite admit that the power of selection is right & valuable but its application should be only rarely had recourse to, excepting as to rejecting an incompetent man."[112]

The CinC's Selection Book began to record alternative promotions from colonel to major general by seniority and by selection from January 1886 onward. In 1889 Stanhope instituted a Selection Board in the hope both of reducing the number of general officers and, as already indicated, of securing promotion only by selection, in effect from 1 January 1891. Selection applied to major generals and lieutenant generals, full generals still being chosen by seniority unless appointed to a particular post carrying general's rank or for distinguished service. The intention was to make generals subject to selection as well, but it was resolved to wait until the reduction of the generals' establishment was completed.[113]

Two remarkably similar apocryphal accounts of the meeting of the board survive, which are worth quoting. At the very least, they suggest a general impression of proceedings. In his memoirs, Maj. Gen. Granville Egerton, then a captain, has Cambridge arriving in a temper:

"Well, I suppose we must get on with this new fangled nonsense, go on, read out the names." At the first name read out, Wolseley said, "He's deaf." "What?" said Evelyn Wood, who was himself as deaf as 40 posts, "Dead?"—"No," replied Wolseley, "D E A F." "Humph," answered Wood, "lot of good officers are deaf." Later on Wood remarked that a certain officer was a VC, on which Wolseley countered, that he did not in the least consider that fact any claim for advertisement—Wood, of course, being a VC. Then the old Duke chipped in, "Whose name was that? Oh! Colonel Brown,—oh! Good old fellow!—Yes, certainly, promote him; but that man Jones, No, scratch him out, nasty fellow—I hate him."[114]

There is then the memoir of Lt. Col. Arthur Richardson. A name is read out:

"Does anyone know anything about him?" asked H.R.H. "Yes, Your Royal Highness"—Shouting, H.R.H. being deaf. "Speak up! I can't hear you." "Yes, Sir. He's one of the So-and-So's of So-and-So. Plenty of stuff, And he's married to a very smart little woman." "Promote him. Who's next?"—"Does anyone know anything about him?" "He's a very good regimental officer, Sir." "What's his wife like?" "I don't know her." "Eh, What? He don't show her?" "No, Sir, I don't know her." "Oh! Don't you? Anything else about him?" "He's a little deaf." "Lately dead! Why's his name here then? Cross him off. Who's the next?"[115]

While vacancies were absorbed without new appointments being made, Cambridge strenuously resisted yielding to selection. In 1894 Cambridge declared he "did not care a damn" about the board's recommendations for promotions in the Royal Artillery.[116] Given Buller's recommendation of either Col. James Alleyne or Maj. Gen. Albert Williams as the next DAGRA in 1892, Cambridge predictably preferred Williams.[117] Williams was not just a friend of Cambridge, but the duke thought "that in him he will have the officer most opposed to change that he can find." The post had never previously been filled other than by a colonel, and there were only five artillery colonels senior to Alleyne, of whom three already had posts.[118] Such was Cambridge's friendship with Williams that he even tried to get the retirement age for major generals raised to sixty-four in order to prolong Williams's tenure in 1893.[119]

In January 1895 Buller threatened to resign as AG when, prompted by the Prince of Wales, Cambridge proposed the unpopular Maj. Gen. "Eddy" Wood for the Shorncliffe command ahead of two other major generals recommended by the board. Buller observed, "seems to me to be advertising to the Army that the Promotion Board is a farce and that an officer only has to ingratiate himself with personages in order to be considered best qualified for good appointments."[120] Campbell-Bannerman was sufficiently convinced of Wood's worthiness to allow it.[121] Similarly, Wolseley had appealed to Campbell-Bannerman to intervene when Cambridge was determined to promote Col. Arthur Harness, showing his utter contempt for the board.[122]

On occasion, other considerations applied. In 1892 the board turned down Col. Alexander Kidston for promotion or further employment as being both dull and stupid—a "gloomy ass."[123] Campbell-Bannerman urged reconsideration on the basis that Kidston was well regarded in Scotland and, if given a Scottish regimental district, might well bring in more recruits. Cambridge, too, wished to overrule the board. Wolseley liked Kidston personally but considered that

> he ought, most certainly, never to be promoted. It would be to go back to our worst period to ever give him any hope or prospect of promotion, but he could do little harm anywhere & none in a Scotch regimental District—please do not send him to Ireland. . . . I don't know if he plays the pipes or can dance a sword dance. If he has these national accomplishments he would do well to send round the town & villages as a Recruiting Agent, for he is very Scots, & looks formidable in a kilt.[124]

As a consequence of the changes in the powers of the CinC upon Cambridge's retirement, promotions to and above the rank of major and staff appointments above the rank of lieutenant colonel were vested in what was now called the Army Board. The CinC was no longer tasked with selecting officers but "proposing fit and proper officers" for promotion and appointments.[125] The board became the Selection Board again when the CinC's committee was renamed the Army Board in September 1899, although its meetings were then suspended with the outbreak of the South African War, leaving appointments once more in the hands of the CinC and the MS.[126]

According to Evelyn Wood in his evidence to the Elgin Commission, the CinC was now only "first among equals" and did not always get his way.[127] Brackenbury, too, suggested that the CinC had "only the same voice as any one of his own staff in promotions & appointments," although Wolseley recorded that "all soldiers wanting employment are nice to a Comd. in Chief."[128]

Wood acknowledged there was general agreement in nine cases out of ten, which is not perhaps surprising given that the members of the board between 1895 and 1899 were all closely associated with Wolseley and were likely to share many of his views. A total of seven men shared the other four offices alongside Wolseley, of whom five—Buller, Wood, Brackenbury, Charles Mansfield Clarke, and Richard Harrison—had been members of the Wolseley ring.

In fact, seniority continued to be of significance. Wolseley's own close adherents were gaining preferment as much through their seniority as through Wolseley's patronage.[129] The WO Committee on Selection recommended in November 1897 that a quarter of promotions to major general still be filled by seniority in 1898 and a fifth in 1899, with full selection only coming into effect in 1900.[130] Salisbury also could still write in 1896 that "seniority goes for a great deal too much in the Army and that machinery of promotion by merit is sorely wanted."[131]

Promotion to full general still went by seniority until such time as the establishment had been reduced to ten (including three in India) not counting those promoted by virtue of appointment or distinguished service. Consideration was given to bringing in selection for the ten generals on the establishment in 1901 in accordance with the original intentions of the 1889 warrant. That in itself was ambiguous insofar as the generals' establishment was concerned. If, for example, a British officer became CinC in India, there might be no other generals in the Indian army for five years.[132] Brodrick, as secretary of state, decided that only the post of CinC, whether at home or in India, should be reserved for a general by virtue of appointment, although in India the supreme command could be held by a lieutenant general holding temporary general's rank. Otherwise, no officer who had not been selected as a lieutenant general could now be considered for promotion to general.[133]

Writing in 1903, George Henderson noted that although progress had been made in selection, it had been too timidly applied and, while staff employment and brevets offered openings for the more able, the rule still held that "good appointments were made for men, and not good men for the appointments."[134] According to James Edmonds, the patronage powers of the MS, "tempered by the wishes of the commander-in-chief," only ceased when the new Selection Board was established under the auspices of the new Army Council in 1904. Edmonds considered the system was still unsatisfactory because officers made appeals to any members of the Board they knew for redress, with a resulting increase in jobbery. Edmonds claimed Cambridge's nephew, the Earl of Athlone, had confirmed the gist of Cambridge's reported comments: "I did a few jobs in the nearly forty years that I was Commander-in-Chief; Wolseley, in four years, did more jobs than I did in forty; but Roberts has already done more than I and Wolseley put together."[135]

Confidential Reports

In truth, there was little for Horse Guards to go on in terms of assessing officers' capabilities. The principal means was the annual report—somewhat similar to the "dossiers" of the medical profession[136]—but the system was deeply flawed. Appearing before the Elgin Commission, Evelyn Wood placed blame for military failure on the annual confidential reports on which the Selection Board relied: "The confidential reports up to recently have not been sufficiently drastic and straight; it is only in recent years that the man making the report has understood that his own character is also at stake for fairness and for telling the facts as they really are."[137]

To Wood, promotion up to the rank of major appeared automatic. Thereafter, it was a matter of seniority tempered by rejection only in the very worst cases despite the fact that selection of higher commands by merit alone had been supposedly in force since 1891.[138] Wood suggested there were three distinct categories of officers that could be identified from confidential reports. There were those whose fitness for advancement was undoubted, and those with such a bad record their unfitness was readily apparent. The great majority were "colourless men," who had been promoted "simply because 'there is nothing known against them'"; he was quoting his own memorandum on selection written in October 1900.[139] The Akers-Douglas Committee suggested in 1902 that at lower levels under the existing system, "the promotion of indolent officers is as rapid as—and may be more rapid than—that of their more industrious comrades."[140]

While relatively small, the officer corps was still large enough for men not to be known to each other. When Henry Warre was appointed to the Bombay command in 1878, the CinC in India, Frederick Haines, had not seen him since 1851.[141] Cambridge wrote in 1880 that he hardly knew Donald Stewart, "& this is a great drawback."[142] In light of this, the reports were all the more important. As military member, Brackenbury, who was new to India, noted in October 1891 that he knew none of those up for promotion and could not offer a real opinion. Two years later, Brackenbury remarked to one applicant for a presidency post that the local CinCs "have before them the confidential reports upon all officers, which give the history of their careers; and through their own knowledge and that of their staffs are able to judge the qualifications of officers far better than I can do."[143]

Criticism of confidential reports was not new. The Penzance Commission noted that, in the first two years of the operation of the new style form introduced in April 1873, only 48 officers in the entire army had been reported as unfit for promotion. A further 143 had been reported on unfavorably but not as unfit for promotion, while 5 officers regarded as unfit had been promoted but immediately retired on the grounds of previous good service; seven more had improved sufficiently to be promoted; 5 more had been passed over.[144]

In October 1888 Sir George Chesney, Brackenbury's predecessor as military member, complained that there was a reluctance to report adversely on subordinates by those "who in their desire to make things pleasant, do not put before A.H.Q. & Govt. their real opinions about officers." According to Chesney, Indian district commanders would not commit to paper what they really thought of individual officers, with the effect that "no one wd. infer from them, what has been notorious for years to everyone in the army, except apparently the General O.C. [of] the district," which officers were "thoroughly useless." Whereas the authorities might be aware of an officer's incompetence, lacking "public vouchers to that effect," they were unable to "establish a case merely on private opinion" without "something official and definite to go on."[145]

In a similar vein, Donald Stewart, soon to become CinC in India, wrote in 1880, "The curse of our service is that people—I mean most people—won't say what they think about an officer till it is too late. Then the authorities who ought to know all about the Army then round and say there is nothing on record against so & so as if that were a sufficient recommendation in his favour."[146] Amid the recriminations following the disaster at Maiwand in Afghanistan in July 1880, Cambridge criticized Henry Warre for his selection of Lt. Gen. James Primrose for the command at Kandahar. Warre tried to deflect criticism by suggesting he should not have been expected to report on someone of equal rank. Cambridge retorted that a candid view should have been given: "In high positions disagreeable things have to be done at times for the good of the public service." Cambridge also suggested he had advanced Primrose in rank previously in the belief he was able, and could not have known otherwise unless properly informed through reports.[147]

When he was CinC, Wolseley complained to Roberts, now commanding in Ireland, in September 1895 that the Selection Board was necessarily guided by confidential reports but that, in the case of officers of the Indian army, they were of little use: "All their geese are swans."[148] Wolseley had earlier used the same phrase regarding confidential reports by his four district commanders when he commanded in Ireland.[149] Roberts was well aware of the problem, having noted previously that, "as a rule, I have observed that whether men behave well or ill, they are spoken of in the same terms, and get the same reward."[150] Neville Lyttelton, who became AMS in 1897, felt too many reports still displayed the old tendencies he had first seen as MS at Gibraltar ten years earlier in reluctance to find fault.[151]

The form of the annual report changed over time.[152] More and more detail was required as to such qualities as general ability, capacity for command, self-reliance, judgement and tact, temper, and practical proficiency, as well as specific knowledge for artillery and engineers. When Paul Methuen was about to be appointed AAG to the Irish command in 1877, his predecessor told him that dealing with the confidential reports for seven cavalry regiments, twenty-one infantry battalions, and three companies of engineers, as well as for all the staff, was "the devil" in terms of work. The process began each August and continued until the following March.[153] One of the points Cambridge made to the Penzance Commission was that, with over six thousand annual reports reaching Horse Guards, he could not adequately adjudicate between them, especially if trying to compare, for example, field service in India with garrison duty in the West Indies. He also believed he would undermine regimental esprit de corps by using confidential reports to pass over officers when it was better to persuade the inefficient to retire.[154]

Surviving Irish command reports suggest Wood was essentially correct: detailed comments recorded in summary returns tended to relate routinely to the OC and second in command of units, but, otherwise only to those with obvious failings. To some extent, it depended on the GOC. Upon assuming the Irish command in October 1880, General Sir Thomas Steele directed that only unfavorable reports should be recorded. By contrast, Wolseley insisted the first four officers in a unit should be reported on as to their fitness for promotion if it was a two-battalion regiment, or the first six officers in the case of a three-battalion regiment. Forms had to be filled in properly and fully.[155] Yet, even in Wolseley's time, every subordinate officer in a regiment could be returned simply as satisfactory.[156]

There is evidence of the reluctance to be specific in comments. In August 1884, Maj. Gen. Lord Clarina, commanding Dublin District, reported Lt. Col. John Blaksley of the First Buffs was not a success "although I am not prepared to give any specific reasons for expressing this opinion, but he is certainly not popular with his officers & is disliked socially according to common report."[157] The MS responded by demanding a full report: "It is necessary that reasons should be fully given for forming an adverse opinion regarding any officer, but Lord Clarina, although he has formed an unfavourable opinion of Lt. Col. Blaksley, states that he is not prepared to give any reasons for having formed it."[158] Clarina replied with details of Blaksley's want of tact and judgment, defending his own original intention as being a desire "to avoid troubling the authorities with unnecessary correspondence." Blaksley had quarreled with his officers and could not command their "esteem."[159] Cambridge concluded from the evidence now presented that Blaksley should be compelled to retire. Blaksley denied being on poor terms with his officers, and entered a heartfelt plea to be allowed to continue in the army, at which point Clarina said he would say no more to damage Blaksley's prospects. He trusted the episode to have taught Blaksley the need for requisite tact.[160]

In the following year, Clarina was again compelled to further elucidate remarks made concerning two officers. Clarina excused himself on the grounds that, with between five hundred and six hundred officers in Dublin District, he "need scarcely observe that it is manifestly impossible for him to become personally acquainted with the qualifications of every individual officer, therefore he is obliged in a great measure, to rely on the information he obtains from Comg. Offs."[161] One of the two officers had been reported previously as satisfactory. Cambridge demanded to know how these reports could be reconciled, noting he "is obliged to rely on the reports received from Genl. Officers to assist him in deciding as to the fitness of an officer for promotion, and specially in the selection of a Lieut. Colonel for the responsible position of the command of a

Battalion, and H.R.H. is placed in a very difficult position, when, after acting on such a report and appointing an officer to a command, he receives an unfavourable report from the same General Officer."[162]

Clarina replied that he felt "no difficulty in reconciling the apparent anomaly of his having in three separate reports rendered in three different years expressed opinions regarding an officer at variance with one another." Rather giving the game away, Prince Edward wrote, "No man can possibly more dislike having to make a disparaging remark as to the capacity of an officer than he (Lord C.) does, and he trusts H.R.H. will credit him with the desire to faithfully discharge the somewhat invidious duties which an Inspg. Gen. Officer is required to perform & that his explanation may be considered sufficient."[163]

Disagreement over the quality of an officer and adverse comment could have its roots in personalities. In 1889 there was a clash between Maj. Gen. Henry Davies, commanding Cork District, and Lt. Col. Thomas St. Clair of the Second Princess Charlotte of Wales's (Royal Berkshire) Regiment. St. Clair reported adversely on Maj. Justinian Ponsonby, after which Davies suggested St. Clair lacked tact. St. Clair claimed Davies's hostility toward him originated from the time they had served together in Southern District. Davies, in turn, took strong exception to any idea he had been influenced by unsubstantiated reports. Cambridge upheld Davies's report, St. Clair having been cited for his temper as far back as 1878. Two years later, St. Clair again reported Ponsonby unfit for promotion, but Davies did not agree. Cambridge found no reason to question Davies's assessment in the light of St. Clair's own record, concluding Ponsonby was fit for promotion.[164] In 1892 there was an acrimonious correspondence between the MS and the now retired Col. Charles Slade over the proposed promotion of Maj. Cecil St. Paul to command a battalion of the Rifle Brigade. Slade was told to justify his private statement that St. Paul was unfit for command when previous confidential reports suggested the latter had the integrity of a Pitt, the virtues of Saint Augustine, and the military genius of Napoleon.[165]

One lasting dispute that played out in the confidential reports was between Roberts and Sir Charles Gough. In December 1879 when Roberts forced his way into Kabul, he was besieged in the Sherpur cantonment. Commanding a brigade on the LOC, Gough was ordered to advance from Jagdalak to reinforce Roberts at Sherpur, some seventy miles away and with snow thick on the ground. Peremptory orders from Roberts contradicted those Gough received from his immediate superior, Maj. Gen. Robert Bright. Gough believed Roberts was "screaming (by every letter he could get through) to me to advance *at all risks* and regardless of anything else but himself, on Kabul—and Bright imploring and *ordering* me in the strongest terms *not* to advance until I got reinforcements!! . . . Roberts thinks I was not half bold enough, and Bright thinks I was insane and rash to guilt and folly!!!"[166]

Roberts thought Gough unnecessarily slow in taking twelve days to get through to him although Gough's achievement was characterized as "perhaps the most adventurous march of the war."[167] Thereafter Roberts went out of his way to damage Gough's reputation. He included derogatory reflections in his correspondence, and did his best to ensure Gough would not get the Madras command in 1890. There was also what Gough took to be a damning slight in Roberts's autobiography, *Forty-one Years in India,* published in 1897.[168] Confidential reports also served Roberts's purpose. In 1888, as commander of the Oudh Division, Gough was characterized as able and energetic by Roberts, who added, "Of his power to act with decision when a crisis arrives I have some doubt." The 1890 report was the same.[169]

Ultimately, what mattered most, as Wolseley and Roberts invariably stressed, was how an individual performed on the battlefield. They expressed themselves freely on the quality of fellow officers in their private correspondence, and postcampaign reports were also common. Maj. Gen. John Davis, for example, complained to Wolseley in April 1884 that Buller had been made second in command at Suakin rather than himself. He received the withering reply that, in view of his own lack of active service experience, he was lucky to get to Suakin at all: his commission was but a parchment title, for only battle conferred the right to command.[170] Writing to Reginald Pole-Carew, Lt. Alexander Fortescue related a story going the rounds in Egypt:

> Said Davis "Beastly country this, no sport, no hunting, no fishing." W[olseley] "No sport, no fishing! Why I am told the natives catch lots of fish in the Canals." D "And do you mean to say Sir you would like to see me, a British Major Genl. squatting on the bank of a canal fishing and doing the other thing at the same time like a d—d native." Genl. Davis is not going up the Nile.[171]

Frederick Appleyard, a brigade commander in the Peshawar Field Force in 1878–79, complained bitterly in 1882 that, as a result of an unfavorable report on him for the loss of transport animals and baggage during a reconnaissance to Tarakai, Cambridge had refused him promotion. Appleyard's appeal proved fruitless, and he was retired as a major general in 1884.[172] At the time, Appleyard had been absolved from blame by an official report, but the viceroy, Lytton, refused to allow him to be reemployed in Afghanistan. Appleyard was also denied a KCB as a result of Lytton's report.[173]

Some who had been praised routinely in successive reports fell short of expectations. Sir John McQueen had received glowing reports and was nominated by Roberts as CoS to the Second Corps in the event of a full war mobilization in India in October 1886.[174] McQueen, however, failed to conduct the 1888 Black Mountain expedition to Roberts's satisfaction. In Roberts's view, McQueen was now "quite the most unsatisfactory commander I have had to deal with and I would never trust him with the conduct of another expedition."[175] True to his word, he told McQueen in 1891 he was not fit for field command.[176]

In 1894 George White found Brig. Gen. Alexander Kinloch at Peshawar "altogether a man of considerable mark, which he would probably make greater on service." A year later, following Kinloch's indifferent performance on the Chitral relief expedition, he had "shown none of the dash or enterprise I expected of him."[177] It was rumored that Kinloch had suffered a total breakdown and only copious bottles of port had kept him going.[178] Buller suggested privately that Kinloch's chance had come too late after prolonged Indian service and exposure to the sun. He should no longer be considered for the Burma command for "it would never do to have a man who proved himself of no use in war, and yet was a great martinet, and very exigent of his Troops, in peace time."[179] Kinloch disputed that he lacked nerve, which opinion he believed had originated with the Chitral expedition commander, Sir Robert Low, whose operational plans he had questioned. Kinloch had thereby lost a first-class district command worth £3,000 a year, promotion to substantive major general, a higher pension, potential honors, further employment, and his reputation.[180]

In the same way, the formerly favorable opinions of Brig. Gen. Francis Kempster ended with his perceived failings during the Tirah campaign of 1897. Perversely, his immediate superior gave him a very favorable report in 1899 on the grounds of the "practical knowledge of his profession gained on active service."[181] Once seen as a coming man, Kempster retired in 1902 when he still had potentially ten years' more service.[182] Kempster, contemptuously referred to by William Nicholson as "this Egyptian hero," was far from popular in his brigade and tended to blame his subordinates for his own mistakes.[183] His errors were compounded by the action on 11 December 1897 when Kempster returned to camp early with his advance guard leaving the rear guard still engaged.[184] According to George MacMunn, the sayings "To be Kempstered" and "I'm Kempstered if I do" became a ribald phrase and an expression of dissent, respectively.[185]

Considerations

Irrespective of how well known an officer was, or how favorable his reports, there were other internal factors at play in the considerations of CinC and the MS. Primarily these concerned the vexed issues of arms of service in relation to command appointments.

There have been various attempts to rank the "smartness" and social precedence of particular regiments on the basis of the ability to attract royal patrons as honorary colonels and colonels in chief, or titled officers. Such listing can only be suggestive and not definitive.[186] Generally speaking, the Guards and Household Cavalry are ranked first together with the Rifle Brigade and King's Royal Rifle Corps. The Tenth and Thirteenth Hussars, the First Royal Dragoons and the Ninth Lancers tended to be toward the top of fashionable cavalry regiments, and some of the Scots regiments toward the top of the infantry. It has been suggested there is a correlation between "smart" regiments and higher command. In 1890 a total of 30 out of 142 officers of major general's rank or above (21 percent) were drawn from the Household Brigade, the KRRC, and the Rifle Brigade. Similarly, the supposed thirty-five least prestigious infantry regiments together provided only 19 percent of senior officers.[187] In 1899 the Scots Guards provided ADCs to the viceroy, the governor-general of Canada, and the governor of Bombay. The highest nonregimental position held by any officer in the Manchester Regiment was head of the Aldershot military prison.[188]

There were certainly suspicions of what the *Broad Arrow* characterized in April 1880 as a "charmed circle." This followed the announcement that all three recent staff appointments would go to the Rifle Brigade. Suggesting the "system" had been "perfected" by Sir Charles Yorke, MS from 1854 to 1860, the paper proclaimed, "for although we cannot be said to have a 'political army,' we have regiments the patronage of which is, to a great extent, 'political,' and whose corporate system is based upon purely political principles, so that the lease of power never runs out, and there is always some representative of it at headquarters."[189] There is no particular evidence, however, that an individual of real ability was necessarily held back once selection became more pronounced, whatever his unit.

Nonetheless, the Guards enjoyed certain privileges. First commissions remained in the gift of regimental colonels.[190] There was also the issue of the vestiges of double rank, whereby the Guards' regimental rank of ensign had carried that of lieutenant in the army; that of regimental lieutenant, the army rank of captain; and that of captain, the army rank of lieutenant colonel. The system was abolished in June 1872, but this only applied to new entrants after August 1871.[191] The term "Captain and Lieutenant Colonel" continued to be used in the

Army List but only when an officer reached the actual rank of lieutenant colonel through seniority. They could not then be promoted to colonel unless they had had staff service or actually commanded a battalion. In 1881 it became possible for Guards majors to be promoted to colonel in the army after four years' company command. Thus significant advantages were retained. In 1886, for example, when promoted to colonel, Maj. Laurence Oliphant of the Grenadiers leapt over thirty-seven cavalry lieutenant colonels alone.[192]

Receiving news of the most recent promotions to field marshal and of the latest appointments to the Bath while in Natal in July 1875, Wolseley commented acidly of Cambridge, "The Guards of course receive his first care, and everything must give way to gratify them & to further their promotion and convenience: they have now had their majors restored to them, entailing great expense upon the Army estimates at a time when every shilling available should be spent upon creating an efficient army."[193] In August 1879 when Lt. the Hon. George Bertie arrived in Zululand suggesting he be made an extra ADC, Wolseley noted all Guardsmen arriving with drafts expected staff employment: "Dear good creatures, how very condescending of them to come here at all!"[194]

Only Guardsmen could be given command of the Home District since it carried with it command of the Brigade of Guards.[195] Cambridge, however, was careful to balance appointments of Guardsmen elsewhere with those from the line.[196] The Coldstreamer Pole-Carew fell afoul of Cambridge's disapproval of young Guards officers receiving potentially important opportunities ahead of other officers. Lytton allowed Pole-Carew, then his ADC, to be attached first as orderly officer to Thomas Baker in Afghanistan and then as ADC to Roberts. While the transfer to Roberts's staff had been approved by Pole-Carew's OC, the MS ordered Pole-Carew to return to his battalion or be regarded as absent without leave.[197] Roberts intervened to ensure Pole-Carew was recorded as absent on duty, but he was denied any Indian pay. Pole-Carew was also refused a brevet for his Afghanistan service as Cambridge regarded him as having been a "loafer."[198]

Appointments to command the rifle depot at Winchester were expected to be alternated between the King's Royal Rifle Corps and the Rifle Brigade.[199] Similarly, Roberts expressed surprise in 1892 that three officers of the Twelfth Lancers in succession should have commanded the cavalry depot at Canterbury as this was unfair to the rest of the army.[200]

Artillery and engineer officers posed a particular difficulty. Certain commands such as the RMA at Woolwich or the School of Military Engineering at Chatham were always going to be occupied by artillerymen and engineers, respectively. The question was how far they might gain any wider opportunities beyond their corps. A return in July 1873 listing all those who had held home or overseas commands between 1850 and 1870 showed few engineers or artillerymen had held appointments as major general or above. Robert Napier had held a major general's appointment in China before being CinC in Bombay and then in India (Bengal). He was exceptional, for only three other engineers had held a major general's appointment, two on Guernsey, and one on Bermuda. Three artillerymen had, not unexpectedly, held the Woolwich command, and four—one from the Bengal Artillery—had held divisional commands in Bengal. William Fenwick Williams had commanded in Canada and at Gibraltar. Other than that, one artilleryman had commanded at Gibraltar, one in Ireland, and one each on Jersey and Bermuda. Even in the Crimea, only two men from each arm had held major general's appointments or above.[201] In raising the lack of staff opportunities for artillery and engineer officers, Lt. Col. George Arbuthnot, MP for Hereford, called for a royal commission in March 1879, but the motion was lost by a single vote.[202]

Maj. Gen. Henry Lynedoch Gardiner complained to Cambridge in June 1879 that there was only one gunner general (at Woolwich) of thirty serving in posts outside India. Replying in the context of what he regarded as the "peculiar" views of artillery officers, Cambridge pointed out Gardiner was overlooking the RMA's lieutenant governor, the IG of the Royal Artillery, and the DAGRA. In addition, he remarked on the number of higher staff positions occupied by gunners in the Royal Arsenal.[203] Cambridge denied he was opposed to artillery and engineer officers in high command, citing his recommendation of Napier to command the expeditionary force in the event of war against Russia in 1878, and perhaps less impressively, of three successive governors of Bermuda since 1867.[204]

On the other hand, the merger of the British and Indian artillery in 1861 opened up greater opportunities for all-arms commands. Whereas in 1861 there was only one British artilleryman holding a district or divisional command in Britain and one elsewhere (in Canada), there were three Indian artillery officers in such positions. Albeit slowly, more commands became available. Between 1874 and 1881 seven artillerymen held senior nonartillery appointments outside India and eleven in India. Between 1882 and 1890 ten artillerymen held senior posts outside India and fourteen in India.[205] In India in 1886 there were artillery officers as CinC in both Bengal (Roberts) and Bombay (Charles Arbuthnot), and as QMG (Edward Chapman). The engineer, George Chesney, was military member.[206] At the time Arbuthnot was selected, Roberts emphasized he was the best candidate lest Cambridge think he was favoring his own branch of the service.[207]

Prejudices remained. In November 1893 Sir Charles Nairne, whose previous appointments had included command of the Meerut District as well as inspector of artillery in India, was incensed that the *Pioneer* deprecated his advancement to the Bombay command "as I was a 'mere gunner,' or some such phrase."[208]

Engineers often lamented their lack of command opportunity, although Wolseley noted how often they claimed colonial governorships: "put one of them into any position no matter what it is, and he at once begins to use his influence in favour of the Officers of his Corps. Make an Engineer a General Commanding anywhere, and you will soon find every post around him filled by officers & N. C. Officers of his own Corps."[209] Wolseley, however, acknowledged the grievance of engineer and artillery officers when they were more highly educated than others. He told the queen he had "always gone out of my way to employ both Gunners & Engineers in high positions in order to break down a system which I felt to be monstrously unjust to individuals & most injurious to the interests of Your Majesty's Army and of the State."[210]

When Gerald Graham was given a brigade for Egypt in 1882, Wolseley told him "that I have to prove that REs can command troops in the field so that my responsibility is greater than that of an officer from the line as the credit of the Corps appears to rest on me." Cambridge advised Graham "not to 'over engineer.'"[211] Subsequently, in March 1884, Wolseley expressed pleasure that both Charles Gordon and Graham were occupying respective command positions at Khartoum and Suakin as a way to overcome prejudices against engineers.[212] Graham expressed the fear that he might be passed over "because I am an Engineer."[213] Gordon and Graham were old friends of Wolseley. He was much less generous to engineers of whom he disapproved, such as Lintorn Simmons and Andrew Clarke.

When consideration was given to the succession to Charles Nairne at Bombay in 1898, one factor militating against George Sanford was that he was an engineer. There could be criticism if Sanford was appointed, given that Bindon Blood, another engineer, was likely to get Meerut and yet another, William Nicholson, the AG post in India. The incoming CinC, Sir William Lockhart, felt that "people will say that I have made my recommendations under Nicholson's influence in favour of men of his own Corps, and the Pioneer newspaper will in all likelihood write in that sense, but I don't think it matters what people say so long as the best man is selected for such posts or at any rate the man whose selection seems to be the most desirable one."[214]

Some wider considerations also applied. Cambridge declined to allow an individual to command a brigade depot in a county with which he was closely associated "as it is considered that he would probably be mixed up with local influences & politics."[215] Serving soldiers' involvement in politics tended to pose difficulties. Gathorne Hardy was annoyed in 1876 when Maj. Gen. Charles

Shute wished to ascertain if his Brighton parliamentary seat was safe before he accepted an Aldershot command.[216] The matter of serving soldiers as MPs came up in the House of Commons in December 1880. Childers suggested that those soldiers elected be seconded perhaps without pay. The Speaker took the view that whereas frequent attendance in Parliament had not been required in the past, increasing public expectations of attendance made it difficult for serving officers to combine military with parliamentary duties.[217] As a result, Sir Henry Havelock-Allan resigned his seat in 1881 to take a brigade command, though he returned to the Commons in 1885.[218]

It was believed undesirable for Col. Sir William Crossman to stand for the parliamentary seat at Portsmouth when he was CRE for the Southern District.[219] Crossman resigned to stand for election for the Liberals. When the IGF, Sir Andrew Clarke, decided to stand for Chatham as a Liberal in 1886, he was also told he must resign, despite arguing that he should be allowed simply to exchange commands. In any event, Clarke failed to win the seat.[220] In 1899 Hugh McCalmont resigned the North Antrim seat he had held since 1895 as a Conservative, in order to take the Cork command, a decision that prolonged his military career at a point when he had anticipated he would be compelled to retire as unemployed.[221] Serving soldiers, however, often made high-profile candidates. Fred Burnaby, for example, stood unsuccessfully for the Conservatives against John Bright and Joseph Chamberlain at Birmingham in 1880, and Andrew Wauchope unsuccessfully against Gladstone in Edinburghshire (Midlothian) in 1892.

There are even hints that religion could be a factor. Cambridge considered the Catholicism of Sir Hugh Clifford VC and Sir Arthur Herbert a potential bar to their postings to Gibraltar and as AG, respectively.[222] William Butler was AAG in the Western District in 1880 when the viceroy, Ripon, offered him the post of PS. Gladstone vetoed it on the grounds both were Catholics. Ripon's appointment "was sufficiently experimental without further endangering the position by the appointment of another of the same creed to a subordinate but still influential post."[223] Nonetheless, Catholicism did not hold back the career of James Dormer, who rose to be CinC in Madras, nor that of Sir Thomas Kelly-Kenny, who ended as AG. One bizarre religious twist occurred when Evelyn Wood was promoted to brevet colonel in 1874 and returned briefly to his regiment. He was not welcomed by the existing lieutenant colonel, Henry Palmer, who insisted on commanding, which left Wood to act in his substantive rank as major. The situation resolved itself in early 1878 when Palmer converted to the pacifist Glasite sect; as a result, Wood took the regiment to South Africa.[224]

Occasionally, physical fitness could be considered. In May 1893 George White felt he could not recommend the otherwise well-qualified Edward

Chapman for one of the new corps commands in India: "I tell you candidly there is no one that I would rather have under me in command than yourself if you were in strong health, but I cannot believe that you are wise in offering yourself for a post with heavy work in India, involving the chances of exposure in the field."[225] In 1895 White complained that Horse Guards had nominated two men for first-class district commands—George Wolseley and Henry Crealock—who were not physically fit enough to stand up to the heat of the Indian plains.[226] Yet, Garnet Wolseley, Roberts, Dormer, and Whitmore were all one-eyed, and Kitchener's squint was so pronounced he could not play any ball games and was a notoriously bad shot.[227] Sam Browne VC, Archibald Alison, and George Corrie Bird were all one-armed. Bird apparently remained a useful cricketer.[228]

India

In the case of India, while the precise boundaries of his authority were not clear, Cambridge regarded himself as solely responsible for higher commands.[229] This included divisional GOCs when they were British officers.[230] Brigade commanders in Bombay and Madras could only be recommended by the local CinC to the CinC of India and then had to go to Horse Guards for approval. Neither could an AG be appointed in the presidential armies without reference to Horse Guards.[231]

Thus, in 1886, after Roberts had suggested Henry Brackenbury and Thomas Baker for divisional commands, Sir Charles Brownlow reported to Roberts that Cambridge "rather resents you naming these men & thinks that he is the best judge of the qualifications of the officers of the British Army!"[232] According to Roberts, Cambridge "clings to the old seniority system, and he has more than once let me know that it is not my business to make any suggestions or recommendations in regard to the selection of officers for high command."[233] Similarly, Roberts wrote to George White in December 1892, when discussing the rearrangement of commands that would follow White's elevation to succeed him, "The Duke of Cambridge resents what he calls my interference in such matters."[234]

The same general procedures were followed for India in terms of the usual consideration of three names for appointments.[235] The IO was also advised by a separate MS there for all Indian appointments. Similarly, an AMS with special responsibility for India was appointed at Horse Guards from 1860.

When he was military member, Brackenbury got agreement on introducing selection in the Indian service to bring it into line with the home army. A

Promotion Board was established in India along the lines of that at home with a major general representing each presidency. The intention was to appoint every fourth vacancy by selection. It proved a sobering exercise. In order to find 18 colonels capable of being promoted to major general from the Staff Corps in 1893, the board had to go down to 175th on the list. For eight vacancies from the wider Indian service, they could find no more than 15 colonels of any quality.[236]

As CinC in India between 1860 and 1865, Sir Hugh Rose, later Lord Strathnairn, favored selection, proclaiming an end to "petticoat influence, intrigue and favouritism" with his declaration that "patronage should go by . . . merit only."[237] His successor, Sir William Mansfield, later Lord Sandhurst, believed firmly in selection being applied to all commands.[238] One dispute that reached the public domain was that involving Lt. Gen. Henry Stannus, whose publicized grievances went well beyond propriety. Stannus was passed over for a divisional command in India in 1874 as a result of being censured five years previously by Mansfield following a trivial dispute over summer uniform codes. It was only when Stannus complained that he became aware that the censure was on the record. Stannus was further incensed that Mansfield's successor, Napier, conveyed through his MS, Col. Martin Dillon, in May 1875, that Stannus had lacked energy as a brigade commander. The AG in India, Sir Peter Lumsden, emphasized that selection rather than seniority now applied. Napier had inherited from Mansfield a list of officers whom the latter felt should not be entrusted with commands but who were likely to be considered by virtue of seniority.[239]

Taking his case to Horse Guards in October 1876 and demanding a court-martial to restore his reputation, Stannus complained of Horsford's discourtesy in not only refusing to rise or shake hands when he entered his office but also flying into a violent rage. Stannus was promoted to lieutenant general in October 1877, but Cambridge took the view that Stannus's increasingly intemperate letters only demonstrated that Mansfield had been correct. Unsurprisingly, Stannus was not selected for a vacant cavalry brigade command in February 1879. He then returned his decorations to Horse Guards, and refused to acknowledge his promotion to honorary general upon his retirement in June 1879. His resentment growing, Stannus lashed out in print: Napier was the greatest jobber yet seen in India; Lumsden was the real power in India and controlled Napier's successor, Haines; Horsford and Dillon were unfit for office; and, as a personal friend of Horsford, Dillon should not have been appointed AMS at Horse Guards. Furthermore, the administration of honors and rewards was corrupt, Stannus charged, with officials in Horsford's department demanding bribes; brevet promotions being awarded through the influence of friends; VCs being solicited; Indian officers in higher commands always providing for their friends; too many men achieving advancement through staff appointments alone; and the five-year rule on tenure being flouted through extensions on the grounds of public good. The litany of abuses included "epidemics of heroism," as demonstrated in the award of the VC to George White for the action at Charasia in October 1879.[240] Publication did Stannus no good at all, however; his charges remained unsubstantiated.

There were particular requirements in India. AGs and QMGs in the presidencies needed to have served five years in any rank in India and at least two years within the previous nine. This could be reduced to three years' previous service in India if an individual had commanded a regiment or seen staff service in a campaign for which a medal had been issued. In addition, they had to have passed at least the lower standard in Hindustani.[241] Even in the case of officers who had achieved the lower standard in Hindustani, absence from India for four and a half years also disqualified them from higher command.[242] Ironically, Hindustani was of little practical use when Urdu and Pashto were those languages most needed on the frontier.[243]

An added complication was the perceived need to balance opportunities between those of the British and the Indian services and between the three presidency armies of Bengal, Bombay, and Madras. Bombay and Madras were seen as inferior to Bengal, a concept that even extended to British regiments serving in the different presidencies.[244]

In September 1872 the CinC in Bombay, the Hon. Sir Augustus Spencer, needed to appoint a successor to a British AG. Another British officer declined the post, so Spencer appointed the DAG, Col. Charles Aitchison, who was of the Indian service. Spencer felt he should balance this by finding a British officer to replace Aitchison. The only realistic candidate was Lt. Col. George Bray of the Ninety-sixth Foot serving in Bengal. Spencer hoped Cambridge would agree since there was no specific rule on the need to balance appointments, and the only actual requirement was that someone possess the requisite language qualification.[245] Spencer viewed the language qualification as a farce that merely prevented able British officers from being appointed.[246] Unfortunately, Bray wanted to retire almost immediately for family reasons, and Spencer had to start the search over again.

Napier agreed with Spencer to some extent but still felt it desirable that senior officers know India and its peoples.[247] He was prepared to waive the language qualification to secure Col. Charles Arbuthnot as DAGRA at Army Headquarters in 1873.[248] Not yet as hostile to Wolseley as he would become later, Cambridge recommended him as AG in India the same year. Wolseley had entered the language examination in 1859 and would have passed, but a cheating case had led to all results being canceled. Wolseley had then been posted to China before he could retake the exam.[249] Since Wolseley had also not spent the required five years in India, Napier considered it unlikely that he could be appointed.[250] Wolseley's candidacy was supported by the viceroy, but by this time Wolseley's success in Asante had alerted Cambridge and Napier to the dangers of Wolseley's reforming instincts. The language test, therefore, became a convenient excuse.[251]

Cambridge was sympathetic to waiving the language qualification, not least during the Second Afghan War, but the government of India was immovable on the matter.[252] When he was CinC, Donald Stewart considered the language test of little practical value since it qualified some officers for higher command who would not otherwise be considered. Thus, in replacing Col. Henry Wilkinson, who had been named to command the cavalry brigade being sent to Egypt in 1882, Stewart was compelled to name Col. Richard Marter, when better and more senior men were available who had not passed the qualification.[253] Stewart then also found himself attacked because Wilkinson was a British officer.[254] Neville Lyttelton, however, believed the government of India authorities waived the language rules generally when it suited them, as in the appointment of Thomas Baker as AG.[255]

The interweaving complexity of language and service was well illustrated by the death of Brig. Gen. Henry Brooke, then also AG in Bombay. Brooke, who died at Kandahar in 1880, was a British officer, and Haines thought his post should be filled by another British officer, Arthur Annesley. This would balance the appointment of an Indian officer as QMG, with the posts to be filled alternately. Some on the Bombay Governor's Council pointed out that, while there had been an unwritten convention to that effect for the last twenty years, only Indian officers had filled the post of QMG because of their greater local knowledge. This implied that no Indian officer could again be AG. Over the last twenty years, only one out of six AGs in Bengal had been of the Indian army and none in Madras. In effect such a convention had supposedly applied only to Bombay. The case went all the way to the IO, with the secretary of state, Hartington, pronouncing that the best men should be appointed and that "it would be highly inexpedient to lay down an absolute rule on the subject."[256]

Cambridge had no time for arguments as to alternating appointments, believing it better for the AG always to be a British officer and the QMG to be from the Indian service.[257] Annesley then faced what was characterized as a clique animated by the perceived slights to Bombay.[258] Henry Warre, who supported Annesley's appointment, noted what he called "family influence" being exerted on Bombay's governor to secure the post for an Indian officer. Warre complained that "these Indians are such cormorants they endeavour to take possession of all the plums."[259]

By 1883 brigade commands in Indian presidencies were no longer restricted to officers of that army or even Indian officers.[260] Local sensitivities still persisted. In 1890 James Dormer, a British candidate for Madras, believed it important that the viceroy supported him against the interests of Indian officers "because I know the India Govt. authorities will do their best to get an Indian Local Forces General appointed on the plea of its being their turn for the next Presidency Command vacancy." The MS, Major General Harman, suggested that Dormer had "a first rate chance provided no Indian officer can be produced who is eligible & suitable & he told me he really did not see where this officer is to be found."[261]

In the case of internal Indian army divisions, the Burma campaign (1885–95) provides an example. Most of the troops deployed were from Madras. When Burma came under a single general officer, it was decided one of the three brigades would be commanded by a Madras officer, one by a Bengal officer, and one by a British officer. In 1891 Roberts proposed Col. Arthur Palmer from Bengal should succeed a British officer, only for Madras to complain despite there being Bengal troops in the country. Not having anticipated such difficulties, Roberts pointed out that those Madras officers who had commanded brigades in Burma were invariably junior to those from Bengal. He was of a mind to meet the objection by transferring a Madras officer from the Hyderabad Contingent, which came directly under the authority of the viceroy, to Burma and putting a Bengal officer into Hyderabad. But this would give Madras four second-class district commands to five for Bengal when there were only 348 officers in Madras compared to 926 in Bengal.[262]

In 1895 White felt he could not appoint Charles FitzGerald from Madras, even though he was bold and energetic, to the overall command of the Hyderabad Contingent as this was normally commanded by an officer from Bengal or the PFF.[263] The PFF in itself was something of a special case, for it did not come under the direct authority of the CinC in India until 1893. Its particular expertise in frontier warfare was not willingly communicated to other parts of the Indian army.[264] In the case of the major uprising on the frontier in 1897–98, White was anxious that there not be too many PFF officers in leading command positions given that George Corrie Bird was in the Tochi; Charles Egerton had the First Brigade under Bird; and William Lockhart, Alfred Gaselee, and Arthur Hammond VC were all appointed to the Tirah campaign. Gaselee had a brigade in the First Division and Hammond commanded the Peshawar Column.[265]

Matters in India generally changed with the replacement of the three presidential armies and the PFF by four corps commands in 1893. The CinC in India lost the patronage of commands up to the rank of colonel, which now passed to the lieutenant generals commanding the corps.[266]

Occasionally, once an individual was selected, a complex game of musical chairs ensued as the example of India in 1888 demonstrates. With the expectation that Maj. Gen. Robert Gillespie would be transferred from Mhow in Bombay to command the Madras troops in Burma, the CinC in Madras, Arbuthnot, proposed to move Maj. Gen. Benjamin Gordon from Burma to command the Secunderabad Division in Madras, with Maj. Gen. Stanley Edwardes moving from Deesa in Bombay to Mhow. All changes would take place when Maj. Gen. William Gib retired from Secunderabad on 1 January 1889. Brig. Gen. Harcourt Bengough from Kamptee in Bombay would replace Maj. Gen. Hugh Rowlands VC at Bangalore in Madras, since Rowlands did not like Bangalore. The viceroy then proposed instead that Rowlands move from Bangalore to Secunderabad, Bengough from Kamptee to Bangalore, and Maj. Gen. Horace Anderson from Nurseerabad in Bombay to Kamptee. As Rowlands had made all the arrangements for the forthcoming camp of exercise at Bangalore and was sufficiently close to retirement for a temporary move to be unwelcome, Arbuthnot declined to act on this recommendation. In any case, Gillespie was no longer being transferred and Gordon wished to stay in Burma.[267]

Promotion and selection, therefore, was a highly complex affair. This complexity was further complicated by the existence of the so-called rings surrounding particularly prominent commanders like Wolseley and Roberts. It is to these personal cliques attention can now be turned.

CHAPTER 3

THE RINGS

A n additional complication in terms of promotion and selection was the existence of the so-called rings around prominent commanders. The rings have been noted as leading to a personalized army, one of "ins" and "outs," and to a "deadly game of musical chairs between the senior British and Indian generals."[1] The rings arose in part from the casual attitude toward the emergence of a general staff. There was no sense in which the British attempted to emulate the Prussian staff system. Cambridge and Wolseley were equally opposed to the emergence of a chief of staff who might challenge the authority of the commander in chief. Politicians were also wary of such a development. Henry Campbell-Bannerman famously remarked in 1890 that a CoS should not "be shut up in a room by himself in order that he might think."[2]

The resulting personalized approach to command and leadership fueled rivalry. Garnet Wolseley's "Ashanti" ring, known to some as the "Mutual Admiration Society," was the best known: the phrase was already current by 1879.[3] Frederick Roberts, too, had his "Indian" ring. Moreover, Cambridge was equally determined to have his own way with regard to appointments, with his own circle of conservatively minded officers.

The struggle between the rings ranged widely over issues of imperial strategy and military reform. In essence, those associated with Wolseley favored Cardwell's wider reforms, notably the short-service introduced in 1870—six years with the Colours and six with the reserve in the case of the infantry, although the terms were always flexible. It was intended not only to stimulate enlistment and reduce wastage, but also to attract a better class of recruit and produce a viable reserve.[4] In reality, it required the army to recruit more men than previously.[5] A system intended for limited colonial commitments paradoxically came to be upheld by its supporters as the best means of meeting extended obligations.[6] Opponents of short-service doubted its suitability for imperial commitments because it seemed likely the ranks would be filled with immature youths. Roberts was a constant critic of short-service, suggesting in a speech at the Mansion House on 4 February 1881 that short-service soldiers were inferior, and that home battalions were too weak under the necessity of supplying drafts to battalions overseas. His solution was separate home and foreign-service armies, the latter based on the revival of long-service engagements.[7]

There were also strategic differences. From an Indian perspective, the steady Russian advance into Central Asia represented the greatest threat. Viceroy Lytton claimed in September 1878 that, while the distance between India and Russian territory had been over 2,500 miles in 1700, it had decreased to 2,000 miles by 1800, to 1,000 miles by 1850, and was now just 400 miles. Roberts remarked in 1883 that Afghanistan was to India what the English Channel was to Britain.[8] It followed that India should be the priority for imperial defense. On the other hand, Wolseley's position, except for a brief period in the late 1870s, when he still hoped for an Indian command, was that any war fought against Russia should be primarily amphibious and aimed at peripheries such as the Baltic Sea, Black Sea, or the Turkestan/Caspian area. Any posture adopted by the Indian army should be primarily defensive.[9]

The likelihood of any Russian invasion of India provoked much debate.[10] The assumption that a Russian invasion was a possibility was continually rebutted by the Intelligence Department in London. Those in London were always more fearful of French ambitions in Africa than Russian ambitions in Asia.[11] The War Office was also obsessed with the threat of invasion to Britain irrespective of the navy's claim as to its impossibility. There had been major invasion scares in 1846–47, 1851–52, and 1858–59. Additional scares occurred in 1871, 1882, and 1888.[12] The celebrated Stanhope Memorandum of 1888 laid down the army's priorities in order as aid to the civil power in the United Kingdom; the provision of drafts for India; the provision of garrisons for colonies and coaling stations; the provision of two corps for home defense; and the possible employment of one of the corps in a European war. The latter was deemed so improbable that nothing need be done to prepare for such an eventuality.[13]

The point has been made that the only real threat to the empire would have come from a European hegemonic bloc and that the real defense of the empire lay in the deterrent effect of global maritime dominance: the "reality of British power was written in stone, at Cherbourg, Cronstadt, New York, and Wilhelmshaven."[14] In that sense, Wolseley's and Roberts's assumptions were equally questionable. That was not how they and their adherents saw it at the time although neither particular issues nor the positions assumed by individuals with respect to them were necessarily constant as the factions attempted to maneuver adherents into particular commands.

It was jostling for position that marked the impact of the rings on the already muddied waters of promotion and selection. The rings were resented by many officers precisely because they posed a challenge to the regimental system in offering a route to advancement independent of regimental promotion.[15] At the same time, they proved an "effective means of exercising meritocratic preferment."[16]

In passing, it should be noted such patronage groups were not confined to the army. In the Royal Navy, Sir John Fisher as first sea lord had his "Fishpond" and his rival Lord Charles Beresford his "Syndicate of Discontent" in his successive commands in the Channel and Mediterranean Fleets. Earlier, there had been the "Malta clique" surrounding Sir Michael Culme-Seymour as CinC in the Mediterranean from 1893 to 1896. In the Great War, Adm. Sir David Beatty had his "Band of Brothers" and his rival, Adm. Sir John Jellicoe, his own adherents.[17] The scientific community had its "X Club," which met regularly to discuss the candidates for the annual election to the Royal Society and those for sectional presidents of the British Association for the Advancement of Science, and wielded considerable influence over the affairs of the Royal Institution and scientific publishing. As suggested earlier, patronage was a fact of life in the London metropolitan engineering profession, dominated by the chief engineer of the Metropolitan Board of Works from 1846 to 1889, Sir Joseph Bazalgette, and his "Great George Street Clique."[18] The reconstruction of South Africa after 1902 was also largely in the hands of Lord Milner's "kindergarten" of young administrators.[19]

Garnet Wolseley

Wolseley became associated with some of his leading adherents almost coincidentally in the Red River campaign in 1870, since the choices of Redvers Buller, William Butler, John McNeill, and George Huyshe were dictated by those officers being available in Canada. Only Hugh McCalmont made his own way there to press his services on Wolseley.[20] Consequently, the Asante War (1873–74) marked the ring's real emergence. It was also the first Victorian colonial campaign to really catch the British public's imagination since the Indian Mutiny. Some, including Cardwell, regarded it as a successful test of short-service enlistment and the abolition of the purchase system.[21] Success on the Gold Coast was actually accomplished with the tools of the old system in terms of officers who had largely bought their commissions, and battalions of long-service soldiers from which younger, raw recruits had been weeded out before embarkation. But Asante was widely seen as a model campaign, won at modest expenditure both in financial cost and in lives. It made a household name of Wolseley, the model for George Grossmith's portrayal of the "very model of a modern Major-General" in Gilbert and Sullivan's *Pirates of Penzance*. Wolseley had also become "our only General."

Wolseley was not the initial choice. Command had been offered first to Col. Sir Andrew Clarke, governor designate of the Straits Settlement. Clarke declined but, in any case, envisaged a far more limited operation than what Cardwell and the colonial secretary, Lord Kimberley, had in mind.[22] There had been speculation, and some support, in the press for the dispatch of Charles "Chinese" Gordon. This was never seriously contemplated although the queen believed Gordon should be kept in mind if Wolseley became incapacitated.[23] According to Frederic Villiers, his fellow war correspondent Archibald Forbes had some impact in advocating Wolseley's appointment over Gordon in the pages of the *Daily News*.[24]

Wolseley undoubtedly pressed for the command. His organizational and logistic ability, his achievements on the Red River, his appointment as a divisional CoS during the 1871 autumn maneuvers, and his recent participation in planning the autumn maneuvers in 1872 were all recommendations in addition to his association with reform. Mutual hostility between Wolseley and Cambridge had not yet arisen although Wolseley did tell his wife his correspondence with the duke was "rather a tax upon my time, as I have to tell him all sorts of fiddling little things."[25]

Butler, Buller, McNeill, Huyshe, and McCalmont duly appeared in Asante. Also selected to sail with Wolseley in September 1873 were Evelyn Wood, Baker Russell, Thomas Baker, Henry Brackenbury, Robert Home, Frederick Maurice, and Lord Gifford. When McNeill was wounded, he was replaced by George Greaves, who had shared the same WO room with Wolseley.[26] Wood had fortuitously met Wolseley while he was planning the operation, telling him his naval knowledge would be useful on the rivers.[27] George Colley arrived subsequently. Huyshe died during the expedition; Home died as a result of service on the Bulgarian frontier delineation commission in 1879; and Gifford entered the colonial service in 1880. The remainder all reached general rank with Wood, like Wolseley, becoming a field marshal. Other officers who served in Asante were also to reach general rank, including John Brabazon, William Dalrymple, Fitzroy Hart, Arthur Paget, and Edward Woodgate; Paul Methuen, too, became a field marshal.

According to his memoirs, Wolseley "had long been in in the habit of keeping a list of the best and ablest soldiers I knew, and was always on the lookout for those who could safely be entrusted with any special military piece of work." In the same vein, when Butler was proving quarrelsome, Wolseley wrote in December 1884 that he would "drop him from my list except for a big war."[28] On the voyage out, Wolseley gave Capt. George Furse "a paper bearing a long list of names, asking him at the same time to mark with a cross any name which he considered to be that of a good and efficient officer."[29]

Some were clearly chosen for their courage: Wood, McNeill, and the expedition surgeon, Dr. Anthony Home, all held the VC: Buller and Gifford won it subsequently. Coolness in action was always a quality Wolseley appreciated, and those whose conduct appeared to betray weakness were suspect.[30] Brackenbury, Robert Home, Maurice, and Colley had all earned intellectual reputations.

Wolseley remarked in his memoirs, "I felt that ordinary men could not be good enough for the work I had undertaken."[31] As Wolseley had not taken men direct from the top of the special service roster, the Staff College commandant, Edward Hamley, accused him of "cutting blocks with a razor" by taking *psc* men to West Africa. Wolseley's old friend, Lt. Col. the Hon. Augustus Anson MP, similarly feared Wolseley was "using the finest steel of our army to cut brushwood." Maj. Gen. Arthur Herbert thought "these brutal niggers are not worth the life of one of our promising young officers."[32]

Of the first twenty-seven officers who went out with Wolseley, eight had the *psc* qualification. Of those sent out subsequently, another five were *psc*'s. Buller's participation prevented him from completing his course at Camberley, and thus he was never granted the *psc* although Cambridge was prepared to accept that Buller had graduated.[33] Wolseley was to favor *psc*'s in all his campaigns. Significantly, he told his brother Richard in 1880 that their nephew, Arthur Creagh, must go to Staff College "for unless he does I cannot help him in the Army."[34] Wolseley, however, was not an uncritical admirer of Camberley. Rather than the mien of the Prussian-style "intellectual technocrat," what appealed to him in men like Brackenbury, Colley, and Maurice was "their capacity to bring logic, intelligence and professional insight to bear on the practical problems of campaigning."[35]

A total of thirty-four *psc*'s served under Wolseley in Egypt in 1882, including fourteen in headquarters and five out of seven in the intelligence section; twenty on the Gordon relief expedition in 1884–85, with six (if counting Buller) in headquarters and seven on the line. In writing to Cambridge that he had taken officers from the list of those applying to the MS for employment in the Sudan, and those he had noted at his most recent levee, Wolseley added, "From them I have selected nearly all the names of those I have asked for officially, giving a preference where possible to those who have passed the Staff College."[36] He pointed out his headquarters staff would be different from that in Egypt two years earlier: "This time, as was also the case in 1882, I have, and then had, a host of new men. My idea is to give every Staff College officer and everyone strongly recommended by a good commanding officer a chance in a subordinate position of showing what he can do and what he is worth."[37]

With Wolseley now CinC, no fewer than eighty *psc*'s were appointed to the staff or dispatched on special service to South Africa in 1899. Wood told the Elgin Commission that Wolseley would always choose Staff College graduates in preference to perhaps abler men without the *psc*. In 1895, indeed, Wolseley directed that, other than in exceptional circumstances, no officer should hold a staff appointment unless he had a *psc*.[38]

Passing the Staff College was of increasing importance. In July 1897 Archibald Alison's son, Capt. Randal Alison, failed to gain entrance for the third time, having also anticipated that success would impress the parents of a girl he wished to marry. Wolseley was unrepentant that the rule of three attempts was absolute: "Men in my position must take care that only the ablest of our candidates are allowed admission to the Staff College." Young Alison committed suicide three days after Wolseley's pronouncement.[39]

Wolseley claimed his staff was selected on merit alone, proclaiming in 1880, "I hate jobs myself; I always endeavour to avoid them & so as you may imagine I don't like to ask others to do what I would not do for them in return."[40] On one occasion, he wrote to Cambridge, "Some think I favour my friends but these are simply officers I pick out on active service as very good men. As soon as I find I have made a mistake, I drop them remorselessly."[41] Again in 1895 Wolseley wrote to the queen that he had "always without any partiality or favour recommended those whom I believed to be the best men for promotion & employment. I have only to point to the fact, that a large majority of those who in high military positions have now the privilege of enjoying Your Majesty's confidence, were originally recommended by me for employment."[42] Not surprisingly, in view of his hostility to selection, Cambridge resented Wolseley's ability to persuade successive secretaries of state of the need to appoint his preferred staff. With Greaves, Baker Russell, Brackenbury, Dormer, and Anthony Home all appointed to the Cyprus expedition in 1878, Cambridge was "angry not being taken into the secret, very angry at my appointment & still more angry at my having selected a staff without consulting him."[43] In the following year when Wolseley superseded Chelmsford in Zululand, Cambridge was infuriated that Frederick Stanley "had sanctioned all Wolseley's friends, a long list of whom he had handed in, to accompany him out to the Cape."[44] Stanley knew the list had not been approved by Cambridge but failed to find either the MS or the AMS in their offices. He decided retrospective approval would do in view of the haste with which the cabinet had decided to send Wolseley. Cambridge objected to what he saw as Wolseley's double dealing in notifying officers of their selection before he had actually authorized it: "The selection of a large number of special friends is a serious blow to my position as Commander-in-Chief. . . . men have gone out *against my judgement* and this is well known to themselves and friends. Consequently, they look to their patron Wolseley & no longer to me as the authority."[45]

Wolseley took the view, as he wrote to Cambridge in September 1879, "I am not the Pope, and like all other men, must therefore make mistakes occasionally;

but as a rule I am tolerably successful in my selections."[46] Cambridge was unconvinced and could not see how the public service "is benefitted by our going out of our way to put some officers prominently forward on all occasions, however valuable they may be, when there are others available quite equal to perform good service also if chance be only given to them."[47]

It was recognized even by his critics that Wolseley had a knack for picking able soldiers. Sir Henry Ponsonby, for one, wrote in November 1882: "He knows a good man and selects him and throws over all other considerations. Therefore his Staff are excellent soldiers."[48] New men did appear in the ring, Herbert Stewart being a case in point. Wolseley first encountered Stewart as a disillusioned captain close to premature retirement while on the LOC in Zululand. Within five years—"this very favoured officer," in Cambridge's view—was a major general although that last promotion came only after he had already been mortally wounded in the Sudan.[49]

Even Wolseley recognized there were failures among his selections, although he noted in April 1880 those he had discarded to date "are Wellingtons compared to those the Horse Gds. people love to honour."[50] In the wake of the failure to save Gordon at Khartoum, Wolseley wrote to Cambridge, "Although I keep a book in which I enter the name & reported character of every officer recommended to me by anyone who I think is likely to be a good judge, in three instances out of four I am disappointed." He singled out fifteen men as examples, suggesting eight were tested under fire, of whom two did well (Brackenbury and Butler), three fairly well (Col. the Hon. Reginald Talbot; Col. Henry "Croppy" Ewart; and Maj. the Hon. George Gough, until he was seriously wounded in the head), and three failed absolutely (Sir Charles Wilson, Lt. Col. the Hon. Evelyn "Star" Boscawen; and Col. Stanley Clarke). Of the seven who were not tested under fire, four had done well (Dormer; Col. the Hon. Everard Primrose, who died from disease shortly after Wolseley commended him; Col. Kennett Henderson; and Col. Henry Blundell, who would be elected a Conservative MP later that year). Three regimental commanders had failed.[51] Interestingly, Buller believed the expedition did not produce "one single new man, who was even average good, except poor [Frederic] Briggs, and now he has gone."[52]

While there was still a prospect of an autumn campaign against the Mahdi in 1885, Wolseley specified exactly whom he wanted sent as part of any buildup to a force of corps strength. If Arthur Fremantle's health broke down—he was at Suakin—then Wolseley wanted Col. Edward Clive, soon to become commandant of the Staff College, or Clive's fellow grenadier, Col. Henry Davies, as brigade commanders, "but don't send me out that poof [Maj. Gen. the Hon.] Percy Feilding or his unpopular brother "Pickles" [Maj.

Gen. the Hon. William Feilding]. [Col.] Philip Smith is a dear good fellow, but he is as slow as a tortoise." Wolseley had noted Lt. Col. the Hon. Raymond Montmorency, commanding the Regimental District at Derby, as another potential brigadier, and wanted George Harman, Buller, and Greaves to command divisions.[53]

On occasion, Wolseley did not have as free a choice as is sometimes supposed. It had been Greaves rather than McNeill whom Wolseley had first chosen for Asante in 1873. The appointment was vetoed by Cambridge on the grounds that feeling in the army would be against "*two* Horse Guards officers going on so small an expedition as first & second in Command."[54] Wolseley did not want Archibald Alison sent out as field commander with the white troops deployed, noting, "I am very sorry for this as I don't care much for him & don't think he is the man I want." Wolseley regarded Alison as "brimfull of maxims borrowed from Jomini and Montecuccioli [*sic*]"—the latter an allusion to Raimondo Montecuccoli, a notably cautious seventeenth-century Habsburg general known for a rigid mathematical approach to the principles of war.[55] There was equally little confidence in Alison among Wolseley's adherents; Greaves told Wolseley five years later that, had Wolseley been incapacitated, it was intended to "put Alison compulsorily on the sick list" and hand over field command to Lt. Col. John McLeod of the Forty-second Foot.[56]

When he went to Zululand in 1879, Wolseley complained that "many of the tools I shall have to work with, are not of my own selection, but are men chosen by H. R. H. & the Horse Guards party."[57] He swiftly disposed of most of Chelmsford's staff, although he retained some, like Butler, who were serving on the LOC. Others whom Wolseley wished to retain, such as Wood, Buller, and Francis Grenfell, chose to go home. Colley, whose services he secured as CoS despite Cambridge's opposition, was recalled to his appointment as Lytton's MS in September 1879 when conflict broke out anew in Afghanistan.[58]

In Egypt in 1882, the principal field commands were taken by those already intended to command at that year's autumn maneuvers—namely, George Willis and Edward Hamley.[59] Wolseley found fault with both. Hamley claimed that Wolseley all but ignored him in the immediate aftermath of the victory at Tel el Kebir and that, in his dispatches, Wolseley deliberately suppressed the role of Hamley's division. Willis equally felt that Wolseley had given undue prominence to Gerald Graham when the latter was acting under Willis's orders.[60]

Wolseley felt obliged to take Cambridge's eldest son, Maj. George FitzGeorge, as PS; the queen's son, Connaught, as a brigade commander; Cambridge's brother-in-law, the Duke of Teck, as a special service officer, albeit Teck was confined to supervising foreign military attachés; the son of Childers, the secretary of state for war, as an ADC; and Childers's private secretaries.[61]

Three years later, Wolseley had to disappoint a number of associates, including Baker Russell, while feeling obliged to accept Col. Stanley Clarke as commander of the Light Camel Corps and Lord Charles Beresford as naval ADC at the request of the Prince of Wales. Clarke's appointment was a particular disappointment to McCalmont, who had expected the command.[62] This time, Cambridge's third son, Augustus FitzGeorge, was accommodated.[63]

It has been argued that the staffing of the Gordon relief expedition showed Wolseley's nepotism and snobbery in taking out relatives like his brother George, and his nephew Arthur Creagh, as well as courtiers such as Clarke and Beresford.[64] Such criticism echoes contemporary claims. Lt. John Spencer Ewart noted of the expedition, "As it was, the theatrical procession of whalers full of Peers, Red Indians, Life Guards, Canadian voyageurs, and Mutual Admirationists of all sorts, arranged as it was for the glorification of a few[,] was foredoomed to failure."[65] Similarly, Ian Hamilton wrote of "the spectacle of most of Debrett's and the elite of London Society riding across the desert on camels."[66] In fact, of Wolseley's original recommendations of officers for the Camel Corps, only 17 percent were titled officers, with the higher proportion of aristocratic officers in the Heavy Camel Regiment (35 percent) and the Guards Camel Regiment (23.5 percent) simply reflecting the greater preponderance of such officers in the parent regiments. By contrast, the Mounted Infantry Camel Regiment, comprising 28 percent of the whole corps, had only two aristocratic officers.[67]

There was in all such criticism a large measure of resentment on the part of those excluded. It was inevitable that Wolseley would be overwhelmed with applications for appointment to his staff. In 1878, when appointed to Cyprus, he was "inundated at present with letters asking for employment. Every idle fellow thinks Cyprus should afford him the means of living without working for his livelihood. I have applications from all quarters of the world from people I have never heard of. How affectionate the world is to one when you have something to give away."[68] Some appeals were "couched in terms that would lead one to imagine that the favor [sic] was to be all on the side of the man who offered his services."[69] Similarly, in 1884, Fred Burnaby reported from the Guards Club that those not chosen were refusing to speak to those selected.[70]

Resentment was always apparent. Writing to Lady Bradford in December 1879, Beaconsfield noted that many hoped Wolseley would fail in his mission: "Nothing can give you an idea of the jealousy, hatred and all uncharitableness of the Horse Guards against our only soldier."[71] In noting the names of those whose services Wolseley had requested for his Camel Corps, Maj. Gen. Reginald Gipps, commanding the Home District, commented on the dissatisfaction of their seniors.[72] "Croppy" Ewart, who commanded the cavalry brigade at Suakin, similarly told Ponsonby that "he never knew such bitterness, jealousy and bickering as exists in London just now about this Camel Corps. Wolseley named his own officers and consequently those who ought to have gone were cut out & resent it."[73]

An interesting perspective is that of a former member of the ring. In 1884 James Dormer was CoS in Cairo to Sir Frederick "Ben" Stephenson. Dormer had been on Wolseley's staff in Cyprus and on the 1882 expedition, having been offered the chance to become CoS in Cairo by Wolseley. In February 1884 Dormer and Stephenson were ordered to prepare an expeditionary force for Suakin but then discovered that Redvers Buller—still a colonel—would be coming to command the infantry brigade rather than any of the three major generals serving in Egypt. As Dormer wrote,

> For my part, having now organised the whole details I have written to Wolseley privately suggesting, after it is all over, that I may be allowed to resign & retire on permanent Half Pay. General Stephenson has also protested in the strongest terms officially to the Sec. of State for War. It is the most monstrous & insulting thing that ever was done to [William] Earle, Genl. [John] Davis, & me sending out a Colonel over our heads to command a Brigade out here.[74]

Earle was also senior to Graham, who had been appointed to lead the expedition.

Dormer received what he called a "humbugging" reply from Wolseley and was incensed that Burnaby had been allowed to come "without any appointment, business or right as an amateur butcher & shooting down these savages with buck shot like he would wild beasts is hardly the duty of an officer of Her Majesty's Blues *on leave*."[75] So far as Dormer was concerned, the subsequent Gordon relief expedition would again see all the major posts going to "the flashy officers who live at home at ease & leave all of us to grill & boil out here & arrange everything nice & pleasant for them." Initially, it seemed Stephenson would have some say, "but this became too sore a trial for our only General who could no longer keep his fingers out of the pie; the consequence is he has commenced appointing all his old clique to all the best posts, & has persuaded that weak man Hartington to allow him to lay out a plan of his own & to upset Genl. Stephenson."[76] John Ardagh, serving with Dormer in Cairo but also close to Wolseley, saw the bitterness "between the old garrison and the new arrivals." He saw himself as "the agent here for Lord Wolseley, and a sort of buffer between the Nile Expedition and the Army of Occupation."[77] Dining with Dormer after his arrival in Cairo, Wolseley wrote, "I wonder there was no arsenic in it, for I am sure he hates me because I have not included him in the list of those to go up the Nile."[78]

Since Stephenson opposed Wolseley's plan, the government believed command should be entrusted to Wolseley. Not surprisingly, Stephenson asked to be relieved of his command but was persuaded to stay on, giving up the Cairo command only in 1887.[79]

An anonymous contributor to the *Army and Navy Magazine* in 1884 defined the "Mutual Admiration Society" as "a small number of persons of the Staff who have obtained rapid promotion by persistently blowing their own trumpets, and knowing nothing about their own or anyone else's regiment, and who abuse all offenders who do not think as they do; but their chief point at all times in belauding the Founder of the Society especially, and each other in particular."[80] It was often a case of reshuffling the pack.

Wolseley's defense was he could rely instinctively on those familiar with his working methods, and in whom he had full confidence. Thus, when urging the selection of Colley, Brackenbury, Butler, and Gifford for Natal in 1875, Wolseley stressed the need for "a few clever men about me whom I could trust implicitly."[81] Similarly, when Cambridge objected to Wolseley's Cyprus choices, he "pointed out how very desirable it was that in carrying out a difficult job, I should be assisted by men in whom I placed the fullest confidence, etc. etc."[82]

Clearly, there was some vindictiveness in the operation of the ring as in the case of the victimization of nonringers such as Capt. John Glover RN in Asante. Glover, who was intended to raise the tribes in the Volta region against the Asante, experienced numerous difficulties and was unable to support sufficiently Wolseley's advance to Kumase. Wolseley remarked that Glover might as well be in Abyssinia or on the Zanzibar coast. In any event, Glover reached Kumase after Wolseley had already left it.[83]

Wolseley's old mentor from his Canadian days, Gen. Sir John Michel, lamented Wolseley's apparent lack of generosity toward Chelmsford in 1879, feeling it had encouraged a "crowd of ignorant, rascally detractors, villainous newspapers & booby soldier's letters, doing their utmost to destroy his reputation & drag him to the earth."[84] Of Chelmsford's victory at Ulundi, Maj. Philip Anstruther of the Ninety-fourth Foot noted, "It is rather amusing to see the way the 'Mutual Admiration Society'—i.e. Sir Garnet's collection—run down Ulundi—and anything that has been done up to the present for our Ulundi finished the war and they were not in it—and they hate that. He has one or two great duffers on his staff and they are always so pleased with themselves."[85]

Sir Charles Wilson was made the scapegoat for the failure to reach Khartoum in time since he had been thrust into command of the Desert Column after the fatal wounding of Stewart at Metemmeh and the earlier death of Burnaby at Abu Klea. As early as 11 March 1885—news of the fall of Khartoum had reached him on 4 February—Wolseley recorded he hated the sight of Wilson: "I have asked that he may be recalled as wanted for his Survey, and when he goes, I hope I may never see him again. He is one of those nervous, weak, unlucky creatures that I hate having near me on active service: yet he is clever."[86] Receiving Wolseley's request on 23 March 1885 to explain the reasons for delay in leaving Metemmeh for Khartoum, Wilson told his wife he was being scapegoated.[87] Hartington declined to publish Wolseley's dispatches castigating Wilson because they also placed blame on the government. Wolseley's critical view of Wilson's command capacity was undoubtedly fed by some of Wilson's subordinates. Wilson was denied any official inquiry into his conduct by Cambridge, who wanted the matter dropped, but the controversy rumbled on through the publication of Wilson's *From Korti to Khartoum* in 1886, Henry Colvile's official history of the campaign in 1889, and Archibald Forbes's critique of Colvile in 1892.[88]

The constant employment of a relatively small number of officers did restrict others' development. In August 1879, in stating his belief to Wolseley that Wood had been rewarded enough for service in South Africa, Cambridge wrote, "Too early promotion is not to my mind beneficial either to an individual or to the Army generally for it damps the ardour of many good men, who are thus superseded and it is far more difficult to find employment for a good man in the General's rank than in that of Full Colonel in which there are many positions which would suit Wood admirably."[89]

Equally, as Cambridge wrote to Wolseley in November 1884, "if the same officers are invariably employed, you have no area for selecting others, and give no others a chance of coming to the front. . . . If you never go beyond this particular batch of men, you work these and bring *nothing* on."[90] Cambridge had a valid point although there is a certain irony for what irked him most was Wolseley ignoring the claims of seniority. From Wolseley's point of view, as he expressed it when appointed to Cyprus, the duke was keeping back younger men and "delighting to honour those of the old cut-and-dry model from whom nothing new is ever to be expected."[91]

It has been argued that Wolseley became something of a prisoner of the initial success of his ring in feeling it desirable to employ the same men lest his rejection of them might reflect adversely on his earlier choice.[92] Wolseley did continue to employ the same men despite his own increasing criticism of their failings. On Cyprus, for example, Baker Russell proved unfit for staff work "for which he has neither the temper nor the aptitude." Wolseley lamented the "scrawling hideousness which will be left to me as the records of my Cyprus campaign."[93] Wolseley was also disappointed to hear Greaves was among those who regretted coming to Cyprus: "I was under the impression I was paying them a great compliment and professionally doing them a great service. I found that apparently the whole army was most anxious to come here. I made my own selections and until last night I had been under the impression that those selected came here rejoicing."[94]

Wolseley frequently commented on Brackenbury's worship of "his own vile body" as on Cyprus in 1878.[95] In South Africa in 1879, Brackenbury appeared increasingly selfish, "his stoicism as regards the miseries of others" being, as Wolseley put it, "admirable."[96] Maurice, to whom Wolseley felt a great debt for nursing him through a serious bout of fever in Asante, had shown little capacity as PS.[97] In Zululand Maurice was "completely useless as a staff officer in every respect." Maurice, whose untidiness constantly amazed Wolseley, appeared so argumentative that Wolseley believed "he would halt halfway up a breech to argue a point if he were aggravated to do so by some one at his elbow who took pleasure in seeing him excited." Wolseley concluded he had "never yet found the hole into which this peg would fit."[98]

Wood was never forgiven for signing the peace treaty with the Boers after Colley's death at Majuba in February 1881. Wolseley was admonished by the queen in December 1884 for referring to Wood's "ignominious" peace.[99] Yet, Wolseley's view of Wood was somewhat ambivalent.[100] He certainly took some pleasure in leaving Wood behind in Alexandria in 1882. According to Archibald Alison, Wood was furious with Wolseley "for refusing to acknowledge that his brigade is entitled to share in the rewards of the campaign in the same way as those who fought at Tel-el-Kebir."[101] By 1884 Wolseley found Wood vain and untrustworthy and a man "who could never run straight . . . or be true to any Chief."[102] Subsequently, Wood felt it keenly that Wolseley had not helped advance his career.[103] Yet, in 1886 Wolseley still believed Wood was an excellent trainer of troops and far better suited for Aldershot than anyone else.[104]

Seemingly, most in the Sudan campaign were failing Wolseley. Butler was furious at Stewart's promotion to brigadier general, and exercising considerable powers of prediction but with the unfortunate trait of never giving "anyone the benefit of his predictions until after the events have occurred."[105] Buller was ready to "belittle everyone who may possibly enter the lists with him in the military race for distinction,"[106] building up imaginary difficulties, and would not again be employed as CoS in any campaign Wolseley might lead.[107] Wolseley glimpsed the essential problem in December 1884:

> Those men are all good in their way, all have some, a few many very good points & talents about them, but not one of them would have been where he is at this moment in the Army List if I had not fought hard with H.R.H. for their advancement. Alison, Graham, Wood, Buller, Dormer, Brackenbury, Butler etc. etc. owe me much in the common acceptance of the word. I don't feel they do myself, because I have fought to push them on, not because I like them, but because I believed it was in the interests of the public service that good men should be placed in high position in the Army. I wonder if there is a man of all the many I have been the means of pushing forward who cares one d— for me

or are the least grateful to me!! One thing is quite certain I never expect any gratitude, so I am never in the least surprised when I meet with the reverse.[108]

Similarly, Wolseley concluded in July 1885, "Nowadays, every man seems to think of himself only, starting with the notion that he is a Napoleon, and apparently entirely indifferent to the interests of the state." On another occasion during this ill-fated campaign to relieve Khartoum, he wrote to his wife, "as soon as they feel they have an assured footing and can do really good staff service they torture themselves with jealousy one of the other and sometimes even in their dealings with me are inclined to kick over the traces."[109]

Certainly, as prominent members of Wolseley's ring became more senior, their willingness to work together was subordinated to their own ambitions. After Buller was apparently willing to accept the office of CinC ahead of Wolseley in 1895, Wolseley wrote that he now intended to have "men about me who will be somewhat more interested in my affairs & less wrapped up in their own selfishness."[110]

What made internal dissension so destructive by 1884 was that Wolseley's command style was built on the basis of individuals willingly filling specific roles in a kind of orchestrated military collective. Wolseley employed larger staffs than his British contemporaries, but his CoS and subordinate commanders were not intended to share in decision making. There were occasions when Wolseley did leave matters to his subordinates and they failed him because the very way he operated militated against the development of initiative. Without him, they floundered.[111]

Wolseley at least persuaded many younger officers including William Robertson and Charles à Court that "hard work," study, and professional knowledge were the way to preferment.[112] He was generally successful in coordinating the diverse talents of his chosen subordinates in a way well suited to colonial campaigning. The problem was that improvisation was no substitute for a proper general staff. Wolseley's capacity to manage affairs decreased in proportion to the growth in the scale of operations.

Frederick Roberts

The critique of the Wolseley ring by Sir Ian Hamilton is well known. Hamilton arrived in the Sudan in 1884 on his way home for leave. For Hamilton, Wolseley's staffing of the Camel Corps drawing from the Guards, cavalry, and rifle regiments was no more than "an urge to do something for his pals." Referring to his initial arrival, Hamilton recalled, "Nothing could have been more inhospitable or forbidding than the response from that special preserve of the Wolseleyites." John Ardagh had responded to Hamilton's request to serve, "I fear I can't take the responsibility; you won't mind if I speak plainly; I fear you might be regarded as an intruder."[113] Yet, Hamilton was permitted to join the First Gordon Highlanders on the expedition. Moreover, when it was proposed that he be left behind at Wadi Halfa, Wood and Buller insisted a named company with its own officer should remain in reserve.[114] Hamilton still wrote that the "Indian Service is a thing apart and the Horse Guards take very good care that none of the outsiders come on these sort of excursions."[115]

Such criticism by Roberts's adherents is not uncommon. One of the more vociferous, William Nicholson, complained to Henry Spenser Wilkinson in December 1894 that his application for a staff appointment at Horse Guards had been declined by Buller, then AG. Nicholson believed he would have succeeded "had it not been for my intimate association with Lord Roberts." It was intolerable that Buller "should be allowed to carry his petty jealousy of a much more famous soldier than himself so far as to debar me from staff employment because I have the honour to be a friend of Lord R."[116] In 1897 another of Roberts's adherents, George Pretyman, felt his prospect of obtaining the Belfast or Woolwich commands likely to be blocked: "But of one thing I feel quite sure, viz. that unless considerable pressure be put on 'the ring' when a vacancy is about to occur, I shall be left out in the cold. I gathered that from Wood's tone & manner to me, which was entirely of the 'we don't know you' style."[117]

Antagonism was not initially apparent. With Wolseley already an established public name and Roberts having only recently made his reputation in Afghanistan, there was no great sense of animosity between them. Wolseley recalled Roberts as a promising officer from the time Roberts had succeeded him as DAQMG on Sir Hope Grant's staff in April 1858—although they had not actually met.[118] Roberts believed Wolseley would be a good choice "to sweep away the cobwebs at Head Quarters" in India.[119] Pretyman similarly recorded that Roberts "has always hoped he [Wolseley] might come out here as C.in. Chief. A strong man and a good soldier is much wanted to sweep away the cobwebs at Head Quarters," a sentiment with which Pretyman concurred.[120] Letters between Roberts and his wife during the Second Afghan War (now lost) also apparently mentioned Roberts's hope that Wolseley would succeed Haines in India.[121]

Roberts cooperated happily with George Colley when the latter was Lytton's adviser and had no resentment toward Evelyn Wood when he was sent out as Colley's second in command in 1881. Roberts wrote to Wood that he was "delighted that my friend Colley should have such an able officer under him. I tell everyone that the country may think itself fortunate that a man like Colley is now in command at Natal."[122] In 1891 Roberts expressed the opinion that, while he had never met Buller, "I am under the impression that he is one of the best soldiers we have."[123]

By the end of 1881, however, hostility had surfaced, not least through Roberts's public declaration at the Mansion House in February 1881 of his criticism of short-service enlistment. Pretyman's views had changed with that of his chief, for Wolseley was now "sadly jealous—of that there is not a shadow of doubt: and I daresay you will hear some sort of rubbish talked now that Sir Fred has left England."[124] In 1888 Roberts was sorry his key ally, Charles Brownlow, the AMS for India, was leaving Horse Guards as it would expose him to "the tender mercies" of Wolseley as AG and Harman as MS, neither of whom he thought liked him. Wolseley would never be a friend: "Our aim and ambitions, views and feelings are absolutely different."[125]

Yet, in 1885 Wolseley still suggested that the Indian command "has been given to a very good man."[126] Likewise, Roberts wrote of Wolseley in 1893, "We are credited with not being well disposed towards each other, but why this should be the general idea I know not. We have never been thrown together, and though there are certain questions about which we do not agree, I see no reason why we should not be good friends."[127] In 1895 Roberts also wrote that Wolseley was "unquestionably the proper person to succeed the Duke of Cambridge, and I hail his advent to the Horse Guards with great satisfaction. Wolseley and I may have differed on matters of detail, but on the main question, viz: the necessity for our Army being thoroughly efficient, we are entirely agreed!"[128]

Wolseley was less generous, characterizing Roberts as a "scheming little Indian who has acquired a great reputation he would never have had but for the necessity of setting someone up to counteract my influence in the Army."[129] Writing of Roberts in February 1900, Wolseley expressed that he knew "nothing in his career, nothing he has done beyond his talent at self-advertisement—and I admit that is great—that in any way proves him to be a military genius."[130] As Wolseley's retirement came closer, Roberts was increasingly a "little charlatan" and a "jobbing charlatan."[131]

The Roberts and Wolseley rings operated in much the same way. Roberts was equally careful in his selections. Discussing command recommendations in December 1885, Roberts wrote, "I want to see the best men appointed and I am strongly of opinion that no one should get a command in peace unless he is considered fit to command in war." Two weeks later, he said that no general should be appointed "who is not in every respect qualified to command troops in the field," suggesting no one should have a divisional command after the age of fifty-five.[132] He also felt that no brigade commander should be aged over forty-eight or fifty when appointed.[133]

Roberts claimed it was immaterial whether a man was his friend or not.[134] Similarly, on 2 August 1887 when reports about his use of patronage were circulating in Horse Guards, Roberts wrote to Martin Dillon,

> I am not ashamed of helping my friends so long as they deserve it, but I would not put my own brother into any place for which he was not, in my opinion, fitted. I knew that men passed over would abuse me, but I am prepared to bear the burden, rather than promote men who I believe to be inefficient. I may, of course, make mistakes, but I do my best, both by personal acquaintance and by carefully weighing opinions, to form a just view of all officers' characters, and I am gratified to find that, as a rule, my selections seem to be approved.[135]

Age and seniority alone were not sufficient recommendations to gain Roberts's support.

Thomas Baker became Roberts's preferred choice for the Poona division in 1885. Roberts hoped Cambridge would agree:

> I have felt all along that His Royal Highness would resent my giving my opinion about officers for commands in this country, but I made up my mind that I would not hesitate to say what I think and to do all I can to get only good men appointed. . . . If I were working for my own friends, I would not venture to force my views upon the Duke of Cambridge, but in no instance are the officers I have recommended more than ordinary acquaintances.[136]

Roberts emphasized that he scarcely knew the newly appointed CinC in Bombay, Charles Arbuthnot, while Herbert Macpherson, whom he had recommended for Burma, was "never what I call a friend." Roberts also maintained the branch of the service to which an individual belonged was of no account.[137]

Nor did he believe in seniority for its own sake.[138] When recommending Pretyman and William Penn Symons for brigades in 1888—both were only regimental majors—Roberts pointed out that he too had only been a regimental major when he commanded the Kurram Field Force.[139] Again in 1889, Roberts acknowledged his recommendations found little favor with Cambridge but noted, "If I am accused of helping my friends, my answer is that I get rid of men who are not superior to their fellows, and only keep those about me who are worth pushing on."[140]

Brackenbury's appointment as military member in 1891 threw him into close proximity to Roberts. In May 1894 Brackenbury specifically compared Roberts's methods to those of Wolseley. Any officer "placed in a great position of authority and responsibility will select as his tools for the work in hand the men whom he has tried, and found never to fail him, and will prefer them to those who he has not tried, or to those who he has tried and not found perfect." Brackenbury asked Roberts about the Wolseley ring, to which Roberts replied, "No officer who has the responsibility laid upon him of carrying out a big job would ever be such a fool as to entrust the details of it to men he did not know he could rely on."[141]

Roberts himself told Brig. Gen. Henry Wilkinson in February 1887 he was guided in his choices by his own knowledge of officers, advice from the HQ staff and higher commanders, the opinion of the army generally, and confidential reports.[142] Interestingly, of Wilkinson's appointment to command the Indian cavalry brigade in Egypt in 1882, Wolseley later noted, "India always was a place for jobbery & I suppose it will continue to be so until the end."[143]

Of course, there was no foolproof method insofar as confidential reports were concerned. In 1891 Roberts sympathized with George Greaves, who had to find a replacement for Maj. Gen. Frederick Solly Flood at Poona: "Isn't it a difficult business to select the right man? I am for ever poring over the Army List only to come to the same conclusion, viz., that very few men are fitted in all respects for high commands or responsible staff appointments."[144]

On the other hand, returning to his regiment in India fresh from Staff College in 1891, Capt. Horace Smith-Dorrien discovered it counted for little. He was told by Nicholson "that much value was not set on the p.s.c. in India, but there was no reason why the holding of such a certificate should prevent my obtaining a Staff appointment."[145] From "this land of jobbery," Smith-Dorrien wrote to his brother saying he had complained to Evelyn Wood: "I had done everything to qualify for staff employ in any Army in the world except the Army in India—but for this latter only one qualification was necessary, viz.: 'Simla interest'—and just like my luck that was the only one qualification I didn't possess & didn't see my way to getting."[146] Of 125 officers holding staff appointments as AAG or DAAG in Bengal alone, only 4 held the *psc*.[147] Wood suggested that Roberts did give preference to *psc*'s. In September 1892, however, Smith-Dorrien attended a dinner for Staff College graduates at Simla. Brackenbury pointed out sarcastically after Roberts had praised Camberley that none out of Roberts, Maj. Gen. William Galbraith (AG), Maj. Gen. Sir James Browne (QMG), and Nicholson (MS) were *psc*'s.[148]

Psc's were fewer in India, which had no Staff College of its own until that established at Deolali in 1905, which moved to Quetta in 1907. Six places were reserved for Indian officers at Camberley from 1875 onward, but expense meant many were not taken up. Thus, on the frontier campaigns in 1897, only twenty-eight out of eighty-five staff officers were actually staff trained.[149]

Kipling's eulogy to "Bobs" from 1892 has a comparative reference to Wolseley in the verse: "e— does— not— advertise— Do yer Bobs?" Less well known is

Kipling's earlier poem, "A General Summary," from *Departmental Ditties* (1886)—
ostensibly about ancient Egypt, and regarded as a satire on Roberts:

> When they scratched the reindeer-bone,
> Some one made the sketch his own,
> Filched it from the artist—then,
> Even in those early days,
> Won a simple Viceroy's praise
> Through the toil of other men.
> Ere they hewed the Sphinx's visage
> Favouritism governed kissage,
> Even as it does in this age.[150]

Kipling also contributed the poem "A Job Lot" to the *Pioneer* in September 1888:

> We've heard it before, but we'll drink once more
> While the army sniffs and sobs.
> For Bobs its pride, who has lately died
> And is now succeeded by Jobs.[151]

As in the case of Wolseley's ring, there were many officers who became closely
associated with Roberts. Rather like Wolseley, Roberts spoke of his "list" in
South Africa in 1900.[152] Certainly, protégés were advanced.

In writing to Viscount "Rowly" Melgund in September 1879, Roberts indicated he would be delighted to see him back under his command, as he was
already accompanied by Pretyman, Hugh Gough, Pole-Carew, "and a few more
of the right sort."[153] In 1884 Roberts tried to get Cambridge to agree to Ian
Hamilton becoming his MS, although he was only a captain when a field officer
would more typically be appointed. Cambridge declined so Pole-Carew, then a
lieutenant colonel, was appointed instead.[154]

Roberts believed the younger Neville Chamberlain not only promising
in every respect, but possibly the most popular man in India, recommending him for a brevet lieutenant colonelcy after only fourteen years' service in
1887.[155] When William Nicholson turned down the opportunity to be George
White's MS in 1892, as he wished for a home posting, Roberts at once suggested
Chamberlain if Hamilton also declined.[156] In the event, Hamilton accepted.
Subsequently, Roberts pressed the claim of Chamberlain to be MS at Horse
Guards in succession to Coleridge Grove; Lansdowne wrote that he would
"take care that his claims are examined."[157]

Service in Afghanistan was a touchstone. William Galbraith, Roberts's
AAG in Afghanistan, was another whose career was advanced. Roberts strongly

recommended Galbraith as AG in India in 1890, which post he duly secured.[158] Galbraith's successor as AG in 1895 was Gerald Morton. He thanked Roberts for his continued support since they had first met in 1872: "You have always been most thoughtful in considering the interests and in helping on the advancement of those officers who served with you."[159]

Charles Gough was amused by Roberts's constant attempts to advance the interests of his younger brother, Hugh Gough, despite the lack of real result, "but you must allow for a little friendly colouring in the hope of pushing him on—still even Bobs can't make very much out of it."[160] Hugh Gough, though disappointed not to be given a brigade, was "really a very lucky fellow to have an independent command although not a Brigade," wrote his older brother. "He is five years and a half junior to me in the Service and has been far more lucky as regards opportunities and pay than ever I have—but there is no satisfying those two. His friend Bobs is doing all he can for him, and will I daresay succeed in getting him made a Brig. Genl."[161]

Roberts's three principal protégés were Ian Hamilton, William Nicholson, and George White. When Hamilton received the DSO and Nicholson the CB in 1891, Nicholson had no doubt these were owed to Roberts.[162] Roberts had pressed strongly already for their promotions to substantive colonel, as they occupied what he deemed to be colonel's appointments: Hamilton was AAG for musketry in India, and Nicholson was Roberts's MS. Hamilton had over eighteen years' service and Nicholson over twenty-six years'. Although both brevet lieutenant colonels, Hamilton was only a regimental captain and Nicholson a major. Cambridge was deaf to Roberts's plea that eighty-six current general officers in the British service had been promoted to colonel before their twenty-sixth year of service. Roberts also pointed out that Wolseley had become a colonel after only thirteen years' service and Hardinge after fourteen years' when both were still regimental captains.[163] Pressure from the viceroy through the IO, however, resulted in Nicholson and Hamilton both securing promotion.[164]

When it seemed possible that Roberts might get the Aldershot command in 1893, he wrote to Hamilton that he would then be able to "work my way quietly round the Horse Guards people, and be able to provide for you and Nicholson."[165] Unexpectedly offered the post of DQMG in India by George White in 1895, Hamilton was careful to consult Roberts before accepting it as he had previously promised Roberts to return to England if Roberts wanted him on his staff in Ireland.[166]

White was picked out early, Roberts describing him after his appointment as Ripon's PS in 1880 as "quite one of the best men I know for such an appointment; clever, gentlemanly and a first rate soldier."[167] Interestingly, White believed the appointment to Ripon's staff was due to the Earl of Camperdown, who was a family friend.[168]

White's relatively long service without promotion caused constant difficulties for Roberts and himself. In 1885, then at Madras, Roberts wanted White to take the Kamptee brigade, pointing out he had thirty-four years' service and would be forced to retire if he remained unemployed.[169] In 1886 Roberts wanted White to be promoted to major general in order to hold the command of Upper Burma. Cambridge opposed White as too junior despite his service:

> This I *could not* by any possibility assent to, as White is quite low down in the list of Colonels, & would by such an arrangement go over the heads of many & such valuable officers, that it would produce the *very worst* impression, & great & reasonable outcry. Believe me, my dear friend, these sort of things had better be left to me, and I never found that Sir Donald Stewart or any other of the several Commanders in Chief who have served under me, ever suggested or interfered with my authority, in such matters.[170]

By Cambridge's calculation, White would jump three hundred colonels and could not even be made a local major general. The army would not benefit from "causing heart burnings & dissatisfaction" among those passed over.[171] In vain, Roberts tried to show that White could be compared to Herbert Stewart, who had received promotion to major general after twenty-one years' service.[172]

Roberts enlisted the help of the viceroy, Lord Dufferin, who had not appreciated White's junior standing in the army. Cambridge told Dufferin he had confidence in Roberts,

> excepting on one point the love & devotion he entertains for *his Friends.* There are a certain number of these whom he never fails to push forward on every occasion, & to this I honestly tell you I *greatly object,* for it upsets the Army, & the good feeling I have happily been able to keep up in it under many difficulties, as you know. The Army I hope, under my authority, has never been *jobbed.* If we don't prevail, Roberts will introduce a system of this sort, & this I cannot stand, & in this I hope to receive your fullest & kindest support, for I am satisfied you take the same view of this question as I do.[173]

Roberts again returned to some comparisons. There were, indeed, 222 colonels senior to White, but 73 of them were either artillerymen or engineers, who counted separately. Of the remaining 149, 97 had entered the army after White, and there were also several major generals who had been commissioned after him. In fact, when White received promotion to major general, he had served not only longer than Herbert Stewart but also longer than Brackenbury, Buller,

Dormer, Wolseley, and Wood. As Roberts wrote to Dufferin, "I fail to see, especially in these days of selection, why the 222 Colonels senior to General White should be protected from supersession by him, when he has proved himself eminently successful in the command of a very difficult operation."[174]

Herbert Macpherson received the Burma command instead but died shortly after arriving. White finally got his promotion to major general in July 1887. He fully expected to be "the best hated man in the Upper Ranks of the Army" by being promoted over so many colonels.[175] Roberts had intended White to take a command in Bengal, but this was rendered redundant by White remaining in Burma. Roberts then wrote to Lord Randolph Churchill asking that he receive White and also urged White to make himself known to Cambridge when he next went home.[176]

White duly saw Cambridge and made a favorable impression.[177] White was offered a brigade at Aldershot, which Roberts thought something of an insult, and it gave him some pleasure to tell Cambridge that White could not accept as he was being extended in Burma by the wish of the viceroy and the chief commissioner.[178] White, who was more hopeful, wrote to Roberts,

> I find there is a very general opinion that he treated me badly in not giving me the division for which you recommended me and I rather think he feels it himself. He was nettled at having to give in to Your Excellency's continued appeals in my interests & having been forced into promoting me. He indulged a little spleen at my expense by refusing me the division. But he is good hearted and I believe fair minded, and I do not think he will throw me aside again.[179]

But White found Cambridge still reluctant to give him the next vacancy that occurred.[180] He was not aware of the efforts taking place on his behalf, for it still took three days of argument by Brownlow for Cambridge to agree to White getting a divisional command for the following year.[181] Roberts also pushed White for the Madras command in 1890, complaining that Dormer, who he had not met in thirty years, did not have sufficient Indian experience.[182]

If Wolseley supposedly surrounded himself with aristocracy in the Sudan in 1884–85, Roberts was equally accused of surrounding himself with an aristocratic staff in South Africa in 1899–1900, including Lansdowne's son, the Earl of Kerry, and the young Duke of Marlborough. Wolseley complained that Roberts "manipulates the views of a democracy on the one hand & plays up to the Aristocracy on the other by surrounding himself with dukes & earls & their sons to the third & fourth generations."[183] He hoped a future generation of authors would show Roberts up "as the little toady & snob & bad general he has proved himself to be."[184] James Grierson referred to Roberts's headquarters as the "House of Lords."[185] Charles Townshend, whose arrival in South Africa from India in 1900 was largely due to Lord Curzon's influence, found that he was not altogether welcome. Townshend characterized the coterie around Roberts as "a sort of extract from the Peerage, with a few names of untitled officers thrown in here and there." He listed eight peers and an honorable, many drawn from the domestic militia or yeomanry, as ADCs or in other staff posts.[186]

The Roberts ring could be just as poisonous as Wolseley's. The case of Charles Gough has been noted already. No friend of Roberts, Gough concluded, "Everybody nowadays seems to me to serve his Personal advancement only and for that will sacrifice anything. . . . Roberts also is a great time server and his principal object is to serve himself and his friends." With his own forward movement halted in October 1879, Gough assumed the reason was "in order to cook up a little dish for some other favourite!!!"[187]

William Dunham "Redan" Massy was another example. Massy was blamed for allowing Afghan forces to escape Kabul on 8 October 1879 and again on 11 December. On the second occasion, he lost two field guns. Massy was clearly incompetent. Yet, Charles MacGregor, who retrieved the guns, suggested that it was Roberts who had effectively ordered Massy to place the guns where they had to be abandoned and that there was no prospect the Afghans had either the means or the intention of taking them.[188] From Roberts's perspective, Massy misrepresented clear orders that left him no discretion and was not justified in departing from them.[189] With Haines fully concurring in Massy's removal, Massy returned to India in March 1880.[190]

The problem was that Massy was "intimately connected with the Press through his father & other sources": his father was the Paris correspondent of the *Pioneer*.[191] As Charles Gough noted, removal would make "so much noise, and he has been so extravagantly puffed in some of the papers, that these same people will assuredly take up the case and *as regards the loss of the guns on the 11th December* there will be a good deal to be said on both sides of the question."[192] As Gough anticipated, the press took up Massy's case despite Massy having "no head, no resolution and no *flint and steel* element in his composition."[193]

Roberts was warned that Massy's friends were putting it about that he had been removed because Roberts wanted to promote his own favorites. Roberts responded that he would "rather be accused of favouring my friends (knowing how absolutely untrue such an accusation is) than bring to favourable notice men who have failed in, or are unfit for, positions of responsibility."[194] He took the precaution of sending Martin Dillon his memorandum on the Massy case.[195] Pretyman thought the public all too gullible in believing Massy's side of the story; for his part, Massy pleaded with Roberts to allow him to return to his brigade command in India. According to Pretyman, Massy was a "low cad" more interested in creature comforts than in soldiering.[196]

Roberts initially thought Massy could temporarily retain his brigade and return to Britain for employment "in the shape of some of the lesser prizes of the service." Haines, however, made an error in publishing charges against Massy.[197] Although Haines had assured him there was no alternative, Cambridge was somewhat suspicious of Massy's instant removal, feeling he could not be wholly to blame. Cambridge urged Haines to be careful to ensure there was a clear case against Massy "so that there may be no mistake as to the view taken for I must tell you that some people fancy, that Sir Frederick Roberts is quite as much to blame in the failure of December 11th as Massy, and you must be very sure, that this will not be brought forward on Massy's side."[198] The publication of Massy's case forced Roberts to go public when he would "infinitely prefer confining the circulation of this memorandum to officials at the Horse Guards, and to a few private individuals, rather than giving it publicity in the newspapers."[199]

Old scores were settled once Roberts succeeded Buller in the supreme command in South Africa in January 1900. Key ring members such as Nicholson, Chamberlain, and Pretyman were brought to South Africa, and others already in South Africa such as Hamilton and Henry Rawlinson were summoned to join Roberts. When Roberts became CinC, the WO was said by some to have become a case of "Bobs, Jobs, Snobs & Co."[200] In February 1902 Wolseley wrote to his brother George, "They say the smell of curry all over the War Office is very overpowering."[201]

Nonetheless, George Wolseley made a career in India, and Brackenbury and Greaves both reached sufficient accommodation with Roberts to hold positions under him in India at varying times, suggesting the rings were not as rigid as often supposed. They were not mutually exclusive, and it was possible for some individuals to maneuver themselves adroitly between them.

One good example is Thomas Baker, who was also well liked by Cambridge. When Baker, who had become QMG, died in February 1893, Cambridge described him as a "most charming man & excellent officer both departmentally & on the Field & I mourn with his loss, a very loyal & devoted friend."[202] When Baker had become Lytton's MS in 1878, Cambridge looked forward to being well informed of events by an "outsider."[203] Subsequently, Cambridge viewed Baker as a voice of reason on the proposed committee to examine the organization of the Indian army.[204] Yet, Cambridge also believed Roberts and Baker "both to be very ambitious & dangerous men, who would sacrifice anything & anybody for their own advancement."[205] Thus, despite describing Baker as a personal friend, Cambridge was reluctant to see him as AG in India when he was recommended for the post by Donald Stewart: "But as Adjt. Genl. I look upon him as extremely dangerous. He is very determined & goes very much ahead in all modern notions of Reform in Army matters, & he is far too much disposed to go with the Powers that be to justify any great reliance being placed upon him."[206] Nonetheless, Cambridge came to believe Baker so valuable as AG that he should not be moved to a divisional command when Roberts suggested it in 1886.[207]

Baker had the unhappy knack for jumping the wrong way at the wrong moment. Posted to South Africa in 1881 as brigadier general in the wake of Colley's death at Majuba, Baker was displeased, in spite of their friendship, to find his junior, Buller, had local rank as major general. One can sense the relish with which Cambridge replied, "But my dear Baker, as you are one who approves of *selection* all I can say to you is, that this is the result of that system, which as you know, I am not myself very fond of, & only accept so much of it, as is inevitable & this is unfortunately one of those cases, when I should have preferred taking a different course, & adhering to the seniority as it existed at the time."[208] Roberts was especially sorry to see Baker quit as AG in India in order to become QMG at Horse Guards.[209] Baker turned down the offer of being MS in 1892 in the belief that remaining QMG would enable him to go anywhere at short notice. Since his health was already bad, any overseas appointment would have been impossible.[210]

As with Baker, it was not unusual for Cambridge to recognize the positive qualities of some of Wolseley's adherents, such as Robert Biddulph, who became DGME in 1888, and Charles Mansfield Clarke, who became CinC in Madras in 1893.[211] That raises the question of Cambridge himself for, notwithstanding his protestations, he certainly indulged in what could equally be called jobbery.

The Duke of Cambridge

When an announcement of members of the royal commission on the abolition of purchase was made in September 1871 without his or the queen's prior approval, Cambridge urged the Keeper of the Privy Purse, Maj. Gen. Sir Thomas Biddulph, to make it clear to Cardwell that the queen "is still at the *head of the Army,* that she has not the slightest intention of giving up this function, and that she equally insists on her Com. in Chief being taken into account on all important subjects concerned with Army matters, even in cases where the actual selection & appointment do not rest with him but are in the gift of the minister of the day."[212] In August 1874 the *World* suggested that Cambridge had "always been surrounded by a little clique, the members of which, finding themselves very comfortable in the positions which with little merit of their own they have secured, wish to retain those positions, and consequently have ever sought to keep down men of energy and originality."[213]

Cambridge clearly had his own friends and clients. Following the death of James Lindsay in 1874, Cambridge indicated to the queen that Alfred Horsford was best qualified to succeed as MS. He was frank and genial but also was "one of my oldest comrades & friends."[214] The duke clung to those he favored. Sir Richard Airey's term as AG was due to expire in 1875, but Cambridge induced him to stay on until Airey wanted to retire: he was seventy-three. Cambridge managed to get Gathorne Hardy to agree to an extension until September 1876, at which time another favored officer, Sir Charles Ellice, QMG for the last five years, succeeded.[215] Cambridge even recommended Airey as field commander in the event of a war against Russia in 1878. Hardy was appalled and did not think the duke's subsequent recommendation of the sixty-eight-year-old Napier of Magdala was much better.[216]

At the time Wolseley was still hoping to replace Haines as CinC in India in 1879, he heard that Ellice believed he would get it instead; he confided to his brother that Cambridge was "a great jobber & a hater of mine but I think that would be rather too much of a joke."[217] Wolseley believed there was a clique around Cambridge including Ellice, Horsford, and Daniel Lysons—"all of whom would gloat over my failure [to get the India command] as they have doubtless gloated over the fact that I arrived here [Zululand] too late to command in the final action of the war."[218] Ellice was identified as a particular foe. Wolseley had once considered him a friend and only came to the conclusion he had misjudged Ellice in June 1879: "I leave him for ever: I have always had the meanest opinion of him as a soldier, & I have now learnt to despise him as a fake friend and a malignant backbiter."[219]

A few months later, Wolseley concluded he had more enemies than he had thought:

> My tongue goes too freely in denouncing the jobbing and the shams that pass current at the Horse Guards; I shall in future endeavour to keep my opinions more to myself. I am not yet strong enough to stand against the Court party who regard me as a radical because I won't put up with men like Chelmsford & [Henry] Crealock. It requires a stronger man than I am to pursue the line I had worked out for myself. I must wait for some big event before I can show up HRH of Cambridge and the lot of incapables he delights to honour.[220]

When there was an attempt to compel Baker Russell to rejoin his regiment in India when Wolseley wanted him to remain in South Africa, Wolseley again wrote of an "old fogy [sic] clique" and "a piece of spite on the part of Ellice,

Horsford & Co to annoy me & one of those who are regarded as 'Wolseley's men.'"[221] He attributed Whitmore's antipathy to George Greaves to the latter being seen as "one of my lot."[222] Nonetheless, Wolseley generally thought that Whitmore was above "jobs," and that his real fault was "he thinks one man is much the same as the other & hates passing any man over because you have a better man available for service."[223]

Alison had been associated with Wolseley in terms of being assigned to command the white troops sent to Asante and then again serving in Egypt in 1882, but Alison was not of the Wolseley ring. Given command of the Army of Occupation in Egypt, Alison hoped for the Aldershot command. When this went to George Willis, Alison suspected that Cambridge and Whitmore

> think they have got rid of me very cleverly. Lord Alexander [Russell] goes to Halifax, Willis to Aldershot, Malta will not be filled up for another year and then must go to some old gentleman. Portsmouth will be given to some Court favourite with lots of money. When I go home from any cause they will say "Oh, We always intended you to command in Egypt during the occupation— everything else is filled up for several years. We are so sorry but you see it is not our fault!"!![224]

Alison was suffering from recurring fever and was ordered home by a medical board. The reception of the news did not suggest any sympathy, but, much to his surprise, he was then given Aldershot after all.[225]

In discussing the appointment of Maj. Gen. Francis Hamilton to a brigade command in May 1886, George Pretyman complained, "It is this accursed jobbery of the Duke & his clique that sickens all professional soldiers of English soldiering."[226] In November 1892 Arthur Bigge suggested to Sir Henry Ponsonby that the "Boulder" (by which he meant the duke) had many "playmates" at headquarters including the DAG, Sir Francis Grenfell; the AMS, Col. Ronald "Rowdy" Lane; and the DAGRA, Albert Williams.[227]

In 1881 Childers insisted it was essential that the AG and other principal officeholders under Cambridge should have a broad sympathy for reforms accepted by all governments since 1869. He pointed out that the recently appointed DAGRA and DAGRE—Cols. Sir Charles Arbuthnot and Sir John Stokes—were both distinctly old-school. According to Cambridge, Arbuthnot and Stokes were good officers, but were not his friends, and he knew little of them.[228] Furious, Cambridge claimed Childers wanted "to perpetuate a job." As for AG, Cambridge claimed there was no soldier other than Wolseley who supported reform. His own choices for AG were Thomas Steele, Lysons, or Hardinge.[229] Others acceptable to him were Sir Alexander Macdonnell, Horsford, and Stephenson.[230] The Prince of Wales's PS, Francis Knollys, also suggested Lysons, as well as other known opponents of reform including Sir William Parke, Sir Beauchamp Walker, and Lord Alexander Russell, the latter two being particularly acceptable to Cambridge. Knollys also listed Stephenson, but Ponsonby felt that, while he might come round to reform, he would not be sufficiently strong.[231] According to the distinguished artillery officer Col. William Reilly, Cambridge surrounded himself with "a parcel of people who do nothing but swear the Army is going to the Devil and apparently intend it should do so."[232]

Ponsonby and the queen's assistant PS, Sir Fleetwood Edwards, both thought that Lintorn Simmons would be suitable as AG but that, as an engineer, he would not find favor with the rest of the army. Ironically, while Cambridge felt Simmons too advanced in his views, Childers felt him not advanced enough.[233] In addition, Hartington strongly advised Childers against selecting the prickly Simmons as a result of the difficulties that had arisen with him during the Eastern crisis.[234] Cambridge remained so opposed to Wolseley as AG that he tried to keep him in Egypt as long as possible in 1882. He even suggested Wolseley was now "too important a man" for AG and should be given a colonial governorship "or something of that sort," or even the lord lieutenancy of Ireland.[235]

Cambridge was hostile to the Staff College, suggesting to the Penzance Commission it was only one qualification for advancement among many. The MS, Horsford, stated that tact was more of a requirement for staff service than talent, while Airey opined that some officers went to Camberley without the intention of advancing in professional knowledge.[236] Cambridge explained after making remarks about the college at a dinner that what concerned him was the "amount of writing going on in the Army" by *psc*'s who pushed their grievances in public and appeared to be "a very dissatisfied class of men."[237] Generally, he felt there was a minority who saw the *psc* solely as a means of advancement rather than attending to the regimental duties he felt more valuable as staff training.[238]

Granville Egerton was ADC to the governor of Malta, Arthur Fremantle, when Cambridge visited the island in 1895 in the company of the MS, Gipps. According to Egerton's memoirs, Cambridge began talking about the Staff College at a luncheon: "You have no brains Fremantle, I myself have no brains, and as for Gipps, he hasn't any brains either, but we all know our duty, and do our duty. But these Staff College fellows, they have brains, oh yes, they have brains, but let me tell you, Fremantle they're nasty fellows, and what's more Fremantle, they're dirty fellows."[239] This was clearly said for effect. Charles Callwell recorded a precisely similar story in which the remarks were addressed to the GOC of a home district.[240]

Cambridge invariably contested the claims of the adherents of both Wolseley and Roberts to preferment. Wolseley's efforts to get Baker Russell rewarded with the positon of ADC to the queen, for example, were rejected in 1877: "HRH has refused my appeal in favor [sic] of B. Russell in a note worded in a nasty tone. I hope I may yet be in a position to have justice done to Russell."[241] In September 1879 Horsford told Buller in discussing Wood's failure to be promoted to major general, "it was only the fact of your having been in Ashanti that stands in your way."[242]

Cambridge was determined that Wolseley should not be considered for the Madras command in 1879, which might lead to pressure for him to succeed Haines as CinC in India. Cambridge was equally opposed initially to George Greaves becoming AG in India, although this was conceded on Haines's recommendation. It would be folly, Cambridge felt, for Wolseley to get to India "when he would be surrounded by Greaves, Baker, Baker Russell, all his *own men* & the Governor-General [Lytton] being in the hands of Colley, also his *creature* in Military matters & views & then the Indian Armies would be destroyed and upset."[243] Cambridge also wrote pointedly on one occasion that Roberts was "a nimble jobber." If Roberts became AG in succession to Wolseley, having been CinC in India, he would not "submit himself to a higher military authority."[244] As indicated earlier, Roberts's attempts to promote Nicholson and Hamilton in 1890 likewise fell afoul of the duke. The same went for Lord William Beresford, who Cambridge believed had already been well rewarded: "his last Brevet has not escaped a great deal of comment, and to make him now a full Colonel would be looked upon by the Army as a tremendous job and would create a howl of dissatisfaction even amongst his best friends."[245]

Other Patrons

There were other patrons within the army. In some cases, those associated with Wolseley were originally linked with others. Edward Hutton initially saw Henry Crealock as his mentor.[246] Hutton even turned down the offer of being Buller's second in command in the Frontier Light Horse in 1879 to remain as Crealock's ADC. Crealock proved a failure in South Africa, but Hutton was taken up by Archibald Alison. Hutton remained with Alison rather than taking up Evelyn Wood's offer of a battalion in the reconstituted EA. Alison and Buller together then advanced Hutton on the basis of his advocacy of the value of mounted infantry. He came to Wolseley's notice through his work with Alison.[247]

Wood and Buller prospered under Chelmsford while others like Grenfell and Butler served on the Nile under Stephenson after Wolseley's departure. Lytton was another who gave impetus to men like Colley, Baker, and Brackenbury. Ardagh became something of a protégé of Lansdowne after becoming his PS in 1891. Salisbury was an influential supporter of Brackenbury after appreciating his work in the Intelligence Division to the extent that Brackenbury believed Salisbury's recommendation had secured him the post of military member.[248] He was right, for Salisbury had written in November 1890 that he had "formed a very high opinion of his ability and clearness of judgement. He is one of the very ablest soldiers we have got—I mean for the Council room."[249] Brackenbury also used his contacts with Stanhope, W. H. Smith, and Lord Knutsford.[250] In turn, Brackenbury built up his own following of capable young officers such as Gleichen, Callwell, Henry Wilson, and William Robertson.[251] Brackenbury also promoted the career of James Grierson, recommending him first as PS to the viceroy, Lord Elgin, and then, with Wolseley's support, as military attaché in Berlin.[252]

Other members of the Wolseley ring also had their own protégés whom they would bring to Wolseley's attention but also assist. Robert Spottiswoode, who was talent-spotted by McNeill and Greaves at Suakin, recalled that he "got my foot" into the ring, though he was already a lieutenant colonel and retired as a colonel in 1890.[253] More significantly, Robert "Stephe" Baden-Powell was brought on by Baker Russell and Evelyn Wood. Unfortunately for Baden-Powell, Baker Russell did not secure the more prominent commands Baden-Powell had hoped for. Nonetheless, he was introduced into Wolseley's circle. Baden-Powell also came to Wolseley's notice through his experiments with Nordenfeld machine guns in 1887. His reputation was then firmly made when Wolseley selected him to command native levies in the Third Asante War in 1895.[254]

Wood favored the career of Horace Smith-Dorrien, and Buller that of John French.[255] French was frequently praised by Wood.[256] Similarly, Wood and Greaves helped promote the career of Douglas Haig, giving him active service experience in the Sudan at a key moment and, in the case of Greaves, supporting Haig's efforts to gain entrance to the Staff College.[257]

When White succeeded him as CinC in India, Roberts wrote to Hamilton he would not use his influence, "It would be unfair—he might not like to refuse, and he of course has his own ideas about 'men,' and his own friends to look after."[258] White was generally regarded as "above jobbery"; as Brackenbury noted, "the one thing he cannot stand is men coming up to Simla to ask for appointments."[259] White had his preferences, though, strenuously supporting Edward Stedman for the Burma command in 1895 but equally prepared, if Stedman preferred, to back him for AMS at the WO.[260] Nicholson believed Ian Hamilton should have been offered the Nerbudda District in Bengal in

1898, but White selected Patrick Jeffreys, who had commanded a brigade in the Malakand Field Force, as White seemed "determined" to provide for his own favorites whatever their merits.[261]

It has also been suggested that the group of Royal Engineers who were so often called on to advise the government on strategic issues, such as Robert Home, Lintorn Simmons, Andrew Clarke, and later, George Clarke, represented a clique of their own.[262] George Clarke's career was assiduously promoted by Andrew Clarke and also by John Cashel Hoey, who had undertaken public service in Australia and New Zealand. Hoey wanted George Clarke to be given a lectureship at Chatham and worked with Andrew Clarke to get him appointed. This was unsuccessful but Andrew Clarke and Hoey were instrumental in rescuing Clarke from routine duties at Bermuda in 1881 to be sent to Gibraltar. Andrew Clarke then sent his protégé to report on the defenses of Alexandria. Subsequently, George Clarke was secretary to the Colonial Defence Committee from 1885 to 1892, a member of the Esher Committee in 1903, and first secretary of the Committee of Imperial Defence.[263]

Rivalries

Irrespective of the rings, the playing out of personal rivalries was hardly unique. One example is afforded by the Suakin expeditions of 1884–85. The dispatch of Buller and Herbert Stewart to join the first expedition under Gerald Graham in 1884 caused resentment when officers already serving in Egypt were passed over. Cambridge regretted "that I did not set my face against this arrangement" in the anticipation of friction, although he recognized Buller was more experienced than Maj. Gen. John Davis and that the commanders of the two cavalry regiments at Suakin were also inexperienced.[264] As he told Stephenson, Cambridge was sorry for those serving in Egypt who had been overlooked, "but you know how these matters are brought about and the difficulties there are to contend with in that respect."[265]

There was objection within the government to Greaves's receiving the local rank of lieutenant general and command of the expedition as this would make him senior to Earle, Wood, Buller, and Stewart if the two forces in the Sudan came into contact. Nor had Greaves seen as much active service as the others.[266] Hartington favored Alison, but Gladstone and Childers preferred Greaves largely on the basis that Cambridge opposed Greaves. Gladstone wanted Wolseley to choose either Graham or Greaves to command, but instead Wolseley was told by Cambridge that Greaves would be CoS and he could choose from Stephenson, Alison, and Graham to command. Wolseley opted for Graham. Gladstone held out for consulting Wolseley again in view of Cambridge imposing the choice, but the cabinet declined to support him.[267] Amid considerable antagonism between Greaves, irascible and foul-mouthed, and everyone else, Wolseley wrote of the staff serving at Suakin in May 1885, "never was there a force in the field that was less of a happy family; every one seemed to desire to play his own hand & to think solely of himself whilst he hated and ridiculed his neighbour."[268]

Another example of personal rivalries is the Tirah campaign of 1897–98.[269] Notwithstanding White's apparent impartiality, there were significant disagreements between him and William Lockhart, who would succeed him as CinC in India. The problem was Lockhart's connection with William Nicholson, a divisive figure throughout his career. Having been Roberts's MS, Nicholson became DAG to Lockhart in the Punjab in July 1895. Although still only fifty-three in 1898, he was already known as "Old Nick."[270] White was prepared to accept Nicholson as Lockhart's DAG because he felt Col. St. John Fancourt Michell, who coveted the post, would be an even more malign influence.[271] Methuen suggested Lockhart was "as simple minded as a child" suggesting how far he could be swayed by powerful characters like Nicholson.[272]

Particular criticism of Nicholson arose in the Tirah. When the tribal uprising erupted, Lockhart was absent in Europe and Lt. Gen. Sir Arthur Power Palmer, commanding the PFF, was also away from India. White had little confidence in Lockhart's temporary successor, George Wolseley. Still DAG in the Punjab, Nicholson was only an ex officio brigadier general and had no field command experience. Lockhart would take time to return even if he was fit. It would be better, White believed, to allow Lockhart to make a full recovery before assuming the chief command in India. Another possible candidate, Maj. Gen. George Sanford, commanding at Meerut, was also not in the best of health and had applied for home leave from November. Indeed, Sanford turned down the chance to command. Accordingly, White proposed to the viceroy that he should take personal command in the Tirah. This was rejected on the grounds of the uncertainty over the course of events and the absence of any "strong man" to deputize for White.[273]

White wanted Maj. Gen. William Penn Symons, who had earned an excellent reputation in Burma and on the Chin-Lushai expedition of 1889–90, to command the LOC, but Lockhart did not. According to Lockhart, there was nothing personal in his objection and his judgement rested on his assessment of Penn Symons's military abilities when commanding a brigade in Waziristan in 1894–95. Lockhart rated him below other district commanders in the Punjab "in the matter of cool judgement & common sense."[274] Nicholson, too, reported that, while he personally recognized the value of both Bindon Blood and Penn

Symons, he felt they had been given previous service opportunities: other major generals commanding districts should have been appointed.[275]

Despite Lockhart's objections, White decided to appoint Penn Symons to command the First Division, and to request the services of Palmer for the LOC. White believed Penn Symons the most capable British officer available, and it was important there should be British representation in command. As CinC, White reserved the right to select staff for the expedition. White telegraphed Lockhart—the message reached Lockhart at Port Said—to suggest Hamilton be appointed CoS with Nicholson taking a brigade command as a means of getting Lockhart "out of difficulty." Nicholson professed not to know what this difficulty might be, which, of course, was Nicholson's perceived influence over Lockhart.[276] Hamilton lacked staff experience, and so the positions were to be reversed with Hamilton taking the brigade and Nicholson as CoS. From Aden, Lockhart telegraphed, in turn, his objection not only to Penn Symons but also to the appointment as AAG of Col. Richard Ridgway VC. Lockhart wanted Palmer for the division rather than Penn Symons, and Michell, who was AAG in the Punjab, rather than Ridgway. If Palmer was not available, then Lockhart suggested Sanford, not realizing White had offered Sanford the command of the whole expedition.

As suggested by his earlier preference for even Nicholson over Michell, White believed Michell to be self-seeking and worried he would make mischief in Lockhart's "ear." White took offense not only at Lockhart's presumption in "going a little out of his province" but also calling it "disloyal."[277] White was not prepared to allow Michell to go on the expedition even in the expectation that Nicholson would "sit on him." At the least, White thought George Barrow, whom Lockhart suggested if Michell was not available, would be a safe pair of hands as AAG, and Barrow was duly appointed. Ridgway became AAG on the staff of the Second Division.[278]

The conduct of the campaign itself was controversial given the poor health of Lockhart and the terminally ill Arthur Yeatman-Biggs, who commanded the Second Division. Charles Nairne attributed "unusual friction" to Nicholson's influence: "There was too much Nicholson & not enough Lockhart & men in Yeatman-Biggs & Symons' position could not stand it & kept away after the earlier stages & Nicholson made many enemies among the Brigadiers." Nairne felt that since Lockhart's health had been impaired, it left Nicholson to "irritate" the senior generals.[279] Subsequently, Nairne's public criticism of Lockhart at the United Service Institution of India resulted in an official reprimand with his comments expunged from the record of the occasion.[280]

The EA was also troubled by rivalries. Col. Josceline Wodehouse rather than Kitchener was the popular choice in the EA to succeed Grenfell as sirdar in 1892. There had been friction between Kitchener and Wodehouse, as well as between Kitchener and Henry Settle, when Kitchener had been AG and Settle QMG of the EA.[281] Consequently, Kitchener's appointment as sirdar was far from popular.[282] According to Archibald Hunter, back in 1891 Grenfell had wanted to get rid of Kitchener as AG of the EA by switching him with Wodehouse, who then commanded the Frontier Force.[283] Grenfell thought Kitchener was capable but ambitious and unpopular as a result of his rapid promotion, even if he had begun to improve in his tact and manner.[284] It was also believed that Kitchener was afraid of Hunter, who had been close to Wodehouse and was a leading exponent of an EA frontier policy akin to the forward school in India.[285] Hunter characterized Kitchener as heartless, inhuman, vain, egotistical, and "a mixture of the fox, Jew and snake and like all bullies is a dove when tackled."[286] According also to Wingate, Leslie Rundle, the EA's CoS, was corresponding with Grenfell without Kitchener's knowledge, prompting Wingate to wonder "when K's eyes will be opened to those who serve him loyally & those who don't."[287] Wingate himself had frequent disagreements with both Hunter and Rundle.

There was also considerable jealousy of Kitchener within the WO, with Cromer interpreting rumors of the sirdar's supposed ill health in February 1898 as being exaggerated, "for the other soldiers are so frantically jealous that they would welcome any excuse to get him away."[288] Later, he viewed the criticism of Kitchener's conduct toward the Mahdi's tomb and skull after Omdurman as inevitable: "The solders are furiously jealous of him, and many of the newspaper people, whom he took no pains to conciliate, have for long been watching for an opportunity to attack him."[289] Capt. Sir Henry Rawlinson, DAAG of the British division in the final advance on Omdurman, assumed that the delay in Kitchener receiving the congratulations of Wolseley and Wood after the successful action at the Atbara River on 8 April 1898 was intentional. Back home, Rawlinson noted the absence of most of the military hierarchy from a celebratory dinner for Kitchener at the "Senior" in November 1898.[290]

Rivalries were perhaps inevitable. Writing to Curzon in February 1901, Clinton Dawkins, chairman of the committee reviewing WO administration, remarked it was not so much the system at fault as the individuals involved: "the greater part of the energies of the leading soldiers is devoted to 'putting each other in the cast.' It is a story which would be tiresome, if not serious of Wolseley, Buller, White, Wood, all trying to knife each other."[291] Dawkins wrote similarly to Lord Milner of "Buller contradicting himself in every sentence, Butler . . . referring all the evils of the Army back to Oliver Cromwell, and Wood sitting on my knee incoherently abusing Wolseley in answer to every question bawled into his ear."[292]

Yet, if the impact of the army's internal dynamics were complicated enough, there were also external influences that played their part in career advancement.

CHAPTER 4

EXTERNAL INFLUENCES

As suggested earlier, military patronage was vested in the Crown. The queen herself initially signed all commissions, declining in 1848 to sanction their replacement with a certificate from the secretary at war.[1] Her signature was limited to first commissions after 1861, but she continued to sign these personally. Yet, as the existence of the "rings" demonstrates, private considerations intruded on appointment, advancement, and reward. While political patronage was of less significance in the army than in other walks of life, politics still played its part. This was especially so as public interest in the army increased, and politicians became wary of public opinion as exercised through the press. More traditional obligations of family and friends were certainly of account. Occasionally, personal wealth and social skills also permeated the process, as did social proprieties. So, too, did perceptions of wives, for all that imperial expansion is sometimes characterized as a masculine affair and the result of the export of surplus emotional energy on the part of inveterate bachelors or worse.[2] All these factors added further levels of complexity to career advancement.

Politicians

Conventionally, British soldiers believed themselves to be apolitical under the constitutional constraints applied to the army since 1689. In reality, they habitually played politics themselves in trying to influence politicians, although they had to accept the limits imposed by parliamentary sovereignty.[3]

The respective powers of the CinC and the secretary of state for war were defined by royal warrant in 1861. The CinC was subordinated to the secretary of state, but the warrant was ambiguous in implying that the CinC had supreme military authority despite being subordinate. In appointing Cambridge in 1856, the queen took the view that it was within her prerogative and that he was not subordinate to the secretary of state. The warrant was never published and was ignored through declining interest in military reform and the frequent change in ministers.[4]

Cardwell was the first to challenge the supposed duality that had existed between CinC and secretary of state since 1855, enforcing the CinC's subordination through the War Office Act in a clear diminution of the royal prerogative. The Order in Council of June 1870 stated that the secretary of state administered "the Royal Authority and Prerogative in respect of the Army." It was a point Childers made forcibly in January 1882 following Cambridge's assertion that command rested with him: "No act of discipline can be exercised, no appointment or promotion can be moved, no payments can be made, without the approval, expressed or implied, of the Secretary of State."[5]

The symbolic end of duality was signified by the removal of Cambridge's office from the Horse Guards building to the War Office in Pall Mall in the summer of 1871. Moving the CinC closer to the secretary of state should have made it easier for soldiers to make their views known and gain more leverage.[6] It was the constant refrain of successive secretaries of state, however, that they did not receive sufficient advice from their principal military adviser. In any case, a degree of duality remained: the massive authority of one who appeared immovable in face of frequent ministerial changes. Whereas only eleven men served as foreign secretary between 1856 and 1914—only three held the office once—twenty-four individuals passed through the WO, of whom only four served more than once. One—W. H. Smith—held the post for only fifteen months in two separate spells.

The domestic political context was one of recurring retrenchment in military expenditure and frequent indifference to military requirements. As Henry Campbell-Bannerman once remarked, his task was "to avoid heroics and keep the estimates down."[7] In reviewing the customary military practice of asking for too much in order to compensate for inevitable reduction, the Stephen Commission on warlike stores memorably concluded in 1887 that a system of "extravagance controlled by stinginess is not likely to result either in economy or efficiency."[8]

Technically, soldiers were not responsible for the result of government economies. Consequently, they refused either to answer for national security policies determined on purely political and financial grounds, or to state definitely what the army's actual requirements might be until such time as they wrested back financial control from the politicians. Stanhope's solution in February 1888 was to dispense with the civilian appointment of SGO established by Cardwell to deal with all questions of matériel. Cambridge was reinvested with authority over all the principal WO departments, with those questions previously overseen by the SGO transferred to the QMG. At face value, soldiers had regained a degree of control but the financial secretary remained the key player, and Stanhope chose to interpret the reorganization as making soldiers responsible for providing an efficient army. The soldiers were understandably horrified when Stanhope publicly declared the army responsible for its own failings. They claimed their responsibility ended with a statement of the army's needs, leaving ultimate responsibility with the politicians.[9] As the war of words escalated, Cambridge insisted it be placed on record in December 1888 that "hitherto he has been more guided in his annual demands for men by what he thought had some chance of getting than by what he knew to be the total military requirements of the country."[10]

The army also confronted socioeconomic conditions and cultural attitudes that impeded recruitment within a system of voluntary enlistment. Campbell-Bannerman had in mind army officers when he suggested in March 1892 that military reformers had to "humour the feelings of those classes from which the Army is supplied" in order to overcome "traditions and prejudices and habits."[11] Insofar as the army was concerned, it was equally valid to recognize the traditions, prejudices, and habits of the middle and working classes. Discussing the impact of a downturn in trade on recruitment in November 1906, William Nicholson pointedly referred to the army's dependence on the "compulsion of destitution."[12]

Yet, politicians had to bow to a growing recognition of the need to take account of public opinion in an age of popular journalism and an expanded electorate. In turn, soldiers were under pressure from politicians, the press, and the public alike, all of whom had raised expectations of rapid and cheap military success.[13] The readiness of ministers to send Wolseley on political missions to Natal in 1875 and to Cyprus in 1878 reflected the increasing significance of public opinion. The general political consensus regarding the preservation of the Cardwell reforms after 1872 also required that reform-minded soldiers be given prominent roles. As Childers wrote in October 1882—when Cambridge was endeavoring to keep Wolseley in Egypt as long as possible—"he does not want Wolseley here, & I must admit that I do."[14] It was on such political grounds that the controversy over Wolseley's peerage and subsequent appointment as AG mattered so much to the government.

Consequently, politicians intervened in appointments. When Sir Edward Selby Smyth, who had previously served at the Cape, offered his services in Zululand, Frederick Stanley immediately rejected the appointment of one who was "hardly well enough known" to take on the job of reversing the defeat at Isandlwana.[15] The Hon. Sir Leicester Smyth (formerly Curzon-Howe), who was sent to command at the Cape after the Zulu War was safely over and no new crises were anticipated, was pointedly instructed not to interfere with George Colley in Natal.

The feeble Smyth was again ignored when Evelyn Wood was sent to be Colley's deputy in February 1881, and was passed over when Colley was killed at Majuba, at which point the public's new hero—Roberts—was sent to take command.[16] Buller saw it as "a sop to the Public."[17] Smyth "quickly recognised that he [Roberts] was universally trusted in England and that therefore it was a matter of much political expediency to send him out." He still objected to Wood's commanding the equivalent of a division while he had but half a brigade after Roberts was ordered home.[18] Smyth was overlooked once more when Charles Warren was appointed to command the Bechuanaland expedition in October 1884, although it was intended Smyth should have general oversight of any regulars needed.[19] Smyth was compensated with a KCMG and, later, a KCB and a good pension. He wrote appreciatively of Cambridge's support: "It is that that has cheered me up through all the dark days I have gone through since I came out here. For it must needs be that the repeated selection of others to do military work in this country has been a heavy blow to my professional reputation in the eyes of the people in this country and the troops stationed in it, and one would not be human if it was not felt."[20] Cambridge would have liked to offer a new command to Chelmsford in 1881—the Northern District was considered—but Childers feared public reaction, suggesting he would have to take the matter to the cabinet.[21] Cambridge recognized the problem when conceding that Chelmsford could not be given Portsmouth in March 1884.[22] In much the same way, Stanhope rejected any notion of Sir John Ross for Aldershot in 1888, as "he is so little known to the public here, in spite of his service, that his appointment would be received with astonishment, if not dismay."[23]

Yet, politicians were not averse to seeking preferment for their relatives. In 1885 the former lord chancellor, the Earl of Selborne, asked Wolseley to help get a musketry instructor's post for his wife's nephew. In 1896 the Earl of Cranbrook, the former secretary of state for war, Gathorne Hardy, wanted his grandson to serve in the Sudan.[24] As viceroy in 1890, Lansdowne felt he could not approach the secretary of state for India, Cross, or Stanhope directly to secure his nephew an ADC's post at Woolwich. Instead, he suggested Cross's PS might have a word with Stanhope's PS.[25] Another viceroy, Dufferin, wanted favors for the Burma chief commissioner's son, his old schoolmaster's son, and even a cousin's son-in-law.[26] As prime minister, Salisbury asked for his son, Lord Edward "Ned" Cecil, who had already been Wolseley's ADC, to be sent to the Sudan once Kitchener requested more subalterns. Salisbury repeated the exercise in 1898.[27]

In February 1888, with tongue firmly in cheek, Salisbury reported to Stanhope he had been visited by Edward Hamley, now the Conservative MP for Birkenhead and the army's senior lieutenant general. Hamley complained of "a mysterious influence at the War Office, which appears to exist for the purpose of wreaking its malignity on him." According to Hamley, the country had realized he was to be retired for nonemployment, and "this catastrophe was

spreading dismay in the ranks of your supporters in the House of Commons—
that it was impossible to foresee what the consequences would be—& in the
meantime their anguish at the thought of what you had done entirely prevented them from giving a proper attention to military subjects in the House
of Commons."[28] Hamley was promoted to full general in 1890 but saw no
more active employment. Local political considerations also were taken into
account. On March 1883 Childers applied to Wolseley for a favorable posting for the son of a "valued constituent."[29] In 1885 Ellis Ashmead-Bartlett MP
urged the appointment of Col. Edward England as AAQMG at Colchester to
gratify Tory "friends."[30]

Politicians likewise impeded operations. In 1881 Colley and Wood suffered
from what has been characterized as the "tortuous transformation" of cabinet policy toward the Boer republics.[31] The same indecision was apparent in
the delay in dispatching Wolseley's expedition to the Sudan three years later.
Arthur Hardinge noted of Wolseley's failure to save Gordon: "it is ungenerous
to forget that nowadays military methods are too often the slaves of political
expediency."[32] Conversely, the government's decision to begin the reconquest of
the Sudan in March 1896 took the soldiers entirely by surprise.[33] Local political
interference was something of a tradition in Indian frontier campaigns where
prominent soldiers like Bindon Blood, Lockhart, and O'Moore Creagh instinctively distrusted the officers of the Indian Political Service.[34]

In any case, commanders increasingly needed to exercise both military
and political judgment. Wolseley, who had a highly prejudicial view of politicians, played the game astutely. He pressed for full military and political powers wherever possible, as in Asante, noting in his valedictory speech at the
Mansion House on 31 March 1874 that "had my operations been encumbered
by the presence with me of a Civil Governor, or of an Ambassador authorised to
give orders I do not think I should ever have reached Coomassie."[35] Wolseley's
view of colonial politicians was even more jaundiced. Generally, Wolseley kept
his more poisonous comments on politicians private. Thus, as he noted in his
diary in December 1877: "In all the old great republics a Dictator was appointed
in times of danger and with us, the same plan should be followed, for it is really
next to impossible for any party to retain power and carry on a great war."[36] In
1887 he longed for "a healthy despotism."[37]

In reality, Wolseley understood the restricted constitutional parameters
and the requirements of his political masters. He wrote that George Greaves,
who had succeeded him on Cyprus, "has yet to learn that it does not do to
insert the whole truth in official correspondence. Despatches should always
be strictly true, but unpleasant truths that can be made use of by the opponents of the Government you are serving should be reserved for one's private

correspondence with ministers."[38] Referring back to Asante, Wolseley wrote in 1880, "I always make it a rule to serve the Govt. in power to the best of my ability & to help them to demolish their opponents who attack them on military matters with which I am concerned, for party purposes." It would differ only if the government itself "directly violated" constitutional principle.[39]

Cardwell thanked Wolseley for the "moderate" tone of his dispatches from Asante regarding government policy.[40] In April 1877 the colonial secretary, Carnarvon, wrote to Wolseley, "you are one of the few in whose hands I personally should wish to see the fortunes of an English army placed."[41] Carnarvon believed old-style colonial governors would not be "capable of appreciating the paramountcy of strategic considerations in the administration of colonial policy."[42]

Like other soldiers, Wolseley was disingenuous in claiming he had no politics.[43] Indeed, Wolseley frequently embarrassed Cambridge as well as his ministers by his public pronouncements, such as at a dinner in April 1888 when he suggested that party politics was the "curse of modern England" and that ministers were trying to gain "some claptrap reputation by cutting down the expenses of the Army and Navy Estimates."[44]

Politicians could be humiliated by leaked confidential information. One extraordinary case arose in 1888 over the dispatch of just one and a half British battalions to Suakin to reinforce the garrison for a projected sortie against encircling Mahdists.[45] Lord Randolph Churchill sprang an adjournment debate, attacking involvement in the Sudan and claiming that partial reinforcement might lead to disaster. What concerned the government was not the motion itself, which was defeated, but Churchill's claim that "he knew the highest military authorities had expressed to me [Stanhope] the opinion that the British force prepared to be sent to Suakin was inadequate."[46] The affair culminated in Salisbury's formal warning to officers that they were "under the strictest obligation to observe silence with respect to all confidential matters coming to their knowledge, including, especially, their own opinion and those of their colleagues, upon the course which, on any military matters, Her Majesty's Government have decided to pursue."[47] Cambridge threatened to resign, but Salisbury was unrepentant:

> It is a matter of record that within thirty-six hours after the military advisers of the War Office had represented to Mr Stanhope that in their judgment the force at Suakin was insufficient, the fact that they had done so was stated by Lord Randolph Churchill in the House of Commons. A fact so secret, and so recent, that at the time he was stating it publicly, it was unknown even to me, could not have come to his knowledge except by indiscretion.[48]

Certain appointments were regarded as being properly political. The viceroy's personal staff was one area over which Horse Guards had little influence although the choice of MS and PS required consent. The viceroy's MS was the principal channel of communication with the CinC and the Military Department as well as the organizer of the viceroy's household, entertainments, journeys, and ceremonials. He also liaised with the CinC over appointments to those forces such as the PFF and Hyderabad Contingent, which lay within the gift of the Foreign Department and, thus, the viceroy.[49] The PS was responsible for civil matters including accounts.

When Colley was chosen for command in Natal in 1880, Lytton requested the services of Brackenbury as PS. Cambridge opposed the selection but could do nothing: "His knowledge & experience of India is nil. Therefore I confess I think the selection, anything but a judicious or a happy one; but I cannot oppose it, for as his *Private* Secretary I can do no more than *warn* him, that he will have a man who knows absolutely *nothing* of India. Brackenbury is a clever fellow no doubt, but he is a man entirely of Wolseley's school, quite as much so as Colley."[50] The viceroy's choice of ADCs was also his to make. The Earl of Northbrook even made it clear that his son's appointment as an additional ADC was a condition of his accepting the viceregal billet.[51]

The Colonial Office (CO) had to be consulted on a number of senior posts overseas, and had power of veto. It was alone responsible for selecting civil governors, and always a party to the choice of higher military commands in the colonies, especially Malta and Gibraltar. Retired officers, in particular engineers, were highly favored as colonial governors.[52] Carnarvon was responsible for Wolseley's appointment to Natal in 1875, prompting Wolseley to note that Cambridge "does not like my being selected for employment without his having anything to say to it."[53]

When the British administrator in Perak in the Straits Settlement was murdered in November 1875, it became necessary to dispatch troops. Cambridge suggested sending Maj. Gen. the Hon. Francis Colborne from Hong Kong. Colborne had sailed immediately with three hundred troops. Carnarvon believed Colborne had forced himself into the command and had no experience of "oriental war." His age, character, lack of ability, and lack of tact also suggested he was unfit for command. Carnarvon preferred John Ross, who had been nominated by the viceroy to take one thousand men from India. Carnarvon suggested Colborne be ordered back to Hong Kong at once on "political grounds."[54]

Cambridge considered this outrageous since he viewed Colborne as "a very respectable officer, not over strong perhaps, but quite *reliable.*" The cabinet agreed to let things stand, but Cambridge harbored a suspicion that Carnarvon wanted to send Wolseley. It mystified Cambridge how Carnarvon "has always some private knowledge about officers for good or bad which he puts forward in a very *positive* way, the moment anything occurs when he wants an officer for some Colonial work."[55] One of Carnarvon's informants was certainly Sir Bartle Frere, the former governor of Bombay now serving on the Council of India. In 1874 Frere supplied Carnarvon with several names of those he felt might govern West Africa following the Asante expedition.[56]

Dealing with colonial politicians raised its own problems. Canada was something of a poisoned chalice. Between 1874 and 1904, of eight officers appointed to command the Canadian militia, only one completed his tenure: one was dismissed, three resigned before they were pushed out, two resigned in frustration, and one left as a result of British rather than Canadian pressure.[57] The Canadians often requested a different officer to the one appointed, prefer-ring retired officers resident in Canada.[58] In 1883, for example, Col. Frederick Middleton seemed ideal as he was married to a French Canadian and had pre-viously served in Canada, but the Canadians favored Maj. Gen. John Laurie, well known in Nova Scotia and later an MP in Canada as well as Britain.[59] Middleton was appointed but was forced to resign in 1890 over allegations he had sold furs looted during the North-West Rebellion in 1885.

Appointed to command the Canadian militia in 1898, Edward "Curly" Hutton had decided views on the need for closer imperial cooperation and proconsular attitudes toward colonial politicians and soldiers. The bitter dis-pute that arose between Hutton and the minister for militia and defense, Frederick Borden, was foreshadowed by the dispute between Hutton and the New South Wales prime minister, Sir George Dibbs, when Hutton had been commandant there in 1893–94.[60] The governor-general, Minto, reported that "there was endless friction, due to informal political jobs that he [Hutton] would not stand, and finally it became impossible to carry on."[61] The post was filled temporarily by Maj. Gen. Richard O'Grady Haly, whose "career had been limited by too many children and too few means."[62] With O'Grady Haly resigning in October 1901, Maj. Gen. the Earl of Dundonald became the last imperial GOC of the militia. As with Hutton, Dundonald was drawn into play-ing politics and recalled.[63]

The Foreign Office (FO) had some say in the selection of military attachés, although Cambridge had the major role. In 1877 Cambridge recommended Lt. Col. Richard Crichton as attaché in Berlin even though he spoke no German. The ambassador objected but, surprisingly, not the FO.[64] In 1892 Cambridge rejected Edward Chapman's recommendation to appoint an able linguist, Captain Wallscourt Waters, to St. Petersburg. Despite Waters's having a bet-ter knowledge of Russia and private means, Cambridge selected Col. Montagu

Gerard as someone of "higher rank and social standing."[65] When Gerard resigned after less than a year, Cambridge wanted an officer who did not even speak Russian, but the foreign secretary, the Earl of Rosebery's intervention saw Waters appointed after all.[66] With private income seen as necessary for Berlin and St. Petersburg, Leopold Swaine was considered the best candidate for the German capital in 1878 as he spoke good German and had "plenty of means of his own."[67] At Vienna, "connection with persons of high rank" was very useful. Thus, in 1878 Capt. the Hon. Everard Primrose, Rosebery's brother, was dispatched there.[68]

The FO also had oversight over Egyptian affairs where the sirdar of the reconstituted EA after 1882 was nominally the khedive's servant. It was thought essential by Cambridge that the GOC in Cairo should have the rank of lieutenant general even with a much reduced force "because otherwise our troops would have no proper representative to stand up for them & hold his own against such powerful aggressive elements as those represented by E[velyn] Baring & even [Valentine] Baker though I believe the latter to take a very proper and English view of all that takes place."[69] When commanding in Cairo in 1883, Archibald Alison considered that the first sirdar, Evelyn Wood, "thinks himself a much greater person in Egypt than I am—and regards our army here as interlopers unfairly occupying his barracks and quarters."[70] Wood was the de facto Egyptian minister of war, which made it awkward to subordinate him to the GOC even when the latter was senior in the British army.[71]

The eventual reconquest of the Sudan was, to quote Cromer, a "Foreign Office war." Responsibility for decisions was vested in Salisbury in his capacity as foreign secretary, a point even the queen did not initially appreciate.[72] The commitment of British troops, which Kitchener accepted reluctantly in December 1897, then caused complications. Reappointed GOC in Cairo in July 1897, Francis Grenfell as a former sirdar found his position a difficult one. Cromer and Kitchener tried to smooth relations, but, according to Wingate, Grenfell had "the awkward habit of telegraphing & informing [Cromer] afterwards that he has done so[me]th[ing]."[73] Under Grenfell's successor, Maj. Gen. the Hon. Reginald Talbot, Kitchener reported directly to the WO on British officers and British troops under his command while Kitchener's own instructions passed through Cromer.[74]

Language was a criterion for the relatively unimportant Guernsey and Alderney District, on which it was usual to consult the Home Office. Maj. Gen. Gaspard Tupper was suggested in 1885 not only as Guernsey-born but also because, as W. H. Smith put it, he spoke French "and we have very few officers of his rank who do."[75] Knowledge of French was more significant for the Cairo command given the large diplomatic community there and the French role in the Suez Canal Company. When Alison's health would not permit him to return to Egypt in 1883, Frederick Stephenson appeared ideal as firm yet conciliatory but also because he spoke French well.[76]

While Ireland was often seen as something of a retirement post, or a convenient place for a prominent soldier for whom nothing else could be found, such as Wolseley in 1890 and Roberts in 1895, there was always the possibility of serious internal disturbances. In January 1886 the incumbent, Prince Edward of Saxe-Weimar, was not thought "best qualified for a really critical condition of things." Accordingly, Maj. Gen. George Young was moved from Cork to the Dublin District, with Maj. Gen. Thomas Stevenson moving to Cork. Young was regarded as having good judgment, while Stevenson was "an exceedingly safe man and has great knowledge of the County."[77] Cambridge also considered Arthur Fremantle, but W. H. Smith suggested Fremantle suffered so much from asthma that he might not be a man in an emergency requiring "exertions."[78]

The perceived deteriorating situation in Ireland at different times also resulted in special measures. Henry Brackenbury was appointed assistant undersecretary for police and crime in May 1882 following the Phoenix Park murders of the chief secretary and the permanent undersecretary. Brackenbury did not wish to accept given the likely crisis in Egypt, but Childers insisted, "It is war in Ireland, the Government have selected you, and I do not think you can refuse."[79] When Brackenbury was soon seduced by the prospects of campaigning in Egypt and resigned, Ponsonby informed the queen he had "abandoned his post at a most critical moment."[80] Finding himself back on half-pay as a regimental major and in disfavor before being posted to Gibraltar, Brackenbury was rescued by Wolseley for the Gordon relief expedition. Surprisingly, Brackenbury was offered the post of special commissioner in Ireland in 1886 but declined it.[81]

Wolseley was suggested as lord lieutenant of Ireland by Carnarvon in June 1885 as a means of threatening the nationalists with coercion if outrages persisted. In the event, Carnarvon briefly took the office. Salisbury suggested Wolseley as Carnarvon's replacement in December 1885, but Carnarvon had changed his mind as to the political message this would send.[82] In August 1886, however, Buller was appointed as special commissioner for Kerry and Clare. His comparative liberalism did not endear him to landlords including Lansdowne, with unfortunate consequences for his future.[83] Unfortunately, no one had thought to inform Prince Edward of Saxe-Weimar of Buller's appointment since it was seen as a civil one, and Smith had to smooth ruffled feathers.[84] Buller reluctantly remained in Ireland until October 1887, latterly as undersecretary.

The Press and Public Opinion

The burgeoning popular press was an increasing factor to be taken into account by politicians and military authorities alike. In 1860 there were 31 daily newspapers in Britain, but by the 1890s, the number had risen to over 150. The reduction in price from a penny to a halfpenny brought weekly newspapers into the reach of many ordinary people, with the first halfpenny mass circulation morning newspaper, the *Daily Mail*, appearing in 1896.[85] With the addition of the periodicals and a host of other popular print media outlets for adults and children, imperial wars proved a popular subject.[86] Napier remarked of the minor Duffla campaign on India's North-East Frontier in 1874 that, judging by the number of correspondents, it would become better known than Waterloo.[87]

In 1886 W. T. Stead wrote grandiloquently, "I have seen Cabinets upset . . . armies sent hither and thither, war proclaimed and war averted, by the agency of the newspaper."[88] Stead was part of what has been characterized as an "informal cabal" including Wolseley, Childers, Andrew Clarke, and Sir Samuel Baker that forced Gladstone into sending Charles Gordon to extricate the Egyptian garrison from Khartoum in January 1884.[89] The Gordon saga was played out day by day in the London press. Even when telegraphic communications with Khartoum were cut off, information was still coming out of Khartoum by one means or another, "and since the flow of information was largely one way—from North Africa outwards, whether from Gordon or Wolseley—it was a flow that they could control, and which they did control with skill."[90] Naval officers like Fisher and Beresford were equally attuned to the potential influence of the press; Fisher's dealings with Stead in the 1880s contributed to the pressure that resulted in the increased naval expenditure introduced by the Naval Defence Act in 1889.[91]

The press was simply a fact of life. In February 1884 the MS, Whitmore, told Martin Dillon that he would most probably get the appointment he was seeking but that Cambridge should not be asked about it so far in advance, "especially in these days when the newspapers get hold of everything which is not guarded by lock & key if they know of an appointment in advance some unfriendly critic may say disagreeable things as happened in case of the military paper which made a nasty remark when the apocryphal announcement was published of your going to Bangalore."[92] Soldiers were well aware of the consequences of bad publicity. Wolseley characterized war correspondents in *The Soldier's Pocket Book* in 1869 as "those newly invented curses to armies."[93] As he wrote from Asante, "I feel so uncomfortable when I read all this 'high talk' about myself in the newspapers & have a sinking feeling within me, when I think how worse would be the abuse of the same writers if I prove a failure here." The press could easily "turn round and abuse me as roundly as it had previously lavished unmerited praise upon me."[94] Yet, he also knew it was important "to keep my name before the public."[95]

Cambridge, too, was attuned to the press, cautioning Chelmsford in March 1879 that "in these days the freedom of the press has taken very large dimensions, and anybody that has a relative or friend receives letters and sends them to the press giving his version of events as they believe them to have occurred."[96] Cambridge repeatedly tried to convey to Chelmsford the need to provide him with the fullest information and "carefully worded & good clear despatches. The Public at home & Parliament particularly requires this."[97]

Generally, the war correspondents known as the "specials" were not overly critical of the army. The relationship was symbiotic for they depended on soldiers for transport, supplies, information, and the means of communication. Archibald Forbes, a former ranker, believed he should record "how our countrymen, our dear ones, toil and thole, vindicate British manhood, and joyously expend their lives for Queen and fatherland."[98] Correspondents shared the dangers. Nine lost their lives in the Sudan between 1883 and 1898, and the influential G. W. Steevens died of enteric while besieged in Ladysmith in South Africa in January 1900.[99] By June 1900 six war correspondents had been killed in South Africa, with three dead from disease, six wounded, and nineteen captured.[100]

Criticism, however, could be directed at soldiers as in the case of Forbes's critique of Chelmsford in 1879.[101] W. H. Russell's criticism of the discipline of British troops in the Transvaal in November 1879 caused Wolseley considerable trouble in refuting the allegations.[102]

During the Tirah campaign in 1897, William Lockhart complained bitterly of "amateur" critics in the press. Faced with criticism in the *Pioneer*, Lockhart commented, "I make no secret of my contempt for newspaper people and their methods, but I have hitherto regarded the Pioneer as something better than the ordinary 'rag.' Its attacks on people whose mouths are shut—attacks based on hearsay or one-sided evidence—do it little credit, and damage it in the opinion of all but the fools."[103] But he recognized that "we live so fast in these days that praise or blame or even ridicule cannot remain in the public memory for more than a few hours."[104] At Suakin in 1884, Gerald Graham had regretted, "I am afraid I am a very bad hand at manipulating the telegraph and see now that I missed a grand opportunity for creating a sensation during the last fight [Tamai]. I ought to have sent a telegram every five minutes describing the ups and downs keeping London in a tremor of excitement."[105]

It became necessary, therefore, to manage the press carefully. Wolseley's employment of his own staff to write for the press in Asante, and Brackenbury's semiofficial account of the campaign, deflected criticism of the major crisis that arose in the native carrier transport system.[106] In South Africa, Russell pointedly complained of Wolseley's staff writing for the press, suggesting it was wrong for generals employing "at the public expense corps of trumpeters to do their flourishes and hymns of praise in the newspapers."[107] Wolseley claimed London newspaper reports were not directed by his staff:

> I have never attempted to influence or control their views regarding my own or your policy. None of them were officers on my staff, but as to what the officers on my staff may or may not write is not my affair. I am only responsible for what I write myself, and I never write to newspapers, or take any notice of what is said in them nor do I ever attempt to influence those who do write to or for them.[108]

Nonetheless, Wolseley's frequent use of the press and public speeches greatly irritated the queen and Cambridge. Cambridge began referring to Wolseley's adherents not as the "Mutual Admiration Society" but as the "Press Gang."[109] The Prince of Wales said Wolseley "& his satellites were all 'press men'—& that he or his immediate friends have consistently inspired the press."[110]

Others also cultivated the press. Wolseley came to believe that Roberts was "much cleverer, *cuter* than I was in understanding public opinion & in playing cleverly upon its unworthy strings a tune that suited human vanity."[111] During the South African War, Wolseley could not "but admire his [Roberts's] adroitness in dealing with public opinion and the clever manner by which he manipulates the views of a democracy on the one hand and plays up to the aristocracy on the other by surrounding himself with dukes and earls and their sons to the third and fourth generation."[112]

Roberts's autobiography, *Forty-one Years in India*, published in January 1897, was a commercial success. The two-volume version had reached its twenty-seventh edition by January 1898, to be followed by a single-volume version in three further printings by September 1898. Supposedly presented by its self-effacing author merely to "contribute towards a more intimate knowledge of the glorious heritage our forefathers have bequeathed to us," it served to present Roberts's political agenda on frontier strategy.[113] Roberts was adept at reinforcing his own image and feeding his views to influential publishers and editors such as Moberly Bell of *The Times*, whose underage son received a commission through Roberts's influence.[114]

Roberts had "an unmitigated cad," Maurice Macpherson of the *Standard*, removed from the Kurram Field Force in 1878 for eluding controls through using the post rather than telegrams submitted for Roberts's countersignature, altering telegrams after counter signature, and keeping the public in Britain "in a state of constant apprehension."[115] Charles Gough noted Roberts's press manipulation:

the correspondent [MacPherson] scores several very severe points agst Bobs—more particularly that of doctoring all the telegrams regarding his operations—and of appointing the officers of his Staff as special correspondents to the Papers, he had Col. Villiers as correspondent to the "Times"— Capt. Pretyman to the "Daily News," Dick Kennedy to the "Daily Telegraph" and "The Pioneer"!!—not only is this directly contrary to his special order!! But of course now it has come out, people will not put much reliance on information furnished entirely by so partial and one sided a source![116]

Roberts used another journalist, Howard Hensman of the *Daily News*, to bolster his reputation, and employed a system of unofficial rewards and punishments to secure press compliance.[117] Ironically, Roberts benefited earlier from the publicity accorded the forcing of the Peiwar Kotal Pass in the Kurram since the news had arrived in London on the morning Parliament was assembling to debate Lytton's policy.[118] Roberts was again criticized by Frederic Harrison of the *Fortnightly Review* and forced to defend his conduct against accusations of atrocities in Afghanistan in 1880.[119]

In South Africa in May 1900, Roberts withdrew the Cavalry Division from Kroonstad so he could personally take the town's surrender in view of the assembled press. He also gave an embarrassingly eulogistic speech to the correspondents in Bloemfontein in March 1900.[120] Roberts insisted his own dispatches go to London before any press accounts of operations, which enabled him to be more relaxed about what correspondents then wrote. Failures could be attributed to subordinates on whose conduct he had already commented.[121]

While ostensibly relaxing rules for correspondents with his own force, Roberts ordered Buller to impose much tighter regulation in Natal. The rules Buller applied at Roberts's behest were guaranteed to alienate the correspondents there, thus ensuring Roberts a more favorable press. Kitchener, however, tightened the rules considerably in May 1901.[122] Even Roberts's manipulation, however, was outshone by Baden-Powell's blatant promotion of his defense of Mafeking.[123]

Buller generally disliked the press and once dragged a correspondent through a thorn bush in Zululand "to teach him manners."[124] As for Kitchener, according to Ernest Bennett, he swept out of his tent past the assembled correspondents on one occasion in the Sudan exclaiming, "Get out of my way, you drunken swabs!"[125] It was only government intervention that compelled Kitchener to allow correspondents south of Assouan during the reconquest. Criticism of Kitchener's treatment of wounded Mahdist fighters after Omdurman and the destruction of the Mahdi's tomb was payback time for the press.[126]

The Egyptian campaign in 1882 was the first time a press censor was officially appointed, the duty falling to Paul Methuen. When Childers complained of one false report appearing in the *Daily News*, Wolseley replied that Methuen could not read everything when a recent single telegram had run to over a thousand words.[127] Similarly, when appointed censor in the Sudan in 1896, Reginald Wingate was faced with reading thousands of words a day. It inevitably delayed copy reaching London, and also meant there was no time to show the cuts to the correspondents.[128]

Censorship did not prevent inconvenient disclosures. Nor did it avoid controversy. In the case of the pacification campaign in Burma in 1885–86, George White wrote that it would be best to keep events out of the press for the "operations we are constantly undertaking which are so necessary would not long attract the tide of public sympathy towards us involving as they do heavy loss nearly always inflicted on the enemy with, I am happy to say, very slight loss on ourselves."[129] The viceroy, Dufferin, argued that the public had expected too much: "They thought that the bloodless campaign of last November, and the capture of Theebaw [King Thibaw Min] and of his capital, had finished off the business; and they were delighted with the idea of having acquired a new Province in so inexpensive a manner. The Government of India, on the contrary, never indulged in these sanguine anticipations."[130]

Unwelcome publicity was given the campaign by Edward Moylan of *The Times*. Moylan was deported from Mandalay in December 1885 for evading censorship regulations. He then used his political contacts to be reinstated, writing increasingly critical reports on the slowness of the campaign and the alleged incompetence of Lt. Gen. Sir Harry Prendergast VC. In January 1886 Moylan happened upon a story that, during executions of *dacoits*, the provost marshal, Col. Willoughby Hooper, had questioned men about to be executed by firing squad to extract intelligence. As an amateur photographer, Hooper also supposedly delayed the order to fire so as to capture the death at the exact moment he exposed his negative. Hooper had photographed executions but when not on duty and had not delayed the order to fire to set up the camera.[131] Dufferin immediately forbade further executions for fear they "[would] strengthen the hands of those who may be disposed to criticise our conquest of the country."[132] Charles Brownlow reported the secretary of state for India, Lord Randolph Churchill, was "hysterical." In three weeks Prendergast, who was removed in March 1886, had gone to "number one" on the list of generals to be removed, "such is British public opinion—equally jumpy in its applause & its censure."[133]

Prior to the beginning of the South African War, Lansdowne asked Wolseley for draft legislation to censor the press in the event of war, but the cabinet declined to introduce it. Censorship could not then be imposed legally until martial law was declared in Natal on 23 October 1899, and not in Cape

Colony until martial law was imposed there in January 1902. The imperfect licensing system soon broke down through the number of official and unofficial correspondents. In October 1899 licensing was tightened.[134] But this also broke down. With Reuter's alone employing over one hundred correspondents and stringers, there were perhaps three hundred operating in South Africa.[135]

Family and Friends

Inevitably those with military, political, and social connections sought to advance relatives' careers. When CoS in the Sudan in 1885, Buller was overwhelmed with letters from "fathers, sisters, cousins, aunts and officers of every grade and position and everybody says his own friend is the one man."[136] Similarly, Brackenbury complained, when first appointed military member, that "my life was made a burden by the applications of my friends, and my friends' friends, and my friends' friends' friends to post their sons to the Bengal Presidency, and one of the first things I did was to place it beyond my power to make these appointments a matter of favour."[137] Both Coleridge Grove and his successor as MS, Ian Hamilton, told the Elgin Commission that external pressure could be applied. Hamilton suggested a strong MS would not be influenced, although, bizarrely, he said he would occasionally oblige mothers if he could do so "without doing harm to anyone else." Sometimes, approaches were made on the understanding that, if he declared it impossible to comply, then those inquiring would rest content that their duty was done and they could pass the blame on to him.[138]

The well-connected guardsman Pole-Carew enjoyed a successive series of appointments to personal staffs between 1877 and 1880. Pole-Carew felt he could not afford to serve in England and was politically averse to being in a "'liberally' governed England" under Gladstone and his "babbling crowd of humbugs." Paradoxically, he hoped to serve the new Liberal viceroy in 1880 provided he was a "decent sportsman." Accordingly, he asked his father to find out who the new viceroy was likely to be and to "ask some pal of his to take me on as an eligible youth with a uniform and a marvellous knowledge of the languages." Pole-Carew thought his father could approach the Duke of Devonshire and the Earls of Selborne and St. Germans, or, perhaps surprisingly, any Conservative peer.[139]

Gleichen owed his selection for the Guards Camel Regiment in 1884 to the fact that his uncle, Lord William Seymour, was AMS.[140] The Hon. Neville Lyttelton owed his appointment as Childers's PS to Gladstone's being his uncle. His Liberal sympathies also recommended him as a possible successor to Charles Gordon as Ripon's PS, though Lyttelton did not wish to take up the offer. Lyttelton was ADC to Sir John Adye in 1882, and Adye took him to Gibraltar as his MS. Subsequently, Lyttelton was also MS to the Bombay governor Lord Reay, another Liberal politician.[141]

The newly commissioned Henry Rawlinson fully expected his father's influence "with the swells at the top of the tree will be invaluable."[142] The ambitious Charles Townshend was equally well connected as a cousin to the Fifth Marquess Townshend, the Second Lord St. Levan, and Redvers Buller's wife. Townshend moved effortlessly through London society and frequently called on his connections. Commissioned originally in 1881 in the Royal Marines, where he fretted at the lack of service opportunities, Townshend was able to transfer to the Central India Horse in 1886. Subsequently, there were opportunities to join the Guards, as suggested by both the Prince of Wales and Lansdowne. In the event, Townshend transferred to the Royal Fusiliers.[143]

Winston Churchill shamelessly used his connections in order to get to the North-West Frontier in 1897 and then to the Sudan in 1898, on both occasions ostensibly as a war correspondent. His mother's influence having failed to move Kitchener, Churchill used his acquaintance with Bindon Blood to join the Malakand Field Force. Blood advised Churchill to come out as a correspondent in the expectation of filling a casualty's billet: "Army Head Qrs make all appointments except personal staff and are very jealous of their patronage. I have hardly managed to get any of my pals on my staff—though I have asked for several. However if you were here I think I could, and certainly would if I could, do a little jobbery on your account."[144] Churchill was eventually attached to the Thirty-first Punjab Infantry. Churchill also managed to join Lockhart's staff for the last stage of the Tirah campaign. With no apparent irony, he complained in October 1897 of the obstacles placed in his way: "It is indeed a vivid object lesson in the petty social intrigue that makes or prevents appointments in this country. Simply because I am not known at Simla and have not been to make my obeisance I am persecuted like this. While every tame cat, lap-dog & ADC is hurried into the best place that can be found."[145]

Much was done for Roberts's intellectually challenged son, Freddie. In 1898 Kitchener applied for Freddie to join his staff in the Sudan. Lansdowne immediately obliged.[146] The following year, at Roberts's request, Wolseley supported Freddie's nomination for Staff College despite his having scored four hundred marks less than any other candidate except one.[147] Freddie was attached to Buller's staff in South Africa but was mortally wounded at Colenso. His VC was made possible by the argument that he had been alive at the time he earned it.

Another example of influence is Maj. Gen. Sir Arthur Ellis, equerry to the Prince of Wales, who used his networks to advance the career of his son, Gerald. Commissioned in February 1894, Gerald wanted to get to the Sudan;

his father agreed saying, "it is the only chance of military advancement, & the *best* of the army pass through the Egyptian mill now." Accordingly, Ellis Sr. spoke to Wolseley in May 1896 and, on his recommendation, wrote to Cromer. Cromer spoke to Kitchener and agreed to telegraph the FO. At this point, Buller "positively & absolutely refused to break thro' the Queen's regulation lately made—that no officer with less than 4 years service be permitted to accept any extraregimental or staff service—wh. this is—& he insisted on a refusal of your services being sent to the Sirdar." Buller also believed, as did the Prince of Wales, that Gerald would be best spared the climate. Two years later, having taken advice from Connaught, Ellis was prepared to accompany his son to the WO to request another posting. With the outbreak of hostilities in South Africa, Arthur Ellis wrote to Lansdowne, who agreed to apply to Wolseley and Coleridge Grove, for a billet on the LOC, urging his son, "Don't say one word of this to yr b[rother] officers or to yr C.O. or he may put a spoke in the wheel."[148] Gerald Ellis duly reached South Africa but had an undistinguished career, retiring as a half-pay captain in 1908, only to be reemployed in the same rank during the Great War.

Commenting in April 1880 on a colleague's failure to gain promotion for the Zulu War, Philip Anstruther suggested friends were not always the answer: "I suspect that the Duke's life has been bullied out of him—still it is hard that because a man gets home he can work it very hard whereas a fellow that can't get home and is, consequently, more deserving of it is left out in the cold and, of course, his friends can't fight his battles as well for him as he can himself."[149] Lack of influence could be potentially disadvantageous. Even Wolseley lamented in December 1879: "I often think, if I had had for my father a Lord Chancellor, as Chelmsford had, instead of being a poor Major in a marching Regiment, what could now have been my position! How many times in my life might not the authorities have pushed me on."[150]

Capt. James Wolfe Murray appealed to Archibald Alison, under whom he had served in the Intelligence Branch, to help him get to Egypt in 1882, writing that "the fact that I have no friends, in military high places, but yourself—if you will allow me to call you such—must serve as my excuse."[151] Wolfe Murray saw no active service until the Asante expedition of 1895–96, although he rose to be CIGS in 1914–15. Despite Roberts's patronage, even George White wrote upon failing to get promotion in 1886, "I have very little interest with the Conservative Government but have written to the few friends I have to put in a word for me."[152] Similarly, Dormer feared in 1889 when he wanted either the Madras or Bombay command, "I shall be elbowed out by people who being at home have more interest to bring to bear, on the spot."[153]

Mention should also be made of the brotherhood of freemasonry. Its incidence has been remarked on as one of a number of connections between naval officers opposed to the "informalization" of naval tactics in the 1880s and 1890s. Certainly, there were many military lodges, and those known to be members in the craft included Mansfield, Staveley, Chelmsford, Roberts, Kitchener, Garnet Wolseley, George Wolseley, Charles Warren, and Arthur Yeatman-Biggs. Warren, for example, was the first master of the Quatuor Coronati Lodge of Masonic Research, while, at the time of his death, Yeatman-Biggs was deputy grand master of Bengal.[154] Connaught was grand master of the United Grand Lodge of England from 1901 to 1939. There is no apparent evidence, however, of any masonic influence in appointments or promotion. Wolseley occasionally mentioned attendance at lodge meetings in his correspondence, but without any added emphasis. It must be assumed, therefore, that like membership in "The Rag" or "The Senior," freemasonry was no more than another opportunity for socializing with fellow officers.

Wealth, Status, and Social Skills

If remuneration was of great interest to soldiers without significant means, certain commands required a greater expenditure than was available in pay and allowances. The most expensive home commands were the Southern (Portsmouth) and North British (Edinburgh) Districts, for the GOC would be required to attend the queen at Osborne and Balmoral, respectively.

In 1896 Wolseley wanted to move the MS, Reginald Gipps, to Edinburgh because he was wealthy, which was "a matter of some consequence for commands of that nature."[155] Gipps declined and took retirement. In the case of Portsmouth, the obvious candidate in 1893 appeared to be Lt. Gen. John Davis, who held the record for the highest sum ever paid for an infantry commission under the purchase system.[156] Davis was also a popular sportsman, pleasant and presentable, and had the advantage of being a line officer when guardsmen had usually secured the post.[157] The Western District at Devonport, due to the naval presence, was also a post "impossible for a poor man."[158] As GOC there from 1890 to 1895, Richard Harrison had to attend naval reviews, attend to official visits whenever new naval commanders were appointed, and greet royal visitors and foreign naval captains.[159]

The Dublin District also carried costs. In 1891 Wolseley asked for Maj. Gen. George Moncrieff to be posted away from Dublin:

> I believe he is very poor & consequently unable to entertain. I think the General Officer Commandg. the Dublin District should be well off & able to keep a good house & entertain, at least the Garrison, very liberally. The

War Office have refused to give him the normal £200 per annum table money which I regard as a breach of faith. It was promised us over & over again, that if the list of General Officers was reduced to reasonable limits, all those employed would be better paid, & that the extra pay would be given in the shape of table allowances.[160]

Among overseas posts, Bermuda had a high cost of living. In December 1876 it was thought Col. Robert Laffan, CRE at Gibraltar, was too impecunious to become Bermuda's governor.[161]

In a wider sense, the ability of an officer to mix socially opened doors. "Stephe" Baden-Powell's prowess at "pig-sticking" introduced him to the social circle of Connaught, then commanding at Meerut, and at Simla to that of the viceroy's MS, Lord William "Bill" Beresford. Baden-Powell's cause was also pushed by his mother and his uncle, Sir Henry Smyth. Baden-Powell was ADC to his uncle in South Africa, enabling him to play a part in Smyth's suppression of the Zulu Rebellion in 1888. Subsequently, he accompanied Smyth to Malta.[162] Beresford himself served four successive viceroys as either ADC or MS. It testified to Beresford's administrative skill, tact, natural humor, and a popularity enhanced by his love of amateur dramatics and horse racing.[163]

More specifically, the ability of a general officer to cultivate a smooth relationship with those civilian authorities and individuals with whom he came into contact was also of importance. In February 1877 Prince Edward of Saxe-Weimar, who had been commanding the Home District, was considered the best candidate for Portsmouth because "his social skills would be a great advantage to him in holding the post."[164]

By contrast, Charles Gordon was impatient with all social niceties, writing to his sister soon after he arrived on Mauritius as CRE in June 1881, "I strike against garden parties, archery and lawn tennis meetings! I cannot go through these fearful ordeals of hours' duration."[165] Following the rejection of William Butler as PS, Ripon chose Gordon. To general astonishment, Gordon resigned just three days after he landed at Bombay. Gordon rapidly concluded that the "white lies that are told in official correspondence, the shams of Court etiquette and ceremony, were not to his liking, nor indeed was the necessary subordination of his own will and judgement to those of another man agreeable to him."[166]

In 1893 Cambridge felt that Robert Biddulph was not the best man for Gibraltar because he was not "civil enough": apparently on one occasion he had not attended a ball in his own house. The CO insisted and Biddulph secured the post. Biddulph claimed he had no objection to entertaining, but was just not in the habit of going to balls in his private capacity.[167] Charles Nairne could not recommend Lt. Col. Edwin Sandys for the Aden command in 1898 "because he is so unsociable & unbending, and at times disagreeable: he would not be able to conciliate the foreign consuls, or conduct with sufficient tact & influence, the many political & quasi diplomatic questions that are always cropping up in Aden, & which to handle successfully require firmness, which he possesses almost to the pitch of obstinacy, as well as geniality, of which he has no trace whatsoever." Cols. William Black and Henry Tanby were also unsuitable. Nairne suggested instead Col. O'Moore Creagh VC as energetic, popular, and a good linguist. Creagh was not only "better able to tackle the foreigners" but also to "do the entertaining & social part" compared to "either Black or Tandy."[168]

A rather different case was that of George Greaves. Greaves's first wife died in 1880 while he was AG in India. He had already made the acquaintance of Julia Venour, wife of the doctor of the Fifteenth Hussars, and she became his mistress. Greaves then took up with Mrs. Rochfort-Boyd in late 1884, living in a ménage à trois with wife and husband.[169] In nonetheless recommending Greaves for Bombay in 1889, Roberts acknowledged Greaves's "domestic arrangements have not unfortunately been always quite irreproachable."[170] Lansdowne was aware of what Roberts called Greaves's "little failing."[171] Greaves gave assurances as to his conduct. As CinC in Bombay, he was sufficiently careful for the governor to report, "I am happy to add that Society has nothing to complain of now."[172] However, past social failings were brought up again when Greaves was a potential successor to Roberts as CinC in India. Greaves married Mrs. Venour in 1908.

Greaves's indiscretions raise generally the issue of scandal, which could naturally inhibit advancement. One case coming to Roberts's attention was that of Col. Alexander Morgan, who had been suggested for a brigade command: "Twice since I have been in command very shady monetary transactions have been brought home to him."[173] Morgan was told to settle his debts or be retired. In 1891 Col. Sir William Gordon-Cumming was accused of cheating at baccarat at a house party at Tranby Croft also attended by the Prince of Wales. The case became public knowledge. Gordon-Cumming sued other guests for slander, with the Prince being forced into the witness box. The Prince demanded Gordon-Cumming be court-martialed, but Buller declined to authorize such a proceeding prior to the civil case.[174] Nonetheless, it finished Gordon-Cumming's career.

Major Lord Arthur Somerset fled overseas after his involvement in the notorious Cleveland Street homosexual scandal in 1889. While some prominent soldiers such as Gordon, Wood, and Kitchener have been claimed as homosexual, there is no evidence to suggest this was so. Undeniably, there is the specter of Hector "Fighting Mac" Macdonald, who committed suicide in a Paris hotel room in March 1903 after being allegedly discovered in flagrante delicto with Sinhalese boys in a railway carriage in Ceylon. His subsequent disgrace made no difference to his reputation in Scotland. An astonishingly large number of people attended his funeral and visited his grave, and a large monument was erected to his memory.[175]

While the undoubted existence of homosexuality within the army must be acknowledged, the evidence for serial womanizing is substantially greater. The greatest sexual controversy affecting the army was not a matter of homosexuality in a railway carriage, but of indecent assault on a young woman. The former commander of the Tenth Hussars, Valentine Baker, AQMG at Aldershot, was one of the army's most promising officers. In August 1875 Baker was convicted of the indecent assault of the young woman in a railway carriage traveling between Woking and Esher: "the bitch in the Railway Carriage" was Wolseley's trenchant comment.[176] The judge ruled that a "kiss that gratifies or incites passion is indecent."[177] Lord Lucan, Airey, and the GOC at Aldershot, Sir Thomas Steele, all made a point of attending Baker's trial, with Airey and Steele addressing the court as character witnesses following the verdict.[178] Baker was fined £500 and sentenced to a year's imprisonment.

Incensed, the queen demanded that Baker be dismissed from the service rather than allowed to resign, regretting what she regarded as the judge's leniency.[179] The cabinet decided upon accepting Baker's unconditional resignation.[180] Cambridge continued to champion Baker, who had other influential friends including the Prince of Wales. They failed consistently to persuade the queen to reinstate him. It was to Baker's disadvantage that the queen associated him with the Prince of Wales's "set." Consequently, after his release from prison, Baker pursued a career in the Turkish and Egyptian services. In 1882 Baker was offered command of the newly reconstructed EA on Wolseley's recommendation. By the time he reached Cairo, the government had decided that British officers could not be expected to serve under one previously dismissed from the service.[181] The queen finally agreed to his reinstatement in June 1887, but Baker died before it was confirmed.

Scandal was never far away. William Butler became involved in the notorious Campbell divorce case in 1886. Lord Colin Campbell accused Butler as one of four men who had enjoyed an adulterous relationship with Lady Campbell. There was little evidence of Butler's involvement, and the case as a whole was dismissed, but Butler's refusal to testify was criticized by the jury to the detriment of his reputation.[182]

One promising career blighted by scandal was that of the Hon. George Villiers, son of the Fourth Earl of Clarendon and a cousin to Lady Lytton. About to be attached to Roberts's staff in Afghanistan in 1878, Villiers became involved with a doctor's wife. Unfortunately, she happened to be the sister of the *Daily Telegraph*'s correspondent in Simla. Villiers had to go home, with the Simla divorce court sanctioning him for £2,000 in damages.[183] An equally damaging case was that of Charles à Court, whose affair in Cairo in the 1890s with Lady Garstin, the wife of a prominent civil servant, forced his resignation from the army.[184] By contrast, the young John Cowans, later QMG, was highly fortunate to avoid the consequences of his many indiscretions, having a penchant for "rough trade" in women—that is, consorting with the lowest class of prostitute.[185]

A rather different kind of scandal was the notorious Jameson Raid in December 1895, which was intended to support a rising by the so-called Uitlanders on the Rand. To the WO's discomfort, thirteen of those captured by the Boers were serving British officers, nine of them regulars. Eight were attached to the Mashonaland Mounted Police, the Bechuanaland Border Police, or the British South Africa Company forces; the other was on leave. Conspirators arrested in Johannesburg included Col. Frank Rhodes, who was on half-pay.[186] The public, however, took a benign view, and, after several adjournments, it took considerable direction by the lord chief justice to persuade the jury to convict Dr. Jameson and five others in July 1896. Wolseley wished to save careers, while Buller took a harder line. Public pressure resulted in the five officers incarcerated being retired rather than forced to resign, and in the other eight being merely admonished. Rhodes also retired. The five had all been released by March 1897. In the longer term, all were reinstated, as was Frank Rhodes after his service as a war correspondent in the Sudan.

Wives

The question of generals' social skills leads naturally to a consideration of their wives. It has become axiomatic that the military wife is an "incorporated wife" subordinated to her husband's career organization and without influence other than in the confines of the domestic private sphere. While wives were subject to the constraints of hierarchy that regulated husbands' careers, the reality was rather different.[187]

The old military adage was "Subalterns must not marry, captains may marry, majors should marry and colonels must marry." Increasing numbers of officers were in fact married, with the proportion rising from 25.4 percent in 1851 to 33.5 percent by 1871, although the proportion under the age of twenty-five remained small.[188] Having married while a captain, Edward May met the MS, Harman, in the street soon afterward. Harman remarked, "I see you've married. I congratulate you, but you're done."[189]

The stereotypical perception that wives merely complemented husbands in the approved manner of Victorian domestic ideology is apparent in many contemporary military memoirs and biographies. The autobiography of Elizabeth Thompson creates such an impression. Better known as the artist Lady Butler, she managed capably the entertainment expected of her at Butler's side in his home appointments, while bringing up five children and enjoying professional success. Given the choice of either Colchester or Dover in 1896, Butler allowed her to decide on Dover.[190] A woman's having a separate career was unusual, but Adela Nicolson, Lt. Gen. Malcolm Nicolson's wife, wrote poetry under the pseudonym "Laurence Hope."[191] Fred Burnaby's wife was also an authoress, although her career blossomed only after his death.[192]

The wife of the GOC at Woolwich in 1882, Lt. Gen. the Hon. Edward Gage, "was a popular figure in local society, the essence of hospitality, and always delighted to have her drawing room congested with visitors; but she was a real terror to talk [to]." Few "could get a word in edgeways, while the General would be formed up on the sofa, scowling at his radiant better-half and muttering to himself, just loud enough for everybody to hear, 'Oh, damn the woman's tongue!'"[193] William Nicholson's wife was said to be a particularly successful hostess at Simla and so "very stately and queenly" that she was nicknamed the Simla Queen Victoria.[194]

Certain appointments absolutely required a wife with appropriate social skills, rather as the medical profession identified a "good medical wife."[195] Roberts recommended Viscount Frankfort de Montmorency for the Presidency (Calcutta) District in 1890 rather than William Elles. Frankfort's wife would be an asset while "the extreme deafness of Mrs. Elles is a serious drawback, as it prevents her going much into society, and would have precluded her from sharing in those social functions which are so frequent at Calcutta during the cold season."[196] As already indicated, Roberts had particular antipathy for Charles Gough, but an additional reason for Gough to be denied the Bombay command in 1890 was "his want of hospitality." By contrast, Hugh Gough "would be admirably assisted by Lady Gough in all the social duties."[197]

Reginald Talbot's appointment as GOC in Egypt in 1898 was entirely due to his wife's perceived domestic competence. In specifically requesting Talbot Cromer said he "thought his wife would do the social work well—and that is really all the General here has to do."[198] Three years earlier, Cambridge had recommended either Maj. Gen. Charles Knowles or Maj. Gen. Reginald Thynne for Cairo as both had "very nice *wives*, an important element in this selection."[199] Cairo had not always required a married man. Frederick Stephenson, GOC from 1883 to 1887, wrote in November 1883 that he was "obliged to entertain here a good deal," at some cost to his limited financial resources. Being single, he had previously relied on his sister, and felt her absence in regulating the household since he had "neither the time nor experience to go into those matters myself." Household management was delegated to an ADC.[200]

It was possible to have the wrong wife. As a subaltern, Aylmer Haldane was tricked into marrying a barmaid. According to Winston Churchill, Haldane had offered his wife "half of all he has in the world" for a divorce but she "wants to be a lady." He continued, "It is impossible that he could fill any high command with such a private life. I questioned him about her health. Excellent. I am afraid I could suggest nothing better than Murder—and there are objections to that course. Poor wretch, he is fettered for life."[201] In fact, Haldane made it to full general's rank. Brackenbury's wife lacked tact and he regretted having married her: she had been a widow of thirty-one and he had been only twenty-one.[202] For all practical purposes, Brackenbury separated from her in 1872 although they never divorced. He had affairs including with Edith Desanges, the daughter of a well-known military artist, whom Brackenbury married soon after his first wife's death in 1905.[203] Ungallantly, Pole-Carew noted on the death of William Penn Symons at Talana in 1899, "his wife is such a terror that I think in some ways it must be a relief to him—poor chap."[204]

By contrast, a useful marriage was advantageous. Charles MacGregor's first wife was Sir Henry Durand's daughter. The marriage, which ended with her death after four years, appears to have been extremely happy, but MacGregor still observed just before the marriage, "I must say I do not care much for any supposed honour there may be in allying myself with any one in the position of Sir H. Durand; if he was a Royal Duke I should think the same, for I am proud enough of my own name to think that no other can add luster [sic] to it. But I do feel proud of the prospect of being allied to such a man."[205] William Robertson married Lt. Gen. Charles Palin's daughter while a lieutenant in 1894, six years after being commissioned from the ranks.[206] "Curly" Hutton married Eleanor Paulet, the wealthy niece of the Marquess of Winchester.[207]

The only part of the army where a wife was positively an encumbrance was among officers seconded to the EA once Kitchener became sirdar in 1892. If officers married or became engaged, they had to place their resignation at his disposal.[208] Archibald Hunter, who kept an Abyssinian mistress, did get engaged briefly. The engagement was broken off and Hunter eventually married a widow in 1910.[209] Kitchener once explained to the queen that he disliked employing married officers because "they are always wanting to go home."[210] Kitchener also told James Edmonds on one occasion that he preferred bachelors or widowers because he got more work out of them.[211] Kitchener's objection to married officers extended to his command in the South African War. William Birdwood was recommended as AAG. Lady Roberts mentioned Birdwood was

married, which had "an electric effect" on Kitchener: "'Married! Good Lord—
that fellow married!' on which Lady Roberts bridled up and said, 'Yes, Lord
Kitchener, and let me tell you like all good officers very much the better for
being so'—to which he could only reply, 'I am glad you think so!'"[212]

It was possible to have married prior to 1892 and stay in the EA, but as
Reginald Wingate wrote to his wife, he disliked having to ask Kitchener for
leave in Cairo for "that always brings about a sneer in which he airs his views on
the mistake of officers marrying, & I am not going to subject you or myself to his
boorish insults."[213] The near vendetta Kitchener pursued against Col. Charles
Parsons in 1899 had little to do, as most believed, with jealousy of Parsons's brilliant seizure of the Mahdist post at Gedaref. It was due to Parsons "marrying
without leave & not at once resigning his position in the EA."[214]

Consideration for wives could impinge on career decisions. Haines had
doubts on becoming CinC in India as his wife was in such poor health. She
died in England in 1880 while he was still abroad. Melgund felt obliged by his
wife's pregnancy to turn down the chance to command the Canadian "voyageurs" being sent to join the Gordon relief expedition in 1884.[215] One reason that
Buller declined the chief command in India in 1892 was his wish not to be separated from his wife, who was in poor health, and his stepchildren.[216] Francis
Grenfell, who initially turned down the Cairo command in 1897 due to his wife's
health, recalled that "my wife hearing of it was very much distressed and most
anxious that I should accept so flattering an offer. So I again communicated with
Sir Coleridge Grove and told him to cancel my refusal and that I was prepared
to go to Egypt whenever the Government desired me to take up my duties."[217]

Whether separated from husbands on service or not, military wives had
other roles to fulfill, which suggest ways they could go beyond the private and
domestic sphere. The well-known "crammer" and military writer Dr. Thomas
Miller Maguire pointedly remarked to the Akers-Douglas Committee in his
written evidence in 1902 that female influence should be kept at a distance: "It
is an abomination that the caprice of titled feminine idlers and intriguers, or of
the wives of generals, should make or mar an officer's career. The nation should
put an end to this monstrosity at once."[218]

Women sprang to their husbands' defense in death as much as in life.
Ardagh, Sir William Gatacre, Donald Stewart, and MacGregor all had posthumous biographies compiled by their widows, while Henry Brooke's journal of
the siege of Kandahar was published by his widow. The Rev. James Adams VC
felt it unfortunate that MacGregor's second wife had so published: "Some men
talk too much to their friends; but poor old MacGregor talked too much to
his diary; and it is very hard upon him that his foolish notions as a boy should
be published, as well as the rather unnecessary notions that influenced him

throughout his career, by his own wife under the impression that she was vindicating his character & reputation."[219]

More practically, Fanny, Lady Cunynghame, sister to Cambridge's predecessor as CinC, Viscount Hardinge, was incensed at the apparent slight to Sir Arthur Cunynghame as GOC at the Cape by Wolseley's appointment as administrator in Natal.[220] She wrote directly to Cambridge demanding either Gibraltar or Malta for Cunynghame as proof of the duke's support. Cambridge felt unable to recommend Cunynghame for Malta as he regarded it as too important a command.[221] Cunynghame himself wrote, "She is a good wife, and is anxious for my benefit."[222] Adria, Lady Chelmsford, also complained bitterly of her husband's treatment after the disasters in Zululand. Chelmsford had been "thrown over by the Govt. without a word of thanks for all his hard work."[223]

Military wives were often said to be ambitious for their husbands, as in the case of Lady Grenfell, whom Evelyn Baring described in 1888 as urging her husband to "acquire the maximum amount of glory with the minimum amount of risk."[224] Consequently, just as political hostesses used their social power to influence those able to dispense patronage, military wives sought to advance their husbands by appeals for employment on their behalf. Wolseley's correspondence contains frequent examples.[225]

As the end of Mahdist rule in the Sudan came closer, Wingate wanted to obtain a post in Cairo with some role in future administration. Consequently, he asked his wife to act in his interests: "If all goes well at Khartoum—you know my views about the future and I hope that you may perhaps . . . be able to put them forward. . . . We must carefully watch events and in case of necessity—I shall probably wire to you what line I want you to take."[226]

By contrast, Dormer warned off his wife, Ella—Archibald Alison's daughter—from trying to see the AG, Ellice, or the MS, Horsford, on his behalf while he was on Cyprus in 1878, "for when these things are done at the proper time, & in the right way, nothing does so much harm as wives or female relatives interfering."[227] Five years later, when Dormer was anxious about a cut in his lodging allowance in Cairo, he again pleaded to her, "for Heaven's sake don't you interfere & go bothering the Horse Guards people, either officially or privately upon the subject. I can do it best myself *if it is to be done.*"[228] Dormer was appalled to hear that Ella proposed to see the QMG, Arthur Herbert, in May 1884, for "as I have told you so often before I would much rather you never bothered them, for you can only do my interests more harm than good by interviewing the officials at the Horse Guards, & I so much prefer looking after my own battles." Just five months later he was again begging Ella not to press his possible candidature for MS on Whitmore and Herbert: "Only please do not put your finger in the pie & go on bothering or writing to or calling on them."[229]

While Lady Randolph Churchill was not successful in getting Winston to the Sudan in 1897, she and Susan, Lady Jeune (later Lady St. Helier), successfully lobbied Evelyn Wood to smooth Churchill's way out there a year later.[230] Lady Jeune also interested herself in the career of Charles Townshend.[231] By contrast, Douglas Haig's sister, Mrs. Henrietta Jameson, and Lady Fingall failed to influence Wood in enabling one of Haig's colleagues in the Seventh Hussars to join him in the Sudan.[232]

The wives of Colley, Wood, Wolseley, and Roberts offer particular insights. Wood married the Hon. Mary Paulina Anne Southwell, sister of Viscount Southwell and a Catholic, in 1867. Wood's frequent pursuit of monetary reward partly reflected her expensive tastes.[233] Together with Wood's sister, Anna Steele, whom Lady Wolseley regarded as an "odious hussy" responsible for writing all Wood's speeches, Paulina Wood was very ambitious.[234] In October 1884 Wolseley claimed Paulina was unpopular in Egypt, where it was believed she was behind Wood's attempt as sirdar to avoid being subordinated to the GOC in Cairo. Wolseley added that Wood lived in so much adulation from her and Mrs. Steele that it would turn anyone's head.[235]

It might be suspected that Wolseley was prejudiced after Wood's role in the capitulation to the Boers following Colley's death, but there is confirmation elsewhere. Colley alluded to Paulina's likely wrath when he was preferred over her husband for appointment to the Staff College in 1876.[236] After meeting Wood in 1879, the queen became godmother to one of Wood's daughters. Paulina then entered into the queen's confidence when Wood was abroad. She acted as a conduit between the queen and her husband during the Egyptian campaign, although not always transmitting what she felt Wood wanted kept confidential.[237] In December 1884, however, according to Lady Wolseley, Paulina offended the queen by pressing her own ideas on Egyptian affairs.[238] But there was something of a problem in Paulina's disordered house. Wood was notoriously untidy. In 1876 at Cambridge's request, Buller conveyed to Wood how close he had come to losing the appointment of AQMG at Aldershot: "Tell him that the Duke objects to him that he is not in his person smart enough for a staff officer and that he really must, if he wishes to get on wear better plain clothes. You will tell him this."[239] While in the Sudan, Wood stuffed telegrams into his pockets and even lost them down the back of his trousers.[240]

In October 1880 Wolseley complained of Wood's Dover house being as filthy as a railway refreshment room, with the deaf Wood himself seemingly oblivious of the noise surrounding him and to the poor food being served.[241] Seven years later, Cambridge complained to Wolseley of an "infamous lunch" with the Woods and later suggested Wolseley advise Wood to arrange for a better cook and attempt to create a "better appointed home."[242] Cambridge commented on the Aldershot command in 1888 not only that Wood was too junior but that he and Paulina made "a very rough couple."[243] Wood secured the appointment as the best military candidate, but Arthur Bigge also observed that the wife of Wood's principal rival for Aldershot, John Ross, possessed even greater shortcomings than Paulina.[244] Wood's most prestigious appointments as QMG and AG came after Paulina's death.

By contrast, Lady Wolseley largely succeeded in supporting her husband's ambitions. Louisa Erskine, whom Wolseley married in 1868, was almost certainly illegitimate. She had a reputation for dressing well and was highly intelligent but plainspoken. She moved with ease in literary circles with the likes of Edmund Gosse, Henry James, and George Du Maurier. She saw herself as her husband's equal.[245]

Loo, as she was known to Wolseley (whose endearments also ran to the distinctly curious "little runterfoozle"), was a capable partner. She was just as determined, so much so that she all but cut her daughter out of her will following a rift between the two of them in 1905. Interestingly, she only performed her social role in home stations, for she declined to accompany Wolseley to overseas postings; her only extended tour with him after his service in Canada ended in 1870 was to Cyprus in 1879, plus a very brief visit to Cairo in April 1885. Wolseley was offered the appointment of MS to the viceroy, Northbrook, in 1872 but turned it down because of Loo's pregnancy.[246]

Loo was jealous of other women who seemed too friendly toward Wolseley, such as Baker Russell's wife, "Pal," and the Duchess of Edinburgh, whose correspondence with Wolseley she returned to the royal family after his death.[247] In September 1884 she complained at not receiving a letter from Wolseley, assuming he was too busy writing to "two or three duchesses" instead.[248] She also disliked several of Wolseley's companions, notably Brackenbury.[249]

Yet, whatever her apparent shortcomings, Loo played a significant role in defending Wolseley's interests at home. In 1879, with Wolseley still in South Africa, she was the intermediary between him and prominent Conservatives over the possibility of a peerage.[250] In February 1880 she was sounding out ministers on Wolseley's desire to leave the Cape.[251] Two years later, Loo was negotiating the peerage anew while Wolseley was still in Egypt, this time reminding Liberals of their failure to secure the promised peerage in the previous year.[252] She visited Windsor in February and March 1885, and was passing messages to Wolseley from the queen.[253]

In 1893 it was she rather than Wolseley who was sounded out by Campbell-Bannerman with regard to the likelihood of Wolseley accepting Malta.[254] After Wolseley's serious illness in 1897, she was especially protective.[255] She was so again in December 1899. Loo recognized that if Wolseley resigned following Roberts's supersession of Buller in South Africa, it would be regarded as pique, yet, if he stayed, it might appear he clung to office "or more probably that his wife does."[256]

In both 1884 and 1899 Loo was besieged by women trying to get husbands or sons to the Sudan—the "camel mammas"—and South Africa, respectively.[257] Clearly, it was believed she might wield some influence over Wolseley. Similarly, one young officer wrote to Arthur Bigge in May 1896 that, at the recent AG's ball, subalterns had "tumbled over each other to dance with Miss Buller & Miss Wolseley. This, they tell me is the right way, to get 'selected' nowadays."[258] Gossip in 1897 suggested that Wolseley had asked his PS, Capt. Cecil Feilden, when he was going to propose to Frances Wolseley. Feilden replied that he had admiration for her but no intention of marrying. Wolseley supposedly asked if Feilden thought he had been made PS on his abilities, and that he could now "go about his business."[259] In reality, there is little to suggest Loo was influential in terms of the selection of officers or in guiding particular decisions by her husband. Wolseley was very much his own man. Loo largely operated within the private sphere, but this did not prevent her from exercising independence on occasions nor from being influential in shaping his career.

Both Lady Colley and Lady Roberts stepped beyond the private sphere and subordination. Colley's engagement and marriage at the age of forty-three to Edith Hamilton, daughter of Maj. Gen. Henry Meade "Tiger" Hamilton, in 1878 came as a surprise to most at Simla.[260] When in Natal, Colley was to write that Edith "seconds me splendidly, and rows or laughs at the people who come to her with long faces or absurd stories."[261] Yet, as Wood confided to the queen just before Colley's death, Edith's ambition for Colley "obliterates apparently every thought of the personal danger which he has undergone."[262] When the first train arrived in Pietermaritzburg in October 1880, Colley stood on the footplate but Edith was at the engine's throttle, symbolically in control of her husband's destiny. Reportedly, she had written to Colley after his defeats at Laing's Nek and Ingogo to urge him into further action, although the letter mysteriously disappeared after his death. No such letter (supposedly found on his body) has ever been traced.[263] Actual surviving letters written to Colley by Edith on both 15 and 24 February 1881 express concern for his safe return.[264] She played the part of the widow to the full, commissioning William Butler's biography of her husband. It was eventually Wolseley's belief that Edith had married Colley as a matter of convenience rather than love.[265]

If Edith Colley ultimately failed to wield influence in the public sphere through Colley's death, Lady Roberts succeeded. Roberts married Nora Bews, youngest daughter of a retired Scottish soldier, in 1859, at the comparatively young age of twenty-seven; she was just twenty. Nora, who was taller than the diminutive Roberts, was, according to Wolseley, "the commonest and most vulgar looking old thing I have ever met." On the same day in a separate letter, Wolseley also remarked, "My eyes, what a woman. I have never seen a more hideous animal in my life."[266] Thereafter, Wolseley always referred to Nora as vulgar and frumpy, writing to his brother, "India to me is & has always been the home of military jobs. Roberts, instead of reforming the system, took his frumply [sic] vulgar old wife into partnership in business & made it worse than ever."[267] At his retirement, Wolseley remarked that he was clearing his office "where she can job & dispense favours to her heart's content, dreadful woman."[268] Wolseley's animosity does not seem to have extended to his wife, for Nora wrote to Pole-Carew on one occasion that Loo, whom she liked, had visited her while Wolseley was absent from London.[269]

Obviously, as with Wolseley's view of Paulina Wood, his impartiality might be questioned, but there is other evidence suggesting he was not alone in viewing Nora as a formidable woman exercising real power over her husband. On one occasion even Lansdowne made fun of Nora's vulgarity. She appeared to Cambridge's nephew, Prince Adolphus of Teck, an "awful female" who frightened everyone. Teck also referred to Roberts as "Sir Jobs."[270]

The queen held a particular view of Nora. In August 1893 Roberts wrote to Sir John Cowell on hearing that the queen believed he had "been influenced by Lady Roberts in making appointments." He acknowledged, "I have consulted her freely on almost every subject, and she has been to me (as I imagine a good wife is to every husband) the greatest possible assistance." But he went on, "The only one subject which we have never discussed is that of an official appointment before it was made, in order that she might truthfully reply to the letters she occasionally received, requesting her to use her influence with me, that she knew nothing about such matters and never interfered in them."[271] Unpleasant remarks in a "low society paper" did not trouble him, but if the queen believed them, then it was a serious matter. The queen was not reassured. When Roberts was an outside choice for CinC in 1895, she wrote that Roberts was "ruled by his wife who is a terrible jobber," and his candidature was impossible "on account of his readiness to listen to his wife, & her notorious favouritism."[272]

Even more pointedly, in August 1900, Lansdowne conveyed the queen's concern at Nora's presence in Pretoria. Lansdowne presented it purely as a matter of the queen's fears about safety.[273] Lansdowne was concealing the queen's real objection, as stated by Bigge: "Endless stories, probably many of which are untrue, reach the Queen respecting Lady Roberts' interference and her influence even exerted on the careers of officers in high command in South Africa." Believing public confidence might be shaken by the rumors, the queen concluded that if Lady Roberts "was *not* at Head Quarters there could be no possible ground for the accusations which are but too common against her."[274]

The queen's intervention regarding ladies going to South Africa "when only inclined to spread hysterical rumours" became generally known. One staff officer remarked, "this coming as it did immediately after Lady Roberts's arrival was to say the least of it rather pointed."[275]

There were others with similar views. Hugh Bixby Luard of the Indian Medical Service wrote in his reminiscences, "it was said that any ambitious officer who wished to get on found it advisable to get favour from Lady Roberts at Simla, who was supposed to have unbounded influence with him [Roberts], and was a person of very strong character." Luard suggested, however, that Roberts had good judgment and "exercised the same discretion in considering Lady Roberts candidates or favourites."[276] Maj. Gen. Granville Egerton recalled the "sobriquet attached to the pair in India, of Sir Bobs and Lady Jobs, was not undeserved."[277] George White also wrote of Nora's influence in July 1888, characterizing her as "a prejudiced woman & nothing is too bad for those she does not like but I think she is a warm friend. One thing is certain, that she takes too much part in Sir Fred's business and that it is generally known."[278]

The young Henry Rawlinson, who was befriended by Nora and her daughters, wrote in September 1888, "I can only regret that Lady R. has any knowledge of the official patronage, which should be solely and entirely under Sir F['s] own thumb."[279] Later, in South Africa, Rawlinson suggested that Roberts "will not subordinate his personal convenience and desires to the public interest. It has always been the same." Rawlinson believed that it was for this reason that Nora had arrived in South Africa with her daughters, adding, "all through his career it has been this inclination which has kept Lady R and the family in close touch behind him and has so militated against his own great name and her individual popularity."[280]

There is indication of Nora's influence, too, in Ian Hamilton's memoirs. In 1886 Roberts "would not enter Mandalay; the place was taboo to him or perhaps Lady Roberts had tabooed it."[281] Hamilton's marriage to Jean Muir, a wealthy woman with literary and artistic tastes, was initially opposed by Nora. Hamilton declined to postpone the marriage as Roberts requested in August 1886 but then had to accompany Roberts to Burma. Jean wrote that Hamilton

> begs me to be nice to Lady Bobs as he says so much depends on this and says: "the best way to do this is to meet her advances more than half way." However, she does not seem likely to make any and if she does I can't meet her more than half way. As well ask me to jump over the moon; she terrifies me. But if I decide to marry Major H. she will just have to lump it [282]

They were finally married in February 1887.

In South Africa there was much talk of "petticoat government" in head-quarters at Pretoria. Roberts's ADC, Kerry, even suggested that Roberts's con-version to a much tougher line toward Boer women and children owed most to Nora's presence.[283] Such influence continued seemingly when Roberts became CinC at home. No stranger to the importance of female influence, Haig com-plained to his sister when he believed he was likely to be passed over for the command of the Aldershot cavalry brigade in September 1902: "no doubt some of Roberts' pals (or? Lady R's pals) have been chosen."[284]

In this context, the destruction of the correspondence that passed between Roberts and Nora by Roberts's biographer, David James, in 1954 is perhaps sug-gestive of a desire to conceal the extent to which she influenced him.[285] Few of Nora's letters survive, but it is interesting to compare those that do with Loo Wolseley's correspondence. While recounting to Wolseley those events at home of immediate professional concern to him, Loo's letters are full of social and domestic events. Nora's letters are detailed discussions of military matters.[286] They certainly suggest she stepped well beyond any notion of separate spheres, and the circumstantial evidence points to the lack of subordination in her rela-tionship with her husband.

On the other hand, in defense of Nora, Charles Nairne recalled in 1896 that when Lt. Gen. David Macfarlan had been IG of artillery in India, he had not got on with Roberts because he would

> insist on resenting what he called Lady R's interference, which need not have troubled him any more than it did me, for in reality it did not affect the affairs of the Army as her enemies chose to think it did if indeed it ever deserved the name of interference at all. She occasionally came into the room while the Chief was at work but it was generally to borrow a pencil or ask Sir F. R. for some trifle that he knew & she did not. Of course, it was wrong but why carp at a woman for not being always right as to official etiquette.[287]

Yet, it is clear the incorporation of women in the army through marriage nei-ther automatically implied their subordination nor constrained their ambition. As has been remarked, "We are perhaps too prone to see limitations where the women of the past saw possibilities."[288]

Royalty

There was one other woman whose views most certainly counted. The queen was well aware she was de jure CinC. Following Prince Albert's death in 1861, she only visited Westminster Palace on seven occasions but resumed appearing at military reviews and parades in 1866. She did so regularly until 1900. She took the keenest interest in military affairs and was always insistent on maintaining Britain's military reputation.[289]

The queen's intervention in military affairs could be over the most trivial of matters. Wolseley was horrified when, in July 1899, the queen proposed to award the Sudan Medal to an officer's dog when it represented the only real reward available to private soldiers.[290] On the other hand, the queen's interest in her favorites was another factor of account in the disposing of commands. All promotions to the rank of major general and above had to be formally submitted for her approval. Bigge wrote to Lansdowne in 1895 that in the queen's view the CinC as her personal representative and the army was decidedly "not the property of Parliament."[291] In 1874 Lord Derby was told of "a fancy of hers to have her name conspicuously printed in the Army list, on the first page, with a page to itself and some note implying that she is the head of the army: with her ADC's names given in the next page, before any mention of the Sec. of State or C.in-C."[292]

The depth of the queen's interest in the army generally can be gauged from the seventeen notes she sent to Childers on a single day in August 1882 regarding the preparations for the Egyptian campaign.[293] William Nicholson complained to Spenser Wilkinson in July 1893, "the Army is regulated not with the view of ensuring efficiency, but of satisfying the personal claims of the personages, Royal & otherwise, who can bring pressure to bear on the responsible authorities." A year later, he believed Campbell-Bannerman so "exceptionally subservient" to the queen and Cambridge that the army appeared to be "a convenient appanage of Royalty."[294]

The queen was well informed of military matters in that key members of her household such as Sir Henry Ponsonby and Sir Thomas Biddulph were soldiers. Most remained nominally so even when long inactive. She was always prepared to make her views known, particularly in delaying her assent to appointments, as when Wolseley was proposed for command of the Gordon relief expedition in August 1884.[295] She was deeply involved in resisting Wolseley's peerage in 1881 as well as his appointments as QMG and AG. Wolseley himself wrote to Methuen in 1880, "I do not see any chance however of the army being effectively reconstituted under present circumstances: the Court influence is too strong for those in power, and the interest of the country is not now enlisted on the side of army reform."[296]

The queen also had her own agenda in promoting the career of her third son, Connaught. From her perspective a royal prince had a special advantage in not being a member of any particular clique.[297] In 1882 the difficulty arose as to how Connaught might be suitably rewarded for his part in the Egyptian campaign. The queen wished to give Connaught the GCB. Childers feared there would be public criticism, especially as Connaught had commanded the Guards Brigade.[298] Childers suggested instead that Connaught be made a personal ADC to the queen.[299]

In 1885 the cabinet decided that Connaught could not be given the Bombay command due to the political responsibilities entailed.[300] Salisbury said his colleagues were not swayed by Lord Randolph Churchill, as the queen suspected, but by forthcoming elections and the likely appointment of the Duke of Edinburgh to command the Mediterranean Fleet.[301] Salisbury prevaricated when the queen requested he telegraph the viceroy to ascertain his opinion; Salisbury claimed not to have access to the IO cypher. The queen then telegraphed direct, leading to Churchill's resignation on the grounds the queen should only communicate with the viceroy through him. The viceroy replied that he, Stewart, and Roberts would accept Connaught at Bombay. Churchill withdrew his resignation on being told the queen routinely communicated directly to India.[302] In the event, Connaught went to Rawalpindi.

So far as the government was concerned, nothing had changed by 1886 when Hardinge retired from Bombay. It was claimed that the political responsibilities of command in India at the time were so high they could not be discharged constitutionally by the queen's son.[303] Connaught was considered for Madras, but the continuing pacification operations in Upper Burma ruled out that posting as the Madras army was nominally responsible for Burma. In the end, Connaught got Bombay.[304]

In April 1890 the possibility of Connaught succeeding Roberts as CinC went to the cabinet, which, according to Salisbury, would resign en masse should Connaught be appointed. Stressing that the likely opposition would be "unfair to him & injurious to the throne," Salisbury pointed out that if Connaught did get the Indian command at the age of forty and then succeeded Cambridge at home, he would be retired at only fifty.[305] Another fear was that if Connaught became QMG, it would imply that he would succeed Cambridge as CinC, when the Commons had only just been persuaded to retain the post and many MPs would follow Hartington in voting for its abolition.[306] The queen was predictably angry at the "*shameful principle* that Princes are to suffer for *their birth* in a monarchical country."[307]

In 1897 the possibility of Connaught as AG was raised. Lansdowne indicated it would be difficult to pass over Wood without a good reason "which will be readily understood by the public & not wholly unintelligible to Wood himself."[308] Roberts's supersession of Buller left the Irish command vacant, and, since the queen was opposed to Connaught going to South Africa, he got the Irish command in January 1900.

Having assumed that Connaught would definitely succeed Wolseley as CinC, the queen expressed surprise when it was proposed in September 1900 that Roberts do so; she noted that the substitution of a subject (Wolseley) for a member of the royal family "has not proved very successful."[309] Salisbury suggested that it was impossible to pass over Roberts when "reforms in our military system are being generally urged in a very democratic spirit, and all the unpopularity which the War Office and many officers of the army have incurred, has exasperated that democratic rancour to a singular degree."[310]

Evelyn Wood became a particular favorite of the queen after being presented to her together with Buller on return from Zululand in September 1879, although due to his deafness he talked incessantly.[311] He almost got off to a bad start in the relationship by implying the queen's favored servant, John Brown, was drunk.[312] Thereafter, Wood was a regular correspondent, penning remarkably obsequious and sycophantic letters to the queen. Despite her dislike of the convention with the Boers, the queen requested that Wood's new daughter be named Eugénie Victoria and stood as the child's godmother.[313] Wood felt able to tell the queen in July 1882 how keen he was to serve in Egypt and of his subsequent distress in seeing Gerald Graham playing a leading role. He also raised the matter of his initial failure to secure any decoration for the campaign.[314] Support for Wood, however, did not mean the queen was willing to see him preferred to Connaught when the Aldershot command was being filled in 1888.

Another royal favorite was Sir John McNeill VC. McNeill became an equerry to the queen on the condition he would be free to take an active command if the opportunity presented.[315] In February 1879 McNeill offered his services in Zululand, but only provided that he could remain an equerry since he needed the additional income to service the debt interest on £80,000 he had borrowed to secure an old family property.[316] McNeill was offered the Scottish command in early 1885, but the question arose as to whether he could continue as equerry, not to mention McNeill's doubts as to whether he could afford Edinburgh.[317] McNeill was then given a brigade command at Suakin, which greatly pleased the queen.[318]

Unfortunately, McNeill was heavily criticized for the conduct of the action at Tofrek on 22 March 1885. The queen felt the press criticism unjustified.[319] McNeill defended his conduct in a letter to the queen, and she made it clear she would "not give him up."[320] She did not want Sir Gerald Graham's dispatch to appear before that of McNeill himself. To the despair of W. H. Smith, she seemed to want to "clear" McNeill's name through some kind of private inquiry that might become a public issue.[321]

McNeill himself called for the publication of his despatch to refute press claims. He also wanted Graham to write to the press saying "that he is shocked at the attacks made on an officer serving under him that every precaution was taken."[322] Graham was approached on the queen's behalf. While reluctant to blame McNeill, Graham was "afraid my view of McNeill's conduct will not be considered satisfactory but if a plain unvarnished tale is of any service to you[,] you are welcome to it."[323] McNeill could not be exonerated without damaging Graham, and neither he nor Graham was entirely without blame. What Ponsonby referred to as "terrible recriminations" in public would do little good to anyone.[324]

Arthur Hardinge, second son of the former CinC, Viscount Hardinge, pointedly reminded Cambridge in November 1876 that he was sure the queen would approve when he asked to be considered for an active command in the event of war in Egypt or Europe.[325] Hardinge was known to have the queen's favor.[326] In 1880 the queen wanted Hardinge, also an equerry, to get the Aldershot command so he could continue to perform his duties at court, whereas the possibility he might be offered Canada would not so allow. Canada would also make it difficult for Hardinge's wife to accompany him, and the queen was concerned at rumors that Hardinge had deserted her.[327] Hardinge got Bombay in 1881 but was allowed to remain an equerry on full pay.[328] Hardinge's tenure at Bombay was complicated by the fact that his promotion to full general was due in 1883. If a vacancy for CinC in India occurred while he was still there, either he must be appointed himself or a more senior officer appointed since he could not be passed over even by a lieutenant general given local rank. No promise could be given Hardinge that he would remain at Bombay.[329] Subsequently, Hardinge was asked to stay for the full five years as a means of enabling the command to be kept open for Connaught.[330]

The Prince of Wales also had his favorites, such as Valentine Baker. In Natal in 1875, having already received correspondence from the Duke of Manchester about his son, Viscount Mandeville, becoming an additional ADC, Wolseley found the latter turning up with a letter of introduction from the Prince. All Wolseley could find for Mandeville to do was to correct dance cards for a ball.[331] In January 1882 Donald Stewart asked Cambridge if he knew much about Col. Henry Delafosse, whom the Prince wanted to see in an Indian command. Stewart had not seen Delafosse for some years but was under the impression his brain had been affected either as the result of sunstroke or mental derangement.[332]

In 1882 the Prince sought a better reward for "Croppy" Ewart, even mentioning it to Loo Wolseley.[333] Although recommending Ewart for a cavalry brigade, Wolseley regarded it monstrous that Ewart was senior to Baker Russell by virtue of his Guards rank when the latter had fought in a campaign before Ewart had even been commissioned.[334] The Prince had also tried to get on the expedition himself, enlisting Loo at one point to plead his case when the queen and Gladstone firmly ruled it out. He then alienated Wolseley by criticizing the appointments he made.[335]

Another favorite was Col. Stanley Clarke, the Prince's equerry from 1878 to 1886, and then secretary to the Princess of Wales. In 1881 with the Prince's support, Clarke sought appointment as a second lieutenant colonel in the Fourth Hussars so as to qualify for promotion to colonel. Cambridge pointed out that since Clarke declined to resign as an equerry, he could not get a regimental appointment.[336] Cambridge feared unfavorable press coverage if the matter was pressed.[337] At the Prince's insistence, Clarke commanded the Light Camel Regiment on the Gordon relief expedition, displacing McCalmont, who then complained of "a piece of jobbery."[338] When Clarke applied to go home, the Prince feared his being sent back early might be misunderstood. Wolseley hoped that "it may be clearly understood that he goes home because I find him useless and a laughing stock in his Regt."[339]

Wolseley refused to support any reward for Clarke, for whom the Prince wanted the CMG. Wolseley argued that if everyone favored by the Prince got a decoration whether they deserved it or not, it would cause considerable dissension. Ponsonby made known only the gist of Wolseley's remarks to the queen, who had raised the matter on the Prince's behalf. Ponsonby was confident the queen would drop the matter. Smith would not act either since Cambridge concurred that Clarke should not be rewarded.[340]

There was also the extended royal family. In 1898 Princess Christian of Schleswig-Holstein appealed successfully to Wolseley to get her son—the queen's grandson—Prince Christian Victor, to the Sudan. Prince Christian also wanted to go to South Africa in 1899.[341] Facing the queen's refusal to allow him to go on the Asante expedition of 1895, her son-in-law, Prince Henry of Battenberg, also appealed to Wolseley.[342] Neither benefited from his overseas posting—Henry dying of malaria contracted in Asante on the voyage back in January 1896, and Christian Victor dying of enteric at Pretoria in October 1900.

Prince Edward of Saxe-Weimar, the nephew of Queen Adelaide, consort of King William IV, was brought up in England and naturalized. In 1876 Cambridge suggested that Prince Edward's command of the Home District be extended, but the prince had already been there for six years. Thomas Biddulph pointed out that this "might lead to unpleasant remarks in connection with his position." Cambridge was compelled to agree.[343] In 1884 Edward's morganatic wife, Lady Augusta Gordon-Lennox, Countess of Dornburg (styled Princess Edward from 1886), was urging Wolseley to appoint Prince Edward as AG in his absence from the WO and to get her nephew, Lord Bingham, to the Sudan.[344] The queen supported Prince Edward as acting AG, suggesting that Arthur

Herbert was overtaxed as acting AG as well as QMG, and that Edward should take over AG duties. Herbert insisted he was not overworked but would retire if it was thought he was performing unsatisfactorily. Cambridge supported Herbert. The queen was informed that Prince Edward did not have requisite familiarity with the duties of AG or QMG.[345]

The queen then wanted Prince Edward promoted to field marshal in 1890, which Wolseley thought a poor joke: "Make him a Duke—a K.G.[,] an archbishop if you will, but to make such a man who just stands above me in the list of English generals a Field Marshal would be to me under any circumstances an absurdity, but to do so until I have been made one would be a cruel slight indeed."[346] It was proposed again in 1897. Lansdowne acquiesced despite Edward's lack of any active service since the Crimean War and the superior claims of far more distinguished soldiers.[347]

To navigate the complexities of internal and external factors bearing on promotion and appointment, therefore, was exceedingly difficult. This difficulty becomes even more apparent from the case studies in succeeding chapters.

Field Marshal HRH the Duke of Cambridge visiting the Indian contingent on Malta, June 1878. Courtesy National Army Museum, 7109-16-1.

Back row (left to right): Capt. John De Lancey (ADC), Col. David Crichton (AMS, Malta), Col. Arthur Annesley (AAG, WO), Col. Richard Bateson (ADC to HRH), Maj. Gen. Robert Radcliffe (DAGRA, WO), Col. St. George Nugent (DAQMG, Malta), Brig. Gen. Herbert Macpherson VC (OC, Indian Infantry Brigade)

Middle row (left to right): Brig. Gen. John Watson VC (OC, Indian Cavalry Brigade); Lt. Gen. Sir James Talbot Airey (OC, Malta Brigade); Field Marshal HRH Prince George, Duke of Cambridge (CinC, WO); Gen. Sir Arthur Borton (governor, Malta); Gen. Sir Alfred Horsford (MS, WO); Maj. Gen. John Ross (OC, Indian Expeditionary Force)

Front row (left to right): Lt. Robert Auld (ADC to Borton), Capt. Henry Greenaway (Tenth Bengal Cavalry), Lt. Arthur Close Borton (ADC to Borton)

Lt. Gen. Sir Sam Browne VC and the staff of the Peshawar Valley Field Force, 1878. Courtesy National Army Museum, 1955-04-41-1.

Back row (left to right): unknown, unknown, Maj. John Slade, unknown, unknown, Brig. Gen. John Doran, unknown

Front row (left to right): Lt. Gilbert Hamilton (ADC), unknown, Col. Charles Macgregor, Lt. Gen. Sir Sam Browne VC, Brig. Gen. Frederick Appleyard, Brig. Gen. Herbert Macpherson VC, Brig. Gen. Charles Gough VC, Brig. Gen. John Tytler VC, unknown

Brig. Gen. Sir Evelyn Wood VC and the staff of the flying column at camp on the White Mfolozi, Zululand, 1879. Courtesy Talana Museum, Dundee, South Africa, 16200/610.

Back row (left to right): Capt. Edward Thornburgh-Cropper (orderly officer), Capt. Lord William Beresford (staff officer), Col. the Hon. Henry Needham (orderly officer), Capt. Edward Woodgate (AAG), interpreter

Front row (left to right): Lt. Henry Lysons (orderly officer), Brig. Gen. Sir Evelyn Wood VC (OC, flying column), Lt. Col. Redvers Buller VC (OC, mounted troops)

Lt. Gen. Lord Chelmsford and his staff, Natal, 1879. Courtesy Campbell Collections, of the University of Kwazulu-Natal, Durban, South Africa, c75-047.

Back row (left to right): Maj. Matthew Gosset (ADC), Lt. Berkeley Milne RN (ADC)

Front row (left to right): Comm. Fletcher Campbell RN (OC, HMS *Active* Naval Brigade), Lt. Gen. Lord Chelmsford, Lt. Col. John North Crealock (assistant military secretary)

Lt. Gen. Sir Frederick Roberts VC and heads of department at Kabul, 1880. Courtesy National Army Museum, 1955-04-41-7.

Back row (left to right): Capt. Alexander Badcock (chief commissariat officer), Maj. Edward Hastings (political officer), Lt. Col. William Lockhart (AQMG), unknown, Rev. James Adams VC, Brig. Gen. Thomas Baker, Maj. Robert Low (director of transport), Col. Charles MacGregor (DAQMG), Col. Benjamin Gordon (CRA), The Rev. John Francis Browne

Front row (left to right): Lt. Col. William Tweedie (political secretary), Surg. Charles Owen, Capt. Gerald Morton (AAG), Maj. Gen. James Hills (military governor), Brig. Gen. Sir Herbert Macpherson VC, Brig. Gen. Hugh Gough VC, Maj. Gen. Sir Frederick Roberts VC, Brig. Gen. Charles Gough VC, Brig. Gen. William Dunham Massy, unknown, Lt. Col. Aeneas Perkins (CRE)

Lt. Gen. Sir Garnet Wolseley and his staff, Egypt, 1882. Courtesy Royal Collection Trust / © Her Majesty Queen Elizabeth II, 2017—RCIN 2501632.

Back row (left to right): Capt. Frederick Wardrop (ADC); Capt. John Adye (ADC); HSH Prince Francis, Duke of Teck (attached to staff); Maj. Leopold Swaine (MS); Bg. Surg. Robert Jackson

Front row (left to right): Lt. Col. George Wolseley (AAG), Lt. Gen. Sir Garnet Wolseley (CinC, Expeditionary Force), Lt. Edmund Spencer Childers (ADC), Lt. Arthur Creagh (ADC)

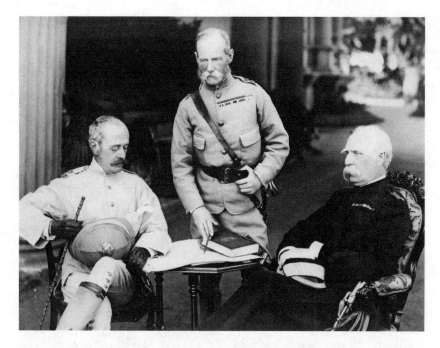

CinCs at the camp of exercise, Bangalore, January 1884. Courtesy Royal Collection Trust / © Her Majesty Queen Elizabeth II, 2017—RCIN 2907272.

From left to right: Gen. the Hon. Arthur Hardinge (CinC, Bombay), Lt. Gen. Sir Frederick Roberts VC (CinC, Madras), Gen. Sir Donald Stewart (CinC, India)

Field Marshal Viscount Wolseley and his staff, 1898. Courtesy National Army Museum 5708-8-6.

From left to right: Maj. Gen. Sir Coleridge Grove (MS), Lt. George Taylour (ADC), Field Marshal Viscount Wolseley (CinC), Capt. the Earl of Cardigan, Col. the Hon. George Gough (PS), Maj. Gen. Sir George Wolseley (GOC, Punjab), Capt. Anthony Weldon (ADC)

PART II

CASE STUDIES

CHAPTER 5

HIGH COMMAND

As suggested in the previous chapter, the commander in chief enjoyed a supposed duality with the secretary of state for war, presiding over the military departments within the War Office. The secretary of state was broadly responsible to Parliament for the supply, equipment, and preparedness of the army; for the conduct of military operations; and for purely political and legislative issues. There were administrative changes in 1888 and 1895, but the CinC broadly advised the secretary of state on military policy, organization, and preparations for operations and was directly responsible for recruiting, appointments and promotion, discipline, education and training, and reserve forces with additional responsibility for command of the forces. Responsibilities for transport and ordnance were added in 1883 and 1888. The principal subordinate offices were those of AG and QMG. As chief staff officer to the CinC, the AG dealt with all matters except those of movement, supply, and (from 1874 to 1888) intelligence devolved to the QMG. The QMG was formerly subordinated to the AG from 1870 until 1888 when the office was restored to independence from the AG.[1] As Cambridge got older and did less work, the AG became de facto head of the army.[2] In any case, the AG was regarded as the second most important post in the army, with that of CinC in India ranked third.[3] With responsibilities for mobilization, training, and discipline, the AG's post was firmly in the hands of Wolseley and his adherents from 1881 until 1901. That set a broadly reformist agenda despite the seeming immovability of Cambridge at the head of the army.

As for the head of the Indian army, there was little enough controversy over the choice of CinCs prior to the emergence of Wolseley. One old India hand, Mansfield, was succeeded by another in Napier. In 1875 the choice was between two British officers with Indian experience—Frederick Haines, CinC in Madras and a former QMG at Horse Guards; and the current QMG, Charles Ellice. Cambridge and his AG, Airey, settled on Haines, who took up the command in April 1876.[4] The question of who was to succeed Haines, however, corresponded with Wolseley's rise. It also threw into sharper focus issues of imperial strategy as well as Indian army reform. These issues continued to color the choice of CinC in India thereafter, in much the same way that the inevitable end of Cambridge's tenure raised issues of the organization of the army's higher command at home. The story of high command after 1881 is largely that of the wider contest between Wolseley and Roberts, but evidence of increasing political interference in high-profile appointments also shaped the narrative.

India

Something has already been said of the strategic issues pertaining to Indian defense, essentially on the desirability or otherwise of securing a "scientific frontier" along the Hindu Kush. The predominant Indian view after the Second Afghan War as articulated by Roberts did not have as much support as has been implied. Lytton was determined that operations in Afghanistan would be sustained without recourse to reinforcements from home to demonstrate to the Russians that no threat to India could draw British forces out of Europe. The WO Council insisted in July 1889 that India must be defended from within its own resources.[5] Charles Brownlow recorded in December 1890 that he had never seen "a single minute" in favor of the massive reinforcements Roberts was calling for up to the time he left the WO in March 1889. Brownlow also offered the considered opinion of one entirely favorable to Roberts's views that no ministry would ever give Roberts the answer he wanted.[6] Salisbury, who largely approved of Roberts's strategic ideas, recognized in March 1891 that India could not possibly be reinforced to the extent Roberts wished. Roberts's demand in 1892 for a first-line reinforcement of 30,000 men in the event of war was met with the reply that India must rely on its own resources.[7]

As viceroy, Curzon received the same response eight years later when claiming that 30,000 men represented only an immediate reinforcement and a further 70,000 men would be required. Even Roberts, now CinC at home, observed in 1904 that no more than 48,000 men could be sent to India in an emergency. The ever increasing forecasts by Kitchener as CinC in India between 1902 and 1911 of the reinforcements needed—ultimately amounting to 211,000 men—prompted the government to seek the diplomatic solution of the Anglo-Russian entente of 1907. Kitchener's earlier demands contributed to the renewal of the Anglo-Japanese alliance in 1905, the negotiations of which embraced the unlikely possibility of deploying Japanese troops on the North-West Frontier of India.[8]

It was beyond the bounds of possibility that enough men could be found to supply Indian demands. In terms of the acceptability of the Indian case, much has been made of the transfer of posts in 1891 whereby Brackenbury became military member of the Viceroy's Council, and Edward Chapman replaced Brackenbury as the WO's DG of military intelligence. It should be explained that the military member was a full member of the Viceroy's Council—the custom was to wear civilian clothes—whereas the CinC only attended for military affairs and had no vote as an "Extra-ordinary Member." The military member was the official channel of communication between viceroy and CinC. The CinC would command in the field but the military member was responsible for all matters of supply and had significant financial powers as head of the Military Department. It is perfectly true that, once in India, Brackenbury was largely converted to Roberts's views, but Chapman was equally confined by the prevailing WO orthodoxy and had little chance to put across his point of view. Moreover, Brackenbury's reform of the Indian Intelligence Branch confined it to information gathering rather than analysis or policy proposals, so it could not challenge the overall analysis made in London.[9]

As for military reform in India, Wolseley and Roberts were of one mind. Both believed that reform of the Indian army was essential, albeit differing in how it should be accomplished. One perceived weakness was the existence of the three presidency armies of Bengal, Bombay, and Madras. Roberts strongly supported the work of the Eden Commission, instituted by Lytton. It was hoped this would recommend abolition of the presidency armies and their replacement with four corps, encompassing the PFF, which would now come under the direction of the CinC. Lytton initially hoped that either Wolseley or Lintorn Simmons would head the commission. In the event, it was chaired by the lieutenant governor of Bengal, the Hon. Sir Ashley Eden. Eden reported in November 1879 despite the continuing war in Afghanistan, which resulted in several original members leaving to take up commands although all signed the final report. Eden duly recommended abolition of the presidency armies and, even more controversially, suggested that the CinC should cease to be a member of the Viceroy's Council. The military member would become the equivalent of the secretary of state at home. Predictably, Cambridge opposed abolition, and his opposition swayed the AG in India, Lumsden, to change his mind. Lumsden and Brig. Gen. Hugh O'Connell of Madras dissented from the recommendations. Haines and Edwin Johnson were also opposed, with Haines trying to postpone it altogether when war was renewed in September 1879.[10] Lytton despaired, memorably writing to Cranbrook, "if all the magnificent mediocrities of the Horse Guards, and all the powerful personal influences, and professional proclivities, which have had their wicked will upon the Zulu campaign, are, with unabashed pretensions, to decide the vital questions of Army Reform in India, then God help us!"[11]

Ripon as incoming viceroy was prepared to support the recommendations, but, with many an old Madras and Bombay man opposing change, the new government dropped reform in July 1881. The idea of abolishing the presidency armies was again taken up in 1885 and rejected anew, but the PFF did come under the CinC's control in 1886. Connaught was a valuable convert to abolition in 1888.[12] It helped also that most senior posts in India were now held by former members of the Eden Commission, including Roberts as CinC. Since the recruitment of the so-called martial races—those classes and sections of the Indian population such as Sikhs deemed to be most warlike—also reduced the significance of the Madras and Bombay armies, there was even greater logic in abolition. Accordingly, legislation was passed in 1893, and the new four-corps scheme came into operation in 1895.[13]

Wolseley coveted the command in India because he thought it the most likely arena in which to display his military skills on the battlefield. When on Cyprus in 1878–79, Wolseley fretted that he was missing the action in Afghanistan, describing India as "the only probable outlet of legitimate ambition" and his "only opening" in view of the hostility to him at Horse Guards.[14] When Wolseley had been sent to Cyprus, thereby leaving the Council of India, Haines opined that he was "rather glad" that Wolseley "has found employment for his undoubted talent elsewhere than at the India Office."[15] As Cambridge wrote to Chelmsford before there was any question of Wolseley going to Zululand,

> I am afraid, between ourselves, there is a strong wish on Colley's part & Lord Lytton's entourage to get Wolseley there to replace him [Neville Chamberlain at Madras], with a view to his subsequently getting the highest military post in India and this I am most anxious to avoid if possible. . . . Wolseley is doubtless a very able man but he is a desperate reformer without looking to the consequences in military matters, which is a great mistake and misfortune and in India perhaps more so than in any other part of the world where you cannot change without serious risk the military arrangements and organisation which have made our power so great in that distant portion of our vast Empire.[16]

Lytton was keen to get Wolseley to India, suggesting him for a proposed wider administrative post with oversight of both the Punjab and Sind. Lytton recognized it would be unpopular with those soldiers "who look upon Sir Garnet as one of Fortune's spoilt children; and, of course, all the Indian officials would resent a selection not made from their own ranks."[17] Disraeli and Salisbury demurred, and Lytton acknowledged that putting Wolseley into the new frontier command might make "too much of a splash."[18] Lytton was still pressing for Wolseley in 1879, stressing that he had only ever met Wolseley "casually for ten minutes in society" and that his support was "entirely on public grounds."[19]

Cambridge and Edwin Johnson, successively military member of the Council of India and of the Viceroy's Council from 1874 to 1880, dreaded that Wolseley's dispatch to South Africa to conclude the Zulu War would give him a stronger claim to India.[20] Apart from its intrinsic value in its own right, Wolseley's hope for a peerage after finishing the Zulu War was also largely entertained on the grounds it would strengthen his claim to succeed Haines.[21] In offering Wolseley the post of QMG in 1880, Stanley was well aware of Wolseley's ambitions but pointed out there was no actual vacancy in India and "there are other persons of high military standing besides yourself who have substantial claims for consideration before anything is decided." Stanley observed that Haines had "not the least intention either of dying or of resigning."[22] As Cambridge admitted, "every endeavour is being made to prevent so *dangerous* a proposal" as Wolseley in India.[23]

Edwin Johnson, Neville Chamberlain, and Charles Ellice were all seen as potential successors to Haines in the determination to deny Wolseley. Ellice's wife resisted the idea, and Johnson and Chamberlain were both in poor health. Johnson suffered a stroke, which gave Wolseley momentary hope that it "may bring me up the batting."[24] According to Wolseley's later account, Chamberlain had the support not only of Cambridge but also of the Duke of Edinburgh.[25] Hartington had not entirely ruled out Chamberlain despite the latter's withdrawal from the Madras command on health grounds. He felt, however, that Ripon "has no confidence in the energy & efficiency of a man whose health has been so completely shattered as is admitted has been the case."[26]

Cambridge told Johnson that he hoped he would succeed Haines as the only alternative candidate to Wolseley, "for you alone as far as I can see, would be at all able to put forward, any very superior Indian claim to so high & responsible a position."[27] Johnson himself foresaw that if Wolseley became CinC, his own views would be set aside as "those of an old fashioned Indian officer who knows nothing of modern requirements and modern organisations."[28]

Apart from Edwin Johnson's ill health, he was also held at least partially responsible for the financial crisis arising from the Second Afghan War, for which he took responsibility as he had been military member when the estimates were prepared. Sir John Strachey, the council's financial member, resigned, and Johnson, having accepted blame publicly, had little alternative but to do likewise.[29] Donald Stewart replaced Johnson, who had been temporarily put into the Madras command, but, as Cambridge reported to Ripon, "Possibly a higher position may ere long be destined for him [Stewart], which however would not sever him from his importance to you."[30]

Stewart's reasonable performance during the Second Afghan War was eagerly seized upon by those "who grasp at the idea of placing Garnett [*sic*] Wolseley out of the running."[31] From the government's point of view, it was advantageous that Stewart did not hold the same strong positions as some of his contemporaries on the need to retain Kandahar.[32] It was later generally held that Stewart was highly dependent on the military member, Thomas Wilson.[33] Melgund believed that Roberts had wanted to be military member—a correct assumption—but his views on Kandahar ruled him out of contention. According to Melgund, Hartington tried to persuade Roberts to change his views, but he was "the last man for that sort of business, stuck to his point, & in all probability his honesty has lost him the appointment."[34]

The combination of Stewart as CinC and Wilson as military member was not viewed with much enthusiasm by Charles MacGregor. While Stewart was notably fair in his dispensing of patronage, he appeared worn out and unprepared to undertake the kind of strategic overhaul MacGregor deemed necessary.[35] Typically waspish, MacGregor opined that he doubted Wilson would give up the post of military member even if he got a KCB for "he is not so indifferent to rupees."[36]

With Wolseley remaining a strong candidate to succeed Stewart in due course, Roberts repeatedly made it known that he would not serve under him.[37] Roberts himself was now a candidate, but his controversial actions at Kabul in 1879 and his resistance to abandoning Kandahar in 1880 suggested he would not be favored by any Liberal government in Britain. Other than Wolseley and Roberts, Henry Norman and Hardinge were also thought to be in the running.[38]

Brownlow hoped Roberts would be appointed before the Liberals potentially returned to office, but "Wolseley is a power in the land and if he insists on it he may get it—indeed I feel sure he will, for bear in mind that he is in a position to make himself very indispensable here, and your best friends may be glad to get him out of the way even at your expense." Brownlow thought Wolseley would be better than Hardinge "with his egotistical fads & follies" although Wolseley would hardly be popular in India. Brownlow's own choice would have been for Wolseley to go to Ireland and, bizarrely, for Chelmsford to succeed Roberts at Madras.[39]

Stewart timed his resignation before the general election so as to give Roberts a better chance. He urged Roberts "to put all your irons into the fire *without delay.*"[40] Roberts agreed for if the Liberals came back into office, he wrote, "I should have no chance then, for I am informed on reliable authority that the Liberals promised Norman the Commander-in-Chiefship in India." Roberts said he knew the Conservative Lord Randolph Churchill only slightly and did not think there was much he could do.[41] Actually, Churchill had begun corresponding with Roberts in 1881 and was favorably impressed when he met Roberts on touring India in February 1885.[42] The advent of a new Conservative administration in June 1885, with Churchill at the IO, enabled Roberts to realize his ambition of becoming CinC.

Salisbury's view was that Roberts had been thoroughly tested in warfare in Afghanistan and that his appointment was not an injustice to Wolseley: "There is a general impression in the army that Wolseley has had much more than his share of opportunities of distinction: & he has certainly been fully rewarded." If Roberts was passed over, then it would create an unfortunate impression while the government could not be "wholly insensible to the consideration that Roberts got less than his desserts five years ago, because he had had the misfortune to serve under Lord Beaconsfield."[43] Salisbury also generally approved Roberts's strategic insights, writing that "the scientific frontier doctrine, which was so much derided some years ago, is master of the field now."[44]

Roberts claimed he would never ask for an appointment.[45] Yet, he had a way of letting it be known he was a candidate almost by means of denying he would lobby for a post. Hardinge, bitterly disappointed by his own failure to gain the command, was scathing at Roberts's protestations that he had exerted no influence on his own behalf.[46]

Roberts was informed of his appointment on 13 October 1885.[47] As he later noted, neither he nor Stewart had been picked by Horse Guards but by the cabinet. Stewart had been picked by Hartington on the advice of Ripon, and Roberts by Lord Randolph Churchill after consulting W. H. Smith and Salisbury. Had Horse Guards had its way, Roberts surmised, it would have been Charles Ellice rather than Stewart, and Hardinge rather than himself.[48]

In normal circumstances, Roberts would have stepped down as CinC in India in 1890 at the same time Wolseley was due to vacate as AG at home. Roberts was anxious to succeed Wolseley, and the post was offered him by Stanhope in December 1889, with Wolseley being offered India. Roberts accepted on 3 January 1890.[49] Cambridge thought this absurd since Wolseley "knew nothing of the Indian Army & Sir F. Roberts less of the English Army."[50] Roberts thought Wolseley's "object is to die a Duke and he would sacrifice India in order to obtain it."[51]

Wolseley, however, was no longer interested in India since he judged there was no "great stirring reason" to go there despite the government stressing the illness of the emir of Afghanistan and Persia's uncertain political future.[52] In any case, his daughter was "coming out" as a debutante that season, the prospect of a war with Russia he judged as the "wildest of dreams," and he was anxious to be on hand to succeed Cambridge, now seventy-two.[53] As Wolseley had also written back in 1885, Loo "loathes even London society, but that of India would I am sure drive her mad."[54]

Wolseley correctly recognized he was being urged to accept India to save the government's face over the queen's pushing for Connaught as Roberts's successor. Stanhope most certainly saw Roberts's appointment to the WO as a means of deflecting criticism from the government's failure to effect the Hartington Commission recommendations to abolish the post of CinC at home and replace it with a CoS in face of determined opposition from Cambridge and the queen.[55]

Wolseley's declining of the India post presented a major problem with no other obvious candidate. Stanhope briefly considered sending Archibald Alison, now aged sixty-four, for a three-year term and even reconsidered Connaught.[56] George Chesney offered himself as a candidate if Roberts did not continue, but he was not taken seriously.[57] On the flimsiest of evidence, meanwhile, Martin Dillon was suggesting to Cambridge that Roberts really wanted to stay in India.[58]

On 21 May 1890 Roberts was informed that the offer of AG was withdrawn due to the claim being advanced for Connaught and the complications arising from the Hartington recommendations. Roberts said he would be prepared to stay in India.[59] Writing confidentially to Roberts, Stanhope said the problem was that "the urgent wish of certain august persons to advance the claims of the Duke of Connaught and the great difficulties which have arisen in consequence of this and of the recommendations of Lord Hartington's Commission, have led at last to this result as the only means which presents itself of extricating ourselves from them."[60] Roberts was far from impressed at the outcome and disappointed the government had reneged on its offer.[61] Roberts would have preferred five years as AG to two more in India given the potential lack of alternative employment in two years' time.[62] Subsequently, he was relieved that he had stayed in India: "I thank my stars that I did not go, and I hope now I shall remain here until the struggle with Russia comes off. That is what I have been preparing for all these years, and I have no wish to let any one step into my shoes just at present.[63]

While Connaught was still under consideration, it was tacitly agreed between Roberts and the viceroy, Lansdowne, that if there was a major war, Roberts would return to India.[64] In accepting prolongation, Roberts also demanded the ability to resign after a year if his health or urgent private affairs dictated, and promotion to substantive general.[65] Unaware of Wolseley's reservations on accepting India, Roberts believed Wolseley "cooked his own goose" by declining the post and hoped his own "star may be in the ascendant."[66] With Roberts's reluctant acceptance of a further two years in India, Buller succeeded Wolseley as AG and Connaught succeeded Buller as QMG. Wolseley took the Irish command.

The CinC was by law not allowed to leave India during his tenure. When the secretary of state for India, Cross, failed to get new enabling legislation through the Commons in 1892, Roberts said he would resign in January 1893 rather than contemplate another extension.[67] Consequently, the problem of finding a successor emerged again. In 1890 considerations of Indian strategy were less significant than domestic political factors. In 1892, by contrast, there was the question for Roberts at least of securing the succession of someone who shared his strategic views and would continue his policies.

There were a number of potential candidates who were unacceptable to Roberts. Greaves, GOC in Bombay, was an associate of Wolseley. As well as possessing a ferocious temper, his colorful private life ruled him out on "social grounds" alone.[68] Back in 1890 Greaves had also been implicated in a curious episode in which some alleged he was responsible for the death of a *syce* (groom), who Greaves insisted had died of pneumonia rather than as the result of an altercation with him.[69] Greaves had secured Bombay partly through seniority as he stood seventh in the list of major generals and, ironically for an adherent of Wolseley, laid his claim to the chief command on this basis.[70] White, who discounted his own prospects, thought Greaves would do well "but he is very free with his tongue and generally has one or two women in tow."[71] White expected Connaught might get the appointment, at which prospect he was content, believing it was likely he would be asked to succeed Chesney as military member.[72] Greaves was clearly disappointed not to succeed. He resigned but was required to stay on until Roberts left India.[73]

Evelyn Wood, commanding at Aldershot, was certainly a candidate. Indeed, when his own term was extended, Roberts anticipated that Wood would succeed him although he thought Wood had too little knowledge of India.[74] Stanhope specifically mentioned Wood's achievements at Aldershot as commanding respect but cautioned, "It is a pie in which unfortunately several persons have a finger, & the choice is not therefore more easy to make."[75] Wood's wife had now died, but he was almost totally deaf. While acknowledged as being a good trainer of troops, he had not served in India since the Mutiny. In addition, there was the lingering issue of the armistice he had negotiated with the Boers after Majuba.[76]

Brackenbury regarded Wood as suffering from "a certain diffuseness & want of concentration" but above all, "he is very quarrelsome & rude, jealousy being always the cause of his rudeness."[77] Wood lamented he did not know Lansdowne "but that not being the case I can only do my level best here [Aldershot], and thus perhaps may obtain a chance of my name being considered when Sir Frederick returns westward."[78] The queen supported Wood but, failing that, hoped Buller might accept.[79] Primarily, this was a means of freeing Aldershot for Connaught.[80] Writing to Wood, Ponsonby said, in the end, Cambridge pressed so strongly for White, as did the Indian authorities, that the queen "had to consent though I may tell you she did her utmost to support your claims."[81]

Thomas Baker, whom Roberts would otherwise have recommended, was in poor health.[82] In 1891 Stewart had considered Baker as White's main rival, "but whether he will be alive & fit at that time who can say?"[83] Baker died in February 1893. Another potential candidate, James Dormer, commanding in Madras, was ruled out in spectacular fashion by being badly mauled by a tiger while out hunting in 1891; ignoring medical advice, he suffered a fatal heart attack as a result.[84] In any case, according to Brackenbury, Dormer had no special ability, lacked tact and judgment, and knew only Madras.[85] Alison was a candidate, for the most part, only in his own mind, although, as indicated earlier, Cambridge did suggest his name.

More realistic candidates were Brackenbury and Buller. There was deep suspicion of Brackenbury, it being widely held that while serving on the Hartington Commission, he had orchestrated the recommendation of a CoS as a means of securing the appointment for himself. Moreover, although having converted to some extent to Roberts's strategic vision, Brackenbury still had serious reservations concerning the number of reinforcements Roberts was demanding from Britain in the event of war. Brackenbury recognized, despite his seniority, that he was not especially known in India. He admitted he was an indifferent horseman and had been now seven years away from commanding troops. Although he felt he would be a better choice than Greaves or Wood, he backed White.[86]

Many, including Roberts, assumed Buller would secure the prize, since Buller's candidacy was being pushed by Cambridge and Campbell-Bannerman. The latter referred to "my Buller whom I back to keep his end up against them all."[87] Buller was offered the command but took a few days to consider it.[88] Like Wolseley, Buller declined the offer on the grounds it would mean too much hardship for his family—he had married his cousin's widow and thereby acquired a family of four young children in 1881, and his wife was not in the best of health. He knew nothing of India. Buller suggested Wood as a better candidate than himself, but in the end he supported White.[89] Buller actually thought Sir Robert Low the best candidate, but this was not realistic.[90]

Buller would only consider taking the Indian command in case of war.[91] Brownlow felt it a pity that Buller did not know India and feared he was so wealthy he might even give up the army altogether.[92] Cambridge and Campbell-Bannerman tried to get Buller to change his mind, but to no avail; Cambridge even offered to reduce the tenure to two years.[93]

Almost by default, therefore, the choice fell on George White despite Cambridge having regarded him as too junior, being only a fifty-seven-year-old major general. He was low on the list of major generals, and it would prove a case of perceived merit or suitability prevailing over seniority. As Brackenbury expressed it, White's appointment represented "another nail in the coffin of the Duke's theory that 'one man is as good as another,' and of selection by seniority."[94] Roberts blamed Cambridge for White's lack of seniority. While Greaves might do, "White is the right man, and I shall work all I know to get him appointed." He believed the Conservatives would never have appointed White had they stayed in office.[95] White himself thought Buller the best man to succeed Roberts, although he felt Buller might be difficult: "There are many ways of giving expression to differences of views but I very much doubt if Buller has the knack of doing it without giving offence."[96] Expecting he might get Madras, White was genuinely surprised to be offered the supreme command.[97]

What recommended White to the politicians was that he was judged "not mad with the idea of a Russian invasion as Roberts was."[98] The secretary of state for India, Kimberley, needed to be assured that White did not "take his politics from Roberts."[99] White was indeed more cautious than Roberts: he had first expressed reservations about the forward policy as early as 1879.[100]

There was still the issue of what to do with Roberts once he ceased to be CinC in March 1893. Roberts was still mentioning the post of AG and found it incomprehensible that Cambridge claimed not to know it had been offered him in 1890.[101] Believing Gibraltar and Malta would be too expensive, Roberts suggested Aldershot "until something better turned up," but Cambridge felt the command unworthy of a former CinC.[102]

Insofar as Cambridge was concerned, the only suitable post was Malta, which would fall vacant in November 1892, but the tenure of Henry Smyth could be extended to give Roberts some home leave before he took it. Roberts was given no alternative. He was informed that "in the event of your not accepting he [Cambridge] is afraid that it may be a considerable time before any other appt. worthy of you will become vacant."[103] Nicholson suggested to Roberts that Cambridge was "perturbed in spirit at the marks of your popularity in India, especially with the Army in that country, and is desirous of getting you out of England as soon as may be," hence the offer of Malta.[104]

Roberts remained unemployed for three years until offered the Irish command in 1895. Cambridge's retirement momentarily seemed to offer the opportunity of Roberts going to the WO, but, while he would have liked him at home, Lansdowne, now secretary of state, was compelled to stand by the arrangement made by Campbell-Bannerman.[105] In July 1897 Roberts and Lansdowne discussed the possibility of Roberts moving from Ireland, but he felt the only post suitable would be Aldershot and that would have to be made a command for a full general to entice him to leave Dublin.[106]

Meanwhile, as Roberts's successor in India, White felt the burden of the challenges facing him—not least the rising costs at a time when the rupee was falling in value, and a legacy of promised military reforms he viewed as misjudged.[107] He also soon faced the greatest challenge on the frontier for some time in the great tribal uprising of 1897–98, an event apparently prompted by Ottoman rather than Russian machinations with some possible involvement on the part of the Afghan emir, Abdur Rahman.[108]

As White's retirement from India came closer, William Lockhart seemed the obvious choice as his successor. According to White, a British officer, it was also the Indian army's turn.[109] White had not been as strong an advocate of the forward policy as Roberts, and there was not quite the same strategic controversy as in the past. Lockhart's lack of strategic vision was not a drawback.[110] He was upset by press speculation that Charles Mansfield Clarke might be preferred, which White felt would result in considerable resentment within the Indian army. He also warned that Brackenbury might be a candidate, though the latter suggested it should be Lockhart.[111] Buller was an outside possibility, but the secretary of state for India, Lord George Hamilton, believed he was "just the man by some sort of folly to incite the native army out of sheer perversity."[112]

As the only serious candidate, Lockhart was backed by Lansdowne in view of his record, his frontier experience, and his knowledge of the native languages. Wolseley was away from the WO due to an illness, but Roberts and Salisbury fully supported the appointment. The queen formally approved the selection on 30 September 1897.[113] As he was in poor health, Lockhart went home for what was intended as an eight months' furlough in February 1897 in order to visit the spa at Bad Nauheim. White himself was to be QMG as Wood was to step up to AG, while Buller replaced Connaught at Aldershot.

Lockhart was sensitive to criticism and disturbed by rumors about his health, believing Baker Russell had put it about that he had cancer to try to assist Brackenbury to become CinC.[114] It was also suggested Lockhart had been under the influence of quinine during the Tirah campaign.[115] Ominously, Lockhart was allowed to vary the usual arrangements for personal staff by taking two ADCs and a personal physician to India instead of three ADCs.[116] He took over formal command in India in November 1898.

Lockhart had little time to make his mark, as he fell ill in February 1900. He took a short sea voyage to try to recover. He discussed resignation with the viceroy on 16 March, but Curzon decided he should not resign for the present. Lockhart was to take a ship home on 21 March to aid his recovery, but he died on 18 March. It is difficult to assess how successful Lockhart might have proven as CinC had he enjoyed a complete term and full fitness. One pressing problem since the establishment of the corps scheme in 1895 had been the tension from the increased centralization inherent in the abolition of the presidency armies. The responsibilities and power of the Military Department grew, with the military member emerging as something of a rival to the CinC. Nairne had been aware of it but had felt powerless to act in the short period of his interim tenure prior to Lockhart's arrival. In any case, Nairne felt he had been kept deliberately in the dark by the military member Edward Collen.[117] White had warned Lockhart of the need to act. Bored by administration and increasingly ill, Lockhart did not have sufficient time to respond.[118]

The problem was one of long standing. As explained earlier, while invariably junior in rank to the CinC, the military member was an ordinary member of the Viceroy's Council where the CinC was an "extraordinary" member. Military Headquarters was always at Simla, but the Military Department moved with the viceroy between Simla and Calcutta. Roberts had not wanted George Chesney to become military member in 1886 because he was an old hand in the department, especially as the viceroy, Dufferin, hesitated to oppose departmental recommendations unless backed by his full council.[119] Roberts also objected to orders for the Burma campaign being issued by the Military Department prior to his appointment as CinC. It was not until he arrived at Mandalay after Herbert Macpherson's death that he was able to ensure complete control.[120] As CinC in Bombay in 1890, Greaves likewise suggested to Cambridge that Chesney's influence over the viceroy was too great.[121]

Collen, who became military member in 1895, was regarded by Curzon as "an obsolete old footler, the concentrated quintessence of a quarter of a century of departmental life" and "mentally composed of Indian rubber."[122] As AG from 1901 to 1903, Smith-Dorrien came close to resigning as a result of what he saw as interference from the Military Department and Curzon.[123] Ironically, Curzon's opposition to the abolition of the post of military member led to his celebrated clash with Kitchener and his own resignation in November 1905. It was a struggle in which Kitchener showed himself just as politically astute as Wolseley or Roberts in utilizing all manner of political and press contacts.[124]

Originally nominated to officiate during Lockhart's illness, Arthur Power "Long P" Palmer was never fully confirmed as his successor and continued to officiate temporarily for another three and a half years.[125] There was an early proposal to send Kitchener to India despite his lack of knowledge of the country, but he was needed in South Africa.[126] Kitchener had expressed his interest in India to Curzon back in December 1898.[127] Roberts felt it would be "rather dangerous to send one who so long has had all his own way." Consequently, he suggested Kitchener should first get a corps in India and serve as military member before becoming CinC. He recommended Bindon Blood as Lockhart's successor.[128] Roberts did not see Palmer as a suitable CinC.[129] Kitchener was not interested in going to the WO as Brodrick, the new secretary of state, wanted, believing he was unsuited for a post there.[130]

Arthur Bigge thought Kitchener's appointment to India might be detrimental to British rule as he was "not perhaps gifted with those special characteristics so essential in dealing with the Native Army."[131] Lansdowne also considered that Kitchener would be too "hard and rough" in his methods for India, and he ruled out either Wood or Brackenbury. Blood struck him as too junior, but he believed Mansfield Clarke would be a safe pair of hands, as would Grenfell.[132] Roberts agreed Grenfell was safe but felt he lacked Indian experience. He suggested that Kitchener take the Punjab command with Palmer being moved to the Council of India, given that Donald Stewart was dying.[133] Salisbury was inclined to favor Kitchener for the Punjab as it would be "nervous work" making him CinC, and suggested Buller could be moved to India.[134] Roberts then concluded Kitchener would be the best candidate after all.[135] Brodrick thought Kitchener's lack of languages a drawback but was prepared to accommodate his wishes. Brodrick felt it would be difficult to dislodge Palmer, and, in any case, Kitchener was still needed in South Africa. Accordingly, Palmer would complete Lockhart's term of office, and Kitchener could then succeed to India after a well-earned rest.[136]

Consideration of the appointment of new CinCs in India after 1880 demonstrates that attitudes toward the "forward policy" had a bearing on those selected. Stewart's preferment in 1880 satisfied a Liberal government anxious not to be dragged into a long-term occupation of Kandahar. Ironically, at the same time, Wolseley's failure to secure the appointment prevented a far more thorough reform of the Indian army and its strategic plans. The choice of Roberts in 1885 signaled the new Conservative government's broad acceptance of a modified forward policy. In 1890 political expediency determined the extension of Roberts's command, albeit only after Wolseley had declined the post, due in part to his increasing belief that war with Russia was increasingly unlikely. In 1892 another Wolseley adherent, Buller, also declined the appointment, and the Liberals took some comfort in the fact that White was perceived to be less extreme in his views than Roberts. So, too, was Lockhart. Lockhart's premature death led to a hiatus before Kitchener arrived in 1902. At that point, military reform took precedence over frontier policy even if Kitchener emulated Roberts in ever more extravagant demands for reinforcements from Britain in the event of war.

Cambridge's Retirement

It was not lost on Wolseley that, following the introduction of compulsory retirement for general officers, Cambridge still clung on. As Wolseley wrote to Maurice in June 1894, "I think we ought now to begin to get public opinion to insist on a certain old Gentleman's retirement, for it is a positive scandal his remaining on at the age of 75 when men ten years (about) younger are ruthlessly retired every year."[137] Back in 1890, Wolseley had suggested to Ponsonby that one means of saving the CinC's post would be to persuade Cambridge to resign and at once appoint Connaught.[138]

Cambridge's opposition to the recommendations of the Hartington Commission was increasingly held against him, and press criticism mounted in the spring of 1895. Both the queen and the Prince of Wales felt Cambridge's position untenable given the determination of the prime minister, Rosebery, and Campbell-Bannerman to effect a change.[139] The queen told Cambridge he must go on 19 May 1895.[140] Having held out initially to remain in post until 1896 and thus complete forty years in his office, Cambridge prevaricated over the exact date of his departure.[141] Ironically, he voiced resentment at a "court intrigue" against him.[142] The general assumption was that if the Conservatives came into government, they might enact the Hartington recommendations in full, whereas the Liberals were prepared to compromise on the CinC's powers.[143]

As Campbell-Bannerman's earlier preference for Buller to succeed Roberts in India suggests, he was not enamored of Roberts. Campbell-Bannerman characterized Roberts as "an arrant jobber, and intriguer, and self-advertiser and altogether wrong in his political opinions, both British and 'Indian.'"[144] Roberts certainly suspected Campbell-Bannerman of pressing Malta on him as a means of getting him out of the way; Buller had supposedly spoken of Roberts's "wickedness" in declining the post.[145] According to Roberts himself, he was embarrassed by Nicholson's apparent efforts to work up parliamentary interest in his future: "I have never had occasion to ask for an appointment, and I would not for the world do anything myself, or ask my friends to do anything to help me in the future."[146] Destined to succeed Wolseley in Ireland, Roberts tried to avoid the post, but, as already indicated, Lansdowne insisted he must go to Dublin as previously arranged.

According to Nicholson, Wood and Buller were not keen to see Wolseley "restored to power," with Buller hoping to persuade Campbell-Bannerman to extend his own tenure as AG until April 1895. By doing so, Nicholson reasoned, Wood would succeed Buller, and Wolseley would have to retire unemployed since Connaught would succeed Cambridge. It might be argued that it would be infra dig for a former CinC in India to become AG and for Roberts thus to be sent to succeed Wolseley in Ireland. Buller would thereby have effectively shelved Roberts as well as Wolseley.[147] Nicholson took some comfort in supposing that Buller "is not as all-powerful as people fancy, and that his obstinacy and dictatorial behaviour are not altogether acceptable to the authorities."[148]

The cabinet recommended Buller's appointment to the queen on 9 May 1895. She formally approved it on 16 June. It was by no means certain the Conservatives would guarantee Buller's appointment.[149] Thus, a stop was put on any early announcement of his appointment on 20 June.[150] The government then fell in the "cordite vote" on 21 June immediately after the announcement of Cambridge's departure. This surprise vote to cut Campbell-Bannerman's salary by £100 due to the decline in cordite stocks was orchestrated by Brodrick, who sprang the trap immediately following the announcement of Cambridge's resignation when most MPs had left the House.[151] Salisbury knew Wolseley's faults but much preferred him to Buller, whom he mistrusted.[152] Bigge explained this to the queen by suggesting that, when in Ireland, Buller had been accused of "having Home Rule or at all events anti-landlord opinions."[153] Since the queen considered Wolseley imprudent, with a "clique of his own," she endeavored to persuade Salisbury that Buller was honest and "has held aloof from the Press which perhaps others have not."[154]

Buller insisted he believed Wolseley should be CinC. Buller told Lansdowne he "would have felt considerable personal difficulty in accepting" the post before Wolseley.[155] In view of future events in South Africa, Buller ominously reported to Campbell-Bannerman, "Personally I am always inclined to think myself a better second fiddle than a leader of thought."[156] Campbell-Bannerman recalled this in 1899 when Buller asked him for a copy of the letter he had written to the latter saying he did not wish to offend Wolseley. Wolseley had "got it into his head that I had plotted against him behind his back, and had tried to supplant him in what he held to be his birth right." Buller believed he had written this in 1897 rather than in 1895, as was actually the case; in any case, Campbell-Bannerman could not find a copy.[157]

Wolseley increasingly believed Buller had played him false. Buller lamented subsequently that Wolseley could never be convinced he had wanted Wolseley appointed. Thereafter, Wolseley ignored him "except when he wanted to get something said disagreeable to the S of S [Lansdowne] when he asked AG to do it."[158] Ultimately, Buller was disappointed that Wolseley "has either got office when he is no longer the man he was, or else he was never the man I thought him."[159]

Wolseley, who insisted he was not lobbying for the post, believed there was "some evil influence at work against me, that I shall yet get to the bottom of." Clearly with Buller in mind, he wrote, "I don't envy the feelings or confidence of the junior comrade who consents at this juncture to be put over my head. But then all men do not look at such points of honour in the old fashioned fashion that I have always felt for the few men who in my early life helped me up some of the difficult rungs of life's ladder."[160]

Several individuals were warning Wolseley about Buller's supposed ambition.[161] Wolseley himself felt Cambridge would support Buller simply as the latter was wealthy and had a wife of high social position. Others also thought the duke would generally want Buller.[162] Much later, Wolseley claimed the reason he wanted the post "was to keep Roberts out of it" as he feared he would "Indianise" the army.[163] Wolseley had another pressing reason—namely, that he would be compelled to retire five years earlier than might otherwise be the case if he failed to be appointed. He felt the tension of the situation, saying, "I don't mind being executed, but being kept on the scaffold with the glint of the axe consistently blurring my power of seeing clearly around me, is a torture worse than that which Damocles underwent."[164]

Some felt Connaught was in the frame until a relatively late stage.[165] The queen hoped the change of government would revive Connaught's claims. The cabinet, however, would never have agreed to appoint Connaught.[166]

Wolseley also saw Roberts as a danger through his friendship with Lansdowne until it became clear he was going to Ireland.[167] Roberts did feel Lansdowne was well disposed toward him, but not the queen.[168] It then seemed that Buller had been extended as AG for a further two years, which gave Wolseley renewed hope until at last the post was confirmed in mid-August.[169]

Asked by Lansdowne for his assessment of the candidates in August 1895, Ardagh indicated that Connaught was not popular in the army, Buller had achieved little as AG, and as an "Indian," Roberts was not acceptable to the army in Britain. Brackenbury, he felt, had proved self-seeking and selfish although he would have been an admirable CoS. Wolseley, therefore, was the preferred choice.[170] Wolseley believed Ardagh had played kingmaker, writing, "I feel that I owe you much more than I care to put on a sheet of paper—for the fact that I am to have a term of office of any sort again."[171]

Believing there was strong pressure for Connaught to succeed Cambridge, Wolseley was prepared to consider the German ambassadorship from which Sir Edward Malet had just resigned or becoming viceroy, as he believed Elgin was about to resign. Lansdowne thought the rapid appointment of Wolseley as CinC with Buller at Aldershot and Connaught as AG would mollify the queen.[172] As previously indicated, the queen opposed Roberts primarily on account of Lady Roberts and demurred at Wolseley's appointment. The Prince of Wales, meanwhile, wanted Cambridge's tenure extended for another year.[173]

Elgin was not about to resign, but, in any case, Salisbury and Lansdowne thought India out of the question insofar as Wolseley was concerned. He could be offered Berlin, although they would support him as CinC.[174] The kaiser proved receptive to the idea of Wolseley in Berlin, a possibility at which the queen instantly grasped. Now firmly given the opportunity to be CinC, Wolseley turned down Berlin since he "would infinitely prefer to be head of the profession in which I have spent my life and with which I am as well acquainted." He accepted the offer on 8 August 1895.[175] The queen reluctantly agreed on 17 August.

Wolseley wanted to become CinC with undiminished powers, his preference being for the AG to act as CoS to the CinC. Lansdowne informed him that there could be no such condition, which Wolseley grudgingly accepted.[176] Lansdowne thought only a direct command would deter Wolseley from becoming CinC and pressed the queen to agree to a five-year term.[177] The queen expressed displeasure at the post being "virtually offered to him without her sanction" and made it clear that Connaught "*must not be kept out of the CinC for long.*"[178] She agreed to a five-year term for Wolseley in the hope this would not prove to be the case. She also insisted that if a royal prince was appointed subsequently, it would be for an indefinite tenure.[179]

Consideration of Wolseley's successor began in 1897, since his term would expire in October 1900. For his own information, Lansdowne drew up notes on the likely candidates in October 1897. Roberts was a year older than Wolseley but, unlike Wolseley, in robust health. The sole argument against him two years earlier had been Wolseley's prior claim. At sixty-two, White would retire in 1902, the sixty-year-old Brackenbury in 1904, the fifty-nine-year-old Wood in 1905, and the fifty-eight-year-old Buller in 1906. At only forty-seven, Connaught would not retire until 1917. Lansdowne was conscious that Wolseley would press for Wood to succeed Buller as AG when Buller's tenure shortly expired, but Wood would not be acceptable to Roberts. Lansdowne believed it would serve Connaught best to be QMG then AG. White was not deemed a success in India and could be given the Malta command in October 1898 or Gibraltar in January 1899, while Brackenbury could fill in as QMG or at Malta or Gibraltar. Buller had been twelve years in the WO and wanted Aldershot, which would be preferable to giving it to White. A few other possible candidates for QMG included Grenfell, Lord William Seymour, and Methuen, but only Grenfell struck Lansdowne as equal to the post, and he was still needed in Egypt. Lansdowne's appreciation was bolstered by Wolseley's observation that those objections that had been put forward with regard to Connaught becoming CinC in India applied equally to his being CinC at home. Lansdowne's solution was Roberts for CinC, Wood as AG, Connaught as QMG, Buller at Aldershot, and White at Malta or Gibraltar.[180]

Roberts, of course, was recalled from Ireland to supersede Buller in the South African command in December 1899. With Roberts still due to replace Wolseley, Lansdowne suggested that those appointed to the WO should be trusted by Roberts and by the public. He toyed with the idea of Kitchener becoming QMG and succeeding Wood as AG. Coleridge Grove did not wish to remain as MS once Wolseley retired. Wood's deafness remained a problem; in Lansdowne's view he was also "bitterly hated and crimes are imputed to him which he does not commit." Both Ardagh and Brackenbury had done a good job, but Nicholson could be either QMG or DMI.[181] Roberts at once proposed Hamilton as MS.[182] With the war in South Africa supposedly over, Roberts arrived home in January 1901 to succeed Wolseley. According to Guy Fleetwood-Wilson, the assistant undersecretary of state, Roberts entered the WO in the belief he had been called on by Providence to cleanse a particularly foul Augean stable.[183] His triumph proved short lived.

CHAPTER 6

THE SECOND AFGHAN WAR, 1878–1881

With the annexation of the Punjab in 1849, British India extended beyond the "natural" frontier of the Indus to the generally mountainous tribal territories separating the extent of British administration from Afghanistan. A line of more than seven hundred miles of indistinctly defined jurisdiction, the North-West Frontier was inhabited by a variety of fiercely independent tribes. Wider strategic concerns were raised by the belief that Afghanistan increasingly represented a buffer zone between British India and advancing Russian influence in Central Asia. Of course, the British had none too successfully intervened in Afghanistan between 1839 and 1842 in an attempt to reduce perceived Russian influence at Kabul.

The Russian threat reemerged with the refocusing of Russian ambitions toward the repudiation of the Crimean War settlement in the Near East as well as expansion in Central Asia. The opening of the Suez Canal in 1869 increased British defense liabilities, though Britain had no Mediterranean naval base farther east than Malta. As indicated previously, there was a steady Russian advance through the 1860s and 1870s with the taking of Tashkent in 1865, Samarkand in 1868, and Khiva in 1873. The rate of advance would be even more marked between 1880 and 1884: the annexation of Merv in the latter year brought the Russians to less than two hundred miles from Herat.[1] There was also an intimate connectivity between events in the Near East and on India's frontiers as demonstrated during the Russo-Turkish War of 1877–78. Cyprus was occupied by agreement with the Ottoman authorities by an Indian expeditionary force, and Wolseley became the island's first high commissioner.[2]

A policy of "masterly inactivity" had been followed on the North-West Frontier since the 1860s. This approach was favored by the Liberals and the so-called Lawrence school, named for Sir John Lawrence, who had initiated the policy as viceroy. Advocates included Northbrook, who became viceroy in 1872, and Sir Henry Norman, now military member on the Council of India. Masterly inactivity did not mean doing nothing but "consisted of a refusal to accept specific commitments to defend or interfere in the affairs of countries outside India, coupled with a belief that Indian security was nevertheless best secured by building up the independence and stability of those countries along the Indian border such as Afghanistan."[3]

Afghanistan, 1878–1880. Map by Erin Greb Cartography.

Insofar as Disraeli's incoming Conservative government in 1874 was concerned, however, the Russian arrival at Khiva necessitated adopting a more active "forward policy" to gain a "scientific frontier." That policy had also been increasingly advocated through the 1860s by men such as Sir Henry Rawlinson, a member of the Council of India from 1858 to 1859 and again from 1868 to 1893, and Sir Bartle Frere, a member of the Viceroy's Council from 1859 to 1862 and Bombay's governor from 1862 to 1867.[4]

Northbrook's refusal to press for a British envoy to be installed at Kabul cost him his viceregal billet. A convinced member of the "forward school," Lytton replaced Northbrook in February 1876. Initially, Lytton and Salisbury had an idea of confronting the Russians in Central Asia, but the logistic difficulties rendered it impossible. For two years, Lytton endeavored to cajole the emir of Afghanistan, Sher Ali, into accepting a British resident envoy. Caught between Russian and British diplomatic pressure, Sher Ali prevaricated until his reluctant acceptance of a Russian mission in August 1878 precipitated a British ultimatum. According to most historians, Lytton exceeded the wishes of Disraeli's government in peremptorily forcing the issue by demanding Sher Ali exclude the Russians and accept a British mission. Actually the decision to intervene in Afghanistan was not taken without due consideration in London. The letter to the queen conveying the arguments rehearsed within the cabinet covered sixteen pages.[5] When the emir declined to reply to the ultimatum sent him in October, hostilities began on 21 November 1878. Nonetheless, Lytton had forced the issue as Bartle Frere and Chelmsford were to do in South Africa, prompting Disraeli, now Earl of Beaconsfield, to comment, "When V-roys and Comms-in-Chief disobey orders, they ought to be sure of success in their mutiny."[6]

The First Phase

While other potential Russian routes to India across the Hindu Kush were to come under discussion by British defense planners in later years, in 1878 two traditional invasion routes utilized since antiquity were regarded as critical. The first was through Kabul and the Khyber Pass to Peshawar and the Punjab; the second went from Herat to Kandahar, and through the Bolan Pass into Sind. Routes from the Caspian, Merv, and Khiva all met at Herat, some five hundred miles north of Quetta, which the British had permanently occupied in November 1876. The occupation of Quetta beyond the key Bolan Pass, following a treaty formally signed with the khan of Kalat in December 1876, marked this distinct change in policy.[7]

Many advocates of the "forward school" regarded the route through Merv as the most likely Russian route for Herat, 220 miles distant, would be the only viable base from which they could then attack India. If the British were to reach Merv before the Russians, then, in turn, Kandahar, 150 miles north of Quetta and 350 miles short of Herat, was the obvious base.[8]

Lytton, however, was arguably most influenced by George Colley, successively his MS and PS, who saw the route through Peshawar and Kabul toward Balkh and Tashkent as the best line of operations in any war against Russia, since Tashkent represented the real seat of Russian power in Central Asia.[9] In Colley's view, Kabul should be the pivot of offensive operations: all of Russia's Central Asian possessions would be vulnerable from it.[10]

Colley had been Lytton's third choice for MS; the services of Col. Frederick Wellesley as military attaché in St. Petersburg were considered too valuable to spare him, while Lytton's cousin, Col. Edward Bulwer, declined the post. Lytton thought Colley was free of "any theory" and not "biased by any tradition, on the subject of military organisation" in India.[11] As Neville Chamberlain noted in November 1878, Colley was always present at conferences, "but sits away and says nothing. I feel all the time that he has given the Viceroy the key to the discourse, and is his real military mentor, and one cannot help admiring his reticence and apparent indifference to all that is said, and his being content to be a nobody."[12] Roberts, appointed acting QMG in 1874 but only a substantive colonel, appreciated the significance of Tashkent, but he believed Herat easier to reach. A force assembled at Quetta could be in Kandahar in less than a month, and at Herat in less than three.[13] On his voyage to India, Lytton had apparently been impressed by a paper Roberts had drafted for Napier advocating a forward defense of India along the Hindu Kush.[14]

According to the future historian of the Second Afghan War Henry Hanna, Roberts was more influential than either Colley or the exotic figure of Maj. Pierre Louis Napoleon Cavagnari in swaying Lytton.[15] Certainly, after Wolseley turned down the appointment of chief commissioner of the frontier provinces of the Punjab and Sind, Roberts accepted; but he first took up the command of the PFF at Lytton's request in March 1878. Roberts was called to Simla for discussions in May and was in close touch with Lytton throughout August 1878. Moreover, Roberts was appointed to the Kurram Field Force in September at Lytton's insistence.[16]

Lytton wished to avoid an occupation of Afghanistan, in order to prove that India could sustain operations without recourse to reinforcements from home, and demonstrate to St. Petersburg that no threat against India would draw British forces out of Europe. There would be an occupation of the Kurram and an advance into the Khyber, a further force placed at Quetta in order to threaten Kandahar, and attempts to detach frontier tribes from the emir. The strategy would pressure Sher Ali to come to terms, accepting an envoy at Kabul and a permanent mission at Herat.[17] The CinC, Haines, wanted to respond to demands from the Madras and Bombay armies for employment by creating a large reserve. With winter approaching, Lytton declined to authorize any such reserve. The unimaginative Haines never quite grasped Lytton's limited intention of simply putting pressure on Sher Ali.[18]

Colley was to describe one conference as five hours of "dull, stolid obstinacy such as I think I never witnessed before" as Haines continued to argue for wider operations.[19] Colley and Cavagnari (now Sir Louis), deputy commissioner at Peshawar, had the intellect and charm to appeal to Lytton in ways well beyond the capability of uninspiring men such as Haines, which only added to the poisonous state of affairs. As deputy commissioner, Cavagnari had personal control of a force drawn from the Corps of Guides and the First Sikhs with, according to Haines, "no allegiance to the officer commanding the troops [at Peshawar], for the political officer seems to have a power of initiative absolutely independent of him."[20] In October 1878 Cavagnari exercised that initiative by conceiving a plan to seize the key to the Khyber, the fortress of Ali Masjid, in advance of the main intervention.

Haines believed such a coup de main "ought not to be undertaken without due deliberation and ample preparation for all its liabilities and consequences."[21] Haines was led to expect the plan had the backing of both Roberts and John Ross, commanding at Peshawar. Roberts was ambivalent, while Ross queried orders appearing to derive from the civil rather than the military authorities. Confusion now reigned, and the attack was cancelled on 8 October. Lytton believed that Haines's objections had been motivated by jealousy of Cavagnari, and his claims that he had not been sufficiently consulted were encouraged by the AG, Lumsden, whose own motivation was resentment at Roberts's preferment for the field command in the Kurram.[22]

In the heated strategic debate that followed through October 1878, it was agreed to establish the Peshawar Valley Field Force as a major formation in its own right rather than as a subsidiary to the operations of the Kurram and the Southern Afghanistan Field Forces. Lytton insisted that Ross's lack of vigor over the Ali Masjid affair and his evident want of what Lytton termed political capacity disqualified him from command.[23] Likewise, Lytton had little faith in the military member, Sam Browne VC, as an adviser. Browne had only become military member in July 1878 when Edwin Johnson suffered a stroke. The creation of the Peshawar force enabled Lytton to get rid of Browne into the field and replace him as military member with Chamberlain.[24] The latter enjoyed poor health after a bout of cholera and recurring fever, but this had the advantage for Lytton of encouraging what Colley described as Chamberlain's "wonderfully gentle and almost deferential manner."[25]

Subsequently, Lytton refused to countenance a divisional command for Browne at the end of the first phase of the war. Even Haines, who believed that to a "certain extent military reputations are being whispered away by means of irresponsible voices," acknowledged that Browne lacked the "far reaching, firm independent grasp of command which a General in Supreme Command ought to have."[26] Charles Gough, whose brigade was attached to Browne's division, found him dilatory: "*Nothing* is well managed here, there is *no* energy no enterprise. 'Sam Browne' is a failure he has no go."[27] Upon Lytton's suggestion that Browne should have been court-martialed for his failures, Beaconsfield mused that he and others Lytton was criticizing "are the men whom, only a few weeks ago, he recommended for all these distinctions. I begin to think he ought to be tried by a court martial himself."[28]

The Cavagnari episode revealed considerable confusion in what Lumsden referred to as "military responsibilities."[29] Haines had seen no action since the Crimea and had been on the staff in Calcutta throughout the Mutiny. To Lytton, he was a "second-rate ordinary military man," and "a weak, well-meaning, but thoroughly wrong-headed man, socially amiable, but intellectually obstinate, prejudiced and ignorant."[30] Naturally, Cambridge thought Haines "an excellent man & the more the Viceroy and he are in direct communication & understand one another the better for all parties concerned, & for the public interest and service."[31] As far as Roberts's ADC, Viscount Melgund, was concerned, Lytton was his own CinC and Haines had "very little to do with the management of the campaign." Any important change in operations would come from Government House and not Army Headquarters.[32]

Haines constantly tried to get to the front to direct operations personally once the war began. An officer was readied to intercept him and order him back to Simla in Lytton's name when he set out for the frontier in November 1878. Fortuitously, Haines unexpectedly returned to Simla and was laid low by fever for a month.[33] Haines was believed to be under the influence of an even more ambitious headquarters staff. Much of the suspicion centered on Lumsden, AG from 1874 to 1879. Indeed, Lytton concluded that Lumsden's influence over Haines was "decidedly obstructive."[34] This was particularly so once Roberts was appointed to command the PFF in March 1878. Haines had intended Lumsden as frontier commissioner and commander in the Kurram, but Lytton vetoed it.[35]

Lumsden was intensely jealous that his former friend, Roberts, should have secured both posts. It was said notably by Colley and Arthur Hardinge that Lumsden retaliated by doing his best to hamper Roberts by ensuring that his column lacked sufficient means of mobility.[36] George Pretyman remarked after Roberts's early successes in the Kurram, "Again the old jealousy of him at Head Quarters: not word or line of congratulation to him from either the Chief [Haines] or Lumsden."[37]

Not the most perceptive of men, Haines was totally mystified by Lumsden's reputation "as the most unpopular man who has held sway at Strawberry Hill," the location of the AG's office in Simla.[38] Having returned to England in early 1880, Lumsden was at pains to convince Cambridge that Haines had been under sustained attack from the "Wolseley school." So far as Lytton and Roberts were concerned, he said, there was "total mistrust in all quarters with regard to both of them," and their telegrams home were "believed to be manufactured to meet the desire of the Ministry."[39]

In March 1880 Haines again tried to take personal control of operations from Peshawar. Initially, Lytton appeared to agree to Haines having more "direct control." Alerted by a personal communication between Lumsden's successor as AG, George Greaves, and Lytton's PS, Brackenbury, on the problems this would create in communications between Haines and Simla, Lytton then argued that Haines could not take "personal command." Haines could not oversee both Donald Stewart and Roberts on top of his duties as CinC: his presence would "excite" the Afghans.[40]

While the choice of AG to succeed Lumsden rested with Haines and Lytton, Cambridge insisted it be a British officer. Rejecting Wolseley's suggestion of George Greaves and Haines's own preference for Col. Robert Stewart, whom Cambridge did not know, the duke recommended either Thomas Baker or Arthur Annesley.[41] Since his command of colloquial Hindustani was somewhat inadequate, Haines acknowledged his need of an AG able to convey his views "in terms more precise and accurate than I could use." Lumsden had spoken Hindustani, Pashto, and Persian, and, from Haines's perspective, Baker lacked local knowledge. At least Greaves had served in India previously.[42] Cambridge accepted the nomination of Greaves to correct the impression that Lumsden "has had a strong leaning towards his local Indian comrades."[43]

Greaves was soon angling to be designated CoS, not only should Haines take the field but also generally, thereby reinforcing his own status vis-à-vis the acting QMG, Charles Johnson. As Lytton told Roberts in March 1880, there was "a disposition at Head Quarters to restrict your authority & cripple your freedom of action but this disposition is intensified by a circumstance which I know you are well aware of, that the Head Quarters staff has never been friendly to you."[44] Lytton warned Roberts to be wary of some on his own staff, specifically Maj. John Brabazon, who was writing to Lytton critically of Roberts's conduct.

James Hills later identified Thomas Wilson as integral to a clique that also embraced Lumsden, Edwin and Allen Johnson, and Charles Brownlow. Edwin Johnson, he felt, had tried to get Roberts removed as QMG when he took command of the PFF so he could move in another of his brothers, Charles.[45] As it happened, Charles Johnson, like Edwin, was also in poor health.[46] Lytton did his best to block Charles Johnson, believing he lacked the "special practical ability, energy, and experience needed" and was "absolutely, notoriously, unfit for the appointment." He would have preferred MacGregor.[47] Cambridge did not know Charles Johnson and wanted Sir Michael Biddulph as acting QMG.[48]

Wolseley was equally suspicious of Edwin Johnson, describing him in January 1877 as "a man without talent but plenty of low sensibility to those in power and a good deal of cunning: he has made it pay well for he goes out now to be Military Member of the Council of India."[49] Another complication was Cambridge's support for both Edwin and Allen Johnson.[50] Lytton viewed Haines and Johnson as rivals in trying to influence Cambridge: "Their first and, as far as I can perceive, their sole, consideration in dealing with any military question is how to compete with each other in anticipating or carrying out the supposed wishes of His Royal Highness."[51] According to Lytton, Edwin Johnson was not physically fit enough to continue on the council following his stroke.[52] Johnson himself had not mentioned any health problems, and Allen Johnson believed his brother's health perfectly satisfactory. Cambridge suspected the hand of Wolseley and Colley, who was a "very clever fellow but to my mind *too clever by half.*"[53] Edwin Johnson was nominated for the Madras command in June 1879, at which point Lytton suggested that Stewart succeed as military member rather than Lumsden, as it would be "practically impossible for him and me to act together as colleagues with any comfort to each other or advantage to the state."[54] Johnson's stroke ended any chance he would get Madras.

Cambridge would have liked to put Allen Johnson into the Madras command instead of his brother, but Allen Johnson felt he could not leave the council at such a time. General Sir James Fraser declined the command, so Cambridge then suggested Donald Stewart, who was acceptable to Lytton. While Stewart was on service in Afghanistan, the senior ranking officer in Madras, William Payn, would be a safe pair of temporary hands.[55] Some years later, Roberts suggested that Allen Johnson "meddles a great deal too much with what he knows nothing about."[56]

It must be acknowledged that Lytton himself interfered in appointments. It was suggested the Kurram Field Force was unnecessary and ordered by Lytton "not because it was required, but to give Roberts[,] an ardent partisan of his, an independent command."[57] Lytton also insisted on moving Frederick Appleyard from a brigade command in Browne's First Division to Frederick Maude's Second Division in December 1878, which transfer Appleyard regarded as being to the benefit of the Staff Corps, by which he presumably meant John Tytler, who replaced him. Appleyard complained to Horse Guards. Horsford indicated he could not intervene, but Haines was directed to ensure that British officers did not suffer. To Tytler's fury, Appleyard was duly returned to command in Browne's division in March 1879.[58] As indicated previously, Appleyard was then again removed by Lytton.

Lytton's unfavorable perception of Haines and Lumsden was undoubtedly fed by Colley and Hardinge. Haines's frequent description of Colley as "the finest theoretical soldier he had ever met" lends itself to more than one interpretation. Haines suggested that Colley's influence was accomplished so judiciously it was never apparent.[59] Haines strongly deprecated Colley being sent in a supposedly private capacity to consult commanders on the Punjab frontier on ways of dealing with incursions by the Jowaki Afridis back in September 1877, stating that "the intervention of an irresponsible officer between me and officers under my command is in my opinion a dangerous measure." Lytton decisively rejected confining Colley to "household accounts."[60]

As for Hardinge, his tenure at Meerut was coming to an end, and he was singularly unsuccessful in securing an active field command. He argued that Haines seemed as prejudiced as Lumsden against officers of the British establishment. In October 1878 Hardinge told the queen that Haines, "under influences, anxious to favour the Indian branch of the Army, has hardly given him the support he might have, as an old friend."[61] Seeing himself superseded by his juniors, Hardinge appealed. Suggesting he needed to balance commands between the British and Indian services, Haines argued that Hardinge was due to leave his command before the field forces were assembled.[62] Cambridge was satisfied with the distribution of commands and felt it "extremely bad taste" for Hardinge to complain when he knew his command tenure was at an end.[63] Subsequently, Cambridge warned Haines of the apparent bitterness abounding and of the contradictory rumors that he was being influenced over appointments either by Lytton and Colley or by Lumsden and Charles Johnson.[64] Haines believed the only malcontents were Frederick Maude and Hardinge, but Cambridge told him that complaints from British officers were "not confined to a few."[65] Cambridge also warned Haines that Lumsden was named "as having sufficient interest to put forward nothing but *local* officers."[66]

Hardinge specifically linked his case to that of Lt. Gen. Frederick Maude VC. Commanding at Rawalpindi, Maude was displaced from the Peshawar Field Force by Browne's appointment in November 1878. Maude had been repeatedly assured in unequivocal terms by the AQMG, Charles MacGregor, that he would have the command.[67] On 4 November, when MacGregor asked Charles Johnson if the orders had been sent off to Maude, he was told Browne had been appointed:

> You may imagine how utterly taken back I was. *I have seen your name actually in orders (proof print)* and I myself drafted the letter of instructions for the approval of the Chief [Haines]. I can't tell you how grieved I am at this. However I hope you will believe that it was only because it appeared so absolutely certain, not only to me but to every one who knew. . . . I cannot conceive what the reason of it is & who the moving power is who suggested it.[68]

Maude's command had been announced in *The Times*, so he was understandably concerned the "change will therefore do me a public injury, which I feel is undeserved." Haines simply telegraphed that there were "*strong political reasons*" for the change.[69]

It was left to MacGregor to explain that Lytton wanted Chamberlain to replace Browne as military member and that this was a convenient means of doing so. In addition, MacGregor detected "a strong prejudice" against Maude instigated by the AAG at headquarters, Lt. Col. Dawson Warren, who had previously served as AAG and acting commander at Rawalpindi before Maude was appointed. Browne had close allies at headquarters, and Lytton, who did not know Maude personally, simply wanted Browne out of the way.[70] Haines excused Maude's supersession by claiming Browne had special knowledge of the Khyber tribes, trusting Maude would be satisfied with the reserve division. He also wrote to Lady Maude regretting the change that had affected her husband but suggesting, "there will be plenty for every one to do before we see the end of this."[71]

Maude had no doubt there was deliberation in giving all three field commands to Indian generals in Browne, Roberts, and Stewart. As he noted in his account of the campaign, "I observe it is sometimes stated that officers of the Indian service are placed at a disadvantage as compared to officers of our Service that their promotion is slower, etc. Unfortunately for me my experience was the reverse." Stewart and Browne were not only younger than Maude but also junior to Maude as major generals. Nonetheless, they achieved the rank of lieutenant general a year before he did.[72] Additionally, Maude lacked the interest in, and the acumen to cultivate relationships with, Lytton and his coterie.[73]

Lytton was well aware of Haines's potential difficulties "in regards to the claims of the British officers" but that felt giving Maude a reserve division "an excellent way of mitigating difficulty."[74] Lytton justified the decision to Cambridge, saying that Maude, "whose assumption of the Khyber Command would, in ordinary circumstances, have been the simplest and most natural arrangement, is a smart energetic officer, in whose purely military capacity I should have felt complete confidence; but he has no frontier experience, he knows nothing of the tribes and territories concerned; he is very deaf and has the reputation of being very hot-tempered."[75] Lytton added that Michael Biddulph had command of the forces at Quetta and that he intended to ask Cambridge for a British officer to command a reserve division for Stewart's force. Lt. Gen. James Primrose from Bombay, a British officer, was given that command so that all three invading columns were led by Indian officers and all three supporting formations by British.

According to Charles Gough, Haines was also wedded to seniority. When a permanent brigade became vacant in July 1880, Gough anticipated that Haines would appoint Charles Palliser despite the latter's military incapacity. Gough consoled himself with the thought that the next vacant command would be that of the Hyderabad Contingent, which was in the viceroy's gift. Palliser got the Silkot Cavalry Brigade but Gough secured the Hyderabad Contingent.[76] Earlier, at the very start of the campaign, Gough complained of "a shocking job" when there was an attempt to maneuver a junior colonel, Francis Jenkins of the Guides, into a brigade. Both Appleyard and Tytler raised such objections that Jenkins had to be returned to regimental duty.[77]

Operations in Afghanistan soon demonstrated the need for field commanders to be capable of exercising political as well as military judgment. Roberts learned the hard way commanding the Kurram Field Force in the first phase of the war. Roberts was vested with full political as well as military powers, but showed little political sense. Roberts issued what was regarded as a highly premature proclamation in December 1878 suggesting British annexation of the Kurram, although he denied having done so.[78] Roberts was reported subsequently to have promised the tribes that Jalalabad and Kandahar would be returned to Afghan control but that the British would retain positions enabling them to intervene in Kabul at any time. Lytton was greatly embarrassed, writing to Roberts that it had placed the cabinet in London "in a very bad humour with me, at a time when it was very desirable that I should, if possible, possess their fullest confidence."[79] It also complicated the negotiations with Yakub Khan leading up to the agreement reached at Gandamak in May 1879. Lytton was forced to place his official disavowal on record.

The Second Phase

The first phase of operations ended with Sher Ali's flight to the Russians and the signing of a treaty at Gandamak on 26 May 1879 by his son, Yakub Khan. Under its terms, Cavagnari would head a mission at Kabul, but he and his escort were massacred in an attack on the residency on 3 September. Following Cavagnari's murder, a hasty meeting was convened at Simla on 5 September 1879 to draw up a plan of campaign. Roberts was appointed to command an advance on Kabul, with Stewart ordered to reoccupy Kandahar. Believing that some of those appointed to commands under him in the Kurram lacked sufficient experience, Roberts insisted that Macpherson and Baker were given his two infantry brigades. The appointment of Brig. Gen. Dunham "Redan" Massy to the cavalry brigade would prove to be less successful.[80] Roberts's next action in January 1880—the mishandling of the summary executions in Kabul of those suspected of complicity in the massacre—only served to reinforce the impression of "the stupidity he has shown in all non-military matters."[81]

Apart from the press criticism previously noted, parliamentary criticism surfaced with regard to the hanging at Kabul in October and November 1879 of (officially) eighty-seven Afghans supposedly implicated in the massacre of Cavagnari and his escort.[82] Although characterizing Roberts as a "cruel Bloodthirsty little brute," MacGregor followed the party line that no one had been executed without definite proof of guilt.[83] Forced to defend the executions, Roberts claimed they had brought stability, checked fanaticism, and halted further attacks on British troops. Martial law was not "terrorism, slaughter, and violence, within such limits as a soldier thinks convenient" but "a means of maintaining order and of preventing collisions between the troops and camp followers and the natives of the country."[84]

Writing to Cranbrook on 28 January 1880, Lytton conceded that Roberts's "management of the political situation has not been altogether as judicious as I had hoped it would be; and, unfortunately, the strongest men about him have hitherto been officers destitute of political or administrative training, and incompetent to give him good advice or assistance in any but military matters."[85] To Roberts's annoyance, Lepel Griffin, chief secretary to the Punjab government, was dispatched to Kabul to exercise political oversight as Roberts's adviser. Irked, Roberts insisted on full political powers when marching subsequently to the relief of Kandahar in August 1880, even threatening to give up his command as soon as he reached the city if he did not get them.[86] The new viceroy, Ripon, conceded the powers requested but ensured that Roberts understood his own views on the situation.[87] Roberts was equally disappointed when Stewart was ordered to Kabul from Kandahar in April 1880 and with political powers he had been denied.[88]

Roberts was not the only soldier with political aspirations; Stewart complained that Biddulph had "an insane desire to enter into political relations with somebody, and thinks I don't trust him properly, because I do not invest him with specific political powers."[89] Stewart had to keep reminding Biddulph that annexation was not the aim of the campaign. Stewart's political officer, Oliver St. John, also believed Biddulph to be an "impulsive gentleman" who courted disaster by splitting his command "into component atoms that know nothing of each other's whereabouts."[90]

Another factor of constant account was the pressure from the Madras and Bombay armies for employment in Afghanistan. Lt. Gen. Henry Warre, commanding at Bombay, complained at the prominence of Bengal officers in higher commands, although he recognized there was difficulty in attracting able men to Bombay, where they had to pass a more difficult language test that was not useful elsewhere.[91] The performance of the Bombay army then caused significant problems through its defeat at Maiwand on 27 July 1880 at the hands of Yakub Khan's brother, Ayub Khan, the former having been deposed when Roberts reached Kabul.

With Stewart's transfer to Kabul, Kandahar had been left in the command of Primrose. Rev. Alfred Cane, who had been at Maiwand, grew impatient with Primrose, finding him "indolent, vacillating & without a single idea beyond extreme caution."[92] From the start, Stewart also fancied Primrose "neither safe nor strong."[93] Haines had insisted on Primrose and Cambridge had thoroughly approved.[94] Warre recognized Primrose was regarded as headstrong but denied knowing of his poor health. Primrose had testified to his fitness although, according to Hills, he was reluctant to take the command.[95] In any case, Warre found that when he tried to counsel Primrose to be cautious, the latter replied he was acting directly under Haines's instructions.

Warre appealed to Haines to be allowed to command the Bombay troops himself but was told,

> I was not in any way to interfere with any troops beyond the Biloochistan [*sic*] Frontier. I was not to alter the numbers or organisation of the Force and there was no place for me and I could not be employed in any way with the Force (composed entirely of Bombay troops) but I was to be held responsible for the discipline! the transport!! and the supply of said force along a line of communication extending 300 miles from Sakker on the Scinde River to Kandahar.[96]

Not surprisingly, Warre felt he was not responsible for Brig. Gen. George Burrows being ordered out from Kandahar with just over twenty-four hundred troops to face thirty thousand Afghans. Primrose also acted under orders from Simla.[97] Based on the accounts of Maiwand reaching him from the first survivors to make it to Kandahar, Primrose's initial telegram—"annihilation" and "rout" were the terms used—took such a gloomy view of the situation that it spread alarm to Bombay. It reached London when sent by Primrose's AQMG, Maj. Frederick Adam, without Primrose's or Warre's knowledge.[98] Ripon believed Primrose must have lost his head.[99]

Burrows had been authorized to cross the Helmand but go no further.[100] Greaves strongly opposed any advance unless Primrose took his full force, although he did not put this in writing as he later claimed.[101] According to Ripon's MS, George White, Haines and Stewart advised an advance and Haines expressed himself satisfied with the strength of Burrows's force. Ripon wanted a much larger force sent but felt he could not impose his will as a civilian.[102] Warre believed Haines ultimately responsible for the defeat and was determined to defend the Bombay army.[103] Subsequently, Warre felt that while promotion to full general obliged him to quit the Bombay command in 1881, his removal had resulted "probably also by my free speaking at a Public Dinner to Lord Ripon when I called his attention to the absolute neglect with which the Bombay Army had been treated by the Govt. of India & the Cmr. in Chief who entirely ignored the very arduous work thrust upon it when Bengal found that its Army was not in a *fit* state or strong enough to maintain their columns with which it hoped to invade Afghanistan."[104]

With the return of the remnants of Burrows's force, Primrose had fewer than five thousand men to defend a large perimeter, defeat having thoroughly roused the surrounding countryside. Although the degree of real danger to Kandahar and of the decline in morale among Primrose's men has been exaggerated, a relief was clearly necessary.[105] In addition, a blow had to be struck against Ayub Khan. Relief and counterblow could be mounted from either Quetta or Kabul. Quetta was closer, and it was logical that relief should be entrusted to the commander there, Maj. Gen. Robert Phayre. However, that reckoned without Roberts, who was determined to reach Kandahar before Phayre and win what became known as the "race for the peerage."[106]

News of Maiwand reached Kabul on 28 July. Stewart was disinclined to weaken Kabul and send forces to Kandahar, unless it could not be more quickly relieved from Quetta.[107] Ripon insisted on a relief force from Kabul led by Roberts.[108] It had been agreed to begin withdrawing the British garrison from Kabul later that month, which meant withdrawal through the Khyber at the height of the hot season. Roberts strongly pressed for a force to be sent from Kabul on the grounds that Phayre had insufficient troops readily available, and that the Bombay army could not be trusted. Stewart was persuaded to give Roberts command since it was evident he himself would be required to oversee the delicate negotiations for the withdrawal from Kabul, for which Roberts had little aptitude. Roberts himself telegraphed to Greaves to urge acceptance of the idea.[109] Not only did Stewart yield command to Roberts; he also gave him the pick of the force available. Moreover, this time Roberts got the political powers he wanted.[110] Upon arriving at Kandahar, he would be senior to Primrose, Roberts's local rank of lieutenant general predating Primrose's by four months.

Charles Gough anticipated taking his brigade with Roberts, but "there was a lot of scheming to get MacGregor a Brigade and all sorts of arguments were used in his favor [*sic*], and he got it."[111] Gough expressed himself appalled by the "horrible favoritism that has been rampant throughout this business."[112] Subsequently, Gough wrote that Roberts was just the man to enjoy the praise when he went home accompanied by Ross, Hills, Baker, and Hugh Gough: "He has no doubt gathered his 'Generals' together to add distinction, however I hope they won't forget that there are others who have done hard and good service and yet are still kept toiling at the mill!!"[113]

Roberts took 10,148 fighting men, 8,143 followers, and 11,224 assorted baggage animals. The march over twenty-four days was not quite the epic portrayed.[114] Even Roberts wrote later that he was surprised by the reaction to his march when he felt his advance to Kabul after Cavagnari's murder had been more difficult.[115] The acerbic MacGregor was particularly critical of the pace, writing on 26 August, "The march of this force is that of a disorganised rabble. An Afghan, seeing it, said we were like an Afghan army whereas Stewart's was like a European."[116] MacGregor's allusion was to the march of Stewart from Kandahar to Kabul between 27 March and 2 May 1880, in which Stewart had taken a force of 7,294 fighting men, 7,273 followers, and 11,000 baggage animals over the same route in reverse in thirty-seven days but in face of stiff Afghan opposition. In comparing the two marches, many have contended that Stewart's was the more difficult, with greater praise being accorded to Roberts arising from the circumstances of the relief of Kandahar, the attendant press attention accorded it as a result, and the prominence given Afghan affairs in the British general election of April 1880.[117]

Just as MacGregor believed Roberts was taking risks to win the race against Phayre, so Ripon feared Phayre "may be very desirous of winning the race between himself & Sir F Roberts for the Kandahar prize."[118] Although Phayre's force had initially been seen as the main relief effort, Haines did not believe Phayre was particularly motivated by the idea of a race. Haines, though, was anxious to push Phayre on as Roberts would be dependent on the supplies Phayre brought into Kandahar.[119]

Phayre encountered severe transport problems, higher temperatures, and more tribal opposition than Roberts. A veteran Bombay officer, Phayre had been Napier's QMG in Abyssinia, and had won plaudits for his energy, enterprise, and organizational skills. But Phayre had been removed as political superintendent in Upper Sind in 1872 after quarrelling with the commissioner in Sind over their respective authority. Phayre was also removed as resident at Baroda in 1873 after an attempt to poison him.[120] He commanded the LOC between Jacobabad and Quetta during the first phase of the war, before being nominated as a Bombay representative on the Eden Commission. Phayre was regarded as a sound choice to defend the Bombay army against possible reduction, as he was "a strong man and has the ability and force of character to make himself heard."[121]

Phayre was considered for the Kandahar command after Stewart's departure for Kabul. Lytton had heard Phayre had a temper and had been unable to cultivate cordial relations with the political officers or the Afghans on the line. Thus, he felt he lacked sufficient tact and judgment for the command. Likewise, Stewart thought Phayre would "go off the rails" if given his head in Kandahar.[122]

News of Maiwand reached Phayre on the same day it reached Roberts, but his available troops were strung out and comprised only Indian units apart from a battery each of the Royal Artillery (RA) and Royal Horse Artillery (RHA).

Phayre soon concluded he could not hope to set out for Kabul for at least fifteen days. In fact, he was unable to leave Quetta until 21 August. Realizing Roberts was already almost at Kandahar, Phayre slowed his advance and reduced his force in order to compensate for the lack of supplies on his own route and in the vicinity of Kandahar. Ripon later praised Phayre's "admirable" self-denial in doing so.[123]

Phayre finally arrived at Kandahar on 6 September, by which time Roberts had dispersed Ayub Khan's army. Given the difficulties he faced, it is remarkable that Phayre got there as early as he did. Despite the exhaustion of his own force upon reaching Kandahar, Roberts believed Phayre's men would have been too spent to fight an action had they arrived first. By contrast, Warre felt that, had Roberts waited for Phayre, he would have gained an even more complete victory over Ayub Khan than was achieved on 1 September 1880.[124] Phayre may or may not have believed himself to be involved in a race with Roberts, but the latter most certainly did. Ironically, there was to be no peerage; Roberts received the GCB and a baronetcy.

Roberts's health was now extremely shaky; he may have been suffering from a duodenal ulcer. Within two days of Phayre's arrival, Roberts departed, following a medical board. He handed command to Phayre but did not believe he should exercise it in the longer term. Ripon shared the earlier view of Lytton that Phayre was not at his best dealing with political matters. In any case, doubts had now arisen about his organizational abilities as a result of the supply problems faced on his march into Kandahar. Although he had no personal knowledge of Phayre, Cambridge also doubted he was prudent or experienced enough to remain in command given he "had frequently been in hot water when employed politically."[125] Consequently, Cambridge favored John Ross for the billet.[126] Ripon suggested that Ross take temporary command but felt Biddulph should be sent to assume command as soon as possible. As Ross was due for home and, technically, no longer on the Indian establishment, Haines considered Maude. He, too, was at the end of his tenure. As a result, Haines suggested Maj. Gen. Robert Hume, a British officer recently recovered from sunstroke.[127] Hume's preferment caused more resentment in Bombay.[128] As CinC in succession to Haines, Stewart suggested the Bombay government and army was more interested in preserving what they deemed their rights than in placing the right man in command of their troops.[129]

Two Bombay officers, Col. John Malcolmson and Maj. Albert Currie, were put under arrest following Roberts's arrival at Kandahar for their alleged culpability in the Maiwand disaster. Primrose had allowed both to do continued duty despite Burrows's accusations against them. Malcolmson, indeed, had distinguished himself in such a way in a sortie that it created obvious complications given his perceived failings at Maiwand.[130] Haines hoped a court-martial would settle the matter, but Warre felt that the inquiry Haines held at Simla was sufficient.[131] Cambridge regretted that Warre had not gone for a court-martial and found the lack of action over Primrose incomprehensible.[132] Matters were not assisted by the uneasy relationship existing between Warre and Haines, and between Warre and Greaves.[133] Warre had also gone out of his way to lavish what most saw as injudicious public praise on the Bombay army in the wake of defeat.[134]

To be fair to Warre, he believed that conflicting evidence would not result in Malcolmson or Currie being found guilty by any court-martial. This proved to be the case.[135] In part, acquittal was due to Burrows and Brig. Gen. Thomas Nuttall foundering under cross-examination. Nuttall, who had commanded Burrows's cavalry brigade, was an infantryman but had previously commanded the largely cavalry-based Sind Frontier Force. He was such a strong horseman that Haines for one had assumed he was a cavalry officer, but he had spent much of his service in civil police appointments.[136] Stewart was not surprised at the courtroom performance of Nuttall, whom he viewed as "one of those puzzleheaded men who is incapable of making an intelligible and connected statement at any time," adding that "the breakdown under cross examination of a man of Genl. Burrows capacity and business experience is simply extraordinary."[137] While Malcolmson soon retired, Nuttall resumed command of the Sind Frontier Force. Burrows did reach the rank of lieutenant general but was not reemployed.

An ailing Primrose was removed from his command on 3 October 1880 on the grounds of "general incapacity for command," as well as being deprived of his Poona command and ordered to present himself to Cambridge in London.[138] Primrose's reputation had been damaged by his insisting on the ill-fated sortie from Kandahar in which Henry Brooke lost his life on 16 August 1880. Annie Brooke published her husband's journal, with critical comments on Primrose by a number of officers.[139] It was Brooke who organized a small force to bring in the survivors of Burrows's force and to render Kandahar more defensible. Neither Primrose nor Stewart before him had taken any particular precaution in the belief that a proper cantonment would be constructed in the event of permanent occupation.[140] Primrose argued that the sortie had restored the garrison's morale.[141]

Withdrawal

There was considerable debate as to whether Kandahar should be retained or not, but the new Liberal government resolved on withdrawal in November 1880. In the light of Cavagnari's death, Lytton conceived of a policy of "disintegration," separating Kandahar from Kabul and perhaps persuading Persia to take Herat. Kabul was evacuated as Roberts marched to Kandahar. Military opinion was divided with Haines, Cambridge, and Napier strongly for Kandahar's retention, in the belief that British prestige demanded it.[142] Cambridge despaired that, if all was given away, "the whole of the War will have been of no value to India & Imperial interests, & we shall have thrown away very large sums of money & many valuable lives."[143] Commercial advantages were also stressed by Conservative politicians. If a strategic railway was extended at least to Pishin, if not to Kandahar itself, it would open up the interior of Afghanistan to commerce. Not surprisingly, the queen fully supported retention on the grounds of prestige. She believed for the Liberals to give up Kandahar simply because it had been their policy while in opposition would be "most deplorable."[144]

Not all soldiers believed Kandahar should be retained. The military member, Thomas Wilson, initially favored retention but went over to the "other camp." Hills later suggested this was intended to win the favor of the new secretary of state for India, Hartington.[145] Of Wilson's change of mind, Roberts commented acidly that he assumed the government "requires to be served by men whose opinions are not quite so unchangeable as mine are."[146]

Nonetheless, for a man who was to become so intimately linked to the concept of the "scientific frontier," Roberts remained strangely muted during the Kandahar debate despite most of those associated with him, such as his ADC, Reginald Pole-Carew, claiming the Kandahar Relief Force was essentially Tory in outlook. Pole-Carew resented having been "shot at for the sake of a lot of ungenerous blackguards who have systematically been doing their best to throw dirt on us and to hold us up before the world as the perpetrators of horrible atrocities, not because they believed it for an instant but merely (ignoring our feelings in the subject) to suit their own paltry purposes."[147] Similarly, George White reported the election result "had called forth a good many d[amn]s from the soldiers here. I fancy Sir F R is about as much put out about it as anyone can be."[148]

At Cambridge's request, Roberts eschewed any mention of Kandahar in his major speech at the dinner in his honor at the Mansion House on 14 February 1881, concentrating instead on the issue of army reform.[149] It may be he thought it better to remain silent rather than imperil his future prospects given that the Liberals strongly disapproved of the executions put in train at Kabul. Even Napier, though effectively retired as governor of Gibraltar, felt it politic not to return to England to actually vote against Liberal policy in the House of Lords.[150] The Liberals also fell gleefully on Roberts's earlier remark—namely, that the less the Afghans saw of the British, the less they would dislike them.[151]

Stewart had never believed Kandahar to be of any value.[152] His known skepticism played no small part in securing his succession to Haines. If Kandahar could be abandoned without "discredit," he would not regret it, "because I am not one of those who attach great strategic importance to that place."[153] Stewart was troubled, however, by the pledges of support made to the local tribes, as well as to the wali of Kandahar: "I do not think a great power like Great Britain can deal lightly or in party spirit with engagements formally sanctioned by such high authority in the Government of India." Stewart also feared the Liberals were intent on quitting Pishin and even Quetta.[154] It was not just the former government's pledge that disturbed Stewart, for he had also personally promised tribal chiefs on 15 March 1880 that there "was no chance of Candahar falling under the authority of a supreme ruler in Cabul."[155]

Others took the view that Kandahar was unnecessary if Sibi and Pishin were retained, since these possessed all the military advantages of Kandahar without the political disadvantages, especially if a railway was completed to Pishin. Stewart had always favored holding Pishin rather than Kandahar. That position was also strongly advocated by James "Buster" Browne, who had acted as Stewart's political officer, and who lectured on the necessity of retaining Pishin while on furlough in London.[156] Colley, now commanding in Natal, was also of such a mind.[157] So, too, was Biddulph.[158] Ripon, indeed, believed that if the government had openly supported Pishin's retention from the beginning, then opposition to withdrawal in his council would have been limited.[159]

Meeting the queen at a presentation in March 1881, Charles Gough was asked his opinion. Without collusion, he and two colonels also recently in Afghanistan who were present all pronounced themselves opposed to retention: "These opinions were mostly contrary to what she had been led to expect, it was an excellent thing she got such strong opinions from all of us. I have no doubt they carried greater weight with her, she seemed satisfied with our reasons."[160]

According to Ponsonby, officers supporting withdrawal hesitatingly put forward their views to the queen in ways that lost her interest, especially when Herbert Macpherson spoke of financial costs. Neville Chamberlain spoke much more passionately of Kandahar as "a hateful, useless, abominable hole which it is dishonourable to stay at one instant longer than we can."[161] While this did not change the queen's opinion, such conviction did move her to listen.

More useful for the Liberals was the significant doubts as to the value of Kandahar within the WO, extending to the AMS, Brownlow, and the Intelligence Department. A paper prepared by Col. Cecil East in August 1880 suggested that, in view of its exertions, the Indian army would not be capable of further sustained operations beyond the Indian frontier for some years. Since the Russians had no greater capacity to get beyond Merv, there was no need to retain Kandahar. Holding Pishin linked to India by rail would suffice to enable the British to return to Kandahar in the event of any hostilities with Russia. Cambridge deplored East's conclusions, but they were endorsed by Alison and Wolseley.[162] In addition, Wolseley penned his own paper against the retention of Kandahar in November 1880, further ruffling the duke's feathers.[163] Gladstone's PS, Edward Hamilton, believed Wolseley's opposition to retaining Kandahar was an additional reason why the queen held out against a peerage for him.[164]

There were also soldiers who openly supported the Liberal case, principally Henry Norman, now military member on the Council of India; Sir John Adye, whom the Liberals appointed to the quasi-political post of SGO; and Maj. Evelyn Baring, Northbrook's nephew and former MS, who was now appointed to the Viceroy's Council.[165] Most of their arguments centered on the financial costs of occupation.

There was a lively public debate in Britain over the merits or otherwise of withdrawal. It was given additional color because the new government was also in the process of capitulating to the Boers as a result of the defeats suffered by Colley in the Anglo-Transvaal War, which had erupted in December 1880. Colley was killed at Majuba on 27 February 1881, an armistice was concluded on 6 March, and an agreement restoring self-government to the Transvaal was signed on 23 March. While defeated in the Lords, the government easily carried the Commons. The withdrawal from Kandahar began on 15 April 1881, although Hartington confirmed Ripon's decision to remain at Pishin and Sibi for the time being.[166] Supposedly only occupied temporarily, Pishin and Sibi were annexed in 1887.

The Second Afghan War cost some £19.5 million.[167] Like the other British involvements in Afghanistan, it has been perceived historically as a failure. It has been argued, however, that reverses implied by withdrawal are not the same as strategic reverses, and the wider strategic prize was to safeguard the British position in India rather than in Afghanistan.[168] That goal was achieved, and the war effectively established Afghanistan as a buffer state as well as subjecting the defense of India to proper analysis for the first time.[169] Privately, Hartington acknowledged that the forward school had not been entirely discredited by the war.[170]

CHAPTER 7

THE ANGLO-ZULU WAR, 1879

The original significance of the Cape of Good Hope lay in its control of the route to India as a "Gibraltar of the Southern Oceans." Its importance was not diminished by the opening of the Suez Canal in 1869. In 1878 trade worth £91 million went round the Cape compared to £65 million through Suez, and the assumption was that canal transit might be problematic in any war.[1] Retention of the Cape increasingly drew Britain into the affairs of the interior, but the primary role of British forces in South Africa remained the defense of its ports against maritime attack. While a permanent military presence was established in Natal in May 1842, the garrison theoretically remained only a temporary expedient throughout Natal's existence as a separate colony from 1856 to 1910.[2]

The British government intended to withdraw the garrison five years after the colony's assumption of responsible government in 1893, a factor that increased the reluctance of Lansdowne to reinforce Natal when the Boer threat increased in 1896. The Intelligence Division concluded that Durban and Pietermaritzburg were worth holding only for reasons of prestige. Lansdowne later questioned whether Natal was worth defending at all.[3]

Only the existing native threats to the eastern frontier and the limited resources of Cape Colony in the 1860s prevented the extension of the policy of withdrawing imperial garrisons that had been applied to Australia, Canada, and New Zealand. Since there was relatively little conflict between the end of the Eighth Cape Frontier War in 1853 and the beginning of the Ninth Cape Frontier War in 1877, there was no imperative to increase the garrison. After the flurry of military activity occasioned by the Ninth Frontier War (1877–78), the Anglo-Zulu War (1879), and the Anglo-Transvaal War (1880–81), there was again little concern for security until relations between Britain and the Boer republics deteriorated in the mid-1890s.

The Ninth Frontier War finally saw off the perceived Xhosa threat. As the British inclination for imperial expansion declined in the 1850s, the two Boer republics of the Transvaal (South African Republic or ZAR) and the Orange Free State (OFS) emerged. What transformed the situation was the discovery of diamonds in 1867 in the loosely defined territory of Griqualand West, to which the Transvaal laid claim. The local Griqua people claimed British protection, and

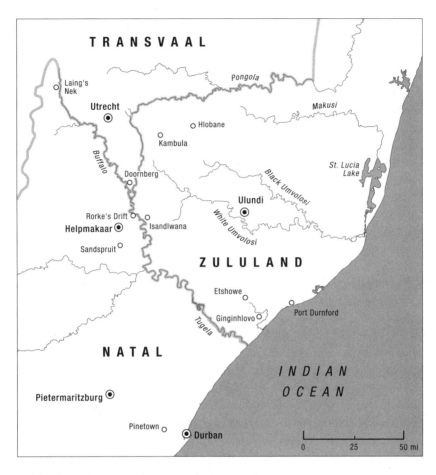

Zululand, 1879–1880. Map by Erin Greb Cartography.

Britain annexed Griqualand in 1871. Settlers in Natal aspired to make Durban a gateway for European goods into the interior and to draw on cheap migrant labor from the north. The Zulu kingdom stood in the way and was increasingly seen as a military threat. The Boers, too, posed a danger to British interests, as did the politically fragmented nature of southern Africa. Carnarvon's solution as colonial secretary was to confederate the British and Boer colonies—hence Wolseley's mission to Natal in 1875. Two years later, when a bankrupt Transvaal could no longer prosecute a border war with the baPedi, it was annexed at the cost of the Boers' deep enmity. By assuming responsibility for the Transvaal, Britain inherited an existing frontier dispute between Boer and Zulu. That provided the high commissioner, Bartle Frere, with the opportunity to find a pretext for acting against the Zulu king, Cetshwayo, while at the same time demonstrating the benefits of British rule to the Boers. Together with his CinC, Chelmsford, Frere deliberately engineered the outbreak of the Anglo-Zulu War in January 1879. Frere's intention was to undertake what he saw as a necessary preemptive strike to ward off any potential Zulu onslaught on Natal. Ostensibly summoned to hear the decision of the border commission on the disputed territory on 11 December 1878, Cetshwayo's representatives were confronted with an ultimatum not only demanding retribution for a recent border incident but also the dismantling of the entire Zulu military system. When Cetshwayo refused to comply with any of the demands, the British army marched into Zululand on 11 January 1879. Recovering from the early defeat at Isandlwana, the reinforced British army mounted a second invasion in May 1879; the Zulu went down to defeat at Ulundi on 4 July 1879. Ultimate Zulu defeat did not reconcile the Transvaal to British rule, however, and its bid for renewed independence resulted in the outbreak of hostilities in December 1880.

Other than during the years 1877–1881, the Cape did not represent a significant command. No serving soldier was appointed governor, CinC, or high commissioner after 1854, and GOCs were frequently undistinguished. When crises arose, the incumbent was often judged unsuitable. As already indicated, Sir Arthur Cunynghame found himself sidelined by the appointment of Wolseley as administrator in Natal in 1875. Cunynghame reluctantly accepted that only a better-known officer would satisfy public opinion, and Wolseley was "by far the most rising."[4] The refusal to contemplate the appointment of Edward Selby-Smyth in 1879 and the bypassing of Leicester Smyth at the Cape when hostilities threatened in 1880 and 1884 have also been noted.

As elsewhere, wartime commanders in South Africa had to demonstrate a capability for exercising both political and military judgment. This was especially so since there was no direct communication between Britain and South Africa until the Zulu War speeded the extension of telegraphic connection to Durban from London via the submarine cable from Aden in December 1879. When Chelmsford was deep in Zululand, his communications with London were sometimes taking more than fifty days. The government had to trust entirely to Wolseley's judgment in Natal in 1875. It also enabled Frere to precipitate a war in 1879 that the government wished to avoid. On the other hand, Wolseley found it irksome to be without government instructions when negotiating with the Transvaal Boers in 1879–80, particularly when the new cable to Aden kept breaking down and dissident Boers cut the telegraph wires.[5]

There were also practical problems in campaigning in South Africa. England was 6,000 miles distant, presenting difficulties of reinforcement. Durban was 730 miles from Cape Town. Imperial troops were invariably few, necessitating reliance on colonial forces, irregulars, and African auxiliaries. South Africa was largely unmapped and communications remained poor, leaving operations largely dependent on oxen given the prevalence of horse sickness.[6]

Friction with colonial administrations was frequent. For example, Cunynghame was removed for "the want of cordiality" existing between him and the Cape authorities in 1878.[7] There were also clashes between the military and local imperial authorities, such as the damaging dispute over the employment of native levies for frontier defense between Chelmsford and Natal's lieutenant governor, Sir Henry Bulwer, in 1879, or that over control of colonial forces between Henry Smyth and the Cape governor, Sir Arthur Havelock, in the suppression of a disturbance in Zululand in 1888.[8]

Opponents could be underestimated, with grave results. While aware of the Zulu military system, Chelmsford expected them to fight much like the Xhosa: they would have to be forced into open battle. Famously, he wrote to Evelyn Wood in November 1878, "I am induced to think that the first experience of the power of the Martini Henrys will be such a surprise to the Zulus that they will not be formidable after the first effort."[9] On the summit of Majuba, Colley is said to have remarked, "We could stay here for ever."[10]

Lord Chelmsford

Cambridge was distressed by Cunynghame's recall but felt he could not intervene "the more so as the difficulties which have occurred are connected with the Civil Government of the Colony, and are not based on purely military considerations."[11] One possible candidate to succeed Cunynghame was Gen. Sir John Bisset, who had experience of the Seventh and Eighth Cape Frontier Wars (1846–47, 1850–53) and was married to a daughter of Natal's Secretary for Native Affairs, Sir Theophilus Shepstone. Cambridge regarded Bisset as well suited for "rough service" but he was too senior. Having been raised in South Africa, he might also be seen as a "Cape man" and his comparatively lowly origins might arouse resentment.[12] Drawing on information from Frere, Carnarvon warned that Bisset was not fondly remembered in South Africa. Frere argued that the Cape needed an officer of "high social & professional standing," judging Bisset as belonging to a bygone era. The Xhosa also held Bisset largely responsible for the supposedly treacherous seizure of Chief Sandile of the Ngqika at Grahamstown back in October 1847.[13]

Carnarvon suggested that George Colley replace Cunynghame, but this choice was rejected by Gathorne Hardy, as Colley was too junior.[14] In Cambridge's view, it "would simply insult the whole Army." Hardy did not favor the appointment of Maj. Gen. Arthur Herbert, so Cambridge suggested either Col. the Hon. Hugh Clifford, currently AAG at Horse Guards, or Col. Richard Glyn as both had Cape experience. A temporary possibility was the QMG, Sir Daniel Lysons.[15] Hardy also rejected the IGAF, James Armstrong, and viewed Patrick MacDougall as not physically fit; therefore, the Hon. Frederic Thesiger, soon to succeed his father as Lord Chelmsford, was selected.[16]

Thesiger was AG in India under Mansfield. Mansfield had given him much latitude, and Mansfield's successor, Napier, evidently felt relief that Thesiger was departing, for they had clashed when Napier reasserted control. Napier found Thesiger liable to "a certain imperiousness in communication with others" during his earlier service on his staff in Abyssinia. He believed that, under his guidance, Thesiger had become more popular, "which would never have been the case had he ruled the business of the army as he did in Lord Sandhurst's time."[17] Thesiger's small staff comprised those who had served under him when he commanded an Aldershot infantry brigade in 1877–78: Maj. John North Crealock, who had been DAAG there; Capt. Matthew Gosset, a brigade major; and Lt. William Molyneux, his ADC.[18] Sir John Michel advised Chelmsford not to take a large staff, as regimental OCs would do any work necessary. Even Chelmsford's appointment of Crealock as AMS was something of an after-thought, as Chelmsford "had never thought of him as my military secretary until he wrote and asked me to take him."[19]

Even Crealock felt Chelmsford had too few staff, writing in April 1879, "We have barely enough to scrape along with now and we have no one to fall back upon except by removing officers from regiments—a serious matter here."[20] Francis Clery, however, reported that Crealock had encouraged Chelmsford to dispense with more staff as he was "indisposed to allow anyone of ability to get near the general."[21] It did not help that Crealock was generally disliked, Sir Henry Bulwer describing him as a "military wasp."[22]

Clery had originally been Evelyn Wood's staff officer but was transferred to Richard Glyn, who commanded the No. 3 Column just before the start of operations against the Zulu even though that left Wood to command the No. 4 Column temporarily without a staff officer since the Hon. Ronald Campbell was laid low with sores.[23] Clery suggested he was sent due to Glyn's general lethargy in order to act as a "blister."[24] Campbell soon enough recovered, Wood having been delighted by his original appointment: "A Guardsman and a peer's son wheeling Clery's cows into column is a source of delight to me!"[25] After Campbell was killed at Hlobane in March 1879, Wood requested that Clery be returned to him as Capt. Edward Woodgate was too slow at office work, while the able Capt. Aubrey Maude could not be spared from regimen-tal duties.[26]

On greater acquaintance with Crealock, Clery wrote after Isandlwana that he doubted Crealock had as much influence as suggested: "As a military secretary I fancy he is very good for he has all the smartness and method that are so useful in such a post, but I do not know that the general really took advice much from anybody, for he certainly seemed—as far as I could see— to discourage anything in the way of suggestion."[27] Writing to Harman in the same vein, Clery noted Chelmsford's "energetic, restless, anxious, temperament led him into very minor matters for he used even to detail the patrols and constantly gave orders direct to commanders of corps, etc."[28] According to Clery, Bvt. Col. William Bellairs's incapacity as DAQMG and the lack of staff generally had still thrown Chelmsford into reliance on Crealock, "who, though an admirable military secretary, was I fear wholly unsuitable as an adviser, for his self-sufficiency, superficiality and flippancy would alone be almost sufficient to deter one from laying any weight on his opinion." For Clery, it marked a distinct difference from Wolseley, who "cannot get too many or too good men about him."[29]

Col. Richard Harrison was made the sole AQMG for the second invasion, but, as Clery noted, he had "never held a staff appointment in his life" and his qualification "appeared to be that he was in the way elsewhere."[30] Chelmsford toyed with the idea of asking for the services of John McNeill and splitting Bellairs's duties. Cambridge did not consider it necessary, although the AG, Ellice, was surprised Chelmsford did not feel a CoS desirable.[31] Bellairs himself argued that dividing his post in the middle of the campaign would be prejudicial to his career as he would be effectively superseded by McNeill and it would be assumed he had some responsibility for Isandlwana.[32] Since McNeill was in Canada, Cecil East was dispatched to act as an additional DAQMG.

Thesiger's command arrangements were not tested by the Xhosa in the Ninth War. There were greater difficulties in the more mountainous region inhabited by the baPedi chief, Sekhukhune, operations against whom were entrusted to Col. Hugh Rowlands VC. According to Clery, Rowlands "made an awful mess of his business."[33] Chelmsford also thought Rowlands a failure and heard "that he sits in his tent & writes all day—That way will not do in S. African warfare." But he did not feel Rowlands should resign.[34] In fact, Rowlands's plans were crippled by horse sickness and Thesiger's own interference.[35] It did not prevent Redvers Buller, commanding the irregulars of the Frontier Light Horse, to send Evelyn Wood a satirical poem:

Oh! For one hour of Wolseley's might
Or well trained Wood to lead the fight

> And quit us of this Rowlands wight
> Who does not understand it quite
> To snair this Sekukuni[36]

Subsequently, as Rowlands was senior to Wood and could not serve under him in Zululand, Chelmsford said that Wood could place Rowlands's force where it would best support him, but that Rowlands should not interfere with Wood's operational independence.[37] Rowlands fared no better in Wood's estimation, and his troops were taken from him.[38] When Col. Charles Pearson went down with typhoid, Chelmsford placed Rowlands in command of his brigade in the First Division since he did not feel that Rowlands was suited to an independent command through his indecisiveness and that he "increases that difficulty by asking advice from everyone about him."[39]

When commanding the No. 1 Column, Pearson had been indecisive himself. He resorted to a council of war at Eshowe to decide what to do after Isandlwana. It was decided to stay at Eshowe and fortify it. A second council of war was then held in February after a dispatch from Chelmsford was received suggesting withdrawal. It was again decided that it was too risky to leave Eshowe. When no further dispatch was forthcoming, Pearson shrank from taking any initiative.[40] Later, when Rowlands commanded a brigade in India, Donald Stewart was sorry to lose his services. Though aware of what had been said about him in South Africa, he averred, "we often find that some of our best peace officers do not shine in the field."[41]

Chelmsford's own operations against the Zulu, of course, met disaster at Isandlwana on 22 January 1879. The attempt by Chelmsford to shift blame elsewhere has been widely discussed.[42] The court of inquiry held on 27 January was deliberately restricted to investigating "the loss of the camp" and not the "circumstances of the disastrous affair."[43] This amounted merely to ascertaining "what orders were given for the defence of the camp, and how these orders were carried out." The inquiry simply recorded the statements of eight individuals: two were so brief as to add nothing to the story, and two were submitted only in writing. Lt. Henry Curling, one of the five imperial officers to escape, later wrote that he had not anticipated the proceedings would be published and that few of those called had taken the trouble "to make a readable statement."[44] Other statements were taken, but Lt. Col. Arthur Harness, presiding, believed there was no point recording "statements hardly bearing on the loss of the camp but giving doubtful particulars of small incidents more or less ghastly in their nature."[45] It might be noted that the evidence and conclusions of the official inquiry into the loss of Maj. Allan Wilson's Shangani Patrol in the Matabele War in December 1893 were never published.[46]

Principally, blame was thrown on the commander of Chelmsford's No. 2 Column, Col. Anthony Durnford. Chelmsford had threatened to remove Durnford from his command on 14 January 1879 when the latter proposed crossing the Thukela into Zululand against Chelmsford's orders.[47] Frere already believed on 27 January that the camp had fallen because Durnford had over-ruled Col. Henry Pulleine, who had been left in command when Chelmsford split his force and marched out earlier in the morning.[48] Similarly, Chelmsford's civilian intelligence officer, the Hon. William Drummond, was still pulling together statements from native sources on 9 February yet already stressing that Pulleine and Durnford had quarreled and Durnford had pulled rank.[49] Bellairs placed the blame firmly on Durnford, urging Chelmsford to publish the results of the inquiry quickly "as calculated to remove many erroneous impressions since entertained."[50]

Chelmsford's own notes on the findings of the inquiry, probably written in April, suggested that Durnford had been ordered to take command of the camp and had ignored instructions by moving out.[51] This was blatantly untrue. Attacked by Archibald Forbes for his conduct of the campaign, Chelmsford responded with a memorandum in February 1880 making the same points. Harness also defended Chelmsford in *Fraser's Magazine* in response to Forbes, although this also served to defend his part in the court of inquiry.[52]

Pressed for more information, Chelmsford tried to shift some of the blame onto Glyn, to whose No. 3 Column Chelmsford had attached himself, for "it would be hardly fair to saddle me with the responsibility of any neglect of details connected with the command of No 3 Column, for the performance of which the Officer Commanding the column was held accountable to me."[53] This attempt had arisen at an early stage, with Crealock writing to his brother on 2 March that "no one of the general's staff did so take upon himself the duty of an executive staff officer." The choice of Isandlwana as a camp, the placing of outposts, and all interior arrangements there were Glyn's responsibility.[54] Even earlier on 20 February, Crealock had drawn Chelmsford's attention to Glyn's contention that Crealock himself had been the conduit for all reports sent to Chelmsford. Chelmsford duly wrote to Bellairs pointing out that Glyn had not objected to any orders given him and that he himself had not interfered with Glyn as regards "outposts, patrolling, and the ordinary precautions for the safety of the Camp."[55]

According to the wily Clery, Glyn commanded only Clery and his orderly officer. Thus, when Glyn and Clery left the camp with Chelmsford in the early hours of 22 January, neither "knew where we were going to or what we were going to do." Clery saw the trap being set for Glyn when he was asked to provide all details of how various camp regulations had been carried out. Clery almost certainly wrote Glyn's carefully crafted replies to Bellairs.[56] It has been suggested that Clery also had a major hand in John Chard's official report on the action at Rorke's Drift and conceivably also Gonville Bromhead's, although this is disputed.[57]

Clery's replies to Bellairs brought what Clery characterized as "quite a lawyer's document" from Crealock as well as another missive from Bellairs. Glyn and Clery "accepted all responsibility for details, but declined to admit *any* responsibility *for the movement of any portion of the troops in or out of camp.*"[58] Clery reiterated the fact that Glyn was a "complete cipher" on 28 April, revealing it was he who had issued some last-minute orders to Pulleine to defend the camp when he realized Chelmsford had left none. Chelmsford expressed his relief that Clery had done so.[59] William Penn Symons later recalled Gosset as well as Crealock throwing blame on Glyn and Clery.[60] Frederick Maurice was appalled at the attempt to blacken Glyn's name, believing Crealock to blame for a maneuver "as feeble as it was unfair."[61]

On behalf of Cambridge, Ellice submitted a detailed list of questions to Chelmsford on 6 March 1879.[62] Chelmsford's reply failed to convince Cambridge, who could not understand why the camp had not been fortified according to Chelmsford's own field regulations.[63] Chelmsford's arguments were rejected.[64]

Chelmsford was subsequently invited to Balmoral. Henry Ponsonby concluded that someone else was always somehow responsible for all that had gone wrong for Chelmsford.[65] Nonetheless, the queen remained supportive. Unsurprised by Chelmsford's favorable reception, Wolseley stated, "he is my Lord, society will back him up, the court included, & because all the Horse Guards clique, the Duke and all his old fashioned set included, and the many enemies I have in the Army, hate me most bitterly, being the bitterness of envy & jealousy, every endeavour will be made by them to cry him up hoping thereby to keep me down."[66]

Wood and Buller followed Chelmsford to Balmoral, both making a very favorable impression on the queen.[67] Wood suggested that he and Buller were pleased Cambridge had shown *"loyalty to his generals"* in not superseding Chelmsford immediately after Isandlwana; nonetheless, they were highly critical of Chelmsford, Crealock, and Rowlands.[68]

Chelmsford was never able to shake off the shadow of Isandlwana. Durnford's brother, Edward Durnford, had no intention of letting matters rest. In 1880 he published a detailed refutation of Chelmsford's speech in the House of Lords and a memoir of his brother in 1882. In 1885 the CRE in Natal, Col. Charles Luard, followed inquiries begun by his predecessor and pursued the rumor that papers had been removed from Durnford's body by Theophilus

Shepstone Jr. when the burial party returned to the scene on 21 May 1879. In January 1885 Luard asked Sir Andrew Clarke to order an inquiry and sent him a lengthy statement of the evidence he had collected.[69] Clarke pressed the matter in February 1886, and the inquiry took place in April 1886.[70] While authorized, it became clear to Luard that it was not intended to delve too deeply and was restricted to ascertaining whether papers had been removed from Durnford's body. Luard was forced to apologize to Shepstone when the latter's evidence that nothing was taken was upheld.[71] Shepstone was most probably lying. Crealock's order book had been found and returned to him in June 1879, but he only revealed this in July 1886. Chelmsford's actual orders to Durnford had been found in a portmanteau by the brother of a former Natal carbineer and given to Luard sometime after June 1885. Supposedly, as Clarke requested, it was agreed in 1887 to review the official history, but it was reprinted in 1907 without correction.

Isandlwana was not the only cover-up, for Evelyn Wood had much to hide after his disastrous raid on the local Zulu stronghold of Hlobane on 28 March 1879. Wood's victory at Kambula the following day fortuitously facilitated his evasiveness. The sacrificial victims on this occasion were Lt. Cols. Cecil Russell and Frederick Weatherley, who was killed.[72]

Wood was not convinced the operation would be a success, but it was a necessary diversion.[73] Weatherley, who commanded the Border Horse, and Russell were accused of cowardice. Weatherley, a former regular with service in the Crimean War and in the Mutiny, was supposedly loath to engage the abaQulusi, who inhabited Hlobane Mountain. Russell retreated prematurely, leaving Redvers Buller and his force stranded on top of the mountain without support. Wood deliberately obscured Weatherley's movements as well as the actual orders given to Russell. His own whereabouts for much of the day remain unknown, and there is no doubt Wood suffered a deep psychological blow when Ronald Campbell and his secretary, Llewellyn Lloyd, were killed.[74]

The Prince of Wales's support for Russell caused significant difficulties. Clery believed Russell had been unnerved by Isandlwana.[75] Wood was already prejudiced against Russell. Following a dispute over the defenses of Utrecht, it was Russell whom Chelmsford had sent to report on the situation. Wood made it known to Chelmsford that he had written officially to complain that "one of my very juniors" had been tasked to report on his arrangements.[76] Wood was generally scathing, accusing Russell of not being strong enough for his command, writing to Crealock, "I could make you laugh by stories of Russell's helplessness on patrol."[77]

In theory, Russell had been sent to command all the mounted volunteers of Wood's column, including Buller. Wood simply ignored the order, giving Buller effective command of the irregular mounted troops, with Russell commanding the mounted infantry and the Natal Native Horse. According to gossip Wood relayed to Chelmsford, Russell wished to avoid serving under Buller.[78] Wood was in no doubt that Russell played a significant role in the disaster at Hlobane.[79] Buller made it clear that he would not serve in any future operation with Russell. Lt. Edward Browne, commanding the mounted infantry, also said the men had lost confidence in Russell.[80] It has been suggested that Wood's recommendation of the VC for Browne was not unconnected with Browne's criticism of Russell.[81]

Wood suggested that Russell could be employed in remount work, and the latter was duly sent to Pietermaritzburg. Russell expressed surprise at his demotion, given he had received no official censure.[82] Marlborough House denied Russell had gone "missing" at Hlobane.[83] The Prince also insisted that Russell be presented to the queen, which raised the likelihood of Wood having to commit to paper the reasons why he found Russell's conduct at Hlobane unsatisfactory.[84] The queen refused to receive Russell on the grounds she would need such an official report if the Prince of Wales persisted. When informed that Buller had withdrawn some charges against Russell, she then refused to receive him on the grounds he was too junior to be presented.[85]

Chelmsford's Second Invasion

As already indicated, there was no direct telegraphic communication to Cape Colony. Consequently, messages were conveyed to Cape Verde by ship and then telegraphed to London via Madeira, Lisbon, and Porthcurno in Cornwall. The news of Isandlwana reached the WO only in the early hours of 11 February. It did not reach Wolseley on Cyprus for another four days, although Haines in India received the news on the same day as the WO.[86]

The secretary of state, Frederick Stanley, summoned the AG, Ellice, and the QMG, Lysons, to meet with him and Cambridge later that morning—Stanley's note to Cambridge was written at 4.30 A.M. Stanley then requested Beaconsfield to call a cabinet meeting shortly after 1 P.M.[87] A telegram from Chelmsford sent on 27 January called for immediate reinforcements of at least three battalions, two cavalry regiments, and a company of engineers. In subsequent letters to Cambridge on 5 and 10 February, Chelmsford requested a designated second in command and an increase to six battalions.[88] Lady Frere, acting under instructions from her husband, also communicated with Cambridge on 4 February, urging the appointment of a second in command and suggesting Alison.[89] Chelmsford himself was annoyed that Crealock had repeated in his official dispatch on 9 February sentiments Chelmsford had conveyed privately to Cambridge that seemed to imply his "state of body and mind was not what it ought to be": he had failed to notice Crealock's inclusion of these damning thoughts when signing the dispatch.[90] Subsequently, Chelmsford complained to Stanley that the press had been able to "distort the truth or misrepresent it, in such a manner as to increase the uneasy feeling regarding my proceedings which has evidently taken possession of your mind, and from which I fear His Royal Highness is not altogether free."[91]

Wood was low on the colonel's list and, in Cambridge's view, already over-rewarded for services in the Ninth Frontier War. He could not succeed to the command. Had Chelmsford been incapacitated, the next senior officer was the CRE, Col. Fairfax Hassard. Hassard had taken temporary command at Helpmekaar after Isandlwana but had not distinguished himself through his inaction. He had served on the court of inquiry but, after a nervous collapse, was sent back to the Cape. Meeting him there subsequently, Wolseley remarked that Hassard had no interest in his profession.[92]

In deciding to send out six battalions, two cavalry regiments, two artillery batteries, and a company of engineers, Stanley and his advisers resolved that three senior officers should accompany them. Since circumstances might arise in which the senior of the three would "find the command has devolved on him," the cabinet initially reserved its judgment on what were clearly Cambridge's personal selections although, as yet, there seemed no grounds for replacing Chelmsford in command.[93] By 13 February the matter was settled, with Cambridge's three selections all accepted—namely, Maj. Gens. Henry Hope Crealock, Edward Newdigate, and Frederick Marshall. Subsequently, a fourth major general, the Hon. Henry Hugh Clifford VC, was added on 27 February 1879.[94]

All four had served in the Crimea. Marshall was ADC to Sir James Scarlett, and Clifford won his VC at Inkerman. Clifford had served in South Africa during the Seventh and Eighth Cape Frontier Wars. Crealock and Clifford had also served in China, where the former had been MS to Lord Elgin. More to the point, all were well known to Cambridge. Clifford and Marshall had been his ADCs, Marshall as recently as 1877. Clifford was AAG at the WO. Crealock had been military attaché at both St. Petersburg and Vienna and, most recently, DQMG in Ireland. Newdigate had held a series of home staff appointments, most recently at the Rifle Brigade depot at Winchester.[95] Opinions on their merits varied. Naturally enough, Cambridge regarded his selections as men of energy and talent, Clifford in particular being "a most agreeable & satisfactory man to deal with."[96] In nominating Newdigate once more to accompany Roberts to South Africa in March 1881, after Colley's death at Majuba,

Cambridge again described him as good and reliable.[97] As might be expected, Wolseley was not overly complimentary toward the commanders he inherited after his own appointment, noting, "Such generals as they have sent out!" Like Clifford and Marshall, the new CRA, Col. William "Tim" Reilly, had also been one of Cambridge's ADCs. Wolseley believed that Marshall and Reilly had been sent out primarily to be awarded the KCB.[98]

Wolseley was particularly acerbic with regard to Henry Crealock, with whom he had served in the Ninetieth Light Infantry, the regiment now commanded by Wood. Crealock had been on Wolseley's Red River expedition. While he regarded Crealock as clever, Wolseley did not believe him fit for a field command and later wrote in the unpublished draft of his memoirs that Crealock had been unpopular with officers, NCOs, and men alike in the Ninetieth.[99] He also found Henry Crealock to be as snobbish as his younger brother, John North Crealock.[100] Once in Zululand, Wolseley recorded the elder Crealock's "manner is so repulsive, that I hate even speaking to him."[101]

Wolseley had not known Newdigate previously, although he had heard he was "sound" but he regarded Marshall as an "idiot." Wolseley took obvious pleasure in writing to Cambridge in July 1879 that even Chelmsford found Newdigate and Marshall "useless" in the field.[102] Unsurprisingly, Clery found both Henry Crealock and Newdigate "awful failures": Newdigate "as a commander is a very feeble old lady—Crealock does the feeble young lady."[103] Crealock's slowness in moving forward with the First Division during the second invasion of Zululand was especially criticized. Francis Grenfell, serving with Newdigate's division, reported that Crealock was a failure adding, "everyone is furious with him—he might have been into Ulundi long before us, and he seems never to have made an attempt to move."[104] Wolseley suggested that Crealock had no "dash," while Clifford also referred to him as "rather too easy going."[105] It may have been a factor that, suffering from a painful ailment—presumably piles—Crealock could not mount his horse for days on end.[106]

Although he found Marshall pleasant, Wolseley's view of his capabilities was not improved by the rumor that Marshall, commanding the cavalry brigade attached to the Second Division, had "fainted from excitement" when the adjutant of the Seventeenth Lancers was killed at eZungeni on 5 June. Wolseley was also surprised that Marshall thought Lt. Col. Drury Drury-Lowe of the Seventeenth competent when he appeared to be a mere "Hyde Park Colonel."[107] Marshall was relegated to commanding the LOC between the Natal frontier and the army in the field on 13 June. The younger Crealock also described Newdigate, commanding the Second Division, as useless. Henry Ponsonby noted in March 1881 that Wood viewed Newdigate as no more than "a steady old adjutant."[108]

A relatively unbiased observer of the selections, Arthur Herbert, wrote to Wood that he did not regard Crealock, Newdigate, or Marshall as sensible choices. Neither Newdigate nor Marshall enjoyed good health. Crealock was "not strong, and never was much on a horse" and, moreover, only excelled "at long letters, and keeping an office in apple pie order."[109] With evident glee, Clifford sent Cambridge a poem from a local newspaper satirizing Crealock being unseated from his horse by a cow. He also forwarded a joke going the rounds about Chelmsford: "Why are the officers and men of Wood's Flying Column Idolaters? Because they do not believe in *the Lord* and make a God of *Wood*."[110]

The one choice commanding considerable support was Clifford. Cambridge thought him the most valuable of the four, particularly through his experience of South African warfare, although this had been twenty-five years previously. Wolseley thought Clifford "zeal itself" and "a bright object in the clouds of confusion that reign supreme in this military chaos"; he even commended Cambridge on his choice.[111] Similarly, Herbert believed that Clifford alone among the four was equal to rough campaigning.[112] He was to receive general praise for his herculean efforts to reorganize the transport system in South Africa.

Clifford's appointment, however, raised the question of the purpose in adding him to Cambridge's original choices. Initially, Crealock—as the senior from himself, Newdigate, and Marshall—was clearly designated as Chelmsford's second in command, but there remained the problem of transport and supply arrangements. Bellairs was struggling to fill the posts of both DAG and QMG. As Cambridge explained to Frere on 27 February, Clifford would take over responsibility for the LOC and the base of operations in Natal.[113] But Clifford was senior to Crealock. The clumsy solution adopted by Cambridge was that Crealock would be second in command to Chelmsford in the field, but Clifford and not Crealock would actually succeed to the command in the event of Chelmsford's death or breakdown. Clifford would also be available to replace Frere as high commissioner. A further complication was that, while Cambridge indicated Chelmsford was free to place Crealock, Newdigate, and Marshall in whatever commands were appropriate, he strongly suggested one of them at least should be made CoS. Chelmsford should also, he wrote, "so arrange as to interfere as little as possible with the very able & distinguished officers at present at the head of your respective Columns"— meaning Wood and Pearson.[114]

Chelmsford's solution to the surfeit of major generals was to give divisional commands to Crealock and Newdigate with the most junior—Marshall— taking the cavalry brigade attached to Newdigate's division. Wood's former command became an autonomous flying column cooperating with Newdigate. Chelmsford accompanied Newdigate, giving Crealock a free hand. After being given a brigade under Crealock, Pearson was invalided home in June after the exertions of the siege of Eshowe and contracting typhoid.

What was not resolved was the respective seniority of Clifford and Crealock. Cambridge tried to clarify the situation on 27 March in the light of the receipt of Chelmsford's dispatch of 9 February, in which he referred to the "strain of prolonged anxiety & exertion, physical & mental" that had been telling on him even the year before. Crealock was instructed that it was expected he would be second in command in the field although Chelmsford was still free to employ his major generals as he wished. If Chelmsford broke down, Clifford would succeed him, with Crealock either remaining second in command or assuming Clifford's duties at base.[115]

Crealock and Clifford remained confused as to their true responsibilities and not just due to the fact that Cambridge's letter did not reach Crealock until 9 May. Clifford had meanwhile written to Cambridge requesting clarification of press reports that he would succeed to the command if anything happened to Chelmsford. Clifford understood from conversations with Cambridge and Stanley before he left London that Crealock had been promised command. From a letter Crealock later sent to Cambridge it would appear that he had spoken to Clifford on the voyage to South Africa: both assumed Crealock would succeed Chelmsford based on the conversations in London. Chelmsford had also conveyed this impression, instructing Crealock to hand his division over to Pearson in the event of having to take overall command, although he must have received Cambridge's letter of 27 February well before Crealock received that of 27 March.[116] It did not mollify Crealock to know that he would come under Clifford's orders should Chelmsford be removed given that he believed he had been promised the chief command in such an eventuality.[117] Curiously, Clifford still sought clarification from Chelmsford on what he had heard from home about the succession two days after the receipt of the Horse Guards letter.[118]

The confusion hardly contributed to harmony among senior officers, which had been damaged in any case by Clifford's growing antipathy toward Chelmsford and Chelmsford's staff. In his first letter to Cambridge on reaching Durban on 17 April, and having spoken to the *Daily Telegraph* correspondent, Clifford reported on the evident dissension arising from John North Crealock's influence over Chelmsford and the poor relationship between the younger Crealock and Bellairs.[119] In a subsequent letter Clifford revealed Chelmsford's disagreements with Bulwer, and how Chelmsford "moves in a very narrow world of his own, as I have told him, shut off by Crealock from many who would give him good sound advice."[120] Cambridge was displeased at Clifford's criticism, writing, "You cannot think what serious mischief must arise in an army where these sort of sentiments are entertained in the highest quarters—and whatever shortcomings there may have been I had rather they had been less remarked upon than they have been."[121]

Clifford resented the restriction of his authority to Natal. There was a particular dispute in June over Clifford altering one of Chelmsford's telegrams that requested additional reinforcements by deleting Chelmsford's reasons for doing so—Chelmsford wanted three more battalions for garrison duty—and also by requesting more ASC personnel.[122] John North Crealock accused Clifford of "back biting and jealousy" and deliberately making mischief.[123] Henry Crealock, meanwhile, resented Clifford "assuming a tone of dictation to me."[124] Clifford kept asking Henry Crealock for reports, and appeared to be "trying to do everyone's duty," leading Crealock to wish to know whether Clifford was entitled to give him orders.[125]

Wolseley accepted Clifford's explanation of affairs when he arrived in South Africa and directed Clifford to control all lines of communication.[126] On 2 July Chelmsford complained that Clifford was communicating with Wolseley about the arrangements made for keeping lines open. So far as Chelmsford was concerned, Clifford knew nothing of the situation in Zululand: "General Clifford seems to imagine that when sitting at his desk in PMBurg he is capable of looking after my lines of communication in the enemys country."[127] Wolseley considered that there was much jealousy of Clifford coming from "some evil influence at Chelmsford's side," by which he meant the younger Crealock.[128] Wolseley soon took exception to the latter continuing to suggest he was MS: "The Military Secretary is in my camp, and as there can be only one General Commanding so there can only be one Military Secretary."[129] Chelmsford suggested he had assumed that, as Wolseley was replacing Frere as high commissioner and CinC, he remained in the same position with respect to Wolseley as he had to Frere.[130]

Crealock consoled himself that Clifford might "have a fall from Colley."[131] Indeed, while Cambridge urged Wolseley to appoint Clifford as his CoS, Wolseley was determined to secure the services of Colley, then Lytton's PS. While recognizing that Clifford was an "indefatigable worker," Wolseley felt he had "no brains & no scientific knowledge of his profession" and lacked a broader view. Colley, on the other hand, was "the ablest man in the Army, and he cannot long be kept back from the high position in the army to which a wise Govt. would appoint such a man, by any amount of Horse Guards jealousy or dread of having first rate men in power."[132] Cambridge could not prevail against the government's support for Wolseley's choice.

Consequently, Colley became Wolseley's CoS. Wolseley failed to get Colley given local rank as major general because Cambridge argued, "no army could stand these sorts of preferences without entirely dampening the energies of senior officers and the balance of the advantage is very decidedly, in my opinion, in favour of the senior officer unless otherwise disqualified."[133] Nonetheless, it was Clifford whom Wolseley recommended should Colley not be available, and he also recommended Clifford as his successor in South Africa (again should Colley not receive the command).[134] Colley was recalled to India following the massacre of Cavagnari's mission in September 1879.

Subsequently, Clifford was somewhat disappointed not to receive the appointment of high commissioner of Natal in preference to Colley in 1880.[135] He also objected to Colley, now given local rank as major general, holding an independent command. Thus, Clifford returned home rather than accept what was now considered a less important command at the Cape. Having come so quickly to South Africa, he had not been able to make satisfactory provision for his family and thought he would find the expense of the Cape command considerable.[136] Clifford also believed he had become fatally associated in Cambridge's mind, to quote Wolseley, as "one of my lot."[137] Clifford was obliged to remain at the Cape until the arrival of Leicester Smyth.[138]

Garnet Wolseley

Arriving at the Cape on 23 June, Wolseley dispensed with the services of Crealock, Newdigate, and Marshall as soon as possible: fourteen officers of rank went home. The *Broad Arrow* suggested that Chelmsford had "an officer of rank for every toe" and that few British armies had taken the field with "such a collection of commissioned inutilities."[139]

Crealock's division—dubbed "Crealock's Crawlers"—was broken up on 23 July, and Newdigate's on 27 July. John North Crealock unwittingly added to criticism of his brother by penning a telegram for Chelmsford that became known to the press and which appeared to suggest the main force's advance had been impeded by Crealock's delay.[140] Arthur Harness maintained that when Wolseley met Crealock he told him he "might as well have been marching between Wimbledon and Aldershot as what you have been doing here."[141] Cambridge voiced astonishment that Wolseley was sending home all his generals and having colonels command his columns.[142]

None of the four major generals sent by Cambridge commanded in the field again. Newdigate, like the remainder of Roberts's reinforcements, was reembarked within twenty-four hours of arriving in South Africa in March 1881. There had been much astonishment at Newdigate's appointment—extending to Roberts himself—when, as a major general senior to both Roberts and Wood, who had only local rank, he was designated to command only a brigade under Roberts.[143] Roberts had wanted Thomas Baker rather than Newdigate, and the queen initially refused to approve the appointment.[144] Newdigate's brother-in-law, Lt. Gen. Henry Lynedoch Gardiner, complained that the press was treating Newdigate badly in suggesting he was superseding Wood when Wood was leaping over at least two hundred major generals.[145] Subsequently, Newdigate turned down the Hong Kong command in 1885 but accepted Bermuda.[146]

Wolseley's own appointment, according to Loo Wolseley, was "sharp work I assure you, just as it *always* is, only told of it on Monday & off on Thursday leaving me to sweep up the debris."[147] When war broke out, Wolseley was still on Cyprus and fretful at his absence from the approaching war in Afghanistan. As he wrote to Salisbury in October 1878, "I grow cold all over at the idea of remaining here whilst I might be leading troops in the field. I have spent my life—I may say since boyhood—in endeavouring to perfect myself in my profession, both scientifically and practically and I now see—or I imagine I see— an opportunity for practising what I have studied so long and so deeply."[148] Cyprus was an appointment Wolseley would give up "at any moment to command the smallest military expedition anywhere."

In February 1879, having just heard the first limited news of Isandlwana, Wolseley declared his immediate availability, while also expressing willingness to replace Haines in India, having heard he was down with fever.[149] Still unaware of his likely appointment to South Africa in March, Wolseley also canvassed the MS, Horsford, on the Madras command as a stepping-stone to replace Haines, trusting that, if unsuccessful, his remaining on Cyprus would not bar him from the highest command in India.[150] By 23 April Wolseley despairingly declared to his mother, "hope has died in me of being sent to the Cape."[151]

The secretary of state for India, Cranbrook, was still considering Wolseley for at least Madras.[152] On 4 April, however, Cambridge wrote to Wolseley indicating the time had not arrived to consider any changes at Madras. In any case, "it is *well known in India*, & therefore *no doubt in Madras* that you *have expressed strong opinions whilst at the India Office*, very adverse to the Madras Army, & I don't know therefore how far this fact might militate against your usefulness in supreme charge in that Presidency."[153] In April Stanley summoned Wolseley back to London, at the same time bringing Sir Patrick MacDougall back from the Halifax command, deliberately to divert attention from the real reason for Wolseley's recall.[154]

Following a conversation with Ellice in London in May 1879, at which Wolseley learned that Napier had also been considered to replace Chelmsford, Wolseley concluded that Chelmsford had been kept on deliberately in the hope he would not be sent to replace him. As he wrote to his brother, "They positively hate me & persuade the Queen that I am a low radical who wishes to upset everything."[155] Certainly, the queen had been concerned at Wolseley's appointment, which she was disposed to sanction rather than approve, while Cambridge had suggested Napier. Beaconsfield first made the government's intentions known on 23 May, but it was only on 3 June the queen finally acquiesced in all respects, despite the public announcement of Wolseley's appointment having been made on 26 May.[156]

Beaconsfield wrote a long letter to the queen on 30 May outlining the cabinet's growing uneasiness as to Chelmsford's conduct of the war. The initial reluctance to replace him had changed with the arrival of his dispatches on 21 May "revealing such a state of affairs—of anarchy & impotence—that your Majesty's Ministers absolutely refused to bear the responsibility of indifference."[157] As there had been six cabinets in eight days and Beaconsfield had also consulted Cambridge (on 25 May), he did not feel Wolseley's appointment had been precipitous. In any case, Napier—judged too old—was not available. Beaconsfield also argued that Frere's authority was not being diminished since he had no authority over Natal and the Transvaal. No one supported Chelmsford's retention. Stanley and Salisbury had strongly pressed for Wolseley's appointment.[158] Subsequently, Beaconsfield refused to see Chelmsford on his return to England. While not accusing Chelmsford of precipitating the war, he did blame him for ignorance, hesitation, and dilatoriness.[159]

Cambridge believed that Salisbury was primarily responsible for Wolseley's appointment since he had "Wolseley on the brain." As Wolseley passed by Cambridge and Ponsonby in Clarence House, the duke remarked, "There goes my master."[160] For Wolseley, it was all too late in the sense it would be difficult to put in place much in the way of new plans so late in the potential campaigning season.[161]

As is well known, Chelmsford managed to defeat the Zulu at Ulundi on 4 July 1879 before Wolseley could reach the front. Chelmsford's brother had urged him, "For God's sake do something! Wolseley supersedes you."[162] Wolseley was further annoyed by Chelmsford's precipitous withdrawal from Ulundi following the battle. Chelmsford claimed that Wolseley had instructed him to do so, but this was nonsense.[163] Chelmsford also wished to leave the country as soon as possible after Wolseley effectively placed him in command of a force smaller than Crealock's. Writing to Stanley on 9 July, having only just received formal notification of his supersession, Chelmsford stated that he "could not accept the inferior command to which he has considered it within his power to reduce me, except under a firm conviction that such sacrifice of dignity & position was required in the public interest. Under such circumstances I should have been ready to set on one side all private interests and would have gladly filled any position in which it was thought I could be useful to my country."[164] Chelmsford duly left South Africa, as did Wood and Buller, who were both exhausted after the campaign.

There remained the question of the settlement of Zululand with Cetshwayo still at large, the unfinished business of the campaign against Sekhukhune, and the unrest evident in the Transvaal. The columns hunting Cetshwayo were entrusted to Cols. Baker Russell and Charles Mansfield Clarke. Cetshwayo was captured on 28 August by one of Clarke's patrols, commanded by Maj. Richard Marter. Wolseley's controversial settlement of Zululand divided the territory between thirteen compliant chiefs answerable to a British resident. It has been argued that the settlement was modeled in part on Indian security concepts and inspired by Colley.[165] Similarly, it has been argued that Bulwer, Theophilus Shepstone, and, especially, John Wesley Shepstone shaped it.[166]

Wolseley conducted the Sekhukhune campaign himself, employing columns commanded by Baker Russell, whom he accompanied, and Maj. Henry Bushman. With the assistance of the Swazi, the Transvaal Field Force assaulted the baPedi strongholds at Tsate and Ntswaneng. Sekhukhune surrendered on 2 December 1879.[167] Following negotiations with the Transvaal Boers, who were informed that annexation was irreversible, Wolseley established an executive council, promising that a legislative council would follow.

As Wolseley anticipated, he received no real reward for his services beyond the GCB, his local rank of full general not being confirmed.[168] A lieutenant general who had acted satisfactorily as a general for five years in peacetime or for any period in active field command could be given the substantive rank on Cambridge's recommendation. Wolseley believed that the absence of confirmation suggested he had failed in South Africa. As he viewed the full general's rank as important in helping him secure command in India, he asked his friend, Alfred Austin, who wrote regularly for the *Standard*, to help: "If you can ventilate my 'grievance,' it will I know do me good."[169] Qualification for the clasp to the South Africa Medal for Zululand was also initially terminated at the date of Ulundi, until Wolseley's protest extended it to the date of the capture of Cetshwayo. He did not succeed in winning a clasp for the Sekhukhune campaign.[170]

Wolseley did not want to stay in South Africa, telling Stanley his ambition was to get to India and not to "settle down as a Colonial Governor."[171] Stanley believed, rightly, that Wolseley was also angling for a peerage. Wolseley's desire to quit Zululand did not meet with Beaconsfield's approval; the latter wrote, "I don't like the state of affairs, but there can be no question, that Wolseley must remain there, and his troops. I hope he has sufficient. It is his own fault if he have not [*sic*]. With regard to himself, he never would give us a moment's peace till we sent him there, and there he must remain until all is settled."[172]

Wolseley finally departed South Africa on 4 May 1880. He took up the post of QMG on 1 July. Meanwhile, Colley became governor of Natal, high commissioner for South-eastern Africa, and CinC for Natal and Transvaal in June 1881. Confronted with rebellion in the Transvaal, he was killed at Majuba on 27 February 1881.[173] Succeeding to the command, Evelyn Wood was directed by Gladstone's government to obtain an armistice. An agreement to restore self-government to the Transvaal under the vague formula of retaining the queen's suzerainty was signed on 23 March 1881. As already indicated, Roberts was dispatched with reinforcements but ordered home as soon as he reached the Cape. Wolseley was refused the command because Childers wanted him at the WO. The intended peerage was intended partly to compensate Wolseley for not being sent out.[174] Wolseley later recorded that the decision not to send him to avenge Colley's death was only the second time in his life he could not sleep: "I should have liked to die, were it not that I felt I should yet be able to show the world that I had better stuff in me than the conduct of the ministers concerned would cause the world to think."[175]

CHAPTER 8

THE SOUTH AFRICAN WAR, 1899–1902

It had been widely assumed that the Transvaal would again slide into bank-ruptcy after regaining its autonomy in 1881, the fiction of nominal British suzerainty being dropped in 1884. The situation was transformed by the discovery of gold on the Rand in 1886. The largest mining companies were British owned, and many of the large number of Uitlanders (foreigners) attracted to the Rand were also British. Afrikaner resistance to granting civil rights to the Uitlanders coincided with the "scramble for Africa" and the extension of British rule to Pondoland, Bechuanaland, and Zululand, and through the auspices of Cecil Rhodes's British South Africa Company (BSAC) to Mashonaland and Matabeleland. Strategic, political, and economic imperatives coalesced. Rhodes's botched conspiracy to organize an Uitlander rebellion, leading to the abortive Jameson Raid of December 1895, not only increased tensions but also contributed to the outbreak of African revolt in Mashonaland and Matabeleland as BSAC police forces had been withdrawn to participate in the raid. Sir Alfred Milner, who was despatched as British high commissioner to restore the imperial position in South Africa, determined to maneuver the intransigent president of the Transvaal, Paul Kruger, into conflict. Efforts at compromise failed due to hard-line attitudes on both sides, with Milner, like Frere in 1878, moving faster than the British government anticipated. The cabinet was still deliberating how to compose a satisfactory ultimatum when Kruger issued his own ultimatum on 9 October 1899 demanding the recall of all British reinforcements sent to Natal since June and the withdrawal of those on the frontier with the Transvaal. On 11 October Boer commandos from both the Transvaal and the Orange Free State invaded Natal and Cape Colony, initiating a war that would not end until peace terms were agreed at Vereeniging on 30 May 1902.

The South African War was a significant shock to army and public alike. Rather than costing the British government no more than £10 million for a three- or four-month campaign utilizing a maximum of 75,000 men, as expected, it lasted thirty-two months and cost £230 million. Britain and the empire eventually fielded over 448,000 men and employed conceivably as many as 120,000 Africans, of whom 30,000 were armed. It cost the lives of 22,000 British and imperial servicemen, the majority from disease. The Boers never fielded more than 42,000 men and, following the defeat of the main Boer

South Africa, 1899–1902. Map by Erin Greb Cartography.

field army in February 1900, never more than 9,000 on commando. It put an additional £160 million on the national debt and dramatically increased government expenditure. Annual army expenditure for the war period peaked at £92.3 million in 1902.[1]

It was a war that confronted soldiers with all the challenges of a transitional military conflict. There were many modern elements with the use of railways, steam tractors, aerial reconnaissance by balloon, electric illumination, breech loaders, smokeless powder, blockhouses, wire entanglements, and entrenchment.[2] Frederick Maurice later wrote that the army "was dealing, as no European army has yet done, with the new conditions of war," amid what George Henderson characterized as the "second tactical revolution" induced by smokeless powder, repeating rifles, and quick firing artillery.[3] Maurice was only partly right; magazine rifles were encountered on the North-West Frontier in 1897, and experimentation had been made already with most other aspects of military modernity.[4] Likewise, there was still reliance on horses, mules, and oxen for transport. Military lessons were highly ambiguous, and different commentators picked examples to fit their own perceptions.

It was the first large-scale war Britain experienced within the context of the emergence of a mass urban-based industrial society. Since the Reform and Redistribution Act of 1884, some 60 percent of adult males enjoyed the franchise. Britain's was also a relatively literate society as a result of the Education Act of 1870, with almost 100 percent literacy among twenty- to twenty-four-year-olds between 1899 and 1914, and 80 percent of those aged forty-five to forty-nine. Patterns of consumption were transformed by new methods of production, distribution, marketing, and advertising. It was a society saturated "with the images, advertising and propaganda of empire."[5] The *Daily Mail* increased its daily circulation from 430,000 in 1898 to almost a million by 1900, and the war saw the launch of more illustrated periodicals. Music halls and other venues of commercial entertainment, commemorative bric-a-brac, children's toys, and a wide variety of print media including sheet music, popular literature, matchbox covers, cigarette cards, and postcards all were utilized in ways that added to the war's impact.

Unsurprisingly, the early defeats of "Black Week" at Stormberg (9–10 December 1899), Magersfontein (11 December), and Colenso (15 December) with their unprecedented casualties were traumatic. Since 1857 the army had lost more than 100 men in a single action only at Isandlwana and Maiwand. Those killed or wounded totaled 102 at Modder River (28 November), 205 at Magersfontein, 171 at Colenso, 383 at Spion Kop (23–24 January 1900), and 348 at Paardeburg (18–27 February 1900). Serious concerns were raised as to the apparent deterioration of the imperial race, resulting in inquiries, investigations of the condition of the working class, new interest in eugenics, and the tentative beginnings of state welfare provision.[6] There were also postwar inquiries into the army's performance chaired by Lord Elgin, into the auxiliary forces chaired by the Duke of Norfolk, and into the WO's structure chaired by Lord Esher.[7]

The army's readiness for war as relations between Britain and the two Boer republics deteriorated was hampered by a complacent cabinet, which believed British aims could be achieved without war. Faced with the unwelcome news on 12 August 1899 that it would take £1 million to reduce the timescale for mobilizing the army corps from four months to three, the cabinet declined to spend money that could not be recovered if there was no war. Wolseley urged the reinforcement of Natal as early as 8 June 1899, but it was not agreed until the colonial secretary, Joseph Chamberlain, forced the issue on 8 September. While Lansdowne claimed to have kept the Army Board fully informed, Wolseley suggested he was never told of the state of diplomacy or what attitude should be taken toward the possibility of hostilities with the OFS as well as the Transvaal.[8] Full mobilization finally commenced on 7 October, four days before the Boers invaded Natal. Parliament had broken up for its summer recess on 9 August and was not recalled until 17 October. By June 1899 there were still only 10,289 regulars in South Africa, although this had been increased to 16,203 by 9 October.[9]

Wolseley, whose relationship with Lansdowne had long since deteriorated, was given more and more to insults.[10] Buller, too, felt the government had been "led into a fool's paradise by their Colonial and War Secretaries." Salisbury's PS, Schomberg McDonnell, was aware that Wolseley and Buller had been repeatedly urging their views on Lansdowne.[11] Buller then approached Salisbury direct through McDonnell, a move Lansdowne resented. It intensified their already uneasy relationship, although, in reality, Buller made no military argument with which the cabinet was not already familiar.[12] Buller had a stormy interview with Lansdowne on 8 September, at which Buller urged sending more troops to Natal.[13]

Operations would be hamstrung by the incomplete railway network in South Africa, difficult climate and terrain, and the all too familiar lack of maps. But the conduct of the war also called into question British generalship itself. In the process, it marked the triumph of Roberts's ring over Wolseley's, for Buller was superseded by Roberts himself.

Redvers Buller

On 3 November 1899, three days after landing in South Africa, Buller wrote a celebrated letter to his brother, Tremayne, in which he stated, "I am in the tightest place I have ever been in, and the worst of it is that it is I think none of my creating."[14] Setting out a defense in advance of operations, Buller recounted his version of events since being informed of his appointment to command the army corps by Lansdowne in the second week of June 1899. Buller maintained he was told "in a most ungracious manner" to the extent he believed that nothing was intended and that it was "a party move in a political game."[15] It was only announced on 15 July that Buller would probably command. He was not formally appointed until 9 October.[16]

One aspect of Buller's defense was his exclusion from any preliminary WO planning: not that there was much in view of the cabinet's reluctance to do anything. The fact of his exclusion remained central to Buller's defense after his supersession by Roberts. Indeed, Buller used much the same terms as in his letter to his brother when appearing before Elgin in February 1903.[17]

Another specific element in Buller's defense was he had no real voice in the selection of his staff or subordinate commanders. It appears as early as a letter written to the Earl of Dundonald on 17 October 1899 from the SS *Dunottar Castle*, which carried Buller to the Cape: "I had, beyond the liberty of suggestions, nothing to do with the appointments, but you know these things are done."[18] On 6 January 1900 Buller included the claim in a wider defense sent to the WO, implying he had been able to secure the employment of only two officers: Col. John French, from the cavalry brigade at Aldershot, to command the Cavalry Division; and Col. Herbert Miles, commandant of the Staff College, as AAG. Buller made the same claim to Bigge in March 1900, although now he suggested that French had been the only one of his choices accepted.[19]

The claim was sufficiently widely known for the MS, Coleridge Grove, to pen an official statement on 7 March 1900. Buller had been frequently consulted on appointments by Wolseley, and told that his wishes would be acceded to. According to Grove, a near complete list of the staff was taken down to Aldershot by Buller's designated MS, Col. the Hon. Frederick Stopford.[20]

On 17 April 1900 Buller again said he had not been consulted. When his suggestion of Henry Settle as CRE was turned down, he did not feel it worth making any others. He also implied the list brought by Stopford had not been one that could be changed: "I assert that I was not consulted as to the selection of my staff and that I had no word in it until I received a printed list in which all the principal appointments were filled up, and the contents of which were generally known."[21] Buller's CRE from Aldershot, Elliott Wood, was appointed instead of Settle. Wood was grouse shooting at the time and only read of his appointment in the press.[22] Buller later claimed, improbably, that he only discovered Wood had been chosen and had been attending WO planning meetings from a chance remark made by Wood three weeks after he had requested Settle's services.[23] Before Elgin, Lansdowne refuted Buller's claim by quoting Grove's statement of three years earlier and, famously, saying that Buller, having seen the list of suggested staff and commanders, had remarked to Grove, "Well, if I can't win with that staff I ought to be kicked."[24]

It was usual to allow field commanders the choice of staff. Evelyn Wood, however, said Wolseley chose the initial brigade and divisional commanders. In his memoir, Wood reiterated that Wolseley and Grove made the appointments, the Army Board being suspended when war was declared. Grove confirmed this to Elgin, saying he and Wolseley chose commanders and staff "to save time." Grove drew up the list and submitted it to Buller, who made "very few" changes.[25]

It would appear the list was not drawn up by Grove, but by the AMS, Neville Lyttelton, whose memoirs imply he did so in July 1899. Lyttelton recalled few amendments were made to his suggestions, although he had to reorganize some brigades and staffs since Wolseley wanted "fancy brigades" such as an Irish Brigade and a Light Brigade.[26] This was not unusual for it was not thought necessary to keep staffs who had worked together in peacetime together in war. Memorably, Leo Amery condemned the practice: "Englishmen who would not dream of sending a crew to Henley Regatta whose members had never rowed together before, were quite content that a general's staff should be hastily improvised at the last moment from officers scraped together from every corner."[27] Amery told Elgin that staff officers shared in their generals' quarrels since there was no staff esprit de corps.[28]

Wolseley reported to Lansdowne on 17 June that a staff list less special service officers had been drawn up in anticipation of a crisis.[29] The earliest extant version is dated 2 September 1899, with an updated version dated a month later.[30] Wolseley sent another version to the queen on 10 October, saying it was now nearly complete.[31] It is not possible to judge when Stopford may have taken the list to Aldershot. The only additions after 2 September were ADCs. Wolseley told Lansdowne on 8 September that everyone had been chosen, although no one had as yet been informed. Consequently, if given the chance to make such amendments as the addition of French and Miles, Buller could only have done so before September.[32]

Buller was appointed on Wolseley's recommendation, although Chamberlain had been advocating his appointment since June.[33] Wolseley had subsequent doubts, twice commenting to his brother that Buller, now sixty, had grown fat and bloated and was not the man he had been ten years previously.[34] Buller expressed his own reservations about accepting command when he would be happier acting as Wolseley's CoS. Buller had seen Wolseley, remarking in Lyttelton's hearing that he had "strong objections to accepting the command, ... that he was sick of South Africa, and if he was forced to go out he would come away as soon as he could."[35] Wolseley felt he could not name himself, but it was made clear to him that he would not be acceptable on the grounds of age. He was sixty-six and had been seriously ill in 1897.[36] Buller had performed badly at the 1898 maneuvers. Commanding the opposing "army," Connaught showed greater capacity to learn from mistakes. Buller repeated his errors in South Africa with the same lack of reconnaissance and a tendency to favor frontal assaults.[37]

Evelyn Wood wished to be considered for the command, but Wolseley had never forgiven Wood for the peace concluded with the Boers in 1881. Buller appears to have believed that Wood would have been a better choice than himself. Wood was not apparently aware of Buller's appointment until Buller informed him. Subsequently, Wood wrote to Lansdowne in August 1899 indicating his wish to have served. He wrote again in October offering to take command at the Cape when Buller decided to go to Natal. After Colenso, Wood offered to serve under Buller, to whom he was senior.[38] Wood was briefly considered for second in command but quickly rejected by Wolseley as "a firework, neither physically nor mentally fit."[39] Interestingly, Brodrick, who became secretary of state in November 1900, seems to have considered asking Wood to go to South Africa.[40] Wood would have been prepared to serve under Kitchener if asked, but only provided he could return to his post as AG at the WO, and also take over if Kitchener was incapacitated.[41]

Another senior officer who felt he should be considered was Roberts, now sixty-seven. Roberts had already offered his services for the Sudan in March 1896.[42] He pressed for command in South Africa in the event of war in March and April 1896, and again in April 1897.[43] On the latter occasion, it would appear that Roberts was prompted to do so by Henry Rawlinson, then brigade major at Aldershot, who had heard only Buller and Wood mentioned.[44] Roberts offered his services thrice more, on 22 October 1899, 8 December, and also 11 December 1899, claiming only the gravity of the situation and his own sense of duty prompted his offer. Of course, he would only go if in supreme command and risk his motives being misconstrued. If the offer was not accepted then, as he wrote on 8 December, "I shall feel the Government have better means than I have of knowing how affairs in South Africa are being conducted, and I shall bow to your decision."[45] Lansdowne replied on 10 December that there was no current justification for Buller's removal.[46]

The queen wanted Kitchener appointed.[47] Kitchener indicated his willingness to go to the Cape in a letter to Lady Cranborne, Salisbury's daughter-in-law, in September 1899: "If you see the chance I hope you will put in a word as if the Cape war comes off it will be a big thing and they might give me some billet." Lansdowne made this known to Arthur Balfour on 17 December 1899.[48] Kitchener's interest was well enough known for his summons to be Roberts's CoS to evince little surprise.

Kitchener was considered as a potential second in command to Buller. Wolseley preferred Francis Grenfell, who had taken over the Malta command in January 1899, arguing that South Africa was not big enough to accommodate both Buller and Kitchener. Salisbury was consulted and suggested Buller be left alone. Buller himself turned down the idea of Kitchener being his second in command.[49] As it happened, Henry Rawlinson and Ian Hamilton had arranged for Kitchener to meet Roberts in Ireland in August 1899, on which occasion

Kitchener said he would be willing to serve under Roberts if Roberts went into the field again.[50] Milner favored Methuen for the command. Recently returned from India, Methuen had acted as press censor for Lockhart during the operations on the North-West Frontier in 1897 while technically merely an observer.[51]

Buller was most certainly consulted on the choice of his actual designated second in command, Sir George White, sent to take command in Natal in September 1899.[52] When Wood was selected to succeed Buller as AG in 1897, Wolseley opted for either Mansfield Clarke or White to fill Wood's billet as QMG, feeling it useful to demonstrate "that we searched outside the ordinary War Office circle for our good men."[53] White had not been a particular success in India. Indeed, Lansdowne felt White might be better employed at Gibraltar or Malta. Lansdowne then changed his mind. White's tenure in India was due to expire in April 1898, but he broke his leg badly in February 1898. The broken bone was reset at Aden with screws inserted on the way home in April, which delayed his arrival at the WO.[54] White, now sixty-four, had recovered from the injury, but was left with a permanent limp.

White's fitness for command in Natal was owing to the bulk of the reinforcements sent there in the autumn of 1899 being drawn from India. Wolseley had been reluctant to draw on the resources of India lest it be thought sufficient resources could not be found from the home army. The viceroy, Curzon, also argued that a brigade of British troops could only be spared for a few months.[55] Wolseley believed, erroneously, that Roberts was behind Lansdowne's willingness to accept the Indian reinforcement.[56]

White had not adjusted to the WO and had already accepted Gibraltar in July, but it would not be vacant for some time. Consequently, dispatching White to Natal—he was warned to be ready to go on 6 September—enabled Mansfield Clarke to succeed him as QMG earlier than would otherwise have been the case. Like Buller, White went without specific instructions. A general instruction was subsequently sent him that cautioned against a forward deployment, but this was intended not for White, but for the existing commander in Natal, Col. (temporary Maj. Gen.) Sir William Penn Symons.[57]

Natal had been a backwater since 1881, and Ladysmith was adopted as a supply base in 1897 on political grounds since a forward position on the much more strategically important Biggarsberg range of hills might antagonize the Boers. Thus, Ladysmith became a de facto operational center through the difficulty of abandoning it.[58] Meanwhile, isolated with four thousand men some forty-two miles north of White's eleven thousand at Ladysmith, Symons felt obliged to defend Dundee, since the governor of Natal, Sir Walter Hely-Hutchinson, feared the impact of its evacuation on Uitlander refugees from the Transvaal and, especially, on the Zulu.[59]

It has been suggested that White clung to Ladysmith after Symons was mortally wounded at Talana on 20 October 1899 when he could still have retreated—first, because he believed he could land a knockout blow on the Boers; and then, after the disaster of Nicholson's Nek on 30 October, where more than eight hundred men were taken prisoner, because he lacked the moral strength to conduct a fighting retreat. White did confide to his wife on 30 October that he felt too old and would be rightly replaced.[60] White thought withdrawal from Ladysmith might lead to a Boer insurrection in Natal as well as having a significant impact on morale. He also felt he could not hold the line of the Tugela River by such a withdrawal, while the Boers could not afford to bypass Ladysmith. Buller had also effectively suggested holding Ladysmith or perhaps Colenso in a telegram on 31 October.[61]

Symons is invariably represented as elderly and headstrong, and as grossly underestimating Boer fighting capacity.[62] His correspondence with White shows he respected Boer mobility and marksmanship, was conscious of the poor training of his own infantry battalions, and believed only offensive action could safeguard the water supplies available to him at Glencoe and Dundee.[63] At fifty-six, Symons was no more elderly than most major generals. He had seen active service in South Africa in 1877–79 and, most recently, commanded a brigade successfully in Waziristan. White concluded in 1896, "I consider him an officer who should be pushed on."[64]

Wolseley claimed that he favored White because "I only knew him by reputation & he was always crammed down my throat as a great General."[65] It is possible Roberts urged White's appointment to Natal. Nonetheless, at the time, Wolseley clearly recommended White to Buller, writing on 7 September 1899 that no one would suit Buller better, and that "I think highly of him."[66] Wolseley and Buller together recommended White's appointment to Lansdowne.[67]

Buller would have preferred Grenfell as his second in command.[68] Buller later claimed that he plumped for White when told Grenfell was not available since the alternative to White was Methuen. Buller would also have preferred Grenfell to Kitchener.[69] Wolseley contemplated removing White from command as early as 3 November 1899, but Lansdowne believed the effect on morale "might be bad."[70] Wolseley thought White was largely to blame for all the disasters, as he had "played the devil" with prewar plans.[71]

Buller later implied that Lansdowne proposed Methuen after White had already been chosen, and it was then he stated his preference for White over Methuen.[72] It is impossible to judge whether this is true, and there is no evidence, as suggested by some historians, that Lansdowne was directly responsible for "many of the key early appointments" including Francis Clery, Arthur Fitzroy Hart, and Charles Long, and that only Henry Hildyard and Lyttelton were Buller's choices.[73] It is equally suggested that French was appointed by Lansdowne without Buller being consulted.[74] Despite being a neighbor in Wiltshire, Lansdowne did not consider Methuen suitable for an independent command. This went, too, for Buller's subsequent decision to send Methuen to relieve Kimberley when he split the army corps in South Africa, but Salisbury said it must be Buller's responsibility.[75]

It should be added there was already a lieutenant general in South Africa as GOC at the Cape. After 1881 the post was filled by a series of undistinguished soldiers until the sudden death of William Goodenough in November 1898, when William Butler was appointed on Wolseley's recommendation. No one could accuse Butler of being undistinguished, but his sympathies lay with the Boers. He dragged his feet in the preparation of defense plans.[76] Butler also displayed frankly anti-Semitic views in alleging Jewish business interests lay at the heart of the evolving political crisis, although he was not alone in this.[77]

Acting as high commissioner in Milner's absence, Butler refused to accept the Uitlander petition calling for British protection following the death of an English boilermaker at the hands of Boer police in December 1898.[78] He clashed with Milner to the extent his position became untenable.[79] Lansdowne, who had supported Butler's appointment, saw no reason to remove him unless he did something "outrageous."[80] Butler then received a letter from an unidentified informant saying how unpopular he was at the WO. Butler's resignation was accepted on 8 August 1899. Methuen was briefly considered but also seemed too sympathetic to the Boers. The best solution was to switch Butler with the GOC at the Western District, Frederick "Shookey" Forestier-Walker. Butler initially turned the offer down but then accepted.[81]

Butler was subjected to such public opprobrium upon his return to England that, in November 1899, it was thought better that he should not accompany the queen on a visit to Bristol.[82] Butler had repeatedly written to Wolseley and others between April and July 1899 putting forth his point of view. Wolseley had chosen not to pass on the correspondence, and Butler would not defend himself "at the risk of putting him [Wolseley] in the cart."[83] Following the Bristol episode, and the accusation he was really responsible for the losses at Nicholson's Nek, Butler requested the opportunity to make his case. Lansdowne replied, "it is not desirable that officers should take note of criticism in the Press as to the manner in which they have discharged their duties."[84] In October 1901 Butler secured a statement that he had not been dismissed for neglect of duty. His performance before the Elgin Commission impressed Esher enough to suggest Butler as QMG in 1903.[85]

No one had much faith in Forestier-Walker's abilities, and he only arrived in South Africa on 6 September 1899. Forestier-Walker has been characterized as a "charming non-entity," but he was regarded as at least a safe pair of hands.[86] He had been promoted to major general by selection in 1887 at the exceptionally young age of forty-three, and had considerable experience of South Africa. Forestier-Walker's responsibilities were reduced by White's appointment, and, with Buller's arrival, he was confined to the LOC.[87] Roberts formed a poor impression of Forestier-Walker and suggested he might be sent to the Scottish command, where he would be popular.[88] In fact, Forestier-Walker remained at the Cape, falling afoul of Kitchener in May 1901 for promulgating appointments without Kitchener's authority.[89] Had Butler turned down Devonport, then it was intended to send sixty-one-year-old Francis Clery, the eccentric former commandant of the Staff College and now DAG at the WO, who had taken to dyeing his prominent side-whiskers blue.[90]

White's staff was primarily from Indian backgrounds, including Ian Hamilton as CoS. Buller's only apparent communication with White regarding staff, on the day before White left for the Cape, was to commend the qualities of Col. Wodehouse Richardson ASC.[91] At Hamilton's suggestion, White asked for Henry Rawlinson as DAAG.[92] Shut up in Ladysmith, Hamilton was soon busy criticizing Buller, while Buller equally characterized Hamilton as a dangerous adviser to White. Buller and Hamilton came into closer contact in September 1900 and became marginally more appreciative of each other.[93]

The choice of a cavalry brigade commander for the Natal Field Force was particularly carefully considered. Wolseley recommended French. While French initially joined White, a decision was subsequently made that he should command the main cavalry division of the army corps, possibly as a result of Buller's intervention.[94] Neither White nor Donald Stewart could recommend anyone from India beyond Lt. Col. Wolseley Jenkins, who was too junior.[95] Wolseley suggested Col. James Babington, who had recently served in India, but he, too, was allocated to the main cavalry division. In the event, the cavalry brigade went to Col. John "Brock" Brocklehurst rather than Dundonald, whom Buller had suggested. Brocklehurst was trapped in Ladysmith, while Dundonald subsequently joined Buller in Natal to command a brigade of mounted infantry and irregulars.[96]

This was not the only change to the original staff plan, for another new arrival on 5 October 1899 was Maj. Gen. Sir Archibald Hunter. Intended to be Buller's CoS, Hunter had only recently been appointed to Quetta from the Sudan. Hunter was not Buller's choice since he believed Hunter was unsuited to office work. Henry Hallam Parr, an old acquaintance of Buller's, believed that he had been considered, but rejected on health grounds.[97] Subsequently, Buller indicated he would have liked Hildyard, a former commandant of the Staff College. He felt unable to reject Hunter "when it was so far settled that he would have known I had refused him." Hunter had also been suggested "in terms which I felt I could not refuse."[98] Pending Buller's arrival at the Cape, it was decided that Hunter should command the Indian contingent in Natal. White then made Hunter his CoS with Hamilton taking a brigade.[99] Interestingly, Hunter was instructed by Buller to report to him independently of White.[100]

With Symons dead and his replacement, James Yule, wounded, White asked to retain Hunter's services. Accordingly, Hunter was trapped in Ladysmith. Arriving at the Cape on 30 October, Buller was left without a CoS. His DAG, Col. Arthur Wynne, acted as such, but Buller found him "in no sense a substitute," though he was "a good little office man." Buller found Wynne "rather a drag than a help—he was so red tapey."[101] Buller left Wynne at the Cape when he decided to move up to the Natal front, taking only Stopford with him. He then acted through Clery's Second Division staff.[102]

While Buller had full discretion to act as he felt necessary, the sudden decision to go to Natal and abandon the original campaign plan to advance through the OFS took many by surprise. Wolseley claimed that Buller went to Natal "on his own hook entirely, and at his own instigation, and I do not know that I even knew, until he had started, or was about to start, that he was going there."[103] The practical effect was to leave Buller short of staff officers in Natal, while he tried to control the whole theater of operations through Wynne issuing orders from Cape Town. After the death of Edward Woodgate at Spion Kop, Buller moved Wynne to the vacant brigade command and made Herbert Miles CoS.[104] According to Charles à Court, who was also on Buller's staff, someone in the WO inquired in early December who Miles actually was.[105]

Buller's designated cavalry divisional commander, French, and his DAAG, Maj. Douglas Haig, were also initially with White. They were ordered out on the last train on 2 November 1899. The designated head of Buller's intelligence service, Maj. Edward Altham, remained in Ladysmith, compelling Buller to rely on a local civilian.[106]

White's investment in Ladysmith and those of the garrisons at Kimberley and Mafeking persuaded Buller to abandon the original plan and to divide his corps into its component divisions. Buller's staff was thus divided. The CRE, Elliot Wood, was dispatched to the Orange River to command "frontier posts"; the DAG, Miles, to De Aar; another DAG, Charles Douglas, to become Methuen's CoS; the DAAG, Charles à Court, to the recruiting depot; and the provost marshal, Julian Byng, to command the South African Light Horse.[107]

The First Division commanded by Methuen was dispatched toward Kimberley, the Second Division commanded by Clery went to Natal, and the Third Division commanded by William Gatacre went to the Eastern Cape. Gatacre's name was omitted from Lyttelton's original suggestions back in July, but added at Wolseley's insistence. Lyttelton, who had commanded a brigade under Gatacre in the Sudan, had deliberately avoided naming him.[108] Gatacre had a decidedly mixed reputation. Lansdowne was clearly aware of some of the doubts concerning Gatacre, writing to the Duke of Devonshire after criticism of Gatacre's defeat at Stormberg that Kitchener had been especially appreciative of him despite his eccentricity, and that working men hard was no reason to be disqualified from command.[109] Significantly, Lyttelton was appointed to one of Clery's brigades.

In 1890 Gatacre was bitten by a jackal, which affected his brain at least temporarily; the incident coincided with the breakup of his first marriage.[110] In India it was said that Gatacre "worries the spirit & go out of his troops. He never rests, they say, and expects perpetual work & motion from all his men and animals."[111] Soon known in the Sudan, where he commanded the British division in 1898, as "Backacher," he was viewed by some as "full of cheap advertisement," prone to long-winded speeches to his men, and too ready to interfere in the work of his subordinates.[112] One subaltern simply regarded Gatacre as a "dangerous lunatic."[113] Churchill perhaps caught Gatacre best in describing him as "disturbed by a restless irritation, to which even the most inordinate activity afforded little relief, and which often left him the exhausted victim of his own vitality."[114]

Roberts pointed out to Lansdowne in December 1899 that none of those sent to South Africa had exercised an independent field command.[115] This was true since only Wolseley, Kitchener, Wood, Lockhart, and Roberts himself had such experience. Yet, the presence of Hunter, Gatacre, Andrew Wauchope, and Lyttelton demonstrated that successful recent experience was regarded as a qualification for field command: all had been in the Sudan. Cromer expressed concerns as early as June 1899 at the prospect of the EA losing the services of Hunter; Rundle; Hector MacDonald, who commanded a Sudanese brigade at Omdurman; and Col. Charles Long, who commanded the EA's artillery. Cromer anticipated all would be sent to South Africa in the event of war.[116]

Lyttelton had taken command of a brigade at Aldershot in September 1899, and the two other brigade commanders from Aldershot, Fitzroy Hart and Hildyard, were also selected. Hart was allocated to Gatacre's division and Hildyard to Methuen's division. French, Elliott Wood, and Buller's CRA, Col. George Marshall, were also from the Aldershot command. The other two brigades were commanded by Maj. Gen. Sir Henry Colvile, now commanding the brigade at Gibraltar but with recent command experience on active service on the Unyoro expedition in Uganda in 1894, and Maj. Gen. Geoffry Barton, who had been unemployed since relinquishing the Chester District command in October 1898. Barton had been one of the special service officers on Wolseley's

Asante campaign, as had Methuen, Wauchope, Hart, Woodgate, and John "Bwab" Brabazon, who was named as the second of French's brigade commanders. Colvile, Gatacre, Barton, Hart, Lyttelton, and Hildyard had all been promoted to major general by selection since March 1898, their average age just over fifty-two years with Colvile only forty-five. Thus, while Hart's tactical acumen was not great, he was hardly the "relic" that some historians have claimed.[117]

In the event, Methuen and Gatacre both suffered serious defeats, while Clery proved hesitant in Natal and urged Buller to come to Natal himself.[118] Buller was also soon dissatisfied with Barton and Long, who made the fatal error of taking his artillery too far forward at Colenso as if he was still facing only Mahdist spearmen.[119] Lyttelton, who was adjudged successful, thought Clery incapable of handling troops, and heard little to commend Hart, Barton, Woodgate, or Maj. Gen. John Talbot Coke, who commanded a brigade in the Fifth Division.[120] Even before the action at the Modder River on 23 November, Wolseley was having doubts about Methuen and recommended his replacement by Grenfell. Lansdowne suggested Kitchener, but Wolseley doubted if Buller and Kitchener could be easily accommodated together.[121] Upon reaching Methuen's division, Reginald Pole-Carew thought him weak and obstinate: "He cannot grasp an idea quickly and he apparently cannot learn by his own awful blunders—a hopeless person."[122] Buller stood by Methuen and saw no place in South Africa for Grenfell or Kitchener while White remained.[123] Buller now envisaged Methuen becoming second in command rather than White, who could not act as such while shut up in Ladysmith.[124]

At home, Wolseley was increasingly exercised by the failures, although he still hoped Buller "will set everything right."[125] He saw the solution in the man appointed to command the Fifth Division, Lt. Gen. Sir Charles Warren, who had offered his services on the outbreak of war.[126] Warren reached South Africa in December 1899 with a dormant commission to succeed to the command in the event of Buller falling.[127] Buller did not wish to be seen to supersede Methuen but accepted Warren as second in command.[128]

Warren was ordered by Wolseley to take over operational command from Methuen, who had served under Warren in Bechuanaland, only for the orders to be countermanded by Buller when Warren was already en route.[129] Methuen, for one, having served under Warren in Bechuanaland, thought him "very impossible," judging that he "knows very little of soldiering." Forestier-Walker was equally dumbfounded, having, or so he claimed, run the Bechuanaland expedition for Warren in 1884–85.[130]

Known as "Jerusalem" Warren for his archaeological investigations in the 1860s, Warren was a curious appointment. Although distinguished, he had courted controversy as commissioner of the Metropolitan Police between 1886 and 1888, and quarreled with the civil authorities when GOC of the Straits Settlement between 1889 and 1894. He had not been employed since relinquishing the Chatham command in 1898, was known to be on poor terms with Buller, and had a notoriously foul temper.[131] Warren had at least exercised independent command not just in Bechuanaland but also at Suakin on the Red Sea coast. The claim that Warren's selection was due to Wolseley's failing memory and that Wolseley "mistook him for some other person" is preposterous.[132] A recent defense of Lansdowne's WO record also suggests that Wolseley's attitude toward the former was because illness had "corrupted his mind."[133]

Buller certainly wrote in early 1899 that Wolseley was not the man he had been and had allowed matters to drift.[134] Wolseley often suffered ill health, notably recurring malaria. There was also the major illness in January 1897, to which Wolseley's declining powers are usually attributed. This illness, which necessitated surgically removing glands from Wolseley's throat, is difficult to pin down after the passage of time.[135] Wolseley's short-term memory was affected, but evidence as to how seriously is circumstantial. Wolseley's correspondence and memoranda show no indication of any drop-off in the continuing expression of his views on military policy. Wolseley's robust attack on Lansdowne's record in the House of Lords in March 1901 and his performance before Elgin in November 1902 do not suggest any real diminution of powers. The poor personal relationship between Wolseley and Lansdowne, not Wolseley's health, led to Wolseley being kept in the dark with regard to Roberts's subsequent appointment.

As all contemporary correspondence suggests, Wolseley was perfectly aware who Warren was.[136] But, as Wolseley wrote to Arthur Bigge in informing him of Warren's dormant commission, generals were born not made and he could only send out the best men he knew of: "I have many young men coming on but the old fashioned lot who were promoted by seniority before I came into office are mostly poor creatures as regards knowledge of war."[137] Warren was one of the youngest unemployed generals in age and seniority available.

While Warren was to contribute to Buller's defeat at Spion Kop, he had not reached the front at the time Buller was defeated at Colenso on 15 December 1899. Buller's injudicious telegram to White following the battle, suggesting that Ladysmith be "let go," was the excuse for which Lansdowne had been waiting. Having refused to supersede either Methuen or Gatacre, Buller fully expected Roberts would be sent out "the first chance." He was relieved for he felt that "this show is too big for one man," and that "it is impossible for me to run this place [Natal] and look after the Cape which is a thousand miles away."[138] Roberts reminded Lansdowne of his availability yet again in a telegram on 15 December, suggesting that "radical change" was required.[139] Unrealistically, Wolseley had previously told his brother that the solution would be for Buller to come home to the WO as CinC and for Wolseley to replace him in South Africa.[140]

Frederick Roberts

Without consulting Wolseley, on the alleged grounds there was no time to do so, Lansdowne and Arthur Balfour, the only other cabinet minister in London, decided the appointment of Roberts with Kitchener as CoS.[141] Balfour's secretary, Jack Sandars, later maintained that Balfour rather than Lansdowne was the "prevailing force." Roberts's telegraphed his willingness to go to South Africa crossed with Lansdowne's request that he do so.[142] Ironically, in view of the role played by Buller's telegram suggesting Ladysmith be given up in his supersession, it is not often noted that Roberts's telegram suggested abandoning Mafeking and Kimberley: Lansdowne kept it to himself.[143] The decision to send Roberts and Kitchener was ratified by the Cabinet Defence Committee on the evening of 16 December and by the cabinet the following morning. Adding Kitchener negated Salisbury's doubts as to Roberts's age.

The queen complained that she and Wolseley had not been consulted and that Roberts was too old.[144] Going to Windsor on 18 December, Balfour conveyed to the queen through Bigge that her advisers "must be permitted to issue important military orders without her previous sanction." It had not been possible to inform Wolseley "as his well known jealousy of Roberts made his advice on such a subject perfectly worthless." According to Balfour, Lansdowne nearly fainted when told Bigge was suggesting that Evelyn Wood replace Roberts in Ireland, Mansfield Clarke succeed as AG, and Connaught come in as QMG. Balfour concluded that Buller should be replaced at once since it seemed "that for the last ten years Buller has allowed himself to go downhill, and, for the moment at least, is not the man he once was."[145] Balfour believed it particularly undesirable to make Connaught QMG when the QMG's office was the most "strained wheel" of the coach in fighting so distant a war.[146]

Kitchener was willing to go as CoS to Roberts although he feared Roberts might be badly affected by Freddie Roberts's death from his wounds received at Colenso.[147] A major general, Kitchener, wanted local rank superior to any divisional commanders in South Africa, but this was initially refused as it would put him over four lieutenant generals and two major generals. It has been suggested that he was then promoted to lieutenant general on 23 December 1899 but not gazetted, or perhaps promoted to lieutenant general on 29 November 1901 on succeeding Roberts but with the immediate temporary rank of full general.[148] Methuen thought Kitchener's appointment in particular "a wretched submission to public opinion."[149] Significantly, in view of the queen's later pointed objection to Lady Roberts's presence in South Africa, Salisbury advised Lansdowne to get the queen's permission for the announcement of the appointment of Roberts and Kitchener, for "as she loves Buller—& does not love R, or rather his wife—she may make a remonstrance."[150]

Roberts's appointment was a bitter blow to Wolseley, who had long viewed Roberts as "a play actor more than a soldier." He added, "The *Hindoo* element is now in the ascendancy & I dread the effect it must have on our regular Army when he rules here in my place." That Roberts—"the greatest toady of peers & big people, a real snob, & the most remarkable jobber of his time"—would also succeed him as CinC added materially to Wolseley's disgust.[151] Wolseley wrote to Buller that he had heard Roberts's headquarters was "a regular *Hindoo* camp."[152]

Warren's dormant commission was promptly canceled by Roberts, who concluded that Warren's "disagreeable temper unfits him for holding an important position in the field."[153] Buller had not removed Warren after Spion Kop in the knowledge Warren held the dormant commission: he did not feel justified as yet in doing so "in the face of the direct instructions which I had received from the Secretary of State for War."[154] Roberts also judged Methuen, Clery, and Forestier-Walker surplus to requirements.[155]

Roberts's arrival marked a change in the power structure within the army as Lansdowne gave him an entirely free hand. Given that Roberts and Kitchener represented the last hope for victory, their appointment significantly weakened the government's own hands in managing the war.[156] According to Wood, no one was sent to South Africa without Roberts's approval once he succeeded Buller despite appointments being made nominally by Wolseley.[157]

Lansdowne gave Roberts a heavy hint that Methuen should be replaced; the queen also made her reservations known.[158] Methuen was reduced to commanding a single brigade in February 1900. Ironically, he recovered his reputation. Despite being captured by the Boers at Tweebosch in March 1902—being wounded, he was soon released—Methuen was one of only three general officers to serve throughout the whole war. The others were French and Lyttelton.

Not unexpectedly, Gatacre was removed on 9 April 1900 following another hint from Lansdowne, and after the convenient surrender to the Boers of five companies Gatacre was judged to have left exposed at Dewetsdorp.[159] In July 1900 Gatacre asked Wolseley to try to get him a command in China that "would enable me to make a fresh start which I fear, I may not get unless I get it now."[160] Immediately before the war, Gatacre had commanded the Eastern District at Colchester, and he was returned to it. Gatacre briefly worked for the WO Remount Department and retired in 1905.

Roberts quickly moved to bring William Nicholson, Neville Chamberlain, and George Pretyman as MS, camp commandant, and ADC/PS, respectively.[161] As it happened, Kitchener disliked Nicholson intensely, with Hamilton suggesting that Kitchener could not bear Nicholson's "envious quality or his habit of detraction however amusingly he expressed himself."[162] The mutual loathing was long lasting. It was suggested by Ian Hamilton's wife, who was present, that Nicholson, who was CIGS from 1908 to 1912, was almost gloating at Kitchener's memorial service in 1916.[163]

To the surprise of most, Kitchener worked well with Roberts, although it has been suggested that most strategic ideas came from George Henderson as Roberts's head of intelligence. Kitchener was not so much CoS as a roving deputy to whom specific tasks were delegated.[164] Kitchener lacked seniority even after his promotion to lieutenant general was backdated. At Paardeburg in February 1900, Kitchener took over the conduct of the battle by virtue of carrying out Roberts's instructions when Thomas Kelly-Kenny was actually senior to Kitchener as a local lieutenant general. The same applied to French and Colvile, who were also both present as local lieutenant generals. Criticism of his headstrong tactics resulted in Kitchener contemplating the possibility of his own dismissal. Roberts, who had been ill, quickly took over the reins once more but made no public censure of Kitchener.[165] With Henderson invalided home, Nicholson assumed charge of transport with James Grierson acting as AAG with responsibility for the work normally undertaken by an AQMG, a post now only existing at the WO.[166]

As soon as Ladysmith was relieved, Roberts summoned Hamilton and Rawlinson to join him. Both were highly critical of Buller although Rawlinson also brought general news of Buller's force, noting that Lyttelton, Clery, and Warren "all crab each other and they say that in the whole force they have not a brigadier worth a damn—the fact is that they are all at loggerheads."[167] Unsurprisingly, Roberts reported most favorably on his own protégés, including Pole-Carew, who got command of the Guards Brigade in February 1900, and Hamilton, who was "quite the most brilliant Commander I have serving under me." Some others were performing satisfactorily, such as Bruce Hamilton, Horace Smith-Dorrien, and, despite his conceitedness, "Curly" Hutton.[168]

Roberts also requested the services of a large number of officers from Egypt and, especially, from India. Due to Curzon's objections, Roberts did not get all of the fifty officers he wanted from India. George Younghusband, for example, was initially refused permission to resign his staff post at Umballa to accompany Hector Macdonald when the latter was summoned to command the Highland Brigade following Wauchope's death at Magersfontein. Younghusband was able to circumvent Curzon's refusal to allow Indian officers to South Africa by calling in the services of the Prince of Wales's equerry, Sir Dighton Probyn, who had been a close friend of his father. The Prince duly sent a telegram to Curzon expressing the desire that Younghusband be transferred to the Imperial Yeomanry. Curzon obliged.[169]

In the case of Egypt and the Sudan, Cromer and Kitchener's successor as sirdar, Reginald Wingate, managed to retain at least a few of those requested, although Cromer was keen to get rid of those most strongly influenced by Kitchener's ideas such as John Maxwell.[170] Wingate was particularly annoyed that Kitchener had refused to allow officers from the EA to go to South Africa, and had then applied for sixteen as soon as he himself reached the Cape.[171] Maxwell was keen to get to South Africa. Cromer saw advantages as Maxwell was engaged in an irreconcilable feud with Wingate. Maxwell duly got the nod for South Africa.[172] As well as Maxwell, Wingate was also happy to be rid of another perceived rival to his authority, Herbert Jackson.[173]

Kelly-Kenny was at least one home-based officer of whom Roberts initially approved, although he soon judged him nervous and overcautious.[174] Kelly-Kenny had succeeded Buller in the Aldershot command. It may be significant that he and Roberts had previously served together on the Abyssinian expedition in 1867–68. Others were marked for removal as circumstances permitted.

Roberts was determined to remove Lt. Gen. Sir Frederick Carrington, who had been appointed to command the Rhodesian Field Force at the specific request of the British South Africa Company only in January 1900. As he had commanded imperial and BSAC forces against the Matabele and Mashona in 1896, Carrington was an obvious candidate to take command in Rhodesia. Carrington's physical condition was poor, and he did not perform well in operations around Zeerust and Brakfontein. Carrington, who threatened to resign if he was sent back to Rhodesia, was duly deprived of any troops to command in August, supposedly because his nerve had gone. What was left of the Rhodesian Field Force was disbanded in December 1900, and Carrington went home.[175]

Of those who had served in the Sudan, Roberts was not impressed by Rundle but felt that Hunter was good.[176] Herbert Chermside, whom Wolseley had recommended after successful service on Crete in 1897–98, was not well regarded by Roberts, who thought him mediocre. Roberts did not think Chermside would be of any use in the WO or in Ireland, suggesting rather that he might be sent as governor to some island.[177]

Baden-Powell, who had become Wolseley's protégé, expressed gratitude to his patron, "I have to thank you for every step in my very rapid promotion— and I am deeply sensible of my indebtedness."[178] He had expected a brigade command in India, but in May 1899 Wolseley intentionally kept him back. On 3 July 1899 Wolseley tasked Baden-Powell with leading a projected raid into the Transvaal from Rhodesia. The scheme proved impracticable, and Baden-Powell defended Mafeking instead. Baden-Powell found Wolseley powerless to help him once Roberts was in the ascendancy. Baden-Powell received promotion to major general in May 1900 but discovered that all those promoted to the rank as a result of Roberts's recommendations had their appointments backdated to July 1899. Fortuitously, those remaining did not have effective seniority over him once he was attached to the South African Constabulary.[179]

Roberts claimed before Elgin that the failure rate among regimental OCs and brigade commanders was due to disinclination to accept responsibility as men got older.[180] Although most victims were ostensibly targeted on the grounds of inefficiency, scores were settled. Pretyman believed there had been an attempt by the "jealous set of jobbers who run the fate of the Army in Pall Mall" to keep him out of employment until he was compulsorily retired. He singled out Evelyn Wood in particular. Now he hoped to see the end of Buller and a clean sweep of "that malicious and jobbing clique."[181] Once released from the confines of Ladysmith, Hamilton was also soon urging the influential military commentator Henry Spenser Wilkinson to use his influence to get Buller removed: "*Buller is no use.* He is indeed far, far worse than useless. You know that, ever since the big manoeuvres when Buller funked fighting on every occasion, I have thought him a duffer. But I think also you know me well enough to be sure I would not strike a man when he's down for the pleasure of it. Now however it is a question of life or death, of our own soldiers here as well."[182] Hamilton also suggested that Buller had spoken violently of Roberts and Kitchener when he had met White after the relief of Ladysmith.[183]

Edward Stuart-Wortley anticipated the same wrangling between Buller and Roberts as had already occurred between Buller and Warren, and between Buller and Long, "as Buller is very jealous of Roberts and is inclined to ignore him instead of working with him."[184] Lyttelton, too, was reported as "full of abuse of Buller."[185] Hunter, who took command of the Tenth Division after the end of the Ladysmith siege, became increasingly critical of Roberts and was soon out of favor. As he wrote on 4 November 1900, "So much is done that I not only don't agree with but which I think to be detrimental to our success & prestige; so many men are pushing their own self advancement by advertisement; Lord Roberts is so weak & vacillating; so short sighted in policy & given to favouritism; & so ruled & badly advised; that I would gladly get away from him, for I never want to serve a day under him again."[186] Hunter left South Africa shortly after Roberts, to take the Scottish command in May 1901.

As early as March 1900, one officer reported a general or colonel was "broke per diem."[187] Conflicting statements were made by Evelyn Wood and even Roberts himself as to the number of men removed from command.[188] The total appears to have been twenty-seven officers, comprising five divisional commanders (Carrington, Clery, Colvile, Gatacre, and Warren), one infantry brigade commander, six cavalry brigade commanders, four infantry battalion OCs, and eleven cavalry OCs.[189]

The cavalry was particularly targeted, conceivably because of Roberts's long-standing reservations about its efficiency going back perhaps to Massy's failures in Afghanistan. Some of its perceived failures in South Africa such as the escape of the Boers at Poplar Grove in March 1900 were at least partly the result of mistakes by Roberts's own staff. Nonetheless, the loss of cavalry horses in South Africa was considerable, and even Methuen removed Bloomfield Gough of the Ninth Lancers, who then committed suicide. While infantry commanders were removed for fairly specific reasons, cavalry dismissals were somewhat more generalized as failures of military capacity.[190]

Babington appears to have been removed largely because he was a friend of Buller, although Roberts claimed he was "sticky."[191] Haig believed Pole-Carew's "evil tales" played a part in Babington's removal.[192] Ultimately, Babington rebuilt his career, ending as a corps commander and temporary theater commander on the Italian front in 1918.

French reported that Brabazon's nerve had gone and that his "characteristic impatience of control and his irrepressible and unrestrained habit of adversely criticising in public the dispositions and plans of his superiors have a very bad effect on any troops."[193] Herbert Miles heard Brabazon was "always having scares" but was surprised by Babington's removal.[194] While Brabazon had served with Roberts in Afghanistan, he considered Brabazon too old for his duties and best suited to take command of the Imperial Yeomanry, where his removal from his brigade would not attract particular attention.[195] Churchill maintained that Brabazon, who had once been French's superior, was too free with his tongue in commenting not only on French's tactics "but on his youthful morals."[196] French was involved in the sacking of several cavalrymen, as well as Wodehouse Richardson, who had miscalculated the grain required by the Cavalry Division.[197]

French himself had a somewhat problematic relationship with Roberts over Roberts's unhappiness with the cavalry's overall performance. French insisted that Haig remain as his CoS, but Roberts wanted to appoint the Earl of Erroll. French simply ignored Erroll. There was a mysterious episode when French removed two brigade commanders only for them to be immediately reinstated. Ironically, Hamilton warned Roberts that French liked to surround himself with his personal friends.[198] Haig himself was critical of Roberts's handling of the cavalry to the extent the Prince of Wales, to whom Haig's letters were shown by his sister, complained of their tone.[199] Roberts thought French lacked the initiative to become a great cavalry commander.[200]

Roberts wanted to avoid any unnecessary "storm" in such cases as that of Brig. Gen. Robert Broadwood, deemed responsible for the loss of two guns in an ambush at Sannah's Post in March 1900. Roberts considered Broadwood at least brave and resolute if not as intelligent as might be hoped.[201] Courts-martial would have attracted too much publicity. Consequently, Broadwood survived. Others sacked included Lt. Col. Bernhard Möller, whose case especially illustrated the unspecific reasons for dismissal. Möller of the Eighteenth Hussars undoubtedly showed manifold failings when forced to surrender at Adelaide farm following the action at Talana in October 1899. On release from Boer imprisonment in June 1900, Möller was exonerated by a court of inquiry and expected to return to command but was sidelined to the LOC as Roberts believed he had shown no command capacity.[202] A solution in many cases was to send an officer to the Remount Department at Stellenbosch, hence to be "stellenbosched."

Roberts sometimes had to tread carefully. As Lansdowne noted in July 1900, "People here are very difficult to deal with. They clamour for a victim whenever a mishap occurs, & are indignant whenever their own friends are dealt with in an exemplary manner."[203] Lansdowne himself suggested that Maj. Gen. Barrington "Bar" Campbell might not be up to commanding a brigade in the Eighth Division but wanted Roberts's view since Campbell was a guardsman and well connected socially.[204] Buller especially remained popular with both the army and the public.[205] Lansdowne counseled that it would be unwise to remove Buller: "With a large section of the army he is very popular, and in the eyes of the public he represents the dogged soldier who in the face of very great difficulties, has persevered and succeeded. His supersession would, I believe, be received in many quarters, some of them very exalted, with indignation. Nor again, do I like the idea of washing our dirty linen in public and before the eyes of a foreigner."[206]

By May 1900 Buller, who was unaware Kitchener had a dormant commission to succeed Roberts in the event of an emergency, considered Roberts had done little but ruin and disgrace officers since his arrival.[207] Buller also believed Roberts was behind the decision to publish the dispatches on Spion Kop without including his memorandum on Warren's part in the disaster, thereby casting greater blame on Buller himself. Roberts's covering memorandum criticized Buller for not taking command from Warren, Warren for not visiting Spion Kop himself, and Col. Alexander Thorneycroft, on whom command devolved after Woodgate was mortally wounded, for assuming too much responsibility in ordering the retreat.[208] In fact, it was Lansdowne's decision to publish, albeit amid considerable confusion as to what the cabinet had decided. Salisbury believed the decision was against publication, while Balfour thought only selective publication had been agreed on. The dispute reflected the absence of a written record of cabinet decisions. Lansdowne assumed he could publish although he later argued he had no recollection of any clear decision one way or the other.[209] Buller suggested he had left Warren alone since "he was sent out after Colenso under such auspices that I did not like to interfere with him."[210] In turn, Warren believed Buller's memorandum, while not intended for publication, had not given him the chance to justify his own conduct as he was not made aware of it.[211] In the end, Buller asked to leave in October 1900 and resumed command at Aldershot.

Others had powerful friends, as was the case with Colvile, whom Roberts appointed to the Ninth Division in February 1900, albeit reluctantly. Roberts then wished Colvile to be removed after the affair at Sannah's Post—Colvile had arrived too late to help Broadwood—and also the disaster that befell the socially exclusive Thirteenth Battalion, Imperial Yeomanry, which was surrounded and captured at Lindley on 27 May 1900. It was a decision the queen wished explained.[212] Colvile was cold in manner and unpopular, and he had not fully recovered from fever contracted in Uganda. Hector Macdonald, whose Highland Brigade served under Colvile, intensely disliked him and repeatedly criticized his conduct behind his back. Gleichen, who served on Colvile's staff, put much of the failure down to the inefficiency of Roberts's own headquarters staff, "the social rank of most of whom was far above their military capacity or training."[213] Colvile refused to resign and was dismissed, but was then retired because he released his criticism of Roberts to the press at Gibraltar while on the way home. His case was well publicized but without redress, for his public profile was not high. Bizarrely, Colvile was killed in 1907 near Bagshot when his bicycle collided with Henry Rawlinson's car.

It was agreed in December 1900 that any officers who surrendered their posts or were deemed responsible for surrenders would be court-martialed.[214] Through parliamentary pressure, such courts-martial were considered in retrospect for the actions at Nicholson's Nek, Lindley, and Nooitgedacht (13 December 1900). Roberts felt that those arraigned for Nicholson's Nek should not be tried again since they had previously been acquitted by a court of inquiry, not least because of the length of time that had elapsed. Brodrick stood firm on the condemnation by the court of inquiry of one officer involved, even threatening to resign if the verdict was overturned.[215]

Feeling Brodrick interfered too much in matters of discipline and honors, Roberts offered his own resignation as CinC in September 1901—it was refused.[216] Indeed, Roberts struggled against the system as much as Wolseley had done, although Brodrick thought he had strengthened the CinC's position through adopting the recommendations of the Dawkins Committee.[217]

Whatever the precise causes, the result in South Africa was a sometimes uneasy mix of officers of different traditions, backgrounds, and persuasions. Buller noted after visiting Roberts in Pretoria in July 1900: "I found Roberts sitting in one building with his Hindu staff, Kitchener in another with his Egyptian staff, and Kelly-Kenny in a third with an English staff, all pulling against each other."[218] An unnamed staff officer described the situation in similar terms, writing from Bloemfontein in March 1900: "Of course I met no end of old friends here for the Staff here is largely composed of men from India, in fact there are quite two factions the English & Indians, the latter are in the ascendant; there is also a small coterie of Egyptians but they are looked down on by both parties. Certainly up to the present they have not done anything but make mistakes."[219] Grierson was critical of Roberts's staff, with its "noblemen swarming everywhere as ADCs or as simple onlookers and loafers." Similarly, Maj. Ivor Maxse saw the staff "growing daily in size but not in competence, some 50 persons mostly ornamental, and all with prodigious appetites—peers predominantly."[220]

Herbert Kitchener

As early as June 1900, the cabinet was considering Roberts's successor in South Africa, the general assumption being that the war was effectively over. In reality, Roberts's faulty strategy in affording too much importance to the capture of the Boer capitals of Bloemfontein and Pretoria, his annexation of the two republics, and his administrative mistakes over such aspects as transport prolonged the war as a guerrilla struggle.

Lansdowne suggested Pole-Carew or Lyttelton as Roberts's successor.[221] Initially, Roberts felt Baden-Powell could undertake the task, but he was too junior. Milner wanted someone acceptable to him. Roberts considered Hamilton the best choice but felt he would not wish to remain in South Africa. In order of suitability, he next recommended Lyttelton followed by Pole-Carew.[222]

Roberts also considered Kelly-Kenny, but he did not want to stay. Hunter was a "fighting general" rather than an administrator, while Clery "sighs for a comfortable seat in his London Club." If not brilliant, at least Lyttelton was a gentleman who would do his part well enough. It was an assessment with which Wolseley agreed, characterizing Lyttelton "as sound & safe as possible."[223] As Kitchener did not want to stay in South Africa, fearing this would jeopardize his appointment to the Indian command, Roberts even suggested in September 1900 that Buller be left temporarily in command, but this was entirely unacceptable to the government.[224]

As it became clear the war was not over, it was deemed necessary to keep Kitchener in South Africa with the ultimate intention that Lyttelton would succeed him.[225] This remained the intention despite Roberts and Kitchener believing subsequently that Lyttelton had "lost his nerve" so far as operations were concerned.[226] Kitchener duly succeeded Roberts in command in November 1900. Hamilton returned to England with Roberts as MS.

Kitchener's unpredictable temperament and his secretive and autocratic working methods had been very evident in the Sudan. Without much success, Cromer counseled Kitchener on one occasion to "encourage your subordinates to speak up and to tell you when they do not agree with you. They are all far too much inclined to be frightened of you."[227] As Rawlinson wrote in January 1898, Kitchener was "very sketchy in the way he fires off telegrams without letting one know sometimes and always without ever keeping a copy. This is no doubt liable to cause errors but K is most obstinate about it, having a firm idea that it is quite unnecessary to have a record of what one sends or of numbering H.Q. telegrams."[228] As Wolseley also wrote on one occasion, Kitchener was a "hardy master."[229] Wingate, who had long experience of dealing with Kitchener, could still be driven to extremes of exasperation by the "boorish insults," steeling himself to "take up the sound line of saying nothing & making no attempt to probe his ostrich-like brain."[230]

As in the Sudan, Kitchener tried to do everything himself in South Africa.[231] Indeed, with the exception of a handful of young officers such as Oswald Fitzgerald and Frank Maxwell VC—"Kitchener's Cubs"—Kitchener never really established anything that resembled the Wolseley or Roberts rings. Fitzgerald died with Kitchener when the HMS *Hampshire* was lost in 1916, and Maxwell was killed in 1917. Arguably only the future Field Marshal Lord Birdwood might count as a significant protégé, acting successively as AMS and MS to Kitchener between 1902 and 1909 following his stint as DAAG in South Africa. Birdwood defended Kitchener's Indian army reforms as QMG in India, and Kitchener then gave him command of the Australian and New Zealand Army Corps in 1914. But as previously suggested, Birdwood was initially recommended to Kitchener by Roberts. Horace Smith-Dorrien recalled being often in "a complete fog" as to Kitchener's intentions.[232] Confusion was apparent in the attempt to trap the elusive Christiaan De Wet in the OFS in December 1900, and it was impossible for Kitchener to try to control as many as thirty columns traversing the veldt. When it was clear Kitchener needed assistance to relieve him of the increasing administrative burden, Hamilton was sent back to South Africa as CoS in November 1901.[233] According to Birdwood, Kitchener's DAAG, Kitchener feared that if he could not end the war, Evelyn Wood would be sent to supersede him.[234] Roberts himself suggested he could return to South Africa if Kitchener felt he needed a rest.[235]

In September 1901 Roberts sought Kitchener's views on the performance of senior officers remaining in South Africa "so that only those that could be trusted in war may be placed in high Commands."[236] Kitchener was supposedly loath to comment on the respective merits of officers until the war was over lest he have reason to modify his view.[237] In fact, Kitchener did report his views to Roberts.[238] Kitchener acted largely by instinct in his choice of commanders. He told Roberts in July 1901, "I think it is a good thing to change [commanders] at times without having any serious cause for doing so against the individuals concerned."[239] Despite criticism of Kitchener's tendency toward centralization, he left Methuen and French to their own devices.[240]

A number of new generals were sent to South Africa from India, including Bindon Blood, Edward Elliott, and Stuart Beatson. Kitchener was pleased with them, but not with Maj. Gen. Mildmay Willson. With pressure for troop reductions in the summer of 1901, Kitchener feared he would have to part with Blood, Beatson, and Elliott but hoped he could dispense with several other commanders, including Barrington Campbell, Barton, Fitzroy Hart, and Babington.[241]

Kitchener's tenure of the command was marked by his increasing feud with Milner, who told Joseph Chamberlain that it was "impossible to guide a military dictator of very strong views & strong character."[242] The dispute centered on the issues of how soon the Boers might be granted self-government after the war, what kind of amnesty could be offered those still in the field, and the amount of compensation to be paid toward the reconstruction of the former Boer republics. Kitchener, who first made direct overtures to the Boer leaders in February 1901, wished to ease the path of Boer reassimilation within a British South Africa. Milner favored a total victory, imposing a harsh, almost unconditional settlement, and firmly excluding the Boer leaders from any role in the future of South Africa.

Milner had given up trying to influence Kitchener by October 1901 and tried to get him replaced with Lyttelton. While some cabinet ministers believed Kitchener was exhausted and should be replaced, others argued that his recall would be regarded as a defeat. Insofar as Salisbury was concerned, there was no evidence that anyone else would conclude the war any quicker. Kitchener's removal would inevitably suggest to the public that there were divisions over policy. Salisbury also feared that such a decision would break the cabinet apart: the recent sacking of Buller from Aldershot was a useful reason for suggesting that things should be let lie.[243] In the end, it was to be Kitchener's version of peace: the Treaty of Vereeniging in May 1902 granted an amnesty, with £3 million allocated for reconstruction, with any question of extending the franchise to nonwhites left for decision once self-government was restored.

Kitchener handed over the South African command to Lyttelton in June 1902. The fact that Lyttelton did succeed Kitchener in South Africa and then became the first CGS in 1904 suggests that the coming to power of the Roberts ring did not necessarily end the prospects of those who had been nominally closer to Wolseley. Similarly, Francis Grenfell was offered a place on the Esher Committee by Balfour in April 1904 but declined it on the grounds he was still a serving soldier, much to the annoyance of King Edward VII.[244] Instead, Sir George Clarke joined Esher and Adm. Sir John Fisher on the influential committee that swept away the post of commander in chief and instituted that of chief of the General Staff.

CONCLUSION

Roberts's triumph over Wolseley's ring provided the subtext of the first major multivolume history of the South African War, namely the six volumes of *The Times History of the War in South Africa*, edited by Leo Amery and published between 1900 and 1909.[1] Buller's response to the criticism of his command in an ill-judged speech at Queen's Hall on 10 October 1901 led to his dismissal from the Aldershot command. Roberts immediately saw the opportunity, writing to Brodrick: "Buller's speech yesterday is really an extraordinary help to us, and I am strongly of opinion that we should take advantage of his indiscretion and remove him from his command."[2] Buller declined to resign, so he was dismissed on 22 October without recourse to any court of inquiry.

Inevitably, controversies were also apparent in the compilation of the official history, which was published in four volumes between 1906 and 1910.[3] Writing to the official historian, Roberts suggested in August 1907, "the history of the Boer War will in all probability be written when we are all in our graves, and it is essential that a true record should exist as to the reasons for the way in which the various forces were employed during the several phases of the war."[4] Roberts's apparent desire for truth concealed the extent to which he wished to manipulate the depiction of events. In October 1906 Pole-Carew wrote that he had distinctly different recollections of one incident involving himself since he saw things "usually through glasses of a different colour" than Roberts.[5] Pole-Carew had fallen out of favor by becoming critical of Roberts. As he wrote to Buller in January 1902, "I think you know that I having had the temerity to tell Bobs what I considered to be the truth, more than once in South Africa, & have been in his black books ever since. He has done a good deal to make me feel small by promoting people over my head etc. etc."[6]

Notwithstanding the controversies, the official history was largely colorless. Its more measured judgments "barely modified the influence exerted by the lively and readable volumes of Amery's history."[7] Thus, the triumph of the Roberts ring was perpetuated at least in print. But in practice it was short lived, for Lord Esher's Committee on War Office Reorganization recommended the abolition of the post of CinC. Roberts was unceremoniously dismissed along with the rest of the Army Council on "Black Monday," 1 February 1904.[8] A chief of the General Staff (later of the Imperial General Staff) replaced the CinC in 1904, with a General Staff being formally established in 1906.

Little really changed. The personnel were different after 1904, but the process of promotion and selection still displayed the same internal and external factors evident in the late Victorian army. The CinC's levees ceased in 1904, but officers could still meet the MS.[9] The annual confidential report and the deliberations of the Selection Board remained central to promotion, but so did patronage. It has been suggested that patronage was the most significant factor in a "personalised army" between 1902 and 1914, with its baneful effects extending into the conduct of the Great War. Many general officers were "degummed" between 1914 and 1918—according to Edmonds, Haig sacked at least a hundred brigade commanders—and some dismissals undoubtedly included a personal element.[10] On the other hand, others have argued that patronage was limited in the Edwardian army and that seniority was still the most important consideration when active-service opportunities were fewer prior to 1914.[11] Either way, the supposed overrepresentation of "cavalry generals" in high command during First World War has been a feature of "popular" history. Cavalrymen were actually underrepresented at the highest levels between 1904 and 1914. Their wartime prominence in most cases was little better than the average statistically.[12] Infantrymen dominated corps and divisional commands.[13]

Examination of the interwar army has suggested that, whatever the apparent role that nepotism, age, and "musical chairs" played in appointments, it was limited by the concern to advance merit. The problem was a lack of higher training for command. The army was readier than was industry to use objective criteria for selection for command. Similarly, while exercised by the CIGS, Alan Brooke, and by Bernard Montgomery, patronage in the Second World War was also intended to promote merit. Judgment of professional competence was not generally clouded by personal considerations, and those who failed were ruthlessly removed.[14]

This begs the question as to the ultimate value of selection as opposed to seniority and whether those changes that were ultimately introduced by the time of the South African War and in its immediate aftermath actually resulted in a better and more professional army. The attributes necessary to thrive in a peacetime army were not those that guaranteed success in war. Although the late Victorian army did have a wealth of colonial campaigning experience, "small wars" were not the same as major conflicts. Major conflict alone would determine the extent and effectiveness of prewar military professionalism, and it has been something of a truism that those in high command at the start of a major war rarely survive in their positions until war's end. Dependence on promotion by seniority alone would have led to military atrophy, but, as has been noted, "Reliance on natural aptitude was the path to amateurism, not to professionalism."[15] In that sense, the system that evolved in the late Victorian army after the abolition of purchase was probably the best that could have been adopted under the circumstances of the army's particular place in state and society. It was more advanced than the position reached in the Royal Navy, where promotion on grounds of seniority survived in theory insofar as flag rank was concerned long after aspiring generals had no such claim to higher rank. It is significant in this regard that the British army confronted its major military challenge in 1899, whereas the Royal Navy did not experience similar trauma until 1914–15.[16]

Of course, that did not mean that the army's system was free of flaws, and soldiers—whether ambitious or otherwise—had to negotiate an extraordinarily complex process. The interplay of internal and external factors threw up both opportunities for, and obstacles to, career advancement. While some soldiers—perhaps even the majority—were undoubtedly content to remain within their regiments throughout their career, many sought to achieve greater promotion through whatever means available to them: to climb what Disraeli called the "greasy pole." Of course, a sense of duty and of service toward sovereign, country, and empire was important. The desire for honors and glory, however, could never be divorced from the reckoning; neither could financial necessity. For many, the realization of ambition fulfilled all requirements. The military profession was not so different after all.

Notes

Abbreviations

APAC	Asia, Pacific and Africa Collection (formerly Oriental and India Office Collection), British Library
BL	British Library (Manuscripts Collection)
BOD	Bodleian Library
CCRO	Cornwall County Record Office
CUL	Cambridge University Library
DCRO	Devon County Record Office
DUDR	Duke University David M. Rubenstein Rare Book and Manuscript Library
EHR	*English Historical Review*
GA	Gloucestershire Archives
HCCP	House of Commons Command Papers
HHM	Hatfield House Muniments
HJ	*Historical Journal*
HPL	Hove Public Library
IHR	*International History Review*
IWM	Imperial War Museum
JAZWHS	*Journal of the Anglo-Zulu War Historical Society*
JBS	*Journal of British Studies*
JICH	*Journal of Imperial and Commonwealth History*
JMH	*Journal of Military History*
JRUSI	*Journal of the Royal United Service Institution*
JSAHR	*Journal of the Society for Army Historical Research*
JSS	*Journal of Strategic Studies*
KCL	Campbell Collections, formerly Killie Campbell Africana Library
KHLC	Kent History and Library Centre
KZNA	KwaZulu-Natal Archives
LHCMA	Liddell Hart Centre for Military Archives
LA	Lincolnshire Archives
MEC	Middle East Centre

NAM	National Army Museum
NLI	National Library of Ireland
NLS	National Library of Scotland
NLW	National Library of Wales
NRS	National Records of Scotland
NWM	National War Museum
QMUL	Queen Mary University Library
RA	Royal Archives
RAM	Royal Artillery Museum
REM	Royal Engineers Museum
SAD	Sudan Archive
SLCM	South Lanarkshire Council Museum
SOTQ	*Soldiers of the Queen*
SRO	Suffolk Record Office
SWI	*Small Wars and Insurgencies*
TNA	The National Archives
UBL	University of Birmingham Cadbury Research Library
VS	*Victorian Studies*
W&S	*War and Society*
WCRO	Warwickshire County Record Office
WH	*War in History*
WL	Wellcome Library
WSA	Wiltshire and Swindon Archives

Introduction

1. Hackett, *Profession of Arms*, 9. There is a slightly different wording in Dyer, *War*, 261.
2. Hackett, *Profession of Arms*, 141.
3. Reader, *Professional Men*, 152–53.
4. *HCCP* 1875 (457); *HCCP* 1872 (315); *HCCP* 1878–79 (15).
5. Spiers, *Army and Society*, 6.
6. Reader, *Professional Men*, 79.
7. Oxford Research Data Services, "Victorian Professions," http://www.victorian professions.ox.ac.uk/.
8. Ian Roy, "The Profession of Arms," in Prest, *Professions in Early Modern England*, 181–219, at 181.
9. Larson, *Rise of Professionalism*, xvii, 219.
10. Corfield, *Power and the Professions*, 176–78; Haig, *Victorian Clergy*, 15–16.
11. Haig, *Victorian Clergy*, 16–18.
12. Gruber, *Books and the British Army*, 3–64.

13. Huntington, *Soldier and the State*; Janowitz, *Professional Soldier*; Finer, *Man on Horseback*; Kourvetaris and Dobratz, *Social Origins and Political Orientation*; Doorn, *Soldier and Social Change*; Perlmutter, *Military and Politics in Modern Times*.

14. Davison, *Challenges of Command*, 20.

15. Pionke, *Ritual Culture of Victorian Professionals*, 6.

16. Reader, *Professional Men*, 44–58, 85–99.

17. Perkin, *Origins of Modern English Society*, 320.

18. Perkin, *Rise of Professional Society*, 359.

19. Lacey, "Way We Lived Then," 599–621.

20. Corfield, *Power and the Professions*, 191.

21. Bourne, *Patronage and Society*, 27.

22. Ibid., 177.

23. Reader, *Professional Men*, 98; Perkin, *Origins of Modern English Society*, 258–59.

24. Haig, *Victorian Clergy*, 249–76.

25. Ibid., 269.

26. Durey, "Ecclesiastical Patronage in Trollope's Novels," 250–70; Morgan, "Background of Anglican Bishops," 295–310.

27. Duman, "Pathways to Professionalism," 615–28.

28. Petersen, *Medical Profession in Mid-Victorian London*, 90–135; Lankford, "Victorian Medical Profession," 511–28.

29. Petersen, *Medical Profession*, 136–93.

30. Ibid., 173.

31. Porter and Clifton, "Patronage, Professional Values," 319–49, at 326. See also Clifton, *Professionalism, Patronage and Public Service*.

32. Davison, *Challenges of Command*, 71–73, 146–56.

33. Bourne, *Patronage and Society*, 176.

34. Davison, *Challenges of Command*, 10, 16.

35. Gordon, *Rules of the Game*, 326–29.

36. Davison, *Challenges of Command*, 42–43, 74–75, 150–56.

37. Ibid., 75.

38. Ferguson, *Empire*, 210–11.

39. Porter, *Thames Embankment*, 166.

40. Meadows, *Victorian Scientist*, 2–3.

41. Corfield, *Power and the Professions*, 211, 224, 237.

42. Reader, *Professional Men*, 73–84; Bourne, *Patronage and Society*, 176–78.

43. See, for example, Spiers, *Late Victorian Army*, 89–117; Harries-Jenkins, *Army in Victorian Society*; Perry, "Irish Landed Class," 304–32.

44. BL, Lansdowne Mss, L(5)48, Lansdowne to Roberts, 5 Oct. 1900.

Chapter 1: The Profession of Arms

1. Strachan, "Early Victorian Army," 782–809.

2. Strachan, *Wellington's Legacy*, 109–45.

3. Harries-Jenkins, *Army in Victorian Society*, 20.

4. Strachan, *Politics of the British Army*, 21–25.

5. Stockings, *Britannia's Shield*, 20; Harries-Jenkins, *Army in Victorian Society*, 8–10.

6. Davison, *Challenges of Command*, 41–48, 117–42.

7. Barczewski, *Heroic Failure and the British*, 12; Collini, "'Character' in Victorian Political Thought," 29–50.
8. Wright, *Life of Colonel Fred Burnaby*, 255.
9. WSA, Methuen Mss, 1742/6335, Staff College, MacGregor to Methuen, 23 Oct. 1876.
10. Dawson, *Soldier-Diplomat*, 63.
11. Gleichen, *Guardsman's Memories*, 110.
12. Luvaas, *Education of an Army*, 212.
13. Bond, *Victorian Army and the Staff College*, 95–96, 107–08, 134–35, 138–39.
14. French, *British Way in Warfare*, 129.
15. Talbot Rice and Harding, *Butterflies and Bayonets*, 10–27.
16. Bailes, "Influence of Continental Examples," 179.
17. Meadows, *Victorian Scientist*, 97–116.
18. Preston, "British Military Thought," 57–74; Luvaas, *Education of an Army*, 101–68.
19. Howard Bailes, "Technology and Tactics in the British Army, 1866–1900," in Haycock and Neilson, *Men, Machines and War*, 23–47; Bailes, "Patterns of Thought," 29–45.
20. Ian Beckett, "Another British Way in Warfare: Charles Callwell and Small Wars," in Ian Beckett, *Victorians at War: New Perspectives*, 89–102.
21. Beckett, "Pen and the Sword," 3–7.
22. Headrick, "Tools of Imperialism," 231–63.
23. Beckett, "Victorians at War," 330–38; Spiers, *Engines for Empire*.
24. Churchill, *River War*, 300.
25. Burn, *Age of Equipoise*, 224.
26. Ian Beckett, "Command in the Late Victorian Army," in Sheffield, *Leadership and Command*, 37–56; Bailes, "Technology and Imperialism," 82–104.
27. Robson, *Road to Kabul*, 51.
28. Cromer, *Modern Egypt*, 2:75.
29. APAC, Lyall Mss, F132/28, St. John to Lyall, 3 Jan. 1879.
30. APAC, Burne Mss, Eur Mss D95111, Colley to Burne, 20 Jan. 1880.
31. NAM, Charles Gough Mss, 8304-32-269, Campaign diary, 11 Apr. 1879.
32. RA VIC/ADDA12/467, Cambridge to Queen, 27 July 1879; VIC/ADDU/351, Pickard to Wood, 28 Sept. 1879.
33. RA VIC/MAIN/B/61/34, Disraeli to Queen, 24 Aug. 1879; Zetland, *Letters of Disraeli*, 2:303.
34. RA VIC/ADDE/1/8882, Johnson to Cambridge, 11 Sept. 1879.
35. Hanna, *Lord Roberts in War*, 57–60.
36. Technically, Cambridge was general and (from November 1862) field marshal commanding in chief until November 1887, when he became commander in chief. The secretary of state for war, Edward Cardwell, forced Cambridge to quit Horse Guards in Whitehall for the WO in Pall Mall in the summer of 1871. The duke insisted on a separate entrance to the building and on addressing his letters from "Horse Guards, Pall Mall."
37. RA VIC/ADDE/1/10073, Lysons to Cambridge, 14 July 1882.
38. TNA, Napier Mss, PRO 30/86/5, Napier to Horsford, 18 May 1877.
39. Preston, *Wolseley's South African Journal*, 34.
40. Arthur, *Letters of Lord and Lady Wolseley*, 78.
41. RA VIC/ADDE/1/10079, Stewart to Cambridge, 21 July 1882.

42. RA VIC/ADDE/1/10134, Cambridge to Wolseley, 18 Aug. 1882.
43. RA VIC/ADDE/1/10981, Cambridge to Wolseley, 12 Dec. 1884. Unless otherwise noted, all emphasis is in the original.
44. Younghusband, *Soldier's Memories*, 293–95; Younghusband, *Forty Years a Soldier*, 133–34.
45. SAD, Wingate Mss, 267/1/12, à Court to Wingate, 13 Jan. 1898.
46. Callwell, *Memoirs of Sir Hugh McCalmont*, 84, 90–92, 95, 181–82, 185–86, 258–60, 264, 272.
47. Churchill, *Churchill*, 1:717.
48. Ibid., 1:971.
49. RA VIC/ADDE/1/11090, Wolseley to Cambridge, 14 Mar. 1885.
50. RA VIC/ADDE/1/11266, Smyth to Cambridge, 12 Aug. 1885.
51. Davison, *Challenges of Command*, 52, 61–66.
52. *HCCP* 1875 (457).
53. Mahaffey, "Fighting Profession," 200.
54. Brice, *Thinking Man's Soldier*, 65.
55. Harries-Jenkins, *Army and Victorian Society*, 98–99.
56. Ibid., 27–28.
57. Mansel, *Pillars of Monarchy*, 78.
58. Razzell, "Social Origins of Officers," 248–61.
59. Otley, "Social Origins of British Officers," 213–40.
60. Spiers, *Army and Society*, 7–8, 10–11, 296–98; Spiers, *Late Victorian Army*, 94, 97–98.
61. Petersen, *Medical Profession*, 199–206; Morgan, "Social and Educational Background of Anglican Bishops," 297; Haig, *Victorian Clergy*, 35–53.
62. Strachan, *Wellington's Legacy*, 100–11.
63. Bruce, *Purchase System*, 158–59.
64. Spiers, *Army and Society*, 24; Spiers, *Late Victorian Army*, 97.
65. Spiers, *Army and Society*, 2–6.
66. Fletcher Vane, *Agin the Governments*, 40–41.
67. Gleichen, *Guardsman's Memories*, 46–47.
68. Farrar-Hockley, *Goughie*, 16–19.
69. Stewart, *My Service Days*, 31–32.
70. Lee, *Soldier's Life*, 7, 8, 10, 21–23.
71. A British Officer [Cairnes], *Social Life in the British Army*, 15–16, 27.
72. Muenger, *British Military Dilemma in Ireland*, 15.
73. Badsey, *Doctrine and Reform*, 68–69.
74. Spiers, *Army and Society*, 25.
75. Riedl, "Brains or Polo?," 236–53.
76. *The Times* (London), 15 Jan. 1900, 4; 22 Jan. 1900, 15.
77. HPL, Wolseley Autograph Collection, Ponsonby to Wolseley, 3 Mar. 1884.
78. Arthur, *Not Worth Reading*, 24–25.
79. Bray, *Mysterious Captain Brocklehurst*, 20–21.
80. *HCCP* 1902 [C. 982], 9, c. 43.
81. *HCCP* 1902 [C. 982], 35–36, c. 153.
82. *HCCP* 1902 [C. 983], 305, c. 8227.
83. *HCCP* 1902 [C. 983], 60, c. 1444; 67, c. 1716.

84. *HCCP* 1903 [C. 1421], 7–9.

85. *HCCP* 1903 [C. 1421], 22–24.

86. Reader, *Professional Men*, 183–206; Petersen, *Medical Profession*, 207–9; Haig, *Victorian Clergy*, 296–318; Barbara Kerr, "Country Professions," in Mingay, *Victorian Countryside*, 1:288–99.

87. Butler, *Autobiography*, 187–88.

88. Brackenbury, *Memories of My Spare Time*, 349–50.

89. Durand, *Life of White*, 1:283–84.

90. DUDR, Wolseley Mss, Wolseley to Turner, 3 Aug. 1893.

91. WSA, Methuen Mss, 1742/6335, Indian Diary, 27 Sept.–1 Oct. 1897.

92. Maurice and Arthur, *Life of Lord Wolseley*, 79.

93. Lehmann, *All Sir Garnet*, 212.

94. Kochanski, *Sir Garnet Wolseley*, 85.

95. HPL, Wolseley Mss, W/P 16/5a, Wolseley to wife, 11 Jan. 1887.

96. HPL, Wolseley Mss, W/P 19/12, Wolseley to wife, 16 Aug. 1890; TNA, WO 32/6302, Wolseley to Harman, 28 July 1890; Harman to Thompson, 28 July 1890.

97. BL, Campbell-Bannerman Mss, Add Mss 41233, Lady Wolseley to Campbell-Bannerman, 14 Nov. 1893.

98. TNA, Ardagh Mss, PRO 30/40/2, Wolseley to Ardagh, 14 Sept. 1895.

99. Buller Family Mss, Buller to wife, 10 Apr. 1900.

100. Melville, *Life of Buller*, 1:148.

101. Powell, *Buller*, 91.

102. CUL, Childers Mss, RCMS 37/5/61, Hartington to Childers, 26 Sept. 1881; RA VIC/MAIN/E/27/171, Ponsonby to Queen, 2 Dec. 1881; ADDE/1/9863, Cambridge to Childers, 7 Dec. 1881.

103. NAM, Cowell Mss, 2009-02-110-396, Roberts to Childers, 10 Oct. 1881.

104. NLS, Minto Mss, MS 12380, Pretyman to Melgund, 24 June and 2–5 Dec. 1887.

105. Robson, *Roberts in India*, 411–12.

106. LHCMA, Hamilton Mss, 1/2/9, Roberts to Hamilton, 18 May 1893; NAM, Roberts Mss, 7101–23–103, Roberts to Brownlow, 4 Feb. 1892.

107. HPL, Wolseley Mss, LW/P 21/47, Lady Wolseley to Wolseley, 4 July 1895.

108. CCRO, Pole-Carew Mss, CO/F10/2, Roberts to Pole-Carew, 29 May 1895; NAM, Roberts Mss, 7101–23–105, Roberts to Lansdowne, 10 July 1897.

109. Elsmie, *Stewart*, 14.

110. Ibid., 268.

111. RA VIC/MAIN/W/73/31, Cambridge to Queen, 3 Nov. 1885.

112. KCL, Wood Mss, KCM 89/9/37/7–8, Harcourt to Wood, 16 Mar. 1882; Herbert to Wood, 17 Mar. 1882.

113. Wood, *From Midshipman to Field Marshal*, 2:180.

114. Wood, *Winnowed Memories*, 157–58.

115. BOD, Alison Mss, Mss. Eng. lett. d.420, Alison to wife, 3–4 Sept. 1882.

116. BOD, Alison Mss, Mss. Eng. lett. d.420, Alison to wife, 28 Sept. 1882.

117. BOD, Alison Mss, Mss. Eng. lett. d.420, Alison to Wolseley, 18 Dec. 1882.

118. WCRO, Dormer Mss, CR895/92, Dormer to wife, 10 and 26 Aug., and 20 Oct. 1878.

119. WCRO, Dormer Mss, CR895/92, Dormer to wife, 23 Jan. and 28 Apr. 1879.

120. WCRO, Dormer Mss, CR895/92, Dormer to wife, 4 June 1879.

121. WCRO, Dormer Mss, CR895/93, Dormer to wife, 9 Feb. 1882.

122. NAM, Chelmsford Mss, 6807-386-18-34, Statement of Service.
123. RA VIC/ADDE/1/11506, Stephenson to Cambridge, 1 June 1886.
124. RA VIC/ADDE/1/11511, Campbell-Bannerman to Cambridge, 10 June 1886; VIC/ADDE/1/11586, Stephenson to Cambridge, 11 Sept. 1886.
125. HPL, Wolseley Mss, 163/iv, Wolseley to brother, n.d. [Dec. 1870 or Jan. 1871].
126. Spiers, *Victorian Soldier in Africa*, 5.
127. HPL, Wolseley Mss, 163/iv, Wolseley to brother, 18 Feb. 1878.
128. Beckett, *Johnnie Gough VC*, 7.
129. Daly, *Sirdar*, 30, 36–37, 40–47, 51, 69–72, 78, 83–84, 87–89, 101–2.
130. RA VIC/MAIN/E/40/24, Bigge to Queen, 14 Aug. 1895.
131. Beckett, *Wolseley in Ashanti*, 371–72.
132. Keown-Boyd, *Good Dusting*, 99–100; Keown-Boyd, *Soldiers of the Nile*, 12, 214–17; Harfield, *Life and Times of Donne*, 169.
133. Haggard, *Under Crescent and Star*, 31–32, 34–35.
134. Doolittle, *Soldier's Hero*, 31–33.
135. Ibid., 96.
136. Bowman and Connelly, *Edwardian Army*, 190.
137. See Clark, *Distributing Status*.
138. BL, Campbell-Bannerman Mss, Add Mss 41209, Ripon to Campbell-Bannerman, 11 May 1894.
139. *The Broad Arrow* 24 (1880): 66–67.
140. Trousdale, *War in Afghanistan*, 54; NAM, Haines Mss, 8108-9-5, Lytton to Haines, 3 Sept. 1877.
141. Trousdale, *War in Afghanistan*, 59, 154–55.
142. MacGregor, *Life and Opinions*, 2:375–78.
143. RA VIC/ADDE/1/7933 and 7939, Carnarvon to Cambridge, 15 and 18 Oct. 1876.
144. BL, Gladstone Mss, Add Mss 44129, Note by Childers, Aug. 1880.
145. RA VIC/MAIN/R/54/22, Campbell-Bannerman to Ponsonby, 5 Apr. 1886; VIC/MAIN/B/37/62, Campbell-Bannerman to the Queen, 11 May 1886.
146. RA VIC/MAIN/R/54/36, Campbell-Bannerman to Queen, 7 July 1886; VIC/MAIN/R/54/42, Ponsonby to Campbell-Bannerman, 14 July 1886; VIC/MAIN/R/54/52, Campbell-Bannerman to Ponsonby, 19 July 1886.
147. RA VIC/ADDE/1/12724, Stanhope to Cambridge, 14 May 1891.
148. TNA, Smith Mss, WO 110/3, Churchill to Smith, 4 Nov. 1886.
149. Lyttelton, *Eighty Years*, 142.
150. SAD, Wingate Mss, 179/6/2, Wood to Wingate, 18 Jan. 1897.
151. Stigger, "Promotion as a Campaigning Reward," 255–59.
152. *HCCP* 1903 [C. 1791], 315, c. 17514.
153. *HCCP* 1903 [C. 1790], 173, c. 4101.
154. Vetch, *Life of Clarke*, 224.
155. Harvie, "Wolseley Ring," 87–88.
156. Ibid., 110n48.
157. *HCCP* 1876 [C. 1569], 30, c. 157–58; 49, c. 654; 96, c. 1966; 103–04, c. 2083–84; 1078, c. 2165.
158. Harvie, "Wolseley Ring," 107.
159. Beckett, *Wolseley in Ashanti*, 378.
160. NAM, Haines Mss, 8108-9-33.

161. RA VIC/ADDE/1/9411, Stewart to Cambridge, 24 Nov. 1881.

162. Elsmie, *Stewart*, 279.

163. RA VIC/ADDE/1/9439, Stewart to Cambridge, 22 Dec. 1881.

164. RA VIC/ADDE/1/9625, Stewart to Cambridge, 22 May 1881.

165. LHCMA, Hamilton Mss, 1/3/4, Roberts to Brownlow, 14 Feb. 1883.

166. HPL, Wolseley Autograph Collection, Smith to Wolseley, 8 Aug. 1885.

167. Burleigh, *Desert Warfare*, 314, 317–18.

168. Wilkinson and Wilkinson, *Memoirs of the Gemini Generals*, 409.

169. Harvie, "Wolseley Ring," 99–100; "Scrutator," *The Times* (London), 17 Sept. 1885, 6.

170. APAC, White Mss, Eur Mss F108/3, White to Roberts, 28 May 1887.

171. NAM, Cowell Mss, 2009-02-110-417, Roberts to Cowell, 5 Aug. 1887.

172. NAM, Roberts Mss, 7101-23-59, Pole-Carew to Roberts, 15 and 28 July 1887; 7101-23-100-1, Roberts to Pole-Carew, 5 Aug. 1887.

173. NAM, Roberts Mss, 7101-23-98, Roberts to Dufferin, 30 July 1886.

174. NAM, Roberts Mss, 7101-23-103, Roberts to Brownlow, 16 Jan. 1887.

175. HPL, Wolseley Mss, 163/4, Wolseley to brother, 17 Oct. 1870.

176. Beckett, *Wolseley in Ashanti*, 375.

177. Ibid., 375, 415–16.

178. Preston, *Wolseley's South African Journal*, 279.

179. HPL, Wolseley Mss, W/P 8/24, Wolseley to wife, 11 Sept. 1879; W/P 9/11, Wolseley to wife, 28 Feb. 1880.

180. HPL, Wolseley Mss, W/P 9/8 and 13, Wolseley to wife, 15 Feb., and 11–13 Mar. 1880.

181. HPL, Wolseley Mss, SSL.10/1, xxxix.

182. RA VIC/MAIN/E/27/1, Gladstone to Queen, 2 Mar. 1881.

183. RA VIC/MAIN/E/27/2, Queen to Gladstone, 3 Mar. 1881.

184. BL, Gladstone Mss, Add Mss 44765, Notes by Gladstone, 24 Mar. and 25 May 1881; Draft letter to Queen, 19 May 1881; Add Mss 44129, Childers to Gladstone, 1 and 7 Mar. 1881.

185. RA VIC/MAIN/E/61/67, Ponsonby to Cambridge, 13 Mar. 1881.

186. HPL, Wolseley Mss, SSL.8, Pt. I, cxciv, ccv–ccvi.; Pt. II, ccl; SSL.10/1, xci, Note by Wolseley, 27 May 1881; W/P 10/6/2, Wolseley to wife, 23 Aug. 1881; RA VIC/ADDA36/20, Ponsonby to wife, 28 May 1881; CUL, Childers Mss, RCMS 37/5/60, Gladstone to Hartington, 25 Sept. 1881.

187. RA VIC/ADDE/1/9797 and 9807, Childers to Cambridge, 19 and 24 Oct. 1881; SLCM, Wolseley Diaries, CAM.H.12, Diary, 16 Nov. 1881.

188. St. Aubyn, *Royal George*, 211.

189. Verner, *Military Life of Cambridge*, 2:252.

190. HPL, Wolseley Mss, W/P 11/22, Wolseley to wife, 25 Sept. 1882.

191. *HCCP* 1881 (311).

192. BL, Gladstone Mss, Add Mss 44130, Childers to Gladstone, 14 and 16 Oct. 1882.

193. RA VIC/MAIN/N/38/227 and 233, Gladstone to Queen, 7 Sept. 1880; Hartington to Queen, 7 Sept. 1880; CUL, Cambridge Mss, Add 8782/I/25, Hartington to Cambridge, 9 Sept. 1880.

194. CCRO, Pole-Carew Mss, CO/F9/3, Roberts to Lytton, 22 May 1883.

195. RA VIC/MAIN/N/39/20, Probyn to Ponsonby, 3 Feb. 1881.

196. BL, Gladstone Mss, Add Mss 44129, Childers to Gladstone, 15 and 23 Sept. 1880.

197. CCRO, Pole-Carew Mss, CP/5, Roberts to Pole-Carew, 5 Aug. 1887.

198. CCRO, Pole-Carew Mss, CO/F9/4, Roberts to Pole-Carew, 8 May 1883.

199. Crook, *Evolution of the Victoria Cross*, 279–89); Smith, *Awarded for Valour*, 207–14.

200. Smith, *Awarded for Valour*, 79–80, 103–4.

201. Manning, "Foreign News Gathering and Reporting," 123–39.

202. Preston, *Wolseley's South African Journal*, 57, 112, 257.

203. Adrian Greaves, "Saving the Colours: Lieutenants Coghill and Melvill," in Greaves, *Redcoats and Zulus*, 41–54; Lieven, "Heroism, Heroics," 419–38.

204. Preston, *Wolseley's South African Journal*, 256–57.

205. Lock, *Blood on the Painted Mountain*, 208.

206. Wood, *Winnowed Memories*, 288–91.

207. Bengough, *Memories of a Soldier's Life*, 133.

208. DCRO, Buller Mss, 2065M/SS4/10, Horsford to Buller, 7 Feb. 1880.

209. Beckett, "Indian Expeditionary Force," 6–11.

Chapter 2: Promotion and Selection

1. Bourne, *Patronage and Society*, 3–9, 12–16, 22–31.

2. *HCCP* 1874 [C. 1018], 14–15.

3. Huffer, "Infantry Officers of the Line," 284.

4. APAC, Napier of Magdala Mss, Eur Mss F114/75, Napier to Baker, 15 July 1872.

5. *HCCP* 1877 [C. 1824], c. 4, 8.

6. *HCCP* 1874 [C. 1018], 11.

7. *HCCP* 1880 (197).

8. BL, Gladstone Mss, Add Mss 44120, Cardwell to Gladstone, 20 Oct. 1873.

9. Bruce, *Purchase System*, 125–26.

10. Spiers, *Late Victorian Army*, 90.

11. Anglesey, *History of the British Cavalry*, 3:89.

12. *HCCP* 1876 [C. 1569], xi.

13. Verner, *Military Life of Cambridge*, 2:221–22; Callwell and Headlam, *History of the Royal Artillery*, 1:51.

14. *HCCP* 1874 [C.1018], Appendix A, 148–49.

15. *HCCP* 1876 [C. 1569], xxxii.

16. Bowman and Connelly, *Edwardian Army*, 34–38.

17. Bruce, *Purchase System*, 139–40, 146–47, 152–54; Mahaffey, "Fighting Profession," 165–67.

18. *HCCP* 1876 [C. 1569], viii, xi.

19. *HCCP* 1876 [C.1569], xv–xxv; xxvii; xliii.

20. Spiers, *Army and Society*, 194–95; Spiers, *Late Victorian Army*, 91–92.

21. *HCCP* 1877 [C.1824]; *HCCP* 1877 [C. 1852].

22. Mahaffey, "Fighting Profession," 183; *HCCP* 1881 (67).

23. Mahaffey, "Fighting Profession," 184–85.

24. Ibid., 194–96; *HCCP* 1899 (90).

25. NAM, Warre Mss, 8112–54–81, Return, 15 Aug. 1871.

26. *HCCP* 1886 (166).

27. NAM, CinC's Selection Book, 1998–06–1997, 25 June 1881; Roberts Mss, 5504–64–43, Note, 26 Apr. 1881.

28. TNA, Smith Mss, WO 110/8, Return, 31 Oct. 1885.

29. TNA, WO 32/6297, MS Note, 22 Feb. 1892.

30. KHLC, Stanhope Mss, 0250/3, Stanhope to Queen, 25 June 1889; 0231/1, Stanhope paper for Cabinet, 28 June 1889.
31. TNA, WO 32/6297, Buller to Thompson, 8 Apr. 1893.
32. TNA, WO 32/6297, Wolseley Memo, 15 May 1893.
33. TNA, WO 32/6297, Brodrick to Lansdowne, 20 Dec. 1895.
34. TNA, WO 32/6297, Wolseley to Haliburton, 21 Jan. 1896.
35. NAM, Roberts Mss, 7101-23-100-3, Roberts to Cambridge, 14 Oct. 1891.
36. Stanley, *White Mutiny*, 266–68.
37. Heathcote, *Indian Army*, 136–39.
38. SRO, Cranbrook Mss, HA43/H/6/1/2, Memo by Norman, 13 May 1879.
39. RA VIC/ADDE/1/9684, Stewart to Cambridge, 22 July 1881.
40. NAM, Haines Mss, 8108-9-46-29, Cambridge to Haines, 23 July 1880.
41. RAM, Brackenbury Mss, MD1085/3, Brackenbury to White, 12 Aug. 1893.
42. APAC, L/MIL/7/7399, Lansdowne to Cross, 14 Oct. 1891; NAM, Roberts Mss, 7101-23-100-3, Roberts to Stewart, 31 Oct. 1891.
43. RAM, Brackenbury Mss, MD1085/2, Brackenbury to White, 1 Aug. 1893.
44. RA VIC/ADDE/1/13119, Nairne to Cambridge, 23 Feb. 1895.
45. RA VIC/ADDE/1/6652, Biddulph to Cambridge, 22 Jan. 1871.
46. BL, Campbell-Bannerman Mss, Add Mss 41209, Cambridge to Campbell-Bannerman, 23 Nov. 1893.
47. RA ADDE/1/10241, Alison to Cambridge, 12 Nov. 1882.
48. LHCMA, Alison Mss, Box 2, Cambridge to Alison, 27 Oct. 1891.
49. RA VC/ADDE/1/12874, Campbell-Bannerman to Cambridge, 11 Nov. 1892.
50. RA VIC/MAIN/E/62/10, Ponsonby to Cambridge, 19 June 1883.
51. RA VIC/MAIN/B/35/36–37, Hartington to Ponsonby, 24 July 1883; Ponsonby to Hartington, 24 July 1883; RA VIC/ADDE/1/10465 and 10466, Hartington to Cambridge, 18 July 1883; Cambridge to Hartington, 19 July 1883.
52. LHCMA, Hamilton Mss, 1/3/4, Roberts to Cambridge, 7 Jan. and 6 Mar. 1884.
53. RA VIC/ADDE/1/12826, Robinson to Cambridge, 22 May 1892.
54. NAM, Warre Mss, 8112-54-92, Horsford to Warre, 19 Oct. 1874.
55. NAM, Warre Mss, 8112-54-986, Warre to Horsford, 28 Feb. 1880.
56. NLW, Hills-Johnes Mss, L10971, Brownlow to Hills-Johnes, 2 Aug. 1888.
57. NLW, Hills-Johnes Mss, L10960, Browne to Hills-Johnes, 13 Feb. 1879.
58. NLW, Hills-Johnes Mss, L13648, Stewart to Hills-Johnes, 23 Nov. 1879.
59. NLW, Hills-Johnes Mss, L14146, Wolseley to Hills-Johnes, 11 July 1882.
60. MacGregor, *Life and Opinions*, 2:118; NAM, MS Letter Book, 1998-06-195, Harman to Hills-Johnes, 4 May 1885.
61. NLW, Hills-Johnes Mss, L12003 and 12004, Grove to Hills-Johnes, 25 Feb. and 10 Mar. 1900.
62. RA VIC/ADDE/1/6801, Cambridge to Airey, 9 Aug. 1871.
63. RA VIC/ADDE/1/6814 and 6816, Cambridge to Airey, 19 and 21 Aug. 1871; VIC/ADDE/1/6842, Note by Airey, 16 Sept. 1871.
64. RA VIC/ADDE/1/6823, Cambridge to Airey, 26 Aug. 1871.
65. RA VIC/ADDE/1/6821, Airey to Cambridge, 26 Apr. 1871.
66. CUL, Cambridge Mss, Add 8782/II/11, Cambridge to Airey, 15 Aug. 1874; RA VIC/ADDE/1/6823, Cambridge to Airey, 26 Aug. 1871.
67. Stannus, *My Reasons for Leaving*, 52.

68. TNA, Ardagh Mss, PRO 30/40/2, Whitmore to Ardagh, 20 Mar. 1885.
69. TNA, Smith Mss, WO 110/3, Smith to Cambridge, 18 Aug. 1885; Cambridge to Smith, 21 Aug. 1885.
70. BL, Hutton Mss, Add Mss 50086, Hamilton to Hutton, 16 Dec. 1902.
71. Waters, *Secret and Confidential*, 57.
72. NAM, Cowell Mss, 2009–02–110–258, Gordon to Cowell, 28 Jan. 1877.
73. NAM, MS Letter Book, 1998–06–194, Horsford to Newdigate, 8 Nov. 1875.
74. NAM, MS Letter Book, 1998–06–194, Horsford to Wilkinson, 16 Aug. 1878.
75. NAM, MS Letter Book, 1998–06–194, Egerton to Chamberlayne, 20 Jan. 1872.
76. NAM, MS Letter Book, 1998–06–195, Whitmore to Templeman, 11 Feb. 1884; Whitmore to Villiers, 17 Dec. 1884.
77. KZNA, Wood Mss, VII/2/4, Wood to Horsford, 22 and 23 Dec. 1877.
78. BL, Hutton Mss, Add Mss 50086, Wood to Hutton, 2 Feb. 1886.
79. TNA, WO 27/489, Wood to Harman, 17 Oct. [1890].
80. CCRO, Pole-Carew, PC/9, Roberts to Pole-Carew, 20 Aug. 1890.
81. Beckett, *Memoirs of Edmonds*, 471.
82. Butler, *Autobiography*, 186.
83. Harrison, *Recollections*, 294.
84. NAM, MS Letter Book, 1998–06–194, Hawley to Paulet, 29 July 1874; MS Letter Book, 1998–06–195, Whitmore to Appleyard, 29 May and 24 June 1882.
85. NAM, MS Letter Book, 1998–06–195, Harman to Seymour, 2 June and 13 Nov. 1890.
86. Maude Mss, Diary, 17 Mar. 1874.
87. Maude Mss, Diary, 24 July 1874.
88. Maude Mss, Diary, 19 May 1882.
89. Maude Mss, Diary, 12 June 1882.
90. Maude Mss, Diary, 2 May 1884.
91. Maude Mss, Diary, 21 May 1885.
92. NAM, MS Letter Book, 1998–06–195, Harman to Maude, 8 Aug. 1885.
93. RA VIC/ADDE/1/10894, Wolseley to Cambridge, 13 Sept. 1884.
94. May, *Changes and Chances*, 200–201.
95. Arthur, *Letters of Lord and Lady Wolseley*, 365.
96. Fortescue-Brickdale, *Hallam Parr*, 169.
97. MEC, Grenfell Mss, GB 165–0319/1, Diary, 11 and 15 Feb. 1876.
98. WCRO, Dormer Mss, CR895/93, Dormer to sisters, 13 Mar. 1883; Dormer to mother, 25 June 1883.
99. BL, Hutton Mss, Add Mss 50078, Gipps to Hutton, 11 Apr. 1895; Hutton to Gipps, 1 July 1895.
100. *HCCP* 1876 [C. 1569], xxxiii.
101. Verner, *Military Life of Cambridge*, 2:21.
102. St. Aubyn, *Royal George*, 154.
103. Preston, *Wolseley's South African Diaries*, 33–34.
104. [Garnet Wolseley], "Our Autumn Manoeuvres," *Blackwood's Edinburgh Magazine* 112, no. 685 (1872): 627–44, at 628.
105. RA VIC/ADDE/1/11172, Cambridge to Wolseley, 1 May 1885.
106. RA VIC/ADDE/1/11181, Wolseley to Cambridge, 11 May 1885.
107. Johnson, *Diary of Gathorne Hardy*, 220.
108. James, *Roberts*, 212.

109. Cavendish, *Cyprus 1878*, 6–9.
110. RA VIC/ADDE/1/9756, Cambridge to Childers, 20 Sept. 1881.
111. RA VIC/ADDE/1/9679, Cambridge to Stewart, 8 July 1881.
112. RA VIC/ADDE/1/9819, Cambridge to Queen, 6 Nov. 1881.
113. TNA, WO 32/6298, Memo by Mansfield Clarke, Dec. 1901.
114. NWM, Egerton Mss, M1994/112/93, "Reminiscences of the 72nd Highlanders," 8–9.
115. NAM, Richardson Mss, 7712-3, 56–57.
116. BL, Campbell-Bannerman Mss, Add Mss 41233, Wolseley to Campbell-Bannerman, 9 Feb. 1894.
117. BL, Campbell-Bannerman Mss, Add Mss 41212, Buller to Campbell-Bannerman, 6 Sept. 1892; Add Mss 41209, Cambridge to Campbell-Bannerman, 9 Sept. 1892.
118. BL, Campbell-Bannerman Mss, Add Mss 41230, Buller to Campbell-Bannerman, 6 Sept. 1892.
119. BL, Campbell-Bannerman Mss, Add Mss 41209, Cambridge to Campbell-Bannerman, 23 Nov., and 3 Dec. 1893, and 6 Jan. 1894.
120. BL, Campbell-Bannerman Mss, Add Mss 41212, Buller to Campbell-Bannerman, 3 Jan. 1895.
121. RA VIC/ADDE/1/13108 and 13110, Campbell-Bannerman to Cambridge, 20 and 26 Dec. 1894; BL, Campbell-Bannerman Mss, Add Mss 41230, Thompson to Campbell-Bannerman, 1 Jan. 1895.
122. BL, Campbell-Bannerman Mss, Add Mss 41233, Wolseley to Campbell-Bannerman, 9 Feb. 1894.
123. HPL, Wolseley Autograph Collection, Fleetwood-Wilson to Wolseley, 14 Nov. 1892.
124. NAM, Fleetwood-Wilson Mss, 7507-55-7, Wolseley to Fleetwood-Wilson, 17 Nov. 1892.
125. *HCCP* 1896 [C. 7987].
126. Wood, *Winnowed Memories*, 374; *HCCP* 1903 [C. 1790], 172–73, 175, c. 4094, 4098, 4153.
127. *HCCP* 1903 [C. 1790], 172–73, c. 4094.
128. NAM, Roberts Mss, 7101-23-11, Brackenbury to Roberts, 17 Dec. 1900; HPL, Wolseley Mss, WP 25/28, Wolseley to wife, 10 Dec. 1896.
129. Harvie, "Wolseley Ring," 128–29, 154–56.
130. TNA, WO 32/6297, Report of WO on Selection, 20 Nov. 1897.
131. BL, Lansdowne Mss, L(5)49, Salisbury to Lansdowne, 26 Oct. 1896.
132. TNA, WO 32/6298, Kelly-Kenny Memo, 3 Dec. 1901.
133. TNA, WO 32/6298, Brodrick to Roberts, 28 Jan. 1902.
134. Henderson, *Science of War*, 404.
135. Beckett, *Memoirs of Edmonds*, 272.
136. Petersen, *Medical Profession*, 122–24.
137. *HCCP* 1903 [C. 1790], 176, c. 4166.
138. *HCCP* 1903 [C. 1790], 176, c. 4166.
139. NAM, Roberts Mss, 7101-23-207, Memorandum by Wood, 15 Oct. 1900.
140. *HCCP* 1902 [C. 982], 29.
141. RA VIC/ADDE/1/8397, Haines to Cambridge, 26 Sept. 1878.
142. NAM, Haines Mss, 8108-9-46-37, Cambridge to Haines, 23 Sept. 1880.
143. RAM, Brackenbury Mss, MD1085/1, Brackenbury to Roberts, 3 Oct. 1891; MD1085/2, Brackenbury to Sartorius, 28 Mar. 1893.

144. *HCCP* 1876 [C.1569], Appendix U, 261–62.
145. NAM, Roberts Mss, 7101–232–14, Chesney to Roberts, 1 Oct. 1888 and 12 Mar. 1889.
146. NLW, Hills-Johnes Mss, L13655, Stewart to Hills[-Johnes], 16 May 1880.
147. NAM, Warre Mss, 8112–54–671, 705, 707, Warre to Whitmore, 5 Dec. 1880; Cambridge to Warre, 11 Nov. and 31 Dec. 1880.
148. NAM, Roberts Mss, 7101–23–89, Wolseley to Roberts, 4 Sept. 1895.
149. NLI, Kilmainham 1313, Note by Wolseley, 30 Dec. 1893.
150. NAM, Roberts Mss, 7101–24–101, Roberts to Dillon, 4 Apr. 1880.
151. Lyttelton, *Eighty Years,* 145, 172–73.
152. Beckett, "Annual Confidential Report," 12–28.
153. WSA, Methuen Mss, 1742/6335, Letters on Appointment to Dublin, Wynne-Finch to Methuen, 19 Mar. 1877.
154. *HCCP* 1876 [C. 1569], 23, c. 33–35.
155. NLI, Kilmainham 1309, Note by Boyle, 2 Oct. 1880; 1313, Note by Childers, 20 May 1893.
156. NLI, Kilmainham 1312, Report, 22 Oct. 1891; 1313, Report, 20–21 July 1893.
157. NLI, Kilmainham 1309, Steele to Whitmore, 27 Aug. 1884.
158. NLI, Kilmainham 1309, Boyle to Clarina, 16 Sept. 1884.
159. NLI, Kilmainham 1309, Clarina to Boyle, 23 Sept. 1884.
160. NLI, Kilmainham 1310, Note by Clarina, 28 Oct. 1884.
161. NLI, Kilmainham 1310, Note by Clarina, 14 Oct. 1885.
162. NLI, Kilmainham 1310, Turner to Clarina, 5 Dec. 1885.
163. NLI, Kilmainham 1310, Edward of Saxe-Weimar to Harman, 12 Dec. 1885.
164. Beckett, "Annual Confidential Report," 24–25.
165. QMUL, Lyttelton Mss, PP5/2/6, Lyttelton to wife, 10 Mar. 1892.
166. NAM, Charles Gough Mss, 8304–32–211, Gough to wife, 28 Dec. 1879.
167. Rait, *Life of Haines,* 279.
168. NAM, Roberts Mss, 7101–23–100–3, Roberts to Stewart, 5 Apr., 30 Aug., and 29 Oct. 1890; Roberts to Newmarch, 9 Nov. 1892; 7101–23–105, Roberts to Gough, 13 Feb. 1897; NAM, Gough Mss, 8304–32–59, Gough to Roberts, 5 Feb. 1897.
169. BL, APAC, L/MIL/7/17038, Bengal Reports, 15 Mar. 1888 and 15 Mar. 1890.
170. HPL, Wolseley Mss, W/PLB 1, Wolseley to Davis, 24 Apr. 1884.
171. CCRO, Pole-Carew Mss, CO/F9/4, Fortescue to Pole-Carew, 2 Oct. 1884.
172. APAC, Sam Browne Mss, Eur Mss F480/13, Appleyard to Browne, 27 June 1882.
173. Appleyard, *Resumé,* 14, 20–25; Appleyard, *Addenda,* 3–11.
174. Robson, *Roberts in India,* 353–56.
175. NAM, Roberts Mss, 7101–23–98, Roberts to Dufferin, 4 Nov. 1888.
176. NAM, Roberts Mss, 7101–23–100–3, Roberts to McQueen, 25 July 1891.
177. APAC, L/MIL/7/17039, Bengal Reports, 15 Mar. 1895, and Covering Note on Kinloch, 4 Sept. 1895.
178. APAC, White Mss, F108/36, Morton to White, 6, 16, and 19 Apr. 1895; Hamilton to White, 28 Apr. 1895.
179. APAC, White Mss, F108/36, Buller to White, 30 May 1895.
180. Letter, Broadfoot to Forbes, 7 Mar. 1898, enclosing "Supplementary Notes on Pamphlet and Correspondence of 1895 by Major-General Alexander Kinloch, CB, December 1897." Lot sold by Clive Farahar & Sophie Dupré Rare Books, 1998.
181. APAC, L/MIL/7/17040, Madras Reports, 1 Jan. 1898; L/MIL/7/17041, Madras Reports, 1 Jan 1899.

182. NAM, Kempster Mss, 1976–07–37–58.

183. NAM, Roberts Mss, 7101–23–52, Nicholson to Roberts, 10 Jan. 1898 and 20 Feb. 1898; WSA, Methuen Mss, 1742/6335, Diary, 11 Dec. 1897.

184. NLS, Haldane Mss, MS 20247, Haldane diary, 16 Nov. and 11 Dec. 1897.

185. MacMunn, *Vignettes from Indian Wars*, 194; MacMunn, *Romance of the Indian Frontiers*, 239.

186. French, *Military Identities*, 165–70; Badsey, *Doctrine and Reform*, 7–8.

187. French, *Military Identities*, 168.

188. Farwell, *Mr. Kipling's Army*, 47–48.

189. "Favoured Corps," *Broad Arrow* 24 (1880): 498.

190. NAM, MS Letter Book, 1998–06–194, Egerton to Burke, 15 Feb. 1872.

191. Bruce, *Purchase System*, 152.

192. TNA, Smith Mss, WO 110/5, Talbot to Smith, 7 Nov. 1886.

193. Preston, *Wolseley's South African Diaries*, 212.

194. Preston, *Wolseley's South African Journal*, 71.

195. NAM, MS Letter Book, 1998–06–195, Whitmore to Marshall, 22 Dec. 1883.

196. RA VIC/MAIN/W/73/3, Cambridge to Ponsonby, 24 Nov. 1879.

197. CCRO, Pole-Carew Mss, CO/F9/4, Fremantle to Pole-Carew's father, 25 Aug., 29 Oct., and 1 Nov. 1880.

198. CCRO, Pole-Carew Mss, CP/9, Thompson to Pretyman, 19 Sept. 1881; Roberts to Pole-Carew, 25 Oct. 1881 and 15 Aug. 1882.

199. BL, Hutton Mss, Add Mss 50086, Buller to Hutton, 9 Feb. 1894.

200. CCRO, Pole-Carew Mss, CP/58, Roberts to Pole-Carew, 24 May 1892.

201. *HCCP* 1873 (415).

202. *Hansard*, 3rd ser., vol. 244 (1878–79), c. 934–63.

203. RA VIC/ADDE/1/8709 and 8710, Gardiner to Cambridge, 8 June 1879; Cambridge to Gardiner, 8 June 1879.

204. RA VIC/ADDE/1/8717, Cambridge to Gardiner, 11 June 1879.

205. Callwell and Headlam, *History of the Royal Artillery*, 1:28–30, 81–82, 106–7.

206. APAC, Lyttelton Letter-book, Eur Mss F102/43, Lyttelton to Godley, 12 Mar. 1886.

207. NAM, Roberts Mss, 7101–23–100–1, Roberts to Churchill, 14 Dec. 1885.

208. BL, APAC, Bombay MS Letter-book, Eur Mss F564, Nairne to Vibart, 13 Nov. 1893.

209. Preston, *Wolseley's South African Diaries*, 214.

210. RA VIC/MAIN/O/18/139, Wolseley to Queen, 27 Dec. 1882.

211. NAM, Cowell Mss, 2009–02–110–347, Graham to Cowell, 27 July 1882.

212. NAM, Cowell Mss, 2009–02–110–334, Wolseley to Cowell, 5 Mar. 1884.

213. NAM, Cowell Mss, 2009–02–110–377, Graham to Cowell, 19 Feb. 1885.

214. APAC, L/MIL/7/15520, Lockhart to Newmarch, 15 July 1898.

215. NAM, MS Letter Book, 1998–06–194, Egerton to Bingham, 4 Oct. 1872.

216. Johnson, *Diary of Gathorne Hardy*, 275.

217. Childers, *Life and Correspondence*, 1:282–83.

218. Strachan, *Politics of the British Army*, 31–32.

219. TNA, Smith Mss, WO 110/2, Smith to Cambridge, 4 Sept. 1885.

220. RA VIC/ADDE/1/11522, Cambridge to Campbell-Bannerman, 22 June 1886.

221. Callwell, *McCalmont*, 272.

222. CUL, Childers Mss, RCMS 37/5/43 and 67, Cambridge to Childers, 4 Sept. and 11 Oct. 1881.

223. Butler, *Autobiography*, 215.
224. Manning, *Evelyn Wood*, 88–90.
225. APAC, White Mss, Eur Mss F108/17, White to Chapman, 17 May 1893.
226. APAC, White Mss, Eur Mss F108/18, White to Gipps, 16 Jan. 1895.
227. Pollock, *Kitchener*, 19.
228. Western, *Reminiscences*, 135.
229. NAM, MS Letter Book, 1998-06-194, Horsford to Kerr, 31 Dec. 1877.
230. RA VIC/ADDE/1/11728, Cambridge to Connaught, 11 Feb. 1887.
231. NAM, Warre Mss, 8112-54-576, Staveley to Warre, 6 Oct. 1878.
232. NAM, Roberts Mss, 7101-23-12, Brownlow to Roberts, 8 Jan. 1886.
233. NAM, Roberts Mss, 7101-23-100-3, Roberts to Stewart, 30 Aug. 1890.
234. APAC, White Mss, Eur Mss F108/22, Roberts to White, 3 Dec. 1892.
235. NAM, Roberts Mss, 7101-23-78, Stewart to Roberts, 20 Jan. 1893; APAC, L/MIL/7/15520, Morton to Barrow, 16 June 1898.
236. RAM, Brackenbury Mss, MD1085/3, Brackenbury to Buller, 4 Sept. 1893; Brackenbury to Newmarch, 5 Sept. 1893; APAC, White Mss, Eur Mss F108/18, White to Brackenbury, 1 Aug. 1893; White to Buller, 9 May 1894.
237. Stanley, *White Mutiny*, 271.
238. *HCCP* 1876 [C. 1569], 111, c. 2244.
239. Napier, *Lord Napier of Magdala*, 266–67.
240. Stannus, *My Reasons for Leaving*.
241. TNA, Smith Mss, WO 110/6, Memo by Brownlow, 17 Dec. 1886.
242. CCRO, Pole-Carew Mss, CP/58, White to Pole-Carew, 4 Apr. 1896; Roberts to Pole-Carew, 11 May 1896; CO/F10/2, Roberts to Pole-Carew, 3 Nov. 1898.
243. Haldane, *Soldier's Saga*, 68–69, 72–73.
244. Stewart, *My Service Days*, 41.
245. RA VIC/ADDE/1/6997, Spencer to Cambridge, 15 Sept. 1872.
246. RA VIC/ADDE/1/7045, Spencer to Cambridge, 18 Jan. 1873.
247. RA VIC/ADDE/1/7053, 7066, and 7076, Napier to Cambridge, 5 and 19 Feb. and 7 Mar. 1873.
248. RA VIC/ADDE/1/7090, Napier to Cambridge, 21 Mar. 1873.
249. APAC, Napier of Magdala Mss, Eur Mss F114/16, Cambridge to Napier, 10 Apr. 1873.
250. RA VIC/ADDE/1/7123 and 7159, Napier to Cambridge, 15 May and 24 June 1873.
251. Beckett, *Wolseley in Ashanti*, 57, 233.
252. NAM, Haines Mss, 8108-9-43-22, Cambridge to Haines, 15 Nov. 1877; RA VIC/ADDE/1/8495, Cambridge to Warre, 3 Jan. 1879; ADDE/1/8600, Cambridge to Haines, 21 Mar. 1879.
253. RA VIC/ADDE/1/10127, Stewart to Cambridge, 11 Aug. 1882.
254. RA VIC/ADDE/1/10151, Stewart to Cambridge, 1 Sept. 1882.
255. APAC, Lyttelton Letter-book, Eur Mss F102/32, Lyttelton to Godley, 17 May 1886.
256. APAC, L/MIL/7/7388, Wardrop to Johnson, 4 Sept. 1880; Ashburner to Fergusson, 10 Sept. 1880; Notes by Warre, 12 and 14 Sept. 1880; Hartington to Ripon, 25 Nov. 1880; NAM, Warre Mss, 8112-54-987, Warre to Annesley, 24 Sept. 1880; Warre to Whitmore, 1 Oct. 1880.
257. RA VIC/ADDE/1/9354, Cambridge to Haines, 8 Oct. 1880.
258. RA VIC/ADDE/1/9584, Hardinge to Cambridge, 4 Apr. 1881.

259. NAM, Warre Mss, 8112-54-570, Notebook, 1881; 8112-54-987, Warre to Annesley, 10 Sept. 1880.
260. LHCMA, Hamilton Mss, 1/3/4, Roberts to Cambridge, 25 Sept. 1883.
261. TNA, Ardagh Mss, PRO 30/40/2, Dormer to Ardagh, 10 May 1890.
262. NAM, Roberts Mss, 7101-23-99, Roberts to Lansdowne, 18 Nov. 1891.
263. APAC, White Mss, Eur Mss F108/20, White to Brackenbury, 7 May 1895.
264. Moreman, "British and Indian Armies," 35–64, at 40–43.
265. BL, APAC, White Mss, Eur Mss F108/20, White to Elgin, 13 Sept. 1897.
266. DUDR, Pole-Carew Mss, White to Pole-Carew, 25 Oct. 1895.
267. NAM, Roberts Mss, 7101-23-2, Arbuthnot to Roberts, 31 Oct., and 26 Dec. 1888.

Chapter 3: The Rings

1. Travers, "Hidden Army," 523–44, at 535–36; Harries-Jenkins, *Army in Victorian Society*, 163; Adrian Preston, "Wolseley, the Khartoum Relief Expedition and the Defence of India, 1885–1900," in Preston and Dennis, *Swords and Covenants*, 89–122, at 113.
2. Hamer, *British Army*, 151.
3. RA VIC/MAIN/Z/201, Note by Queen, Nov.–Dec. 1879; VIC/ADDA36/18, Ponsonby to wife, 11 Sept. 1879; NAM, Anstruther Mss, 5705-22, Anstruther to wife, 24 Sept. 1879.
4. Spiers, *Army and Society*, 183–84.
5. Bond, "Recruiting the Victorian Army," 331–38, at p. 334.
6. Burroughs, "Imperial Defence," 55–72, at 70.
7. Sir Frederick Roberts, "Free Trade in the Army," *Nineteenth Century* 15 (1884): 1055–74.
8. HCCP 1881 [C.2811], 4–21, Note by Lytton, 4 Sept. 1878, enclosed in Lytton to Cranbrook, 9 Sept. 1878; HPL, Wolseley Mss, W/MEM/2.17, Memorandum by Roberts, 31 Dec. 1883.
9. Preston, "Frustrated Great Gamesmanship," 239–65.
10. Johnson, "Russians at the Gates," 697–744; Preston, "MacGregor and Defence of India," 58–77.
11. Beaver, "Development of the Intelligence Division," 337–41.
12. Gooch, *Prospect of War*, 1–34.
13. Beckett, "Stanhope Memorandum of 1888," 240–47.
14. Andrew Lambert, "The Royal Navy and the Defence of Empire, 1856–1918," in Kennedy, *Imperial Defence*, 111–32, at 116.
15. Strachan, *Politics of the British Army*, 197–200.
16. Harvie, "Wolseley Ring," 203.
17. Marder, *From the Dreadnought*, 2:38–40; Gordon, *Rules of the Game*, 27–29, 40, 299–302, 364–67.
18. Jenson, "X Club," 63–72; Porter and Clifton, "Patronage, Professional Values," 319–49.
19. Dubow, "Colonial Nationalism," 53–85.
20. Callwell, *McCalmont*, 47–48.
21. Biddulph, *Lord Cardwell at the War Office*, 224.
22. McIntyre, "British Policy in West Africa," 19–46; McIntyre, *Imperial Frontier in the Tropics*, 97–99; Vetch, *Life of Clarke*, 115.
23. Pollock, *Gordon*, 131–32; RA VIC/MAIN/E/20/160, Ponsonby to Queen, 21 Sept. 1873.

24. Villiers, *Peaceful Personalities and Warriors Bold*, 251–52.

25. Beckett, *Wolseley in Ashanti*, 175.

26. Greaves, *Memoirs*, 121.

27. Beckett, *Wolseley in Ashanti*, 51; Wood, *Midshipman to Field Marshal*, 1:254–55.

28. Wolseley, *Story of a Soldier's Life*, 2:201; HPL, Wolseley Mss, W/P 13/38, Wolseley to wife, 23–29 Dec. 1884.

29. Douglas, *Life of Wauchope*, 63.

30. Cavendish, *Cyprus 1878*, 56; HPL, Wolseley Mss, W/P 7/20, Wolseley to wife, 12 Aug. 1878; W/P 11/11–12, Wolseley to wife, 22–26 and 28 Aug. 1882; W/P 13/26, Wolseley to wife, 14–15 Oct. 1884; W/P 14/8, Wolseley to wife, 11–15 Mar. 1885.

31. Wolseley, *Soldier's Life*, 2:278.

32. Brackenbury, *Some Memories*, 228–29; Bond, *Victorian Army and the Staff College*, 128–29; BOD, Alison Mss, Mss. Eng. lett. c.450, Herbert to Jane Alison, 24 Nov. 1873.

33. Melville, *Life of Buller*, 1:55, 58–59.

34. HPL, Wolseley Mss, 163/5, Wolseley to brother, 21 Apr. 1880.

35. Harvie, "Wolseley Ring," 58.

36. RA VIC/ADDE/1/10894, Wolseley to Cambridge, 13 Sept. 1884.

37. Verner, *Life of Cambridge*, 2:273.

38. *HCCP* 1903 [C. 1790], 173, c. 4101.

39. NLS, Blackwood Mss, 4655, Alison to Blackwood, 30 Oct. 1897; Wolseley to Alison, 28 July 1897.

40. HPL, Wolseley Mss, 163/5, Wolseley to brother, 17 June 1880.

41. RA VIC/ADDE/1/10953, Wolseley to Cambridge, 9 Nov. 1884.

42. RA VIC/MAIN/E/40/80, Wolseley to Queen, 31 Oct. 1895.

43. SLCM, Wolseley Diaries, CAN.H.9, entry, 9 July 1878; Cavendish, *Cyprus 1878*, 2, 4.

44. St. Aubyn, *Royal George*, 178.

45. RA VIC/ADDE/1/8691, Cambridge to Stanley, 31 May 1879.

46. HPL, Wolseley Mss, S.A.2, Wolseley to Cambridge, 28 Sept. 1879.

47. RA VIC/ADDE/1/8938a, Cambridge to Wolseley, 12 Nov. 1879.

48. RA VIC/ADDA36/21, Ponsonby to wife, 4 Nov. 1882.

49. RA VIC/MAIN/O/23/28, Cambridge to Queen, 19 Sept. 1884; TNA, Smith Mss, WO 110/10, Coleridge Grove, "Rough Notes on the Nile Expedition," 6–11 Aug. 1885.

50. Preston, *Wolseley's South African Journal*, 273.

51. RA VIC/ADDE/1/11123, Wolseley to Cambridge, 4 Apr. 1885.

52. TNA, Ardagh Mss, PRO 30/40/2, Buller to Ardagh, 3 Oct. 1885. Captain Frederic Briggs was mentioned in dispatches but died of disease.

53. LHCMA, Alison Mss, Box 1, Wolseley to Alison, 30 Apr. 1885.

54. RA VIC/ADDE/1/7184, Cambridge to Airey, 25 Aug. 1873.

55. Beckett, *Wolseley in Ashanti*, 263.

56. Cavendish, *Cyprus 1878*, 58.

57. Preston, *Wolseley's South African Journal*, 38.

58. HPL, Wolseley Autograph Collection, Lytton to Wolseley, 12 Nov. 1879; Preston, *Wolseley's South African Journal*, 122–23.

59. Adye, *Soldiers and Others*, 60–61.

60. Shand, *Life of Hamley*, 2:148–51, 166–74, 194–208.

61. Lehmann, *All Sir Garnet*, 303–4; HPL, Wolseley Mss, W/P 11/17, Wolseley to wife, 7 Sept. 1882.
62. Symons, *England's Pride*, 95; Callwell, *McCalmont*, 233.
63. Lehmann, *All Sir Garnet*, 353.
64. Preston, "Wolseley, Khartoum and Defence of India," 97.
65. NRS, Spencer Ewart Mss, GD527/1/1/135/4, Added Note to Diary, 6 Feb. 1885.
66. Hamilton, *Happy Warrior*, 61.
67. Winrow, "British Regular Mounted Infantry," 125–28.
68. HPL, Wolseley Mss, 163/4, Wolseley to mother, 19 Aug. 1878.
69. SLCM, Wolseley Diaries, CAM.H.9, Diary, 12 July 1878.
70. HPL, Wolseley Autograph Collection, Burnaby to Wolseley, 27 Sept. 1884.
71. Zetland, *Letters of Disraeli*, 2:334.
72. RA VIC/MAIN/O/23/22, Gipps to Ponsonby, 19 Sept. 1884.
73. RA VIC/ADDA36/23, Ponsonby to wife, 23 Sept. 1884.
74. WCRO, Dormer Mss, CR895/93, Dormer to wife, 19 Feb. 1884.
75. WCRO, Dormer Mss, CR895/93, Dormer to wife, 11 Mar. 1884; Dormer to "Eva," 18 Mar. 1884.
76. WCRO, Dormer Mss, CR895/93, Dormer to wife, 1 and 14 Sept. 1884.
77. Malmesbury, *Life of Ardagh*, 194.
78. HPL, Wolseley Mss, W/P 13/20, Wolseley to wife, 20 Sept. 1884.
79. Stephenson, *At Home and on the Battlefield*, 39–41, 324–27.
80. Bailes, "Patterns of Thought," 35–36.
81. Lehmann, *All Sir Garnet*, 208.
82. Cavendish, *Cyprus 1878*, 4.
83. Beckett, *Wolseley in Ashanti*, 99–100, 193, 252–53, 370–71.
84. KCL, Wood Mss, KCM 89/9/30/7, Michel to Wood, 9 Sept. 1879.
85. NAM, Anstruther Mss, 5705–22, Anstruther to wife, 24 Sept. 1879.
86. Preston, *In Relief of Gordon*, 164–65.
87. Watson, *Life of Wilson*, 341–42.
88. Snook, *Beyond the Reach of Empire*, 20–30.
89. RA VIC/ADDE/1/8864a, Cambridge to Wolseley, 26 Aug. 1879.
90. RA VIC/ADDE/1/10955, Cambridge to Wolseley, 14 Nov. 1884.
91. Cavendish, *Cyprus 1878*, 5.
92. Preston, *Wolseley's South African Diaries*, 88.
93. Cavendish, *Cyprus 1878*, 117; HPL, Wolseley Mss, W/P 7/19, Wolseley to wife, 5 Aug. 1878; SSL.8, Pt. I, civ.
94. BL, Wolseley Letter-Book, Add Mss 41324, Wolseley to Greaves, 14 Jan. 1879.
95. Cavendish, *Cyprus 1878*, 17.
96. Preston, *Wolseley's South African Journal*, 149.
97. Beckett, *Wolseley in Ashanti*, 44.
98. Preston, *Wolseley's South African Journal*, 96, 109.
99. HPL, Wolseley Mss, W/P 14/1, Wolseley to wife, 15–19 Dec. 1884.
100. NAM, Wolseley-Steele Correspondence, 8701–113, Wolseley to Steele, 12 Nov. 1881; KZNA, Wood Mss, IV/2/4, Wolseley to Wood, 3 July 1882.
101. BOD, Alison Mss, Mss. Eng. lett. d.420, Alison to wife, 11 Oct. 1882.
102. Preston, *In Relief of Gordon*, 4–5.
103. SAD, Wingate Mss, 233/4/31, Wood to Wingate, 18 Nov. 1894.

104. Buller Family Mss, Wolseley to Buller, 30 Nov. 1886.
105. Preston, *In Relief of Gordon*, 75–76, 171.
106. HPL, Wolseley Mss, W/P 13/31, Wolseley to wife, 24–27 Nov. 1884.
107. Preston, *In Relief of Gordon*, 112–13.
108. HPL, Wolseley Mss, W/P 13/38, Wolseley to wife, 23–29 Dec. 1884.
109. Preston, *In Relief of Gordon*, 233.
110. HPL, Wolseley Mss, W/P 24/94, Wolseley to wife, 14 Aug. 1895.
111. Beckett, "Wolseley and the Ring," 14–25; Beckett, "Command," in Sheffield, *Leadership and Command*, 37–56.
112. Robertson, *From Private to Field Marshal*, 17; Repington, *Vestigia*, 74–75.
113. Hamilton, *Listening for the Drums*, 172–73.
114. LHCMA, Hamilton Mss, 1/2/10, Hamilton to father, 29 Nov. 1884; Hamilton, *Listening for the Drums*, 175.
115. LHCMA, Hamilton Mss, 1/2/10, Hamilton to father, 31 Dec. 1884.
116. NAM, Wilkinson Mss, OTP13/13, Nicholson to Wilkinson, 12 Dec. 1894.
117. NAM, Roberts Mss, 7101-23-57, Pretyman to Roberts, 25 Dec. 1897.
118. HPL, Wolseley Mss, S.A.2, Wolseley to Cambridge, 2 Jan 1880.
119. NLS, Minto Mss, MS 12380, Pretyman to Melgund, 20 July 1880.
120. NLS, Minto Mss, MS 12380, Pretyman to Melgund, 20 July 1880.
121. James, *Roberts*, 176.
122. KCL, Wood Mss, KCM 89/9/35/1, Roberts to Wood, 6 Jan. 1881.
123. APAC, Lyall Mss F.132/44, Roberts to Lyall, 16 June 1891.
124. NLS, Minto Mss, MS 12380, Pretyman to Melgund, 14 Nov. 1881.
125. NAM, Roberts Mss, 7101-23-103, Roberts to Brownlow, 5 Oct. and 17 Nov. 1888.
126. DUDR, Wolseley Mss, Wolseley to Bentley, 29 Sept. 1885.
127. APAC, White Mss, Eur Mss F108/22, Roberts to White, 21 Feb. 1893.
128. BL, Lansdowne Mss, L(5)47, Roberts to Lansdowne, 21 Aug. 1895.
129. HPL, Wolseley Mss, W/P 24/76, Wolseley to wife, 1 Aug. 1895.
130. HPL, Wolseley Mss, W/P 29/14, Wolseley to wife, 7 Feb. 1900.
131. HPL, Wolseley Mss, W/P 29/47 and 63, Wolseley to wife, 13 July and 28 Sept. 1900.
132. NAM, Roberts Mss, 7101-23-103, Roberts to Brownlow, 15 and 28 Dec. 1885.
133. NAM, Roberts Mss, 7101-23-100-6, Roberts to Chesney, 4 Apr. 1889.
134. NAM, Roberts Mss, 7101-23-103, Roberts to Brownlow, 5 Feb. 1886.
135. Robson, *Roberts in India*, 379.
136. NAM, Roberts Mss, 7101-23-100-1, Roberts to Brownlow, 5 Feb. 1886.
137. James, *Roberts*, 212–13.
138. NAM, Roberts Mss, 7101-23-103, Roberts to Brownlow, 10 May 1886.
139. NAM, Roberts Mss, 7101-23-100-2, Roberts to Harman, 26 July 1889.
140. NAM, Roberts Mss, 7101-23-100-2, Roberts to Lockhart, 19 July 1889.
141. RAM, Brackenbury Mss, MD 1085/3, Brackenbury to Buller, 9 May 1894.
142. NAM, Roberts Mss, 7101-23-100-4, Roberts to Wilkinson, 22 Feb. 1887.
143. LHCMA, Alison Mss, Box 1, Wolseley to Alison, 30 Apr. 1885.
144. NAM, Roberts Mss, 7101-23-100-7, Roberts to Greaves, 5 Jan. 1891.
145. Smith-Dorrien, *Memories*, 72.
146. IWM, Smith-Dorrien Mss, 19600 (87/47/5), Smith-Dorrien to "Algy," 30 May 1891.
147. IWM, Smith-Dorrien Mss, 19600 (87/47/5), Smith-Dorrien to "Algy," 9 June 1891.

148. IWM, Smith-Dorrien Mss, 19600 (87/47/5), Wood to "Algy," 21 Sept. 1891; Smith-Dorrien, *Memories*, 72.

149. Tim Moreman, "Lord Kitchener, the General Staff and the Army in India, 1902–14," in French and Holden Reid, *British General Staff*, 57–74, at 59.

150. Julian Moore, "Kipling and Lord Roberts," http://www.kiplingsociety.co.uk/rg_lordroberts_moore.htm.

151. John McGivering and John Radcliffe, "One Viceroy Resigns," http://www.kipling society.co.uk/rg_viceroy1.htm.

152. BL, Lansdowne Mss, L(5)48, Roberts to Lansdowne, 29 Aug. 1900.

153. NLS, Minto Mss, MS 12378, Roberts to Melgund, 7 Sept. 1879.

154. LHCMA, Hamilton Mss, 1/3/4, Roberts to Cambridge, 12 Apr. and 21 June 1884.

155. NAM, Roberts Mss, 7101-23-100-1, Roberts to Brownlow, 2 Sept. 1887.

156. NAM, Roberts Mss, 7101-23-100-3, Roberts to White, 20 Dec. 1892.

157. BL, Lansdowne Mss, L(5)47, Lansdowne to Roberts, 23 Nov. 1898.

158. NAM, Roberts Mss, 7101-23-100-3, Roberts to Harman, 9 Aug. 1890; 7101-23-99, Roberts to Lansdowne, 14 Sept. 1890.

159. NAM, Roberts Mss, 7101-23-44, Morton to Roberts, 23 Apr. 1895.

160. NAM, Charles Gough Mss, 8304-32-117, Gough to wife, 16 Jan. 1879.

161. NAM, Charles Gough Mss, 8304-32-138, Gough to wife, 9 Feb. 1897.

162. CCRO, Pole-Carew Mss, CO/F9/4, Nicholson to Pole-Carew, 31 May 1891.

163. LHCMA, Hamilton Mss, 1/2/17, Roberts to Harman, 20 Nov. 1890; Harman to Roberts, 1 Jan. 1891; Roberts to Stanhope, 28 Jan. 1891; NAM, Roberts Mss, 7101-23-59, Pole-Carew to Roberts, 17 Oct. and 27 Nov. 1890; 7101-23-100-3, Roberts to Harman, 18 Nov. 1890; Roberts to Stanhope, 5 Jan. 1891.

164. Hamilton, *Listening for the Drums*, 212–16.

165. LHCMA, Hamilton Mss, 1/2/9, Roberts to Hamilton, 22 June 1893.

166. LHCMA, Hamilton Mss, 1/2/20, Hamilton to wife, 17 and 23 Aug. 1895.

167. APAC, Lyall Mss, F.132/24, Roberts to Lyall, 8 May 1880.

168. APAC, White Mss, F108/101, White to wife, 8 and 14 May 1880.

169. LHCMA, Hamilton Mss, 1/3/4, Roberts to Cambridge, 30 Jan. 1885.

170. RA VIC/ADDE/1/11444, Cambridge to Roberts, 12 Mar. 1886.

171. RA VIC/ADDE/1/11458 and 11467, Cambridge to Roberts, 2 and 16 Apr. 1886.

172. NAM, Roberts Ms, 7101-23-98, Roberts to Dufferin, 26 Aug. 1886.

173. RA VIC/ADDE/1/11529, Cambridge to Dufferin, 2 July 1886.

174. NAM, Roberts Mss, 7101-23-98, Roberts to Dufferin, 4 Sept. 1887; 7101-23-100-4, Roberts to White, 4 Sept. 1886.

175. APAC, White Mss, Eur Mss F108/98/101, White to brother, 21 Nov. 1887.

176. NAM, Roberts Mss, 7101-23-100-2, Roberts to Churchill, 31 Mar. 1888; 7101-23-100-4, Roberts to White, 18 Mar. 1888; APAC, White Mss, Eur Mss F108/109, Roberts to White, 25 Jan. and 10 Mar. 1888.

177. NAM, Roberts Mss, 7101-23-12, Brownlow to Roberts, 1 June 1888.

178. NAM, Roberts Mss, 7101-23-98, Roberts to Dufferin, 2 Feb. 1888; 7101-23-100-4, Roberts to White, 14 Feb. 1888.

179. NAM, Roberts Mss, 7101-23-90, White to Roberts, 5 May 1888.

180. NAM, Roberts Mss, 7101-23-90, White to Roberts, 22 Oct. 1888.

181. NAM, Roberts Mss, 7101-23-12, Brownlow to Roberts, 12 Sept. 1888; Durand, *Life of White*, 1:374.

182. NAM, Roberts Mss, 7101–23–100–3, Roberts to Harman, 8 Oct. 1890; Roberts to Stewart, 29 Oct. 1890.

183. HPL, Wolseley Mss, W/W.4/124, Wolseley to brother, 20 Apr. 1900.

184. HPL, Wolseley Mss, W/W.4/133, Wolseley to brother, 27 July 1900.

185. Macdiarmid, *Life of Grierson*, 153.

186. Sherson, *Townshend*, 184, 186–89, 191, 206.

187. NAM, Charles Gough Mss, 8304–32–180, 198, Gough to wife, 22 June 1879 and 18 Oct. 1879.

188. Trousdale, *War in Afghanistan*, 62, 159–61.

189. NAM, Roberts Mss, 7101–23–101, Memo, 29 Feb. 1880.

190. Robson, *Roberts in India*, 158–60.

191. APAC, Baker Mss, Eur Mss D567, Baker to Cambridge, 21 Apr. 1880; Robson, *Roberts in India*, 171–72.

192. NAM, Charles Gough Mss, 8304–32–220 and 222, Gough to wife, 29 Feb. and 15 Mar. 1880.

193. NAM, Charles Gough Mss, 8304–32–234, Gough to wife, 23–24 May 1880.

194. NAM, Roberts Mss, 7101–23–101, Roberts to Dillon, 4 Apr. 1880.

195. Robson, *Roberts in India*, 203–4.

196. NLS, Minto Mss, MS 12380, Pretyman to Melgund, 10 June and 20 July 1880.

197. NAM, Roberts Mss, 7101–23–101, Roberts to Greaves, 25 Feb. 1880; Roberts to Hughes, 3 May 1880.

198. NAM, Haines Mss, 8108–9–46–9, Cambridge to Haines, 27 Feb. 1880.

199. NAM, Roberts Mss, 7101–23–101, Roberts to Ellice, 10 June 1880.

200. Lehman, *All Sir Garnet*, 388.

201. HPL, Wolseley Mss, W/W.4/171, Wolseley to brother, 6 Feb. 1902.

202. RA VIC/MAIN/E/32/7, Cambridge to Queen, 10 Feb. 1893.

203. RA VIC/ADDE/1/8580, Cambridge to Baker, 7 Mar. 1879.

204. NAM, Baker Mss, 7804–25, Cambridge to Baker, 23 May and 12 Aug. 1879.

205. RA VIC/ADDE/1/9174, Cambridge to Johnson, 23 Apr. 1880.

206. RA VIC/ADDE/1/10830, Cambridge to Stewart, 25 July 1884.

207. RA VIC/ADDE/1/11396, Cambridge to Roberts, 28 Jan. 1886.

208. RA VIC/ADDE/1/9639, Cambridge to Baker, 2 June 1881.

209. NAM, Roberts Mss, 7101–23–100–3, Roberts to Stewart, 30 Aug. 1890; Roberts to Cambridge, 1 Sept. 1890; Roberts to Harman, 15 Sept. 1890.

210. NAM, Roberts Mss, 7101–23–7, Baker to Roberts, 2 Apr. 1892 and 30 Jan. 1893.

211. KHLC, Stanhope Mss, 0254/1, Cambridge to Stanhope, 5 Dec. 1887; 0254/3, Cambridge to Stanhope, 26 Dec. 1891.

212. RA VIC/MAIN/E/19/1, Cambridge to Biddulph, 2 Sept. 1871.

213. St. Aubyn, *Royal George*, 170–71.

214. RA VIC/MAIN/E/21/93, Cambridge to Queen, 5 Sept. 1874.

215. RA VIC/MAIN/E/22/12, Cambridge to Queen, 26 Jan. 1876.

216. Johnson, *Diary of Gathorne Hardy*, 356–57.

217. HPL, Wolseley Mss, 163/v, Wolseley to brother, 14 Oct. 1879.

218. HPL, Wolseley Mss, W/P 8/24, Wolseley to wife, 11 Sept. 1879.

219. Preston, *Wolseley's South African Journal*, 37.

220. HPL, Wolseley Mss, W/P 8/32, Wolseley to wife, 31 Oct. 1879.

221. HPL, Wolseley Mss, W/P 8/35, Wolseley to wife, 24 Nov. 1879.

222. HPL, Wolseley Mss, W/P 14/8, Wolseley to wife, 11–15 Mar. 1885.

223. LHCMA, Alison Mss, Box 1, Wolseley to Alison, 22 Mar. 1885.

224. BOD, Alison Mss, Mss. Eng. lett. d.420, Alison to wife, 28 Mar. 1883.

225. BOD, Alison Mss, Mss. Eng. lett. d.420, Alison to wife, 13 June 1883.

226. NLS, Minto Mss, MS12380, Pretyman to Melgund, 11 May 1886.

227. RA VIC/ADDA34/87, Bigge to Ponsonby, 6 Nov. 1892.

228. RA VIC/MAIN/E/27/54 and 55, Childers to Cambridge, 13 Sept. 1881; Cambridge to Queen, 15 Sept. 1881.

229. RA VIC/ADDA36/20, Ponsonby to wife, 16 Sept. 1881.

230. CUL, Cambridge Mss, RCMS 37/5/54, Ponsonby to Childers, 19 Sept. 1881; 37/5/66–67, Cambridge to Childers, 11 Oct. 1881.

231. RA VIC/ADDA36/20, Ponsonby to wife, 19 Sept. 1881.

232. RA VIC/ADDA36/20, Ponsonby to wife, 17 Sept. 1881.

233. RA VIC/ADDA36/20, Ponsonby to wife, 18 Sept. 1881; VIC/MAIN/E/27/58, Ponsonby to Queen, 17 Sept. 1881.

234. Beaver, *Under Every Leaf*, 80–81.

235. BL, Gladstone Mss, Add Mss 44130, Childers to Gladstone, 12 Oct. 1882; RA VIC/MAIN/E/29/218, Cambridge to Queen, 17 Dec. 1882.

236. *HCCP* 1876 [C. 1569], 24, c. 55; 42, c. 413–16; 44, c. 500; 50–51, c. 705–6.

237. KZNA, Wood Mss, III/4/4, Cambridge to Horsford, 1 June 1878.

238. St. Aubyn, *Royal George*, 116–17.

239. NWM, Egerton Mss, M1994/112/92, "Reminiscences of the 72nd Highlanders," 59.

240. Callwell, *Stray Recollections*, 1:289.

241. SLCM, Wolseley Diaries, CAM.H.22, Diary, 6 Apr. 1877.

242. KZNA, Wood Mss, VII/1/3, Buller to Wood, 29 Sept. 1879.

243. SRO, Cranbrook Mss, HA43/H/4/14, Cambridge to Hardy, 2 Apr. 1879.

244. RA VIC/MAIN/W/12/10, Cambridge to Ponsonby, 17 Feb. 1890.

245. NAM, Roberts Mss, 1998-06-195, Harman to Roberts, 24 Oct. 1890.

246. BL, Hutton Mss, Add Mss 50112, "Memoirs," 71.

247. Stockings, *Britannia's Shield*, 48–55.

248. KHLC, Stanhope Mss, 0259, Brackenbury to Stanhope, 6 Nov. 1890.

249. BL, Cross Mss, Add Mss 51264, Salisbury to Cross, 6 Nov. 1890.

250. Brice, *Thinking Man's Soldier*, 191n21.

251. Ibid., 175–76.

252. RAM, Brackenbury Mss, MD 1085/3, Brackenbury to Grierson, 1 Nov. 1893 and 11 Feb. 1895.

253. Spottiswoode, *Reminiscences*, 109.

254. Jeal, *Baden-Powell*, 55, 71–72, 106, 113, 122, 126–27, 154–57.

255. Ballard, *Smith-Dorrien*, 74; Holmes, *Little Field Marshal*, 40–42.

256. TNA, WO 27/489, Reports on French by Wood, 18 June 1891 and 14 Sept. 1893.

257. De Groot, *Douglas Haig*, 54; Hussey, "Very Substantial Grievance," 169–80, at 179. Haig contributed an appreciative foreword to Greaves's posthumous memoirs. See Greaves, *Memoirs*, v–vi.

258. Hamilton, *Listening for the Drums*, 221.

259. RAM, Brackenbury Mss, MD1085/2, Brackenbury to Buller, 20 May 1893; MD1085/3, Brackenbury to Buller, 10 July 1894.

260. APAC, White Mss, Eur Mss F108/19, White to Stedman, 13 May and 13 July 1895.

261. NAM, Roberts Mss, 7101-23-52, Nicholson to Roberts, 14 Mar. 1898.

262. Preston, *Wolseley's South African Diaries*, 81, 88, 101; Preston, *Wolseley's South African Journal*, 14, 17–18; Preston, *In Relief of Gordon*, xxix–xxx.

263. Sydenham, *My Working Life*, 17–20; Vetch, *Life of Clarke*, v–vi.

264. RA VIC/ADDE/1/10659, Cambridge to Stephenson, 29 Feb. 1884.

265. RA VIC/ADDE/1/10676, Cambridge to Stephenson, 7 Mar. 1884.

266. BL, Gladstone Mss, Add Mss 44147, Hartington to Gladstone, 10 Feb. 1885.

267. Bahlman, *Diary of Hamilton*, 2:793; HPL, Wolseley Mss, W/P 14/8, Wolseley to wife, 11–15 Mar. 1885; Cooke and Vincent, *Governing Passion*, 194–97.

268. HPL, Wolseley Mss, W/P 14/13, Wolseley to wife, 20–27 May 1885.

269. Ian Beckett, "Sir William Lockhart," in Brice, *Forgotten Victorian Generals*; Churchill, *Churchill*, 965.

271. NAM, Roberts Mss, 7101-23-90, White to Roberts, 20 Feb. 1895.

272. Miller, *Methuen and the British Army*, 57.

273. APAC, Elgin Mss, Eur Mss F84/71, Elgin to White, 27 Aug. 1897.

274. APAC, White Mss, Eur Mss F108/38, Lockhart to White, 30 Sept. 1897.

275. NAM, Roberts Mss, 7101-23-52, Nicholson to Roberts, 14 Sept. 1897.

276. NAM, Roberts Mss, 7101-23-52, Nicholson to Roberts, 10 Oct. 1897.

277. APAC, White Mss, Eur Mss, F108/98A, White to John White, 14 May 1897.

278. BL, APAC, White Mss, Eur Mss F108/20, White to Elgin, 10 and 13 Sept. 1897; Lockhart to White, 12 Sept. 1897.

279. NAM, Roberts Mss, 7101-23-48, Nairne to Roberts, 29 Jan. 1898; NLW, Hills-Johnes Mss, L13001, Nairne to Hills-Johnes, 9 Feb. 1898.

280. BL, Lansdowne Mss, L(5)37, Lansdowne to Wolseley, 22 Aug. 1898; Wood to Knox, 17 Aug. 1898; L(5)28, Lansdowne to Lord George Hamilton, 24 Aug. 1898; L(5)38, Lansdowne to Wood, 18 Aug. 1898.

281. SAD, Wingate Mss, 233/7/11 and 51, Wingate to wife, 10 and 27 July 1889.

282. TNA, Kitchener Mss, PRO 30/57/93, Reminiscences by Sir John Maxwell.

283. Doolittle, *Soldier's Hero*, 32.

284. Pollock, *Kitchener*, 84.

285. SAD, Wingate Mss, 102/1/80, Wingate Diary, 5 Feb. 1898; Cecil, *Leisure of an Egyptian Official*, 181; HHM, Salisbury Mss, Cecil Diary, 2 Sept. 1896.

286. Hunter, *Kitchener's Sword-arm*, 52–54.

287. SAD, Wingate Mss, 233/5/45, Wingate to wife, 8 June 1898.

288. HHM, Salisbury Mss, A/111/17, Cromer to Barrington, 5 Feb. 1898.

289. HHM, Salisbury Mss, A/112/17, Cromer to Salisbury, 2 Mar. 1899.

290. SAD, Wingate Mss, 266/11/15, Rawlinson to Wingate, 9 Nov. 1898.

291. Satre, "Brodrick and Army Reform," 117–39, at 126.

292. Keith Surridge, "Lansdowne at the War Office," in Gooch, *Boer War*, 21–40, at 39.

Chapter 4: External Influences

1. Bourne, *Patronage and Society*, 71.

2. Hyam, *Britain's Imperial Century*, 135–48.

3. Strachan, *Politics of the British Army*, 1–19.

4. Farrell, *Military and the Monarchy*, 107–8, 163–67, 211–12; Omond, *Parliament and the Army*, 97–99.

5. Childers, *Life and Correspondence*, 2:57; Omond, *Parliament and the Army*, 128–30.

6. Strachan, *Politics of the British Army*, 119.

7. Bond, "Effect of the Cardwell Reforms," 515–24, at 523.

8. Hamer, *British Army*, 66.

9. Ibid., 132–34.

10. TNA, WO 163/4, A418a, WO Council, 8 Dec. 1888.

11. Hamer, *British Army*, 83.

12. TNA, Roberts Papers, WO 105/41, Nicholson to Roberts, 10 Nov. 1906.

13. Collins, "Defining Victory in Victorian Warfare," 895–929.

14. BL, Gladstone Mss, Add Mss 44130, Childers to Gladstone, 12 Oct. 1882.

15. RA VIC/ADDE/1/8596, Stanley to Cambridge, 20 Mar. 1879.

16. RA VIC/ADDE/1/9532 and 9547, Cambridge to Smyth, 24 Feb. and 4 Mar. 1881.

17. Buller Family Mss, Buller to Henrietta, 6 Mar. 1881.

18. RA VIC/ADDE/1/9577 and 9583, Smyth to Cambridge, 29 Mar. and 4 Apr. 1881.

19. RA VIC/ADDE/1/10947, Cambridge to Smyth, 30 Oct. 1884.

20. RA VIC/ADDE/1/11233, Smyth to Cambridge, 1 July 1885.

21. RA VIC/MAIN/E/26/37, Ponsonby to Queen, 26 Feb. 1881.

22. RA VIC/MAIN/E/30/65, Cambridge to Queen, 3 Mar. 1884; VICMAIN/W/10/19–20, Queen to Ponsonby, 9 Mar. 1884; Hartington to Ponsonby, 10 Mar. 1884.

23. RA VIC/ADDE/1/12314, Stanhope to Cambridge, 25 Nov. 1888.

24. HPL, Wolseley Autograph Collection, Ripon to Wolseley, 6 Sept. 1885; Selborne to Wolseley, 6 Nov. 1885; Cranbrook to Wolseley, 13 Mar. 1896.

25. BL, Cross Mss, Add Mss 51277, Lansdowne to Maitland, 23 May 1890; Fleetwood-Wilson to Maitland, 4 June 1890.

26. HPL, Wolseley Autograph Collection, Dufferin to Wolseley, 30 Oct. 1887, and 21 Aug. and 23 Nov. 1892.

27. HPL, Wolseley Autograph Collection, Salisbury to Wolseley, 23 Mar. 1896; BL, Lansdowne Mss, L(5)49, Salisbury to Lansdowne, 4 Jan. 1898; Lansdowne to Salisbury, 4 Jan. 1898.

28. LA, Stanhope Mss, RA 4/C/2/54, Salisbury to Stanhope, 11 Feb. 1888.

29. HPL, Wolseley Autograph Collection, Childers to Wolseley, 5 Mar. 1883.

30. TNA, Smith Mss, WO 110/2, Ashmead-Bartlett to Smith, 2 Sept. 1885.

31. Brian Bond, "The South African War of 1880–81," in Bond, *Victorian Military Campaigns*, 199–240, at 215.

32. RA VIC/MAIN/N/41/78, Hardinge to Queen, 12 Feb. 1885.

33. Ian Beckett, "Kitchener and the Politics of Command," in Spiers, *Sudan*, 35–53.

34. W. Murray Hogben, "British Civil-Military Relations on the North West Frontier of India," in Preston and Dennis, *Swords and Covenants*, 123–46.

35. Beckett, *Wolseley in Ashanti*, 422.

36. SLCM, Wolseley Diaries, CAM.H.22, Diary, 31 Dec. 1877.

37. HPL, Wolseley Mss, W/P 16/84, Wolseley to wife, 28 Aug. 1887.

38. HPL, Wolseley Mss, W/P 8/19, Wolseley to wife, 8–13 Aug. 1879.

39. Preston, *Wolseley's South African Diaries*, 272.

40. HPL, Wolseley Autograph Collection, Cardwell to Wolseley, 18 Nov. 1873.

41. HPL, Wolseley Autograph Collection, Carnarvon to Wolseley, 19 Apr. 1877.

42. Preston, *Wolseley's South African Diaries*, 100–101.

43. RA VIC/MAIN/E/27/144, Wolseley to McNeill, 17 Nov. 1881.

44. KHLC, Stanhope Mss, 0314, Stanhope to Cambridge, 26 Apr. 1888; Wolseley to Stanhope, 27 Apr. 1888.

45. Beckett, "Edward Stanhope," 278–307.

46. RA VIC/ADDE/1/12324, Stanhope to Cambridge, 4 Dec. 1888.

47. KHLC, Stanhope Mss, 0308, Salisbury to Stanhope, 7 Jan. 1889.

48. RA VIC/ADDE/1/12380, Salisbury to Cambridge, 23 Jan. 1889.

49. Heathcote, *Military in British India*, 133.

50. RA VIC/ADDE/1/9090, Cambridge to Haines, 20 Feb. 1880.

51. RA VIC/ADDE/1/7009, Northbrook to Cambridge, 23 Oct. 1872.

52. Gann and Duignan, *Rulers of British Africa*, 170.

53. HPL, Wolseley Mss, M2/41/8/4, Diary, 17 Feb. 1875.

54. RA VIC/ADDE/1/7746 and 7747, Carnarvon to Cambridge, 11 and 12 Nov. 1875; Gordon, *Political Diaries of Carnarvon*, 271–76; Vincent, *Diaries of Stanley*, 4:251.

55. RA VIC/ADDE/1/7748 and 7750, Cambridge to Airey, 12 and 13 Nov. 1875.

56. BL, Carnarvon Mss, Add Mss 60797, Frere to Carnarvon, 2 May 1874.

57. Stockings, *Britannia's Shield*, 164.

58. Morton, *Ministers and Generals*, 53, 69, 133, 194; Preston, *Canada and Imperial Defence*, 141.

59. RA VIC/ADDE/1/10521, Lorne to Cambridge, 17 Oct. 1883; VIC/ADDE/1/10744, Lansdowne to Cambridge, 11 May 1884.

60. Stockings, *Britannia's Shield*, 80–85.

61. CCRO, Pole-Carew Mss, CP/21, Minto to Pole-Carew, 2 June 1900.

62. Morton, *Ministers and Generals*, 167, 173.

63. Ibid., 174–92.

64. RA VIC/ADDE/1/8160, 8163 and 8170, Hardy to Cambridge, 28 Oct., 1 Nov., and 8 Nov. 1877.

65. TNA, Chapman Letter Book, WO 106/16, Walton to Eliot, 24 Feb. 1892.

66. TNA, Chapman Letter Book, WO 106/16, Chapman to Gipps, 8 Feb. 1893; Chapman to Buller, 11 Feb. 1893; Chapman to Villiers, 11 Feb. 1893; Chapman to Waters, 15 Apr. 1893; Waters, *Secret and Confidential*, 5, 40, 55.

67. HHM, Salisbury Mss, E/Cambridge/54, Cambridge to Salisbury, 29 Oct. 1878.

68. RA VIC/ADDE/1/8417 and 8420, Salisbury to Cambridge, 20 Oct. 1878; Stanley to Cambridge, 24 Oct. 1878.

69. RA VIC/ADDE/1/10553, Cambridge to Stephenson, 23 Nov. 1883.

70. BOD, Alison Mss, Mss. Eng. lett. c.452, Alison to Cambridge, 9 Apr. 1883.

71. RA VIC/ADDE/1/10648 and 10649, Hartington to Cambridge, 21 Feb. 1884; Cambridge to Stephenson, 22 Feb. 1884.

72. Cromer, *Modern Egypt*, 2:106; BL, Lansdowne Mss, L(5)42, Lansdowne to Bigge, 9 June 1896.

73. SAD, Wingate Mss, 102/1/76, Wingate Diary, 19 Jan. 1898.

74. BL, Lansdowne Mss, L(5)43, Bigge to Lansdowne, 7 Dec. 1898; Lansdowne to Bigge, 8 Dec. 1898; RA VIC/MAIN/E/33/35, Wolseley to Queen, 9 Dec. 1898.

75. TNA, Smith Mss, WO 110/1, Smith to Cross, 10 Aug. 1885.

76. RA VIC/MAIN/E/30/27, Cambridge to Ponsonby, 30 Apr. 1883.

77. TNA, Smith Mss, WO 110/3, Smith to Carnarvon, 9 Jan. 1886.

78. TNA, Smith Mss, WO 110/4, Smith to Cambridge, 17 Oct. 1886.

79. Brackenbury, *Some Memories*, 312.

80. RA VIC/MAIN/D/34/58, Ponsonby to Queen, 21 July 1882.

81. Brackenbury, *Some Memories*, 353.

82. Gordon, *Political Diaries of Carnarvon*, 51, 62, 381.

83. Thomas, "Sir Redvers Buller," 56–88.

84. RA VIC/ADDE/1/11570, Prince Edward to Cambridge, 22 Aug. 1886; VIC/ADDE/1/11574, Smith to Cambridge, 27 Aug. 1886.

85. Streets, *Martial Races*, 119–20; Stephen Badsey, "New Wars, New Press, New Country? The British Army, the Expansion of the Empire and the Mass Media, 1877–1918," in Beckett, *Victorians at War*, 34–46.

86. Paris, *Warrior Nation*, 49–82.

87. RA VIC/ADDE/1/7516, Napier to Cambridge, 15 Jan. 1875.

88. Stearn, "War Images and Image Makers," 149.

89. Nicoll, *Gladstone, Gordon and the Sudan Wars*, 42–57.

90. Matthew, *Gladstone*, 145.

91. Davison, *Challenges of Command*, 34–37.

92. NAM, MS Letter Book, 1998-06-195, Whitmore to Dillon, 4 Feb. 1884.

93. Wolseley, *Soldier's Pocket Book*, 178–80.

94. Beckett, *Wolseley in Ashanti*, 177, 200.

95. HPL, Wolseley Mss, 163/4, Wolseley to brother, 18 Feb. 1878.

96. RA VIC/ADDE/1/8593, Cambridge to Chelmsford, 20 Mar. 1879.

97. RA VIC/ADDE/1/8576 and 8577, Cambridge to Frere, and Cambridge to Chelmsford, 6 Mar. 1879.

98. Spiers, *Army and Society*, 213; Stearn, "War Images and Image Makers," 249–58.

99. Stearns, "War Images and Image Makers," 368–80.

100. *Daily Express*, 6 June 1900.

101. Walford, *Forbes and the Zulu War*.

102. Preston, *Wolseley's South African Journal*, 199, 212, 245, 260; Atkins, *Life of Russell*, 2:289–92, 294–97, 300–305; Lehmann, *First Boer War*, 74–76.

103. BL, APAC, White Mss, Eur Mss F108/38, Lockhart to White, 27 Dec. 1897.

104. KCL, LHCMA, Hamilton Mss, 1/2/24, Lockhart to Hamilton, 16 May 1898.

105. NAM, Cowell Mss, 2009-02-110-357, Graham to Cowell, 22 Mar. 1884.

106. Ian Beckett, "Manipulating the Modern Curse of Armies: Wolseley, the Press, and the Ashanti War, 1873–74," in Miller, *Soldiers and Settlers in Africa*, 221–34.

107. Atkins, *Life of Russell*, 2:297.

108. HPL, Wolseley Mss, S.A.1, Wolseley to Frere, 9 Dec. 1879.

109. St. Aubyn, *Royal George*, 196.

110. RA VIC/MAIN/E/27/156, Ellis to Ponsonby, 22 Nov. 1881.

111. HPL, Wolseley Mss, W/P 29/49, Wolseley to wife, 1 Aug. 1900.

112. HPL, Wolseley Mss, W/W.4/124, Wolseley to brother, 20 Apr. 1900.

113. Streets, *Martial Races*, 129.

114. Streets, "Military Influence," 231–56.

115. RA VIC/ADDE/1/8476, Baker to Cambridge, 22 Dec. 1878; NAM, Roberts Mss, 7101-23-160, Roberts to Dillon, 7 Feb. 1879; 7101-23-101, Collette to Macpherson, 6 Feb. 1879; Roberts to Lumsden, 2 Sept. 1879.

116. NAM, Charles Gough Mss, 8304-32-155, Gough to wife, 2 Mar. 1879.

117. Robson, *Roberts in India*, 61–68, 81–83, 85–87, 92–93.

118. Atwood, *Life of Roberts*, 80–82.

119. NAM, Roberts Mss, 7101-23-147, Stanhope to Roberts, 26 Feb. 1880; 7101-23-101, Memo on Kabul Atrocities, 19 June 1880.

120. Wessels, *Roberts and South Africa*, 63–65.

121. Beaumont, "British Press and Censorship," 267–89, at 276.

122. Stephen Badsey, "War Correspondents," in Gooch, *Boer War*, 187–202.

123. Morgan, "Boer War and the Media," 1–16.

124. Melville, *Life of Buller*, 1:131.

125. Bennett, *Downfall of the Dervishes*, 70.

126. TNA, Kitchener Mss, PRO 30/57/14, Kitchener to Cromer, 1 Feb. 1899; Cromer to Salisbury, 12 Mar. 1899; Alford and Sword, *Egyptian Soudan*, 231–35.

127. Childers, *Life of Childers*, 2:119, 122.

128. Hugh Cecil, "British Correspondents and the Sudan Campaign of 1896–98," in Spiers, *Sudan*, 102–27, at 109–11.

129. APAC, White Mss, Eur Mss F108/3, White to Roberts, 19 June 1886.

130. Stewart, *Pagoda War*, 173.

131. RA VIC/MAIN/N/43/124, Dufferin to Queen, 5 Mar. 1886; APAC, White Mss, Eur Mss F108/3, White memo, Apr. 1886.

132. Stewart, *Pagoda War*, 127–28.

133. NAM, Roberts Mss, 7101-23-12, Brownlow to Roberts, 28 Jan. 1886.

134. Stephen Badsey, "War Correspondents in the Boer War," in Gooch, *Boer War*, 187–202.

135. Ibid., 190–91.

136. BL, Hutton Mss, Add Mss 50086, Buller to Hutton, 7 Aug. 1885.

137. RAM, Brackenbury Mss, MD1085/4, Brackenbury to Grenfell, 20 Feb. 1895.

138. *HCCP* 1903 [C. 1790], 399, c. 9435-36; 470–71, c. 10919-20.

139. CCRO, Pole-Carew Mss, CP/5, Pole-Carew to father, 6 Apr. 1880.

140. Gleichen, *Guardsman's Memories*, 24.

141. Lyttelton, *Eighty Years*, 98–99, 130, 143–44, 149.

142. Maurice, *Rawlinson*, 8.

143. Sherson, *Townshend*, 7, 17–18, 47, 49, 81–82, 119, 121, 123–24, 178, 181, 183–84, 192–93.

144. Churchill, *Churchill*, 780.

145. Ibid., 806.

146. BL, Lansdowne Mss, L(5)47, Roberts to Lansdowne, 6 Aug. 1898.

147. HPL, Wolseley Autograph Collection, Roberts to Wolseley, 13 Oct. 1899; NAM, Roberts Mss, 7101-23-91, Wood to Roberts, 29 Sept. and 11 Oct. 1899; 7101-23-110-1, Roberts to Wood, 29 Aug. 1899.

148. Author's collection, Ellis Mss, Arthur Ellis to Gerald Ellis, 26 May, 17 June, 15 July, and 30 Aug. 1896; 24 Aug. 1898; and 4 Oct. 1899.

149. Butterfield, *War and Peace in South Africa*, 106.

150. Preston, *Wolseley's South African Journal*, 197.

151. BOD, Alison Mss, Mss. Eng. Lett. c.420, Wolfe Murray to Alison, 21 July 1882.

152. APAC, White Mss, Eur Mss F108/3, White to Roberts, 24 Sept. 1886.

153. WCRO, Dormer Mss, CR895/94, Dormer to brother, 4 Nov. 1889.

154. Gordon, *Rules of the Game*, 326–29; Gould, *Military Lodges*, 107–10.

155. RA VIC/MAIN/O/28/265, Wolseley to Edwards, 6 Apr. 1896.

156. RA VIC/MAIN/W/12/141, Connaught to Ponsonby, 17 Oct. 1893.

157. RA VIC/MAIN/W/12/140 and 142–143, Cambridge to Ponsonby, 11 and 18 Oct. 1893; Gipps to Ponsonby, 19 Oct. 1893.

158. Hamilton, *Listening for the Drums*, 162.
159. Harrison, *Recollections*, 318–27.
160. RA VIC/ADDE/1/12738, Wolseley to Cambridge, 25 June 1891.
161. RA VIC/ADDE/1/7998, Hardy to Cambridge, Dec. 1876.
162. Jeal, *Baden-Powell*, 38, 55–56, 71, 75, 110–13, 128–29, 135–37.
163. Menzies, *Lord William Beresford VC*, 124–31.
164. SRO, Cranbrook Mss, HA43/H/4/13, Cambridge to Hardy, 12 Feb. 1877.
165. Gordon, *Letters of Gordon*, 173.
166. Vetch, *Life of Clarke*, 218.
167. BL, Campbell-Bannerman Mss, Add Mss 41209, Cambridge to Campbell-Bannerman, 7 and 20 July 1893; Add Mss 41230, Thompson to Campbell-Bannerman, 11 July 1893.
168. BL, APAC, Bombay MS Letter-book, Eur Mss F564, Nairne to Duff, 10 and 20 Jan. 1898.
169. HPL, Wolseley Mss, 10/28, 30, Lady Wolseley to Wolseley, 27 Nov. and 25 Dec. 1884.
170. NAM, Roberts Mss, 7101-23-99, Roberts to Lansdowne, 20 Sept. 1889.
171. NAM, Roberts Mss, 7101-23-99 Roberts to Lansdowne, 12 Oct. 1889.
172. RA VIC/ADDE/1/12798, Harris to Cambridge, 12 Mar. 1892.
173. NAM, Roberts Mss, 7101-23-99, Roberts to Lansdowne, 29 May 1890.
174. St. Aubyn, *Royal George*, 287–94.
175. Spiers, *Scottish Soldier and Empire*, 146–50, 206–7.
176. SLCM, Wolseley Diaries, CAM.H.22, Diary, 12 Mar. 1878.
177. Baker, *Question of Honour*, 88.
178. Anderson, *Baker Pasha*, 41; Baker, *Question of Honour*, 88.
179. SRO, Cranbrook Mss, HA43/5/1, Note on the Queen's remarks to Salisbury.
180. SRO, Cranbrook Mss, HA43/5/1, Note by Hardy on Cabinet decision, 7 Aug. 1875.
181. RA VIC/MAIN/O/18/90, Ponsonby to Queen, 27 Nov. 1882; VIC/ADDE/1/10247 and 10250, Cambridge to Alison, 17 and 24 Nov. 1882.
182. McCourt, *Remember Butler*, 187–99; Ryan, *William Francis Butler*, 133–49.
183. RA VIC/ADDE/1/8408 and 8448, Hardinge to Cambridge, 11 Oct. 1878; Baker to Cambridge, 13 Nov. 1878; APAC, Burne Mss, Eur Mss D951/8, Lytton to Burne, 24 Dec. 1878; NLS, Minto Mss, MS 12538, Melgund to mother, 30 Apr.–2 May 1879.
184. Jeffery, *Wilson*, 48–53.
185. Ibid., 24–25.
186. Beckett, "Daring a Wrong Like This," 3–9.
187. Beckett, "Women and Patronage," 463–80.
188. Trustram, *Women of the Regiment*, 32, 34.
189. May, *Changes and Chances*, 141.
190. Butler, *Autobiography*, 205.
191. MacMunn, *Behind the Scenes*, 7–8.
192. Wright, *Burnaby*, appendix, iv.
193. Callwell, *Stray Recollections*, 1:218.
194. Greaves, *Memoirs*, 168–69.
195. Petersen, *Medical Profession*, 107.
196. NAM, Roberts Mss, 7101-23-100-3, Roberts to Cambridge, 15 Nov. 1890.
197. NAM, Roberts Mss, 7101-23-100-3, Roberts to Newmarch, 9 Nov. 1892.
198. HHM, Salisbury Mss, A/112/19, Cromer to Barrington, 3 Mar. 1899.

199. BL, Lansdowne MSS, L(5)17, Cambridge to Lansdowne, 27 July 1895.
200. Stephenson, *At Home and on the Battlefield*, 307.
201. Churchill, *Churchill*, 908.
202. HPL, Wolseley Mss, LW/P 5/4a, Lady Wolseley to Wolseley, 21 July 1879.
203. Brice, *Thinking Man's Soldier*, 68–74.
204. CCRO, Pole-Carew Mss, CP/59, Pole-Carew to mother, 28–29 Oct. 1899.
205. MacGregor, *Life and Opinions*, 1:320.
206. Leask, *Sir William Robertson*, 45–46.
207. Stockings, *Britannia's Shield*, 64–65.
208. NAM, Broadwood Mss, 7508-34-4, Broadwood's contract with EA, 2 Oct. 1894; SAD, Wingate Mss, 262/1/167, Rundle memorandum, 14 Dec. 1896; 233/3/6, Maxwell to Wingate, 9 July 1892.
209. Hunter, *Kitchener's Sword-arm*, 38–39, 41–42, 90, 202, 234.
210. RA VIC/MAIN/O/31/20, Note by Queen, 3 Nov. 1898.
211. Beckett, *Memoirs of Edmonds*, 187.
212. Birdwood's preface to Arthur, *Not Worth Reading*, ix; Birdwood, *Khaki and Gown*, 118.
213. SAD, Wingate Mss, 233/5/17, Wingate to wife, 16 May 1898.
214. SAD, Wingate Mss, 269/7/25, Cromer to Wingate, 18 July 1899; 269/3/45, Gleichen to Wingate, 17 Mar. 1899; 269/6/21, Bigge to Wingate, 21 June 1899; 269/6/26, Benson to Wingate, 28 June 1899.
215. HPL, Wolseley Autograph Collection, Lansdowne to Wolseley, 4 Sept. 1884.
216. BL, Campbell-Bannerman Mss, Add Mss 41209, Cambridge to Campbell-Bannerman, 8 Nov. 1892; Add Mss 41212, Buller to Campbell-Bannerman, 7 and 8 Nov. 1892.
217. MEC, Grenfell Mss, GB165-0319/30, Diary, 4 June 1897.
218. *HCCP* 1902 [C. 982], App. XV, 85.
219. NLW, Hills-Johnes Mss, L10703. Adams to Hills-Johnes, 14 May 1889.
220. RA VIC/ADDE/1/7656, Lady Cunynghame to Cambridge, 14 July 1875; VIC/ADDE/1/7691 and 7697, Carnarvon to Cambridge, 18 and 25 Aug. 1875.
221. RA VIC/ADDE/1/8160, Hardy to Cambridge, 28 Oct. 1877; VIC/ADDE/1/8234, Cambridge to Carnarvon, 30 Jan. 1878.
222. BL, Carnarvon Mss, Add Mss 60800, Cunynghame to Carnarvon, 28 Nov. 1877.
223. KCL, Wood Mss, KCM 89/9/27/17, Lady Chelmsford to Wood, 3 June 1879.
224. HHM, Salisbury Mss, A/53/68, Baring to Salisbury, 8 Dec. 1888.
225. HPL, Wolseley Mss, W/P 13/20, Wolseley to wife, 20 Sept. 1884; W/P 16/64, Wolseley to wife, 6 June 1887.
226. Daly, *Empire on the Nile*, 41.
227. WCRO, Dormer Mss, CR895/92, Dormer to wife, 28 Oct. 1878.
228. WCRO, Dormer Mss, CR895/93, Dormer to wife, 1 July 1883.
229. WCRO, Dormer Mss, CR895/93, Dormer to wife, 23 June and 28 Oct. 1884.
230. Churchill, *My Early Life*, 150–52, 156–57, 165–66.
231. SAD, Wingate Mss, 263/1/261, Townshend to Wingate, 13 Dec. 1896; Sherson, *Townshend*, 123–24.
232. NLS, Haig Mss, Acc. 3155/6g, Wood to Haig, 26 July 1898.
233. Stephen Manning, "Evelyn Wood," in Corvi and Beckett, *Victoria's Generals*, 28–50, at 30.

234. HPL, Wolseley Mss, LW/P 8/14/1, Lady Wolseley to Wolseley, 19 Oct. 1882.
235. HPL, Wolseley Mss, W/P, 13/22, Wolseley to wife, 1 Oct. 1884.
236. KCL, Wood Mss, KCM 89/9/24/7, Colley to Wood, Jan. 1876.
237. RA VIC/MAIN/O/16/24, Lady Wood to Queen, 14 Sept. 1882.
238. Arthur, *Letters of Lord and Lady Wolseley*, 152.
239. KCL, Wood Mss, KCM 89/9/24/13, Buller to Wood, 7 Apr. 1876.
240. TNA, Buller Mss, WO 132/2, Wolseley to Buller, 31 Jan. 1885.
241. HPL, Wolseley Mss, W/P 9/33, Wolseley to wife, 4 Oct. 1880.
242. HPL, Wolseley Mss, W/P 16/85, Wolseley to wife, 11 Oct. 1887; W/P 18/8, Wolseley to wife, n.d. [July] 1889.
243. RA VIC/MAIN/W/10/82, Cambridge to Ponsonby, 19 Nov. 1888.
244. RA VIC/ADDA34/40, Bigge to Ponsonby, 27 Nov. 1888.
245. James, *Master*, xxvi–xxxii.
246. BL, APAC, Northbrook Mss, C/144/20, Wolseley to Northbrook, 1 Mar. 1872.
247. HPL, Wolseley Mss, LW/P 4/4, Lady Wolseley to Wolseley, 16 Aug. 1878 and attached note by Frances Wolseley; LW/P 11/32/1, Lady Wolseley to Wolseley, 25 June 1885; RA VIC/ADDA20/1164, Lady Wolseley to Miss Cope, n.d., 1917.
248. HPL, Wolseley Mss, LW/P 10/18, Lady Wolseley to Wolseley, 16 Sept. 1884, and attached note by Frances Wolseley.
249. HPL, Wolseley Mss, LW/P 4/4, Lady Wolseley to Wolseley, 16 Aug. 1878; 6/3, Lady Wolseley to Wolseley, 12 Feb. 1880; W/P 8/4, Wolseley to wife, 4 June 1879.
250. HPL, Wolseley Mss, LW/P 5/10, Lady Wolseley to Wolseley, 22 Oct. 1879; W/P 8/24, 29, 34, and 36, Wolseley to wife, 11 Sept. , 13–17 Oct., 16 Nov., and 30 Nov–1 Dec. 1879.
251. HPL, Wolseley Mss, LW/P 6/1–3, Lady Wolseley to Wolseley, 29 Jan., 5 Feb., and 12 Feb. 1880.
252. HPL, Wolseley Mss, LW/P 8/11, 12, Lady Wolseley to Wolseley, 29 Sept. and 6 Oct. 1882; 8/13/3, Lady Wolseley to Childers, 9 Oct. 1882.
253. HPL, Wolseley Autograph Collection, Queen to Lady Wolseley, 5 Mar., 25 Mar., and 15 May 1885; LW/P 11/15/1, 3, Lady Wolseley to Queen, 3 and 4 Mar. 1885; 11/15/2, Horatia Stopford to Lady Wolseley, 3 Mar. 1885; 11/15/6, Queen to Lady Wolseley, 5 Mar. 1885; 11/16/1, 19/1, Lady Wolseley to Wolseley, 4 and 26–27 Mar. 1885.
254. BL, Campbell-Bannerman Mss, Add Mss 41233, Campbell-Bannerman to Lady Wolseley, 10 and 15 Nov. 1893; Lady Wolseley to Campbell-Bannerman, 14 Nov. 1893.
255. RA VIC/MAIN/W/73/158, Lady Wolseley to Bigge, 18 July 1897.
256. RA VIC/MAIN/W/15/124, Lady Wolseley to Bigge, 22 Dec. 1899.
257. HPL, Wolseley Mss, LW/P 11/7, Lady Wolseley to Wolseley, 11 Feb. 1885; 25/73, Lady Wolseley to Wolseley, 20 Dec. 1899.
258. RA VIC/MAIN/W/13/26, Ponsonby to Bigge, 16 May 1896.
259. NAM, Roberts Mss, 7101–23–52, Nicholson to Roberts, 2 Mar. 1897.
260. APAC, Burne Mss, Eur Mss D951/8, Lytton to Burne, 7 Mar. 1878.
261. Butler, *Life of Pomeroy-Colley*, 279.
262. RA VIC/MAIN/O/38/276, Wood to Queen, 27 Feb. 1881.
263. Lehmann, *First Boer War*, 88, 234.
264. Laband, *Transvaal Rebellion*, 189.
265. HPL, Wolseley Mss, W/P 20/23, 84 and 85, Wolseley to wife, 8 Feb. 1891, 28 May, and 31 May 1891; DUDR, Wolseley Mss, Wolseley to brother, 28 May 1891.

266. HPL, Wolseley Mss, W/P 24/76 and 77, Wolseley to wife, both 1 Aug. 1895.

267. HPL, Wolseley Mss, W/W.4/74, Wolseley to brother, 21 July 1897.

268. HPL, Wolseley Mss, W/W.4/140, Wolseley to brother, 1 Nov. 1900.

269. CCRO, Pole-Carew Mss, CP/9, Nora Roberts to Pole-Carew, 5 Jan. 1883.

270. HPL, Wolseley Mss, LW/P 21/47, Lady Wolseley to Wolseley, 2 July 1895; RA QM/ PRIV/CC50/193, Prince Adolphus to his parents, 12 Nov. 1888; RA QM/PRIV/ CC50/223, Adolphus to Princess Augusta, Grand Duchess of Mecklenburg-Strelitz, 14 Feb. 1890.

271. NAM, Roberts Mss, 7101-23-104, Roberts to Cowell, 9 Aug. 1893.

272. RA VIC/ADDU/32, Queen to Princess Royal, 26 Aug. 1895; BL, Lansdowne Mss, L(5)54, Salisbury to Lansdowne, 5 Aug. 1895.

273. BL, Lansdowne Mss, L(5)48, Lansdowne to Roberts, 17 Aug. 1900.

274. BL, Lansdowne Mss, L(5)44, Bigge to Lansdowne, 18 Aug. 1900.

275. CCRO, Pole-Carew Mss, CP/128, Diary of a Staff Officer, 11 Apr. 1900.

276. APAC, Luard Mss, Eur Mss C262, 7-8, Diary of Hugh Bixby Luard (written ca. 1937).

277. NWM, Egerton Mss, M1994/112/92, "Reminiscences of the 72nd Highlanders," 16 Feb. 1931, 4.

278. APAC, White Mss, Eur Mss F108/101(f), White to wife, 17 July 1888.

279. Rodney Atwood, "'So single minded a man and so noble-hearted a soldier': Field Marshal Earl Roberts of Kandahar, Waterford and Pretoria," in Beckett, *Victorians at War*, 59–74, at 67.

280. Atwood, *Roberts and Kitchener*, 295n17.

281. Hamilton, *Listening for the Drums*, 193.

282. Lee, *Soldier's Wife*, 6.

283. Pakenham, *Boer War*, 448–49.

284. NLS, Haig Mss, Acc. 3155/6c, Haig to sister, 17 Sept. 1902.

285. James, *Roberts*, xiv.

286. NLS, Minto Mss, MS 12378, Lady Roberts to Melgund, 27 Oct. 1879, 24 Mar., 19 May, and 24 Aug. 1880; 13 May 1884.

287. NLW, Hills-Johnes Mss, L12996, Nairne to Hills-Johnes, 20 Mar. 1896.

288. Prochaska, *Women and Philanthropy*, 1.

289. Arnstein, "Warrior Queen," 1–28; St. John, "Queen Victoria as a Politician," 24–31.

290. RA VIC/MAIN/W/15/92, Wolseley to Bigge, 22 July 1899.

291. BL, Lansdowne Mss, L(5)42, Bigge to Lansdowne, 26 Aug. 1895; Hardie, *Political Influence of Queen Victoria*, 178–82.

292. Vincent, *Diaries of Derby*, 177.

293. Omond, *Parliament and Army*, 103.

294. NAM, Wilkinson Mss, OTP 13/13, Nicholson to Wilkinson, 1 July 1893 and 7 June 1894.

295. Preston, *In Relief of Gordon*, 9.

296. WSA, Methuen Mss, 1742/6335, Berlin Correspondence, Wolseley to Methuen, 18 Dec. 1880.

297. BL, Lansdowne Mss, L(5)43, Lansdowne to Queen, 16 July 1898.

298. Frankland, *Witness of a Century*, 107.

299. TNA, Childers Mss, PRO 30/61/1, Childers to Ponsonby, 18 Dec. 1882.

300. RA VIC/ADDE/1/11307, Churchill to Cambridge, 26 Sept. 1885; 11312, Smith to Cambridge, 9 Oct. 1885.

301. RA VIC/MAIN/W/73/14, Salisbury to Queen, 9 Oct. 1885; VIC/MAIN/W/73/19, Salisbury to Queen, 13 Oct. 1885.
302. Frankland, *Witness of a Century*, 137–38.
303. TNA, Smith Mss, WO 110/3, Churchill to Cambridge, 26 Sept. 1886.
304. TNA, Smith Mss, WO 110/5, Roberts to Smith, 25 Oct. 1886; Cambridge to Roberts, 3 Nov. 1886; Smith to Queen, 3 Nov. 1886; Smith to Roberts, 5 Nov. 1886; NAM, Roberts Mss, 7101-23-2, Arbuthnot to Roberts, 20 Nov. 1886.
305. RA VIC/MAIN/E/31/144, Memo by Ponsonby, n.d., quoting Salisbury letter of 1 May 1890.
306. Frankland, *Witness of a Century*, 184.
307. Bond, "Retirement of the Duke," 544–53, at 548.
308. BL, Lansdowne Mss, L(5)42, Lansdowne to Bigge, 14 July 1897.
309. RA VIC/MAIN/E/33/105, Queen to Salisbury, 27 Sept. 1900.
310. RA VIC/MAIN/E/33/106, Salisbury to Queen, 28 Sept. 1900.
311. RA VIC/MAIN/E/61/27, Ponsonby to Cambridge, 20 July 1879; VIC/MAIN/R/8/82, Note by Queen, 9 Sept. 1879; VIC/ADDA12/485, Queen to Cambridge, 19 Sept. 1879.
312. HPL, Wolseley Mss, LW/P 5/13, Lady Wolseley to Wolseley, 13 Nov. 1879.
313. RA VIC/MAIN/O/40/225, Queen to Wood, 16 June 1881; VIC/MAIN/O/40/230 and 231, Wood to Queen, 17 and 18 June 1881; VIC/MAIN/O/40/242, Lady Wood to Queen, 26 June 1881; VIC/MAIN/O/38/70, Lady Wood to Lady Ely, 14 Jan. 1882.
314. Manning, *Evelyn Wood*, 162, 167; Manning, "Evelyn Wood," in Corvi and Beckett, *Victoria's Generals*, 39.
315. RA VIC/MAIN/E/61/16, Biddulph to Cambridge, 20 Feb. 1878.
316. RA VIC/ADDE/1/8536, McNeill to Cambridge, 11 Feb. 1879.
317. RA VIC/MAIN/E/62/54 and 56, Ponsonby to Cambridge, 5 and 9 Feb. 1885.
318. RA VIC/MAIN/E/62/59, Ponsonby to Cambridge, 12 Feb. 1885.
319. RA VIC/MAIN/E/62/67 and 70, Ponsonby to Cambridge, 4 and 5 Apr. 1885.
320. RA VIC/MAIN/E/62/71, McNeill to Queen, 5 Apr. 1885; VIC/MAIN/E/62/72 and 74, Ponsonby to Cambridge, 27 Apr. and 10 May 1885.
321. TNA, Smith Mss, WO 110/2, Ponsonby to Smith, 20 June 1885; Smith to Ponsonby, 30 June 1885; RA VIC/MAIN/E/62/75 and 76, Ponsonby to Cambridge, 25 and 28 June 1885.
322. NAM, Cowell Mss, 2009-02-110-385, McNeill to Cowell, 13 June 1885.
323. NAM, Cowell Mss, 2009-02-110-388, Graham to Cowell, 16 June 1885; Vetch, *Life of Graham*, 420–24.
324. RA VIC/ADDA36/24, Ponsonby to wife, 14 July 1885.
325. RA VIC/ADDE/1/7959, Hardinge to Cambridge, 17 Nov. 1876.
326. APAC, Napier of Magdala Mss, Eur Mss F114/24, Napier to Dillon, 10 Feb. 1879.
327. RA VIC/MAIN/E/61/42 and 43, Ponsonby to Cambridge, 27 Feb. and 2 Mar. 1880.
328. RA VIC/MAIN/E/62/54, Ponsonby to Cambridge, 5 Feb. 1885.
329. RA VIC/ADDE/1/9493, Hartington to Cambridge, 31 Jan. 1881.
330. RA VIC/ADDE/1/10362, Cambridge to Hardinge, 23 Mar. 1883.
331. HPL, Wolseley Mss, W/P 5/8, Wolseley to wife, 16 Apr. 1875.
332. RA VIC/ADDE/1/9887, Stewart to Cambridge, 2 Jan. 1882.
333. Arthur, *Letters of Lord and Lady Wolseley*, 90; HPL, W11/22, Wolseley to wife, 25 Sept. 1882.

334. RA VIC/MAIN/T/8/89, Wolseley to Prince of Wales, 24 Sept. 1882.

335. M. J. Williams, "The Egyptian Campaign of 1882," in Bond, *Victorian Military Campaigns*, 241–78, at 255.

336. NAM, MS Letter Book, 1998-06-195, Clarke to Whitmore, 11 Oct. 1881; Whitmore to Clarke, 21 and 24 Oct. 1881.

337. RA VIC/ADDA5/27, Cambridge to Prince of Wales, 22 Nov. 1881.

338. Callwell, *McCalmont*, 230.

339. HPL, Wolseley Mss, W/P 14/8, Wolseley to wife, 11–15 Mar. 1885.

340. TNA, Smith Mss, WO 110/1, Ponsonby to Smith, 10 and 16 Oct. 1885; Wolseley to Smith, 13 Oct. 1885; Smith to Ponsonby, 4 and 18 Oct. 1885; RA VIC/MAIN/E/62/81, Ponsonby to Cambridge, 10 Oct. 1885.

341. HPL, Wolseley Autograph Collection, Princess Christian to Wolseley, 6 Jan., 12 Jan., and 28 July 1898; Prince Christian to Wolseley, 24 Aug. 1899.

342. HPL, Wolseley Autograph Collection, Prince Henry to Wolseley, 17 Nov. 1895.

343. RA VIC/MAIN/E/22/14, Biddulph to Queen, 27 Jan. 1876.

344. HPL, Wolseley Mss, W/P 13/20, Wolseley to wife, 20 Sept. 1884.

345. HPL, Wolseley Mss, LW/P 10/30, Lady Wolseley to Wolseley, 25 Dec. 1884; RA VIC/MAIN/E/62/43–45, Ponsonby to Cambridge, 17, 19, and 21 Dec. 1884.

346. HPL, Wolseley Autograph Collection, Wolseley to Fleetwood Wilson, 30 Aug. 1890.

347. BL, Lansdowne Mss, L(5)42, Bigge to Lansdowne, 10 and 17 June 1897; Lansdowne to Bigge, 16 June 1897.

Chapter 5: High Command

1. The best overview of administrative structures is to be found in Michael Roper, *The Records of the War Office and Related Departments, 1660–1964*, 95–105, 125–26, 139–41, 151–52.

2. RAM, Brackenbury Mss, MD1085/1, Brackenbury to Campbell-Bannerman, 25 Oct. 1892.

3. NAM, Wilkinson Mss, OTP 13/13, Nicholson to Wilkinson, 23 Dec. 1894.

4. Verner, *Military Life of Cambridge*, 2:119.

5. TNA, WO 163/4, minute, 30 July 1889.

6. NAM, Roberts Mss, 7101-23-12-95, Brownlow to Roberts, 13 Dec. 1890.

7. BL, Cross Mss, Add Mss 51264, Salisbury to Cross, 17 Mar. 1891; D. R. Gillard, "Salisbury and the Indian Defence Problem, 1885–1902," in Bourne and Watt, *Studies in International History*, 236–48.

8. Mahajan, "Defence of India," 168–93; Gooch, *Plans of War*, 198–232; Wilson, "Anglo-Japanese Alliance," 314–56.

9. Johnson, *Spying for Empire*, 199.

10. Robson, *Roberts in India*, 134–36; Robson, "Eden Commission," 4–13.

11. SRO, Cranbrook Mss, HA43/T/501/31, Lytton to Cranbrook, 16 Aug. 1879.

12. Robson, *Roberts in India*, 385–87.

13. Heathcote, *Military in British India*, 154–56.

14. BL, Wolseley Letter-Book, Add Mss 41324, Wolseley to Salisbury, 16–18 Feb. 1879.

15. RA VIC/ADDE/1/8388, Haines to Cambridge, 18 Aug. 1878.

16. RA VIC/ADDE/1/8630, Cambridge to Chelmsford, 17 Apr. 1879.

17. APAC, Lytton Mss, Eur Mss E218/18, Lytton to Salisbury, 30 July 1876.

18. APAC, Lytton Mss, Eur Mss E218/18, Lytton to Salisbury, 28 Sept. 1876.
19. APAC, Lytton Mss, Eur Mss E218/21, Lytton to Cranbrook, 7 Feb. 1879.
20. RA VIC/ADDE/1/8645, Johnson to Cambridge, 1 May 1879; VIC/ADDE/1/8848, Johnson to Cambridge, 11 Aug. 1879.
21. HPL, Wolseley Mss, W/P 8/24, Wolseley to wife, 11 Sept. 1879; W/P 9/1, Wolseley to wife, 2 Jan. 1880.
22. RA VIC/MAIN/E/25/31, Stanley to Wolseley, 19 Feb. 1880.
23. RA VIC/MAIN/E/25/36, Cambridge to Ponsonby, 21 Feb. 1880.
24. HPL, Wolseley Mss, W/P 8/16, Wolseley to wife, 31 July 1879.
25. HPL, Wolseley Mss, SSL.8, Pt. I, cxci; M2/41/8/6, Letter to Wolseley from Allahabad, 30 Dec. 1880.
26. CUL, Cambridge Mss, Add 8782/I/26, Hartington to Cambridge, 22 Dec. 1880.
27. RA VIC/ADDE/1/8702, Cambridge to Johnson, 6 June 1879.
28. RA VIC/ADDE/1/8848, Johnson to Cambridge, 11 Aug. 1879.
29. RA VIC/ADDE/1/9273, Hartington to Cambridge, 1 Aug. 1880; VIC/ADDE/1/9347, Ripon to Cambridge, 5 Oct. 1880; VIC/ADDE/1/9381, Hartington to Cambridge, 31 Oct. 1880.
30. RA VIC/ADDE/1/9404, Cambridge to Ripon, 19 Nov. 1880.
31. NAM, Haines Mss, 8108-9-41-11, Lumsden to Haines, 4 May 1880.
32. RA VIC/MAIN/N/39/24, Hartington to Queen, 6 Feb. 1881.
33. NLS, Minto Mss, Ms 12380, Pretyman to Melgund, 18 Jan. 1892.
34. NLS, Minto Mss, MS 12506, Diary, 15 Apr. 1881.
35. NAM, Roberts Mss, 7101-23-38, MacGregor to Roberts, 25 May and 10 Sept. 1893.
36. NAM, Roberts Mss, 7101-23-38, MacGregor to Roberts, 25 May 1883.
37. NLS, Minto Mss, Ms 12380, Pretyman to Melgund, 29 Jan. 1882; APAC, Lyall Mss, F132/44, Roberts to Lyall, 6 July 1885; Robson, *Roberts in India*, 283–86.
38. NAM, Roberts Mss, 7101-23-57, Pretyman to Roberts, 25 July 1885.
39. NAM, Roberts Mss, 7101-23-12, Brownlow to Roberts, 9 July 1885.
40. Robson, *Roberts in India*, 325.
41. LHCMA, Hamilton Mss, 1/3/3, Roberts to Stewart, 26 July 1885.
42. Atwood, *Life of Roberts*, 132–33.
43. RA VIC/MAIN/E/30/179, Salisbury to Ponsonby, 25 July 1885.
44. Johnson, "Russians at the Gates," 719.
45. NAM, Roberts Mss, 7101-23-103, Roberts to Brownlow, 10 Feb. 1884 and 12 June 1885.
46. RA VIC/ADDE/1/11347, Hardinge to Cambridge, 30 Nov. 1885.
47. NAM, Roberts Mss, 5504-64-48, Cambridge to Roberts, 13 Oct. 1885.
48. NAM, Roberts Mss, 7101-23-100-3, Roberts to Dilke, 1 Aug. 1892.
49. Robson, *Roberts in India*, 394–96, 398.
50. RA VIC/MAIN/E/65/24, Ponsonby to Queen, 6 May 1890.
51. NAM, Roberts Mss, 7101-23-100-6, Roberts to Chapman, 1 Feb. 1889.
52. RA VIC/MAIN/W/12/52, Wolseley to Ponsonby, 30 Apr. 1890.
53. KHLC, Stanhope Mss, 0292/2, Wolseley to Stanhope, 29 Apr. 1890; RA VIC/MAIN/W/12/53, Wolseley to Ponsonby, 5 May 1890.
54. NAM, Wolseley-Steele Correspondence, 8701-113, Wolseley to Steele, 3 June 1885.
55. KHLC, Stanhope Mss, 0292/2, Wolseley to Stanhope, 12 May 1890; Stanhope to Salisbury, 13 May 1890.

56. HHM, Salisbury Mss, E/Stanhope/166, Stanhope to Salisbury, 1 May 1890.

57. NAM, Roberts Mss, 7101-23-14, Chesney to Roberts, 15 June 1890.

58. NAM, Roberts Mss, Pole-Carew to Roberts, 5 Sept. 1890.

59. Robson, *Roberts in India*, 400–403.

60. NAM, Roberts Mss, 7101-23-82, Stanhope to Roberts, 26 May 1890.

61. NLS, Minto Mss, MS 12380, Pretyman to Melgund, 7–8 Mar. 1891; APAC, Lyall Mss, F132/44, Roberts to Lyall, 28 July 1890.

62. CCRO, Pole-Carew Mss, CP/9, Roberts to Pole-Carew, 30 Sept. 1890.

63. CCRO, Pole-Carew Mss, CP/58, Roberts to Pole-Carew, 7 Sept. 1891.

64. NAM, Roberts Mss, 7101-23-100-3, Roberts to Bradford, 5 and 10 June 1890.

65. NAM, Roberts Mss, 7101-23-100-3, Roberts to Stanhope, 21 June 1890.

66. CCRO, Pole-Carew Mss, CP/58, Roberts to Pole-Carew, 7 July 1890.

67. Roberts, *Forty-one Years in India*, 535–36.

68. RA VIC/MAIN/W/73/105, Connaught to Ponsonby, 18 July 1892.

69. CCRO, Pole-Carew Mss, CP/9, Nicholson to Pole-Carew, 18 Aug. 1890.

70. Greaves, *Memoirs*, 214.

71. APAC, White Mss, Eur Mss F108/98B/105, Write to brother, 6 Dec. 1891.

72. Durand, *Life of White*, 1:393.

73. Greaves, *Memoirs*, 215, 228–31.

74. CCRO, Pole-Carew Mss, PC/9, Roberts to Pole-Carew, 20 Aug. 1890; NAM, Roberts Mss, 7101-23-99, Roberts to Lansdowne, 13 Aug. 1890.

75. KCL, Wood Mss, KCM 89/9/48/20, Stanhope to Wood, 26 Oct. 1891.

76. NLS, Minto Mss, MS 12380, Pretyman to Melgund, 18 Jan. 1892.

77. APAC, Brackenbury Mss, Eur Mss D735, Note by Brackenbury, 19 July 1892.

78. TNA, Ardagh Mss, PRO 30/40/2, Wood to Ardagh, 1 Aug. 1891.

79. RA VIC/MAIN/E/64/24, Ponsonby to Stanhope, 16 Nov. 1892.

80. NAM, Roberts Mss, 7101-23-78, Stewart to Roberts, 4 and 10 Nov. 1892.

81. DUDR, Wood Mss, Ponsonby to Wood, 21 Nov. 1892.

82. APAC, Brackenbury Mss, Eur Mss D735, Note by Brackenbury, 19 July 1892; DCRO, Buller Mss, 2065M/SS4/27, Brackenbury to Lansdowne, 19 July 1892; CCRO, Pole-Carew Mss, CP/58, Roberts to Pole-Carew, 31 July 1892.

83. NAM, Roberts Mss, 7101-23-78, Stewart to Roberts, 11 Dec. 1891.

84. WCRO, Dormer Mss, CR895/94, Lord Abingdon to Fergusson, 3 May 1893; Countess of Abingdon to Mary Dormer, 9 May 1893.

85. APAC, Brackenbury Mss, Eur Mss D735, Note by Brackenbury, 19 July 1892.

86. RAM, Brackenbury Mss, MD1085/1, Brackenbury to Chapman, 22 Oct. 1892; MD1085/2, Brackenbury to Newmarch, 28 Jan. 1893; NAM, Roberts Mss, 7101-23-11, Brackenbury to Roberts, 18 July 1892; DCRO, Buller Mss, 2065M/SS4/27, Brackenbury to Lansdowne, 19 July 1892; Brackenbury to Buller, 17 Sept. 1892.

87. Spender, *Life of Campbell-Bannerman*, 1:130.

88. RA VIC/ADDE/1/12868 and 12869, Campbell-Bannerman to Cambridge, 5 and 7 Nov. 1892.

89. RA VIC/MAIN/W/34/40, Ponsonby to Queen, 23 Nov. 1892; BL, Campbell-Bannerman Mss, Add Mss 41212, Buller to Campbell-Bannerman, 7, 8, and 15 Nov. 1892; Malmesbury, *Life of Ardagh*, 252.

90. NAM, Roberts Mss, 7101-23-11, Buller to Roberts, 29 Sept. and 7 Dec. 1892, and 20 Jan. 1893.

91. BL, Campbell-Bannerman Mss, Add Mss 41212, Buller to Campbell-Bannerman, 9 Nov. 1892.

92. NAM, 7101–23–12, Brownlow to Roberts, 15 Mar. 1890.

93. RA VIC/ADDE/1/12873 and 12874, Campbell-Bannerman to Cambridge, 10 and 11 Nov. 1892; BL, Campbell-Bannerman Mss, Add Mss 41209, Cambridge to Campbell-Bannerman, 6, 8, 11, and 12 Nov. 1892.

94. NAM, Roberts Mss, 7101–23–11, Brackenbury to Roberts, 6 Dec. 1892.

95. CCRO, Pole-Carew Mss, CP/58, Roberts to Pole-Carew, 31 July 1892 and 24 Jan. 1893.

96. NAM, Roberts Mss, 71010–23–90, White to Roberts, 2 Sept. and 1 Nov. 1892.

97. Durand, *Life of White*, 1:408; NAM, Roberts Mss, 7101–23–90, White to Roberts, 28 Nov. 1892.

98. DUDR, Wood Mss, Ponsonby to Wood, 21 Nov. 1892.

99. BL, Campbell-Bannerman Mss, Add Mss 41221, Kimberley to Campbell-Bannerman, 7 and 14 Oct. 1892.

100. Durand, *Life of White*, 1:176–77, 218.

101. RA VIC/ADDE/1/12867, Cambridge to Roberts, 4 Nov. 1892; Robson, *Roberts in India*, 417–20.

102. BL, Campbell-Bannerman Mss, Add Mss 41233, Roberts to Campbell-Bannerman, 9 June 1893; LHCMA, Hamilton Mss, 1/2/9, Roberts to Hamilton, 4 July 1893.

103. NAM, MS Letter Book, 1998–06–195, Gipps to Roberts, 27 July 1892.

104. LHCMA, Hamilton Mss, 1/2/9, Roberts to Hamilton, 28 Apr. 1893.

105. BL, Lansdowne Mss, L(5)47, Roberts to Lansdowne, 12 July 1895; Lansdowne to Roberts, 18 July 1895.

106. BL, Lansdowne Mss, L(5)54(3), Roberts to Lansdowne, 10 July 1897; Lansdowne to Roberts, 12 July 1897.

107. APAC, White Mss, Eur Mss F108/98(b), White to brother, 25 Apr. 1893.

108. Surridge, "Ambiguous Amir," 417–34.

109. NAM, Roberts Mss, 7101–23–90, White to Roberts, 24 Nov. 1896.

110. Durand, *Life of White*, 1:444.

111. NAM, Roberts Mss, 7101–23–90, White to Roberts, 24 Nov. 1896; 7101–23–52, Nicholson to Roberts, 5 Jan. and 16 Mar. 1897.

112. BL, Lansdowne Mss, L(5)54(3), Hamilton to Lansdowne, 4 Aug. 1897.

113. BL, Lansdowne Mss, L(5)42, Lansdowne to Queen, 5 Aug. 1897; Bigge to Lansdowne, 8 Aug. 1897; Lansdowne to Bigge, 14 Aug. 1897.

114. NAM, Roberts Mss, 7101–23–52, Nicholson to Roberts, 14 Mar. 1898; DUDR, Pole-Carew Mss, Lockhart to Pole-Carew, 11 and 30 Mar. 1898.

115. NAM, Roberts Mss, 7101–23–78, Stewart to Roberts, 18 Feb. 1898.

116. APAC, Elgin Mss, Eur Mss F84/71, Lockhart to IO, 8 Aug. 1898.

117. BL, APAC, Sam Browne Mss, Eur Mss F486/13, Nairne to Browne, 12 May 1898.

118. Durand, *Life of White*, 1:440; CCRO, Pole-Carew Mss, CP/F9/4, Lockhart to Pole-Carew, 1 Mar. 1899.

119. NAM, Roberts Mss, 7101–23–100–1, Roberts to Churchill, 12 Jan. 1886; Roberts to Cambridge, 8 July 1886.

120. Robson, *Roberts in India*, 341–44.

121. Greaves, *Memoirs*, 201.

122. Atwood, *Roberts and Kitchener*, 195.

123. Smith-Dorrien, *Memories*, 310–14.

124. Strachan, *Politics of the British Army*, 104–8.

125. Smith-Dorrien, *Memories*, 297.

126. BL, Lansdowne Mss, L(5)48, Lansdowne to Roberts, 9 Feb. 1900.

127. APAC, Curzon Mss, Eur Mss F111/405, Kitchener to Curzon, Dec. 1898.

128. BL, Lansdowne Mss, L(5)48, Roberts to Lansdowne,5–8 Feb., 20 Mar., and 21 Aug. 1900.

129. NAM, Roberts Mss, 7101–23–117–1, Roberts to Lansdowne, 25 Mar. and 15 Apr. 1900.

130. Pakenham, *Boer War*, 492; Arthur, *Life of Kitchener*, 2:118–21.

131. RA VIC/MAIN/W/16/72, Bigge to Lansdowne, 27 Sept. 1900.

132. BL, Lansdowne Mss, L(5)48, Lansdowne to Roberts, 23 Mar. 1900.

133. BL, Lansdowne Mss, L(5)48, Roberts to Lansdowne, 15 Apr. 1900.

134. BL, Lansdowne Mss, L(5)49, Salisbury to Lansdowne, 12 Apr. 1900.

135. BL, Lansdowne Mss, L(5)48, Roberts to Lansdowne, 20, 25, and 26 Mar. and 18 July 1900.

136. Wessels, *Kitchener and South Africa*, 54–56, 74–75.

137. LHCMA, Maurice Mss, 2/2/20, Wolseley to Maurice, 11 June 1894.

138. St. Aubyn, *Royal George*, 284–87; Bond, "Retirement of Cambridge," 549.

139. RA VIC/MAIN/E/41/20, Knollys to Bigge, 9 May 1895; VIC/MAIN/E/41/28 and 47, Memos by Bigge, 12 and 15 May 1895.

140. Bond, "Retirement of Cambridge," 551.

141. RA VIC/MAIN/E/41/56, Campbell-Bannerman to Bigge, 19 May 1895; VIC/MAIN/E/41/68, Buller to Bigge, 26 May 1895.

142. RA VIC/MAIN/E/41/73, Davidson to Buller, 1 June 1895.

143. RA VIC/MAIN/E/41/68, Buller to Bigge, 26 May 1895.

144. Atwood, *Roberts and Kitchener*, 13.

145. LHCMA, Hamilton Mss, 1/2/9, Roberts to Hamilton, 12 and 18 May 1893.

146. NAM, Wilkinson Mss, OTP 13/14, Roberts to Wilkinson, 4 Jan. and 16 July 1895.

147. NAM, Wilkinson Mss, OTP 13/13, Nicholson to Wilkinson, 23 Dec. 1894; Roberts Mss, 7101–23–52, Nicholson to Roberts, 6 June 1894.

148. NAM, Roberts Mss, 7101–23–52, Nicholson to Roberts, 18 June 1894.

149. TNA, Buller Mss, WO 132/5, Campbell-Bannerman to Buller, 19 June 1895.

150. RA VIC/MAIN/E/41/109, Bigge to Queen, 20 June 1895.

151. Midleton, *Records and Reactions*, 89–91.

152. RA VIC/MAIN/E/40/16, Salisbury to Queen, 11 Aug. 1895.

153. RA VIC/MAIN/E/40/17, Bigge to Queen, 11 Aug. 1895.

154. RA VIC/MAIN/E/40/15 and 20, Queen to Salisbury, 11 and 12 Aug. 1895.

155. BL, Lansdowne Mss, L(54)(2), Lansdowne to Queen, 14 Aug. 1895.

156. BL, Campbell-Bannerman Mss, Add Mss 41212, Buller to Campbell-Bannerman, 18 June 1895.

157. Melville, *Life of Buller*, 1:274–75.

158. RA VIC/MAIN/W/13/164, Buller to Bigge, 12 Dec. 1897.

159. BL, Campbell-Bannerman Mss, Add Mss 41212, Buller to Campbell-Bannerman, 5 Jan. 1899.

160. DUDR, Wood Mss, Wolseley to Wood, 7 and 11 July 1895.

161. HPL, Wolseley Mss, LW/P 21/46, 53, and 56, Lady Wolseley to Wolseley, 2, 15, and 17 July 1895; W/P 24/81, Turner to Wolseley, 3 Aug. 1895.

162. HPL, Wolseley Mss, W/P 24/63, Wolseley to wife, 6 July 1895; 24/86/4, Mount Stephen to Wolseley, 19 July 1895; 24/73/3 and 24/75/3, Swaine to Wolseley, 26 and 29 July 1895.

163. RA VIC/MAIN/E/33/110, Wolseley to Bigge, 26 Oct. 1900.

164. TNA, Ardagh Mss, PRO 30/40/2, Wolseley to Ardagh, 5, 12, and 16 July 1895.

165. HPL, Wolseley Mss, W/P 24/73/2, Wood to Wolseley, 26 July 1895; 24/80/2, Grove to Wolseley, 2 Aug. 1895; 24/83, Wolseley to wife, 6 Aug. 1895; W/W.4/61, Wolseley to brother, 7 Aug. 1895.

166. RA VIC/MAIN/E/40/16, Salisbury to Queen, 11 Aug. 1895.

167. HPL, Wolseley Mss, LW/P 21/48, 55, and 57, Lady Wolseley to Wolseley, 4, 15, and 19 July 1895; W/P 24/61 and 62, Wolseley to Lady Wolseley, 3 and 5 July 1895.

168. APAC, White Mss, F108/36, Roberts to White, 5 July 1895.

169. HPL, Wolseley Mss, LW/P 21/58, 73/1, and 82, Lady Wolseley to Wolseley, 20 July, 4 Aug., and 17 Aug. 1895; 21/65/2, Jessop to Lady Wolseley, 23 July 1895; 21/73/2, Grove to Lady Wolseley, 2 Aug. 1895.

170. Beaver, *Under Every Leaf*, 270–71.

171. TNA, Ardagh Mss, PRO 30/40/2, Wolseley to Ardagh, 14 Sept. 1895.

172. BL, Lansdowne Mss, L(5)54(2), Wolseley to Ardagh, 28 July 1895; Salisbury to Lansdowne, 2 Aug. 1895; Ardagh to Lansdowne, 2 Aug. 1895; HHM, Lansdowne to Salisbury, 4 Aug. 1895; TNA, Ardagh Mss, PRO 30/40/2, Wolseley to Ardagh, 10 Aug. 1895.

173. BL, Lansdowne Mss, L(5)54(2), Salisbury to Lansdowne, 5 Aug. 1895.

174. BL, Lansdowne Mss, L(5)54(2), Lansdowne to Queen, 7 Aug. 1895.

175. BL, Lansdowne Mss, L(5)54(2), Bigge to Lansdowne, 8 and 10 Aug. 1895; Wolseley to Lansdowne, 8 and 9 Aug. 1895.

176. HHM, Salisbury Mss, Lansdowne to Bigge, 10 Aug. 1895; Lansdowne to Wolseley, 10 Aug. 1895; Lansdowne to Salisbury, 11 Aug. 1895.

177. BL, Lansdowne Mss, L(5)42, Lansdowne to Bigge, 16 Aug. 1895.

178. BL, Lansdowne Mss, L(5)54(2), Bigge to Lansdowne, 11 Aug. 1895.

179. BL, Lansdowne Mss, L(5)42, Queen to Lansdowne, 22 Aug. 1895.

180. BL, Lansdowne Mss, L(5)54(3), Notes by Lansdowne, Oct. 1897; memo by Wolseley, n.d.; memo by Lansdowne, n.d.

181. BL, Lansdowne Mss, L(5)48, Lansdowne to Roberts, 28 Sept. 1900.

182. BL, Lansdowne Mss, L(5)48, Roberts to Lansdowne, 11 Oct. 1900.

183. Wilson, *Letters to Somebody*, 121.

Chapter 6: The Second Afghan War, 1878–1881

1. Beckett, "Soldiers, the Frontier," 280–92, at 281.

2. Beckett, "Indian Expeditionary Force," 6–11.

3. Robson, *Road to Kabul*, 38.

4. Thornton, *For the File on Empire*, 171–218; Ewans, *Securing the Indian Frontier*, 53–69.

5. Mahajan, *British Foreign Policy*, 55.

6. Eldridge, *Victorian Imperialism*, 110–11.

7. Heathcote, *Balochistan*, 210–23.

8. Hamley, "Our Indian North-West Frontier," 1027–46.
9. APAC, Burne Mss, Eur Mss D951/7, Lytton to Burne, 22 Apr. 1877; Preston, "MacGregor and Defence of India," 70–72; Preston, "British Military Policy," 91–94.
10. NAM, Cooper Mss, 6112–596–14, Colley to Cooper, 24 Feb. 1879.
11. RA VIC/ADDE/1/7813, Lytton to Cambridge, 11 Feb. 1876.
12. Forrest, *Chamberlain*, 485.
13. Robson, *Roberts in India*, 10–17.
14. Roberts, *Forty-one Years in India*, 328; NAM, Roberts Mss, 7101–23–225, "Some Turning Points of My Career."
15. Hanna, *Second Afghan War*, 1:279.
16. Atwood, *March to Kandahar*, 52; Roberts, *Forty-one Years in India*, 336–37.
17. RA VIC/MAIN/N/35/67, Lytton to IO, 19 Oct. 1878; NAM, Haines Mss, 8108–9-15, Lytton to Haines, 4 Nov. 1878.
18. RA VIC/ADDE/1/8397, Haines to Cambridge, 26 Sept. 1878; VIC/ADDE/1/8433, Lytton to Cambridge, 7 Nov. 1878; APAC, Lytton Mss, Eur Mss E218/20, Lytton to Haines, 27 Oct. 1878; Lyall Mss, Eur Mss F132/21, Lytton to Cranbrook, 3 Aug. 1878.
19. APAC, Burne Mss, Eur Mss D951/11, Colley to Burne, 3 Nov. 1878.
20. Rait, *Life of Haines*, 244.
21. NAM, Haines Mss, 8108–9-12, Haines to Lytton, 3 Oct. 1878.
22. Beckett, "Cavagnari's Coup de Main," 24–28.
23. RA VIC/ADDE/1/8433, Lytton to Cambridge, 7 Nov. 1878.
24. APAC, Burne Mss, Eur Mss D951/8, Lytton to Burne, 10 Dec. 1878.
25. APAC, Burne Mss, D951/11, Colley to Burne, 3 Nov. 1878.
26. RA VIC/ADDE/1/8863, Haines to Cambridge, 25 Aug. 1879; APAC, Sam Browne Mss, Eur Mss F486/10, Lumsden to Browne, 14 Aug. 1879.
27. NAM, Charles Gough Mss, 8304–32–80, Gough to wife, 7 Dec. 1878.
28. Atwood, *March to Kandahar*, 78.
29. NAM, Haines Mss, 8108–9-12, Lumsden to Haines, 15 Oct. 1878.
30. APAC, Lytton Mss, Eur Mss E218/21, Lytton to Cranbrook, 21 Feb. and 7 Sept. 1879.
31. NAM, Baker Mss, 7804–25, Cambridge to Baker, 30 Jan. 1879.
32. APAC, Minto Mss, Eur Mss D1227/1, Melgund to mother, 22 Jan. 1879.
33. RA VIC/ADDA36/17, Ponsonby to wife, 31 Oct. 1878; APAC, Burne Mss, Eur Mss D951/11, Colley to Burne, 22 Dec. 1878.
34. APAC, Lytton Mss, Eur Mss E218/21, Lytton to Cranbrook, 21 Feb. 1879.
35. RA VIC/ADDE/1/8421, Haines to Cambridge, 24 Oct. 1878.
36. RA VIC/ADDE/1/8453, Hardinge to Cambridge, 17 Nov. 1878; VIC/MAIN/N/35/83, Hardinge to Queen, Nov. 1878; APAC, BL, APAC, Burne Mss, Eur Mss D951/11, Colley to Burne, 3 Nov. 1878.
37. NLS, Minto Mss, MS 12380, Pretyman to Melgund, 25 Oct. 1879.
38. NAM, Haines Mss, 8108–9-23, Haines to Dillon, 2 Feb. 1881.
39. NAM, Haines Mss, 8108–9-41-8 and 9, Lumsden to Haines, 9 and 28 Jan. 1880.
40. NAM, Haines Mss, 8108–9-26A, Lytton to Haines, 20 and 23 Mar. 1880; Haines to Lytton, 22 and 24 Mar. 1880; APAC, Lytton Mss, Eur Mss E218/21, Lytton to Cranbrook, 16 and 25 Mar. 1880.
41. RA VIC/ADDE/1/8421 and 8618, Haines to Cambridge, 24 Oct. 1878; Cambridge to Haines, 4 Apr. 1879.
42. RA VIC/ADDE/1/8632 and 8638, Haines to Cambridge, 17 and 23 Apr. 1879.

43. RA VIC/ADDE/1/8682, Cambridge to Haines, 23 May 1879.

44. Robson, *Roberts in India*, 177–79.

45. NLW, Hills-Johnes Mss, L14221, Hills-Johnes to Malleson, 15 Nov. 1885.

46. RA VIC/ADDE/1/9383, Haines to Cambridge, 2 Nov. 1880.

47. NAM, Haines Mss, 8108-9-19, Lytton to Haines, 18 Mar. 1879; APAC, Lytton Mss, E218/21, Lytton to Cranbrook, 21 Feb. 1879.

48. NAM, Haines Mss, 8108-9-45-25, Cambridge to Haines, 31 July 1879.

49. SLCM, Wolseley Diaries, CAM.H.22, Diary, 24 Jan. 1877.

50. APAC, Lytton Mss, Eur Mss E218/3, Cranbrook to Lytton, 18 July and 21 and 29 Sept. 1879.

51. Heathcote, *Military in British India*, 145.

52. RA VIC/ADDE/1/8750, Lytton to Cambridge, 23 June 1879; APAC, Lytton Mss, Eur Mss E218/21, Lytton to Cranbrook, 7 and 22 Sept. 1879.

53. SRO, Cranbrook Mss, HA43/H/4/14, Cambridge to Hardy, 16 Sept., 10 Oct., and 19 Dec. 1879.

54. RA VIC/ADDE/1/8882, Cranbrook to Cambridge, 11 Sept. 1879.

55. SRO, Cranbrook Mss, HA43/H/4/14, Cambridge to Hardy, 19 Dec. 1879, and 24 Jan., 3 Feb., and 4 Feb. 1880.

56. NAM, Roberts Mss, 7101-233-100-6, Roberts to Chapman, 1 Feb. 1889.

57. LHCMA, Alison Mss, Box 2, Gerard to Lady Alison, 19 Jan. 1880.

58. Appleyard, *Resumé*, 12, 77, 87–88.

59. RA VIC/ADDE/1/8501, Haines to Cambridge, 8 Jan. 1879.

60. NAM, Haines Mss, 8108-9-5, Lytton to Haines, 7 and 9 Oct. 1877.

61. RA VIC/MAIN/N/35/58, Hardinge to Queen, 4 Oct. 1878.

62. RA VIC/ADDE1/8400, Haines to Cambridge, 3 Oct. 1878.

63. RA VIC/ADDE/1/8428, Cambridge to Haines, 1 Nov. 1878.

64. RA VIC/ADDE/1/8497, Cambridge to Haines, 3 Jan. 1879.

65. RA VIC/ADDE/1/8522, Haines to Cambridge, 31 Jan. 1879; VIC/ADDE/1/8566, Cambridge to Haines, 28 Feb. 1879.

66. NAM, Haines Mss, 8108-9-45-13, Cambridge to Haines, 11 Apr. 1879.

67. Goldsbrough, "Passed Over," 151–66.

68. Maude Mss, MacGregor to Maude, 4 Nov. 1878.

69. Maude Mss, Maude to Haines, 4 Nov. 1878; Haines to Maude, 7 Nov. 1878.

70. Maude Mss, MacGregor to Maude, 5 and 8 Nov. 1878; APAC, Lytton Mss, Eur Mss E218/20, Lytton to Cranbrook, 8 Nov. 1878; Hanna, *Second Afghan War*, 1:336–37.

71. RA VIC/ADDE/1/8437, Haines to Cambridge, 7 Nov. 1878; Maude Mss, Haines to Lady Maude, 14 Nov. 1878.

72. Maude Mss, Maude's Campaign Account.

73. Goldsbrough, "Passed Over," 165.

74. APAC, Lytton Mss, Eur Mss E218/35, Lytton to Haines, 3 Nov. 1878.

75. APAC, Lytton Mss, Eur Mss E218/20, Lytton to Cambridge, 7 Nov. 1878.

76. NAM, Charles Gough Mss, 8304-32-241, 260, and 266, Gough to wife, 6–7 July and 21 Nov 1880, and 1 Jan. 1881.

77. NAM, Charles Gough Mss, 8304-32-269, Campaign Diary, 23 Mar. 1879.

78. APAC, Lyall Mss, F132/24, Lyall to Roberts, 3 Jan. 1879; Robson, *Roberts in India*, 26–28, 32–34, 39–40, 54–56.

79. Robson, *Roberts in India*, 97–99.

80. Roberts, *Forty-one Years in India*, 385–86.
81. APAC, Strachey Mss, Eur Mss F127/1, John Strachey to Richard Strachey, 28 Jan. 1880.
82. Johnson, "General Roberts," 300–22; Robson, *Roberts in India*, 112–13, 119–21, 136–37, 148–50, 154, 162–68; Trousdale, *War in Afghanistan*, 60, 97, 101, 112–14, 124–26, 167n261, 169–171, 195.
83. Trousdale, *War in Afghanistan*, 101.
84. Robson, *Roberts in India*, 164–68.
85. Ibid., 432n9.
86. Ibid., 115, 207–10.
87. Ibid., 214–16.
88. Ibid., 186–88.
89. APAC, Lyall Mss, F132/26, Stewart to Colley, 5 Feb. 1879.
90. APAC, Lyall Mss, F132/27, St. John to Lyall, 2 Mar. 1879.
91. RA VIC/ADDE/1/8466, Warre to Cambridge, 1 Dec. 1878; NAM, Warre Mss, 7212-10–22, Diary, 29 July 1879.
92. Robson, "Kandahar Letters," 146–60, 206–20, at 217.
93. NLW, Hills-Johnes Mss, L13651, Stewart to Hills-Johnes, 7 Mar. 1880.
94. NAM, Warre Mss, 8112-54–672, Warre to Whitmore, 4 Dec. 1880; 8112-54–700, Brownlow to Warre, 19 Mar. 1880; 8112-54–701, Cambridge to Warre, 30 July 1880.
95. NAM, Warre Mss, 7212-10–23, Diary, 25 Feb. 1880; 8112-54–986, Warre to Brownlow, 28 Feb. 1880; RA VIC/ADDE/1/9480, Warre to Cambridge, 22 Jan. 1881; Robson, "Maiwand," 194–223, at 195.
96. NAM, Warre Mss, 8112-54–572, Memo on Maiwand, 1881.
97. NAM, Warre Mss, 8112-54–987, Warre to Fergusson, 20 June 1880; Primrose Mss, 1/2/4, Memo for Cambridge. n.d.
98. RA VIC/ADDE/1/9277 and 9279, Haines to Cambridge, 3 Aug. 1880; Ripon to Cambridge, 3 Aug. 1880; NAM, Warre Mss, 8112-54–987, Warre to Primrose, 31 July 1880; Warre to Phayre, 13 Aug. 1880; 8112-54–609, Warre to Primrose, 18 Sept. 1880; Primrose Mss 1/2/4, Memo by Adam, Sept. 1880.
99. NAM, Haines Mss, 8108-9-30–1, Ripon to Haines, 1 Aug. 1880.
100. NAM, Haines Mss, 8108-9–29, Ripon to Haines, 15 July 1880.
101. NAM, Haines Mss, 8108-9-32–2 and 3, Greaves to Haines, 2 Oct. 1880.
102. APAC, White Mss, Eur Mss F108/2, White memo, 22 July 1880; Ripon memo, 31 July 1880; White to Camperdown, 4 Aug. 1880; White printed account, 26 Oct. 1880.
103. NAM, Warre Mss, 7212-10–23, Diary, 26 Oct. 1880.
104. NAM, Warre Mss, 7212-10–24, Diary, 31 Dec. 1881.
105. NAM, Fox Mss, 8211-62–7, Notes on Roberts's *Forty-one Years in India*, n.d.
106. Beckett, *Victorians at War*, 45–52.
107. NAM, Haines Mss, 8108-9–29, Stewart to Foreign Dept., 29 July 1880; 8108-9-30–3, Haines memo, 1 Aug. 1880; 8108-9-30–20, Stewart to Ripon, 31 July 1880.
108. Atwood, *Life of Roberts*, 103–4.
109. James, *Roberts*, 151; Roberts, *Forty-one Years in India*, 472–73.
110. Robson, *Roberts in India*, 206–14.
111. NAM, Charles Gough Mss, 8304-32–246, Gough to wife, 11 Aug. 1880.
112. NAM, Charles Gough Mss, 8304-32–249, Gough to wife, 5 Sept. 1880.

113. NAM, Charles Gough Mss, 8304-32-257, Gough to wife, 24–29 Oct. 1880.

114. Chapman, "March from Kabul," 282–315.

115. Roberts, *Forty-one Years in India*, 495–96.

116. Trousdale, *War in Afghanistan*, 236.

117. Hoskyns, "Narrative of the Afghan Campaigns," 431–55; Robson, *Road to Kabul*, 190–98, 251.

118. NAM, Haines Mss, 8108-9-30-46, Ripon to Haines, 17 Aug. 1880.

119. RA VIC/ADDE/1/9301, Warre to Cambridge, 19 Aug. 1880.

120. Heathcote, *Balochistan*, 156–63, 170–74.

121. RA VIC/ADDE/1/8862, Johnson to Cambridge, 25 Aug. 1879.

122. NAM, Haines Mss, 8108-9-24, Lytton to Haines, 21 Feb. 1880; APAC, F132/26, Stewart to Lyall, 29 Jan. 1880.

123. RA VIC/ADDE/1/9326, Ripon to Cambridge, 7 Sept. 1880.

124. APAC, Lyall Mss, F132/24, Roberts to Lyall, 9 Sept. 1880; RA VIC/ADDE/1/9360, Warre to Cambridge, 15 Oct. 1880.

125. RA VIC/ADDE/1/9380, Cambridge to Haines, 29 Oct. 1880.

126. RA VIC/ADDE/1/9354, Cambridge to Haines, 8 Oct. 1880.

127. NAM, Haines Mss, 8108-9-32-4, Ripon to Haines, 2 Oct. 1880; 8108-9-32-5 Haines to Ripon, 2 Oct. 1880.

128. NAM, Haines Mss, 8108-9-32-28, Ripon to Haines, 25 Oct. 1880.

129. RA VIC/ADDE/1/9411, Stewart to Cambridge, 24 Nov. 1880.

130. RA VIC/ADDE/1/9339, Haines to Cambridge, 21 Sept. 1880; Robson, *Roberts in India*, 222–23.

131. RA VIC/ADDE/1/9386, Haines to Cambridge, 9 Nov. 1880.

132. RA VIC/ADDE/1/9429, Cambridge to Warre, 15 Dec. 1880; VIC/ADDE/1/9433, Cambridge to Haines, 17 Dec. 1880.

133. RA VIC/ADDE/1/9454, Cambridge to Stewart, 31 Dec. 1880; VIC/ADDE/1/9585, Annesley to Cambridge, 7 Apr. 1881.

134. RA VIC/ADDE/1/9430, Stewart to Cambridge, 15 Dec. 1880; VIC/ADDE/1/9479, Cambridge to Haines, 21 Jan. 1881.

135. NAM, Warre Mss, 8112-54-620, Warre to Greaves, 23 Oct. 1880; 8112-54-987, Warre to Cambridge, 12 Nov. 1880; RA VIC/ADDE/1/9555, Warre to Cambridge, 10 Mar. 1881; VIC/ADDE/1/9596, Stewart to Cambridge, 19 Apr. 1881.

136. RA VIC/ADDE/1/9397, Haines to Cambridge, 14 Nov. 1880.

137. RA VIC/ADDE/1/9615, Stewart to Cambridge, 15 May 1881.

138. NAM, Warre Mss, 8112-54-987, Warre to Mrs. Primrose, 2 Oct. 1880; Warre to Cambridge, 15 Oct. 1880; Primrose Mss, 1/2/4, Memo for Cambridge, n.d.

139. Brooke, *Journal of Henry Brooke*.

140. Primrose Mss, 1/2/1, Diary, 21 Apr. 1880.

141. Primrose Mss, 1/2/4, Memo for Cambridge, n.d.

142. Beckett, "Road from Kandahar," 1263–94.

143. NAM, Baker Mss, 7804-25, Cambridge to Baker, 11 June 1880.

144. Buckle, *Letters of Queen Victoria*, 3:139.

145. RA VIC/ADDE/1/9642, Cambridge to Stewart, 3 June 1881; NLW, Hills-Johnes Mss, L14221, Hills-Johnes to Malleson, 15 Nov. 1885.

146. APAC, White Mss, Eur Mss F108/109, Roberts to White, 12 May 1881.

147. CCRO, Pole-Carew Mss, CP/5, Pole-Carew to his father, 6 Apr. 1880.

148. APAC, White Mss, F108/98A/64, White to brother, 13 Apr. 1880.

149. NAM, Roberts Mss, 7101-23-15, Cambridge to Roberts, 14 Feb. 1881.

150. Napier, *Lord Napier of Magdala*, 94–97.

151. Holland, *Life of Devonshire*, 1:314; APAC, L/PS/18/A43, "Narrative of Events in Afghanistan and Connected Correspondence," 231.

152. Elsmie, *Stewart*, 263–65, 269.

153. RA VIC/ADDE/1/9375, Stewart to Cambridge, 26 Oct. 1880.

154. Beckett, "Road from Kandahar," 1280–81; Elsmie, *Stewart*, 263–66.

155. *Hansard*, HL Deb v. 259, cc. 787–92, Strathnairn, 11 Mar. 1881; HC Deb. v. 259, c. 1841, Stanhope, 24 Mar. 1881.

156. McLeod Innes, *Buster Browne*, 195–97, 208–9.

157. APAC, Burne Mss, Eur Mss D951/11, Colley to Burne, 15 Nov. 1880.

158. RA VIC/MAIN/N/38/124, Biddulph Memo, 24 Aug. 1880.

159. APAC, Northbrook-Ripon Correspondence, Eur Mss C144/1, Ripon to Northbrook, 20 Mar. 1881.

160. Hubert Gough Mss, "Miscellaneous Ideas," Charles Gough to George Gough, Mar. 1881.

161. Ponsonby, *Henry Ponsonby*, 82.

162. Beckett, "Road from Kandahar," 1282.

163. Ibid., 1283.

164. Bahlman, *Diary of Hamilton*, 1:115.

165. NAM, Haines Mss, 8108-9-46-49, Cambridge to Haines, 24 Dec. 1880; 8108-9-47-8, Cambridge to Haines, 25 Feb. 1881; Bahlman, *Diary of Hamilton*, 1:43.

166. Beckett, "Road from Kandahar," 1290.

167. Robson, *Road to Kabul*, 277.

168. Tripodi, "Grand Strategy," 701–25.

169. Robson, *Road to Kabul*, 280; Preston, "British Military Policy," 513.

170. BL, Ripon Mss, Add Mss 435660, Hartington to Ripon, 11 Feb. and 11 Mar. 1881.

Chapter 7: The Anglo-Zulu War, 1879

1. Robinson, Gallagher, and Denny, *Africa and the Victorians*, 59–60.

2. Dominy, *Last Outpost*, 43.

3. Ibid., 164; Surridge, *Managing the South African War*, 21–31; BL, Lansdowne Mss, L(5)40, Lansdowne to Wyndham, 15 Aug. 1899.

4. RA VIC/ADDE/1/7569, Cunynghame to Cambridge, 20 Mar. 1875.

5. HPL, Wolseley Mss, W/P 9/3, 9/10, Wolseley to wife, 13 Jan. and 23 Feb. 1880; GA, Hicks Beach Mss, D2455/X4/3/2/63/22, Wolseley to Hicks Beach, 17 Feb. 1880.

6. Ian Beckett, "Military High Command in South Africa," in Boyden, Guy, and Harding, *Ashes and Blood*, 60–71.

7. BL, Carnarvon Mss, Add Mss 60800, Hardy to Cunynghame, 29 Jan. 1878; RA VIC/ADDE/1/8261, Cunynghame to Horsford, 12 Mar. 1878.

8. John Laband, "Bulwer, Chelmsford and the Border Levies: The Dispute over the Defence of Natal, 1879," in Laband and Thompson, *Kingdom and Colony at War*, 150–66; Laband, "Danger of Divided Command," 339–55.

9. KZNA, Wood Mss, II/2/2, Chelmsford to Wood, 23 Nov. 1878.

10. Bond, "South African War, 1880–81," in Bond, *Victorian Military Campaigns*, 199–240, at 227.

11. NAM, MS Letter Book, 1998-06-194, Cambridge to Cunynghame, 24 Jan. 1878.

12. SRO, Cranbrook Mss, HA43/H/4/13, Cambridge to Hardy, 12 Nov. 1877.

13. TNA, Carnarvon Mss, PRO 30/6/12, Frere to Carnarvon, 24 Sept. 1877; Carnarvon to Hardy, 31 Oct and 16 Nov. 1877; RA VIC/ADDE/1/8147, Frere to Cambridge, 10 Oct. 1877.

14. RA VIC/ADDE/1/8227, Hardy to Cambridge, 23 Jan. 1878.

15. SRO, Cranbrook Mss, HA43/H/4/14, Cambridge to Hardy, 23 Jan. 1878.

16. Johnson, *Diary of Gathorne Hardy*, 351.

17. RA VIC/ADDE/1/7354, Napier to Cambridge, 3 Apr. 1874.

18. Gon, *Road to Isandlwana*, 147.

19. Knight, *Zulu Rising*, 137.

20. Clarke, *Zululand at War*, 53, 170.

21. Ibid., 61.

22. Clarke, *Invasion of Zululand*, 213–14.

23. KCL, Wood Mss, KCM 89/9/26/9, Thesiger to Wood, 2 Nov. 1878; KZNA, Wood Mss, II/2/2, Chelmsford to Wood, 16 Dec. 1878.

24. Clarke, *Invasion of Zululand*, 116.

25. NAM, Chelmsford Mss, 6807-386-9, Wood to Crealock, 5 Dec. 1878.

26. NAM, Chelmsford Mss, 6807-386-14, Wood to Chelmsford, 1 Apr. 1879.

27. Clarke, *Zululand at War*, 81.

28. Ibid., 82.

29. Ibid., 124.

30. Ibid., 207.

31. NAM, Chelmsford Mss, 6807-386-7, Ellice to Chelmsford, 2 Apr. 1879.

32. NAM, Chelmsford Mss, 6807-386-18, Bellairs to Chelmsford, 17 Mar. 1879.

33. Clarke, *Zululand at War*, 44.

34. Laband, *Chelmsford's Zululand Campaign*, 37.

35. Williams, *Commandant of the Transvaal*, 124–31.

36. KZNA, Wood Mss, II/2/1, Buller to Wood, 22 Oct. 1878.

37. Laband, *Chelmsford's Zululand Campaign*, 72, 85, 104; Jones, *Boiling Cauldron*, 230–31.

38. NAM, Chelmsford Mss, 6807-386-9, Wood to Chelmsford, 16 Feb. 1879; Laband, *Chelmsford's Zululand Campaign*, 114.

39. RA VIC/ADDE/1/8681, Chelmsford to Cambridge, 23–25 May 1879.

40. Castle and Knight, *Fearful Hard Times*, 80–81, 91; Whitehouse, "*Widow-Making War*," 90–91, 100–101.

41. RA VIC/ADDE/1/9887, Stewart to Cambridge, 2 Jan. 1882.

42. Lock and Quantrill, *Zulu Victory*, 233–83; Smith, *Studies in the Anglo-Zulu War*, 201–21.

43. F. W. D. Jackson and Julian Whybra, "Isandlwana and the Durnford Papers," in Whybra, *Studies in the Zulu War*, 1–53, at 46.

44. Greaves and Best, *Curling Letters*, 121.

45. Clarke, *Invasion of Zululand*, 118–19.

46. Keppel-Jones, *Rhodes and Rhodesia*, 285; Glass, *Matabele War*, 230–33.

47. Laband, *Chelmsford's Zululand Campaign*, 68.

48. RA VIC/ADDE/1/8514, Frere to Cambridge, 27 Jan. 1879.

49. NAM, Chelmsford Mss, 6807-386-8, Drummond to Chelmsford, 9 Feb. 1879.

50. NAM, Chelmsford Mss, 6807-386-8, Bellairs to Chelmsford, 5 Feb. 1879.
51. Laband, *Chelmsford's Zululand Campaign*, 92–98.
52. Ibid., 220–26; Clarke, *Invasion of Zululand*, 252–62. Chelmsford again defended his conduct in *The Times* (London) in August 1880—see Smith, *Select Documents*, 448–50.
53. RA VIC/ADDE/1/8629, Chelmsford to Cambridge, 15 Apr. 1879.
54. Clarke, *Zululand at War*, 99.
55. TNA, WO 33/34, Crealock to Chelmsford, 20 Feb. 1879; Chelmsford to Bellairs, 20 Feb. 1879.
56. TNA, WO 33/34, Glyn to Bellairs, both 26 Feb. 1879.
57. Greaves, *Rorke's Drift*, 174–83, 353–81; Holmes and Johnson, "Stylometric Foray," 310–23.
58. Clarke, *Zululand at War*, 100–102.
59. Ibid., 128–29.
60. NAM, Roberts Mss, 7101-23-86, Symons to Chamberlain, 19 Aug. 1888.
61. Clarke, *Zululand at War*, 272.
62. Smith, *Select Documents*, 240–41.
63. Ibid., 242–44; RA VIC/ADDE/1/8646, Cambridge to Chelmsford, 1 May 1879.
64. Smith, *Select Documents*, 244–46.
65. RA VIC/ADDA36/18, Ponsonby to wife, 6 and 7 Sept. 1879.
66. Preston, *Wolseley's South African Journal*, 107.
67. Buckle, *Letters of Queen Victoria*, 3:44–45.
68. RA VIC/ADDA36/18, Ponsonby to wife, 11 Sept., 12 Sept., and 19 Oct. 1879.
69. REM, Durnford Mss, 4901.31.1, Luard to Clarke, 22 Jan. 1885.
70. REM, Durnford Mss, 4901.31.11, Clarke to MS, 23 Feb. 1886.
71. REM, Durnford Mss, 4901.31.6, Luard to Vetch, 8 May 1886; Greaves, *Isandlwana*, 199–202; Lock, *Zulu Victory*, 242–43; Greaves, "Curious Case of Luard," 25–29; Jackson and Whybra, "Isandlwana and the Durnford Papers," in Whybra, *Studies in the Zulu War*, 1–53.
72. Huw Jones, "Hlobane: A New Perspective," in Smith, *Studies in the Anglo-Zulu War*, 223–46, Jones, *Boiling Cauldron*, 259–82, 307–39.
73. NAM, Chelmsford Mss, 6807-386-14, Wood to Chelmsford, 27 Mar. 1879.
74. Jones, "Hlobane," in Smith, *Studies in the Anglo-Zulu War*, 239–41; Wood, *Midshipman to Field Marshal*, 2:48–51.
75. Clarke, *Invasion of Zululand*, 92; Clarke, *Zululand at War*, 135.
76. NAM, Chelmsford Mss, 6807-386-9-101, Wood to Chelmsford, 11 Feb. 1879.
77. NAM, Chelmsford Mss, 6807-386-9, Wood to Crealock, 18 Mar. 1879.
78. NAM, Chelmsford Mss, 6807-386-9-110, Wood to Chelmsford, 11 Mar. 1879.
79. NAM, Chelmsford Mss, 6807-386-14, Wood to Chelmsford, 1 Apr. 1879.
80. NAM, Chelmsford Mss, 6807-386-14, Wood to Chelmsford, 1 Apr. 1879; 6807-386-23, Buller to Crealock, 15 Apr. 1879; Smith, *Select Documents*, 331–32; Jones, *Boiling Cauldron*, 316–35.
81. Jones, *Boiling Cauldron*, 329–31.
82. Clarke, *Zululand at War*, 160.
83. RA VIC/ADDA36/18, Ponsonby to wife, 26 Dec. 1879.
84. KZNA, Wood Mss, II/2/7, Ponsonby to Wood, 30 Dec. 1879.
85. RA VIC/MAIN/E/61/36 and 37, Ponsonby to Cambridge, 17 and 22 Jan. 1880.

86. RA VIC/ADDE/1/8535, Stanley to Cambridge, 11 Feb. 1879; VIC/ADDE/1/8540, Haines to Cambridge, 13 Feb. 1879; HPL, Wolseley Mss, CYP.1, Wolseley to Stanley, 16 Feb. 1879.

87. RA VIC/ADDE/1/8535, Stanley to Cambridge, 11 Feb. 1879; BOD, Hughenden Mss, B/XXI/S/558, Stanley to Beaconsfield, 11 Feb. 1879.

88. RA VIC/ADDE/1/8526, Chelmsford to Cambridge, 5 Feb. 1879; VIC/ADDE/1/8534, Chelmsford to Cambridge, 10 Feb. 1879.

89. RA VIC/ADDE/1/8525, Lady Frere to Cambridge, 4 Feb. 1879.

90. Clarke, *Zululand at War*, 94; NAM, Chelmsford Mss, 6807-386-28, Chelmsford to Cambridge, 14 May 1879.

91. French, *Chelmsford and the Zulu War*, 263.

92. RA VIC/ADDE/1/8668, Marshall to Cambridge, 14 May 1879; Clarke, *Zululand at War*, 133–35; Preston, *Wolseley's South African Journal*, 43.

93. RA VIC/MAIN/O/33/89, Stanley to Queen, 11 Feb. 1879.

94. RA VIC/ADDE/1/8542, Cambridge to Chelmsford, 13 Feb. 1879; VIC/ADDE/1/8562, Cambridge to Frere, 27 Feb. 1879.

95. Beckett, "Such Generals," 16–19.

96. RA VIC/ADDE/1/8562, Cambridge to Frere, 27 Feb. 1879.

97. RA VIC/MAIN/O/39/37, Cambridge to Queen, 3 Mar. 1881.

98. Preston, *Wolseley's South African Journal*, 36.

99. LHCMA, Maurice Mss, 2/2/1, Wolseley to Maurice, 2 Apr. 1879; HPL, Wolseley Mss, S.A.2., Wolseley to Cambridge, 18 July 1879; SS1.8, Pt. II, cccclxxvii.

100. HPL, Wolseley Mss, 163/5, Wolseley to brother, 4 June 1879.

101. HPL, Wolseley Mss, W/P 8/9, Wolseley to wife, 10–11 July 1879.

102. HPL, Wolseley Mss, S.A.2., Wolseley to Cambridge, 18 July 1879; Wolseley to Stanley, 18 July 1879.

103. Clarke, *Zululand at War*, 243.

104. QMUL, Lyttelton Mss, PP5/GRE/26/2, Grenfell to Pascoe Grenfell, 17 July 1879.

105. Preston, *Wolseley's South African Journal*, 47; RA VIC/ADDE/1/8633, Clifford to Cambridge, 17 Apr. 1879.

106. Blood, *Four Score Years and Ten*, 191.

107. Preston, *Wolseley's South African Journal*, 57, 64–65.

108. Clarke, *Zululand at War*, 230–31; RA VIC/ADDA36/20, Ponsonby to wife, 3 Mar. 1881.

109. KCL, Wood Mss, KCM 89/9/27/9, Herbert to Wood, 3 Apr. 1879.

110. RA VIC/ADDE/1/8776 and 8791, Clifford to Cambridge, 6 and 13 July 1879. Wolseley had a slightly different version—see Preston, *Wolseley's South African Journal*, 68.

111. HPL, Wolseley Mss, Wolseley Mss, S.A.1., Wolseley to Beach, 10 Oct. 1879; S.A.2, Wolseley to Cambridge, 30 June and 18 July 1879.

112. KCL, Wood Mss, KCM 89/9/27/9, Herbert to Wood, 3 Apr. 1879.

113. RA VIC/ADDE/1/8562, Cambridge to Frere, 27 Feb. 1879.

114. RA VIC/ADDE/1/8542, Cambridge to Chelmsford, 13 Feb. 1879; VIC/ADDE/1/8607, Cambridge to Chelmsford, 27 Mar. 1879.

115. RA VIC/ADDE/1/8606, Cambridge to Crealock, 27 Mar. 1879; NAM, MS Letter Book, Horsford to Crealock, 27 Mar. 1879.

116. Laband, *Chelmsford's Zululand Campaign*, 102–3; RA VIC/ADDE/1/8642, Clifford to Cambridge, 1 May 1879; ADDE/1/8665, Crealock to Cambridge, 9 May 1879.

117. NAM, Chelmsford Mss, 6807-386-15, Henry Crealock to John Crealock, 9 May 1879.
118. NAM, Chelmsford Mss, 6807-386-17, Clifford to Chelmsford, 11 May 1879.
119. RA VIC/ADDE/1/8633, Clifford to Cambridge, 17 Apr. 1879.
120. RA VIC/ADDE/1/8648, Clifford to Cambridge, 21 Apr. 1879.
121. RA VIC/ADDE/1/8852, Cambridge to Clifford, 12 Aug. 1879.
122. Laband, *Chelmsford's Zululand Campaign*, 190–94; Clarke, *Zululand at War*, 174, 203–5, 247; Smith, *Studies in Anglo-Zulu War*, 340–44; RA VIC/ADDE/1/8715, Chelmsford to Cambridge, 10 June 1879.
123. Clarke, *Zululand at War*, 247.
124. French, *Chelmsford and the Zulu War*, 225.
125. NAM, Chelmsford Mss, 6807-386-15, Henry Crealock to John Crealock, 6 May 1879.
126. Smith, *Select Documents*, 405–9.
127. Laband, *Chelmsford's Zululand Campaign*, 204–7.
128. HPL, Wolseley Mss, S.A.2, Wolseley to Cambridge, 11 July 1879.
129. HPL, Wolseley Mss, S.A.2, Wolseley to Chelmsford, 12 July 1879.
130. Laband, *Chelmsford's Zululand Campaign*, 218–19.
131. Clarke, *Zululand at War*, 251.
132. HPL, Wolseley Mss, S.A.1, Wolseley to Beach, 11 Nov. 1879.
133. RA VIC/ADDE/1/8851A, Cambridge to Wolseley, 12 Aug. 1879.
134. Beckett, "Such Generals," 16–19.
135. HPL, Wolseley Mss, S.A.2, Wolseley to Cambridge, 2 Apr. 1880; Preston, *Wolseley's South African Journal*, 228.
136. RA VIC/ADDE/1/9144, Clifford to Cambridge, 2 Apr. 1880.
137. Preston, *Wolseley's South African Journal*, 265.
138. NAM, MS Letter Book, 1998-06-195, Whitmore to Smyth, 21 May 1880; RA VIC/ADDE/1/9367, Cambridge to Clifford, 21 Oct. 1880.
139. *Broad Arrow* 23 (1879), 205–6.
140. BL, Hutton Mss, Add Mss 50110, Chelmsford to Henry Crealock, 17 and 19 Feb. 1880; memo by John North Crealock, 18 Feb. 1880.
141. Clarke, *Invasion of Zululand*, 164.
142. HPL, Wolseley Mss, W/MISC/2, Cambridge to Wolseley, 18 Aug. 1879.
143. RA VIC/MAIN/O/39/55, Whitmore to Ponsonby, 5 Mar. 1881; VIC/MAIN/Z/391, Queen Victoria's Journal, 3 Mar. 1881.
144. RA VIC/ADDA36/20, Ponsonby to wife, 3 Mar. 1881; VIC/ADDE/1/8545, Childers to Cambridge, 4 Mar. 1881.
145. RA VIC/MAIN/O/39/92, Gardiner to Ponsonby, 10 Mar. 1881.
146. WCRO, Newdigate Mss, CR764/249 and 250.
147. KZNA, Wood Mss, II/2/11, Lady Wolseley to Wood, 21 June 1879.
148. BOD, Hughenden Mss, B/XXI/W/505a, Wolseley to Salisbury, 22 Oct. 1878.
149. HPL, Wolseley Mss, CYP.1, Wolseley to Stanley, 16 Feb. 1879.
150. HPL, Wolseley Mss, CYP.1, Wolseley to Horsford, 19 Mar. 1879.
151. HPL, Wolseley Mss, 163/v, Wolseley to mother, 23 Apr. 1879.
152. RA VIC/ADDE/1/8616, Cranbrook to Cambridge, 2 Apr. 1879.
153. RA VIC/ADDE/1/8671, Cambridge to Wolseley, 4 Apr. 1879.
154. Preston, *Wolseley's South African Journal*, 31.

155. HPL, Wolseley Mss, 163/v, Wolseley to brother, 4 June 1879.
156. RA VIC/MAIN/O/34/83, Summary extracts of correspondence on Wolseley's appointment.
157. RA VIC/MAIN/O/34/111, Beaconsfield to Queen, 30 May 1879.
158. Preston, *Wolseley's South African Journal*, 308n25.2; 310n26.12.
159. RA VIC/ADDA36/18, Ponsonby to wife, 2 Sept. 1879.
160. RA VIC/MAIN/O/34/99, Ponsonby to Queen, 27 May 1879.
161. WL, Wolseley Mss, MS. 7043/3, Wolseley to Austin, 5 June 1879.
162. Clements, *Glamour and Tragedy*, 109.
163. Laband, *Chelmsford's Zululand Campaign*, 215–16.
164. Ibid., 217.
165. Charles Ballard, "Sir Garnet Wolseley and John Dunn: The Architects and Agents of the Ulundi Settlement," in Duminy and Ballard, *Anglo-Zulu War*, 120–47.
166. Wright, *British Lion in Zululand*, 182–89.
167. Laband, *Zulu Warriors*, 265–77.
168. Preston, *Wolseley's South African Journal*, 298.
169. WL, Wolseley Mss, MS. 7043/5, Wolseley to Austin, 12 June 1880.
170. HPL, Wolseley Mss, S.A.2, Wolseley to Cambridge, 2 Mar. 1880; Wolseley to Stanley, 2 Mar. 1880; W/P 9/12, Wolseley to wife, 5–6 Mar. 1880.
171. BOD, Hughenden Mss, B/XXI/W/508, Wolseley to Stanley, 11 Sept. 1879.
172. GA, Hicks Beach Mss, D2455/X4/1/1/1, Beaconsfield to Hicks Beach, 20 Nov. 1879.
173. Ian Beckett, "George Colley," in Corvi and Beckett, *Victoria's Generals*, 74–91.
174. HPL, Wolseley Mss, M2/41/8/2, Spencer Childers to Wolseley, 18 Nov. 1903.
175. HPL, Wolseley Mss, SSL.10/1/xxxix.

Chapter 8: The South African War, 1899–1902

1. Beckett, "Britain's Imperial War," 1–29.
2. Howard Bailes, "Military Aspects of the War," in Warwick, *South African War*, 65–102; Spiers, *Late Victorian Army*, 305–33.
3. Maurice and Grant, *War in South Africa*, 2:204; Henderson, *Science of War*, 24, 74, 179, 372.
4. Spiers, "Learning Curve," 1–17.
5. Stephen Badsey, "A Print and Media War," in Wilcox, *Recording the South African War*, 5–16.
6. Beckett, *Victorians at War*, 213–30.
7. John Gooch, "Britain and the Boer War," in Andreopoulos and Selesky, *Aftermath of Defeat*, 40–58; Ian Beckett, "The South African War and the Late Victorian Army," in Dennis and Grey, *Boer War*, 31–44; Hew Strachan, "The Boer War and Its Impact on the British Army, 1902–14," in Boyden, Guy, and Harding, *Ashes and Blood*, 85–98.
8. Kerry, "Lansdowne at the War Office," 175, 264.
9. *HCCP* 1903 [C. 1789], 21–22; BL, Lansdowne Mss, L(5)57, Return of Land Forces in South Africa by Week, 21 Jan. 1900.
10. HPL, Wolseley Mss, W/P 28/30 and 50, Wolseley to wife, 24 June and 6 Sept. 1899.
11. DCRO, Buller Mss, 2065M/SS4/14, McDonnell to Buller, 6 Sept. 1899; Buller to Stopford, 7 Sept. 1899.
12. Powell, *Buller*, 117, 122–25; Surridge, "Lansdowne," in Gooch, *Boer War*, 28; Kerry, "Lansdowne at War Office," 176.

13. Pakenham, *Boer War*, 97.
14. TNA, Buller Mss, WO 132/6, Buller to brother, 3 Nov. 1899.
15. TNA, Buller Mss, WO 132/6 and 24, Buller to brother, 3 and 18 July 1899.
16. HPL, Wolseley Mss, W/W.4/96, Wolseley to brother, 6 July 1899; BL, Lansdowne Mss, Proceedings of the Army Board, 15 July 1899.
17. *HCCP* 1903 [C. 1791], 169–70, c. 14963; 185, c. 14967.
18. NRS, Dundonald Mss, 233/146, Buller to Dundonald, 17 Oct. 1899.
19. TNA, WO 132/6, Buller to WO, 6 Jan. 1900; Pakenham, *Boer War*, 212.
20. TNA, WO 32/7902, Grove Statement, 7 Mar. 1900.
21. TNA, WO 32/7903, Buller to WO, 17 Apr. 1900.
22. Wood, *Life and Adventure*, 131.
23. TNA, WO 32/7903, Buller to WO, 17 Apr. 1900.
24. *HCCP* 1903 [C. 1791], 515–16, c. 21253.
25. *HCCP* 1903 [C. 1790], 399–400, c. 9438; *HCCP* 1903 [C. 1791], 177, 186, c. 4171–72, 4388; Wood, *Winnowed Memories*, 374.
26. Lyttelton, *Eighty Years*, 200.
27. Amery, *Times History*, 2:37–38.
28. *HCCP* 1903 [C. 1791], 468–69, c. 20494–96.
29. TNA, WO 32/7846, Wolseley to Lansdowne, 17 June 1899.
30. RA VIC/MAIN/P/1/225; VIC/MAIN/P/2/7.
31. RA VIC/MAIN/P/2/200.
32. TNA, CAB 37/50, Wolseley to Lansdowne, 8 Sept. 1899.
33. Pakenham, *Boer War*, 96.
34. HPL, Wolseley Mss, W/W.4/96, 104, Wolseley to brother, 6 July and 28 Sept. 1899.
35. Melville, *Life of Buller*, 2:1–3; Lyttelton, *Eighty Years*, 200–201.
36. HPL, Wolseley Mss, W/P 28/80, Wolseley to wife, 17 Dec. 1899.
37. Leeson, "Playing at War," 432–61.
38. Wood, *Winnowed Memories*, 291–93; KCL, Wood Mss, KCM 89/9/50/18, Buller to Wood, 27 Dec. 1899; BL, Lansdowne Mss, L(5)38, Wood to Lansdowne, 11 Aug. 1899.
39. BL, Lansdowne Mss, L(5)57, Wolseley to Lansdowne, 9 Mar. 1900.
40. KZNA, Wood Mss, V/1/1, Mrs. Brodrick to Wood, n.d. [1900].
41. NAM, Roberts Mss, 7101-23-91, Wood to Grove, 1 Feb. 1901; Wood, *Midshipman to Field Marshal*, 2:256–57.
42. BL, Lansdowne Mss, L(5)47, Roberts to Lansdowne, 27 Mar. 1896; NAM, Wilkinson Mss, 9011-42-14-43, Roberts to Wilkinson, 6 Apr. 1896.
43. BL, Lansdowne Mss, L(5)47, Roberts to Lansdowne, 27 Mar. and 20 Apr. 1896; L(5)60, Roberts to Lansdowne, 25 Apr. 1897.
44. NAM, Roberts Mss, 7101-23-61, Rawlinson to Roberts, 22 Apr. 1897.
45. BL, Lansdowne Mss, L(5)47, Roberts to Lansdowne, 22 Oct., 8 Dec., and 11 Dec. 1899.
46. BL, Lansdowne Mss, L(5)47, Lansdowne to Roberts, 10 Dec. 1899.
47. BL, Lansdowne Mss, L(5)44, Bigge to Lansdowne, 27 Sept. 1900; RA VIC/MAIN/P/6/88, Queen to Salisbury, 10 Feb. 1900.
48. Pakenham, *Boer War*, 615n20; Atwood, *Roberts and Kitchener*, 75.
49. BL, Lansdowne Mss, L(5)49, Lansdowne to Salisbury, 8 Nov. 1899; TNA, WO 132/12, Lansdowne to Buller, 9 Nov. 1899; Buller to Lansdowne, 10 Nov. 1899; Spies, *Methods of Barbarism?*, 24.

50. Atwood, *Roberts and Kitchener*, 74–75.

51. Symons, *Buller's Campaign*, 137; Miller, *Methuen and the British Army*, 57–58, 74.

52. BL, Lansdowne Mss, L(5)16, Buller to Lansdowne, 9 Sept. 1899.

53. BL, Lansdowne Mss, L(5)54(3), Wolseley to Lansdowne, 26 July 1897.

54. Durand, *Life of White*, 2:4–5.

55. RA VIC/MAIN/P/1/188, Wolseley to Bigge, 15 Aug. 1899; Halik Kochanski, "Wolseley and the South African War," in Gooch, *Boer War*, 56–69, at 60.

56. NAM, Fleetwood-Wilson Mss, 7507-55-29, Fleetwood-Wilson to Lansdowne, and added Lansdowne note, 31 Aug. 1899.

57. Pakenham, *Boer War*, 96; APAC, White Mss, Eur Mss F108/111, Lansdowne to White, 8 July 1899; Amery, *Times History*, 2:108; HCCP 1903 [C. 1790], 219–20, 373–75, c. 5234–36, 8865, 8867–71; HCCP 1903 [C. 1791], 169, c. 14952–54.

58. *HCCP* 1903 [C. 1790], 22, 27, c. 531, 659, and 663; 374, c. 8880–82.

59. QMUL, Lyttelton Mss, PP5/2/10, Lyttelton to wife, 22–25 Dec. 1899; APAC, White Mss, Eur Mss F108/52, Symons to White, 2 Sept. and 17 Oct. 1899; Hunter, *Kitchener's Sword-arm*, 120–21; Pakenham, *Boer War*, 108.

60. Pakenham, *Boer War*, 155.

61. Durand, *Life of White*, 2:100, 104–5.

62. Powell, *Buller*, 127; Pakenham, *Boer War*, 76, 108–9.

63. APAC, White Mss, F108/52, Symons to White, 2 Sept., 17 Oct., and 18 Oct. 1899.

64. APAC, L/MIL/7/17039, Bengal Reports, 15 Mar. 1896.

65. HPL, Wolseley Mss, W/P 28/71, Wolseley to wife, 31 Oct. 1899.

66. DCRO, Buller Mss, 2065M/SS4/14, Wolseley to Buller, 7 Sept. 1899.

67. RA VIC/MAIN/P/2/112, Lansdowne to Prince of Wales, 15 Oct. 1899.

68. Melville, *Life of Buller*, 2:2.

69. TNA, Buller Mss, WO 132/12, Lansdowne to Buller, 9 Nov. 1899, and Buller to Lansdowne, 9 Dec. 1899; WO 32/7903, Buller to WO, 17 Apr. 1900.

70. HHM, Salisbury Mss, Lansdowne to Salisbury, 3 Nov. 1899.

71. WL, Wolseley Mss, MS. 7043/24, Wolseley to Austin, 8 Feb. 1900.

72. TNA, WO 32/7903, Buller to WO, 17 Apr. 1900.

73. Jay Stone, "The Anglo-Boer War and Military Reforms in the United Kingdom," in Stone and Schmidl, *Boer War and Military Reforms*, 55.

74. Miller, *Methuen and the British Army*, 75–76.

75. TNA, Lansdowne Mss, FO 800/115, Salisbury to Lansdowne, 8 Nov. 1899.

76. Surridge, *Managing the South African War*, 35–39.

77. Butler, *Autobiography*, 436; Surridge, "All you soldiers," 582–600.

78. Ryan, *Butler*, 174–76.

79. RA VIC/MAIN/P/1/155, Lansdowne to Queen, 4 Aug. 1899.

80. Kerry, "Lansdowne at the War Office," 162–64.

81. Butler, *Autobiography*, 456; BL, Lansdowne Mss, L(5)25, Grove to Lansdowne, 8 Aug. 1899; L(5)40, Lansdowne to Wyndham, 15 Aug. 1899.

82. RA VIC/MAIN/W/15/119, Butler to Bigge, 13 Nov. 1899.

83. LHCMA, Maurice Mss, 2/3/68, Butler to Maurice, 20 Nov. 1899.

84. McCourt, *Remember Butler*, 233.

85. Ryan, *Butler*, 196–98, 202–3.

86. Pakenham, *Boer War*, 96.

87. RA VIC/MAIN/P/1/155, Lansdowne to Queen, 4 Aug. 1899.

88. BL, Lansdowne Mss, L(5)48, Roberts to Lansdowne, 25 Oct. 1900.
89. NAM, MS Precedent Book, NAM 2001–05–606–1, Note by Kitchener, 3 May 1901.
90. RA VIC/MAIN/E/33/76, Wolseley to Queen, 15 Aug. 1899; P/1/153 Lansdowne to Queen, 4 Aug. 1899; UBL, Chamberlain Mss, JC 5/51/61, Lansdowne to Chamberlain, 15 Aug. 1899.
91. APAC, White Mss, Eur Mss F108/111, Buller to White, 15 Sept. 1899.
92. Atwood, *Roberts and Kitchener*, 88; Maurice, *Rawlinson*, 44.
93. Lee, *Soldier's Life*, 54–55, 64; Pakenham, *Boer War*, 161.
94. RA VIC/MAIN/P/1/280, Wolseley to Queen, 12 Sept. 1899.
95. BL, Lansdowne Mss, L(5)28, Lansdowne to Hamilton, n.d.; Lansdowne to Hamilton, 12 Sept. 1899.
96. BL, Lansdowne Mss, L(5)43, Lansdowne to Queen, 7 Nov. 1899; NRS, Dundonald Mss, 233/146, Buller to Dundonald, 17 Oct. 1899.
97. KCL, Wood Mss, KCM 89/9/50/18, Buller to Wood, 27 Dec. 1899; Fortescue-Brickdale, *Hallam Parr*, 285.
98. TNA, WO 32/7903, Buller to WO, 17 Apr. 1900; Buller to Lansdowne, 25 June 1900.
99. BL, Lansdowne Mss, L(5)28, Lansdowne to Hamilton, 8 Sept. 1899; HCCP 1903 [C. 1791], 104, 133, c. 13840–1, 14471–3; Doolittle, *Soldier's Hero*, 191–92; Hunter, *Kitchener's Sword-arm*, 117–18.
100. *HCCP* 1903 [C. 1791], 618.
101. KCL, Wood Mss, KCM 89/9/50/18, Buller to Wood, 27 Dec. 1899.
102. Pakenham, *Boer War*, 214.
103. *HCCP* 1903 [C. 1790], 91, c. 1913.
104. Buller Family Mss, Buller to wife, 30 Jan. 1900; Symons, *Buller's Campaign*, 137–38.
105. TNA, Ardagh Mss, PRO 30/40/3, à Court to Ardagh, 6 Dec. 1899.
106. Fergusson, *British Military Intelligence*, 152.
107. Wood, *Life and Adventure*, 233–34; Melville, *Life of Buller*, 2:66.
108. Lyttelton, *Eighty Years*, 200.
109. BL, Lansdowne Mss, L(5)24, Lansdowne to Devonshire, 13 Dec. 1899.
110. Gatacre, *General Gatacre*, 98–99.
111. NAM, Roberts Mss, 71010–23–86, Symons to Roberts, 26 May 1895.
112. NAM, Rawlinson Mss, 5201–33–5, Rawlinson to Douglas, 12 May 1898; Rawlinson to Roberts, 18 May and 8 Aug. 1898; Beckett, *Johnnie Gough*, 38; Edward Spiers, "Campaigning under Kitchener," in Spiers, *Sudan*, 54–81, at 58, 65.
113. NWM, Egerton Mss, M1994/112/82, Egerton to mother, 3 Mar. 1898.
114. Churchill, *River War*, 214.
115. BL, Lansdowne Mss, L(5)47, Roberts to Lansdowne, 8 Dec. 1899.
116. BL, Lansdowne Mss, L(5)21, Cromer to Lansdowne, 10 May 1899; Lansdowne to Cromer, 2 June 1899.
117. Symons, *Buller's Campaign*, 157.
118. BL, Lansdowne Mss, L(5)57, Buller to Lansdowne, 9 and 10 Nov. 1899.
119. Pakenham, *Boer War*, 213.
120. LHCMA, Lyttelton Mss, 1st Accession/26, Stuart-Wortley to Talbot, 26 Dec. 1899; 2nd Accession, NGL/KL/553, Lyttelton to wife, 1 Feb. 1900.
121. BL, Lansdowne Mss, L(5)49, Lansdowne to Salisbury, 8 Nov. 1899.
122. CCRO, Pole-Carew Mss, CP/59, Pole-Carew to mother and sister, 21 Dec. 1899.
123. BL, Lansdowne Mss, L(5)57, Buller to Lansdowne, 16 Dec. 1899.

124. Buller Family Mss, Draft Statement for Official History, n.d.

125. WL, Wolseley Mss, MS. 7043/23, Wolseley to Austin, 3 Nov. 1899.

126. BL, Lansdowne Mss, L(5)57, Wolseley to Forestier-Walker, 14. Dec. 1899; HPL, Wolseley Mss, W/W.4/112, 115, and 120, Wolseley to brother, 15 Dec. 1899, and 5 Jan. and 8 Feb. 1900.

127. RA VIC/MAIN/P/4/28, Bigge to Queen, 3 Dec. 1899.

128. BL, Lansdowne Mss, L(5)57, Lansdowne to Buller, 17 Dec. 1899; L(5)16, Lansdowne to Buller, 1 Dec. 1899; Buller to Lansdowne, 4 Dec. 1899, Lansdowne to Buller, 15 Dec. 1899.

129. HPL, Wolseley Mss, W/W.4/112, Wolseley to brother, 15 Dec. 1899; RA VIC/MAIN/P/4/127, Wolseley to Bigge, 14 Dec. 1899; HCCP 1903 [C. 1791], 515–16, c. 21253–59.

130. WSA, Methuen Mss, 1742/47, South Africa Correspondence, Methuen to Forestier-Walker, 16 Dec. 1899; Forestier-Walker to Methuen, 3 Jan. 1900.

131. Williams, *Life of Warren*, 250; Beckett, *Victorians at War*, 53–63.

132. Lock, *Hill of Squandered Valour*, 80, 94–95; Lock, letter to the editor, *SOTQ* 152 (2013), 13.

133. Kerry, "Lansdowne at the War Office," 255.

134. BL, Campbell-Bannerman Mss, Add Mss 41212, Buller to Campbell-Bannerman, 5 Jan. 1899; RA VIC/MAIN/W/15/33, Buller to Bigge, 27 Feb. 1899.

135. Beckett, "Wolseley and Warren," 10–14.

136. BL, Lansdowne Mss, L(5)57, Wolseley to Buller, 12 Dec. 1899, and Lansdowne to Buller, 17 Dec. 1899; L(5)16, Lansdowne to Buller, 1 and 15 Dec. 1899, and Buller to Lansdowne, 4 Dec. 1899; HPL, Wolseley Mss, W/W.4/112, Wolseley to brother, 15 Dec. 1899.

137. RA VIC/MAIN/P/4/127, Wolseley to Bigge, 14 Dec. 1899.

138. Buller Family Mss, Buller to wife, 18 Dec. 1899.

139. Wessels, *Roberts and South Africa*, 17–18.

140. HPL, Wolseley Mss, W/W.4/11, Wolseley to brother, 16 Nov. 1899.

141. HPL, Wolseley Mss, W/P 28/80, Wolseley to wife, 17 Dec. 1899; RA VIC/MAIN/P/4/152, Wolseley to Bigge, 17 Dec. 1899; VIC/MAIN/P/4/159, Bigge to Lansdowne, 18 Dec. 1899; Buller Family Mss, Wolseley to Lady Buller, 17 Dec. 1899, and Wolseley to Buller, 21 Dec. 1899; BL, Lansdowne Mss, L(5)37, Wolseley to Bigge, 17 Dec. 1899.

142. NAM, Roberts Mss, 7101–23–181, Sandars to Lady Aileen Roberts, 7 and 11 May 1921; Note by Aileen Roberts, 23 Apr. 1921.

143. Pakenham, *Boer War*, 244–45.

144. BL, Lansdowne Mss, L(5)44, Bigge to Lansdowne, 18 Dec. 1899.

145. HHM, Salisbury Mss, 3M/E, Balfour to Salisbury, 19 Dec. 1899.

146. RA VIC/MAIN/W/73/196, Balfour to Bigge, 19 Dec. 1899.

147. HHM, Salisbury Mss, A/112/58, Cromer to Salisbury, 21 Dec. 1899.

148. Wessels, *Kitchener and South Africa*, 7, 10, 13, 22.

149. Miller, *Methuen and the British Army*, 168.

150. BL, Lansdowne Mss, L(5)49, Salisbury to Lansdowne, 17 Dec. 1899.

151. DUDR, Wolseley Mss, Wolseley to brother, 17 May and 2 Aug. 1900.

152. Buller Family Mss, Wolseley to Buller, 19 May 1900.

153. TNA, Buller Mss, WO 132/12, Note by Stopford, 28 Jan. 1900; BL, Lansdowne Mss, L(5)47, Roberts to Lansdowne, 29 Jan. 1900.

154. Melville, *Life of Buller*, 2:159–60.

155. NAM, Roberts Mss, 7101–110–1, Roberts to Lansdowne, 9 Feb. 1900.

156. Surridge, *Managing South African War*, 67.

157. *HCCP* 1903 [C. 1790], 175–76, c. 4154–55.

158. BL, Lansdowne Mss, L(5)44, Lansdowne to Bigge, 11 Jan. 1900; Wessels, *Roberts and South Africa*, 24–25.

159. BL, Lansdowne Mss, L(5)48, Lansdowne to Roberts, 6 Apr. 1900; Gatacre, *Gatacre*, 286–88.

160. HPL, Wolseley Autograph Collection, Gatacre to Wolseley, received 9 July 1900.

161. BL, Lansdowne Mss, L(5)57, Roberts to Lansdowne, 17, 18, and 19 Dec. 1899; Lansdowne to Roberts, 18 Dec. 1899; NAM, Roberts Mss, 7101–23–110–1, Roberts to Lockhart, 26 Dec. 1899.

162. Atwood, *Life of Roberts*, 205.

163. Lee, *Soldier's Wife*, 159–60.

164. Robertson, *From Private to Field Marshal*, 112–13; Wessels, *Kitchener and South Africa*, 39–40.

165. Atwood, *Roberts and Kitchener*, 132–33; Pakenham, *Boer War*, 335–38.

166. Macdiarmid, *Life of Grierson*, 152–53; Robertson, *From Private to Field Marshal*, 121–22.

167. Pakenham, *Boer War*, 368.

168. NAM, Roberts Mss, 7101–23–188, Chamberlain to Lansdowne, 28 Aug. 1900.

169. Younghusband, *Soldier's Memories*, 160–63; Younghusband, *Forty Years a Soldier*, 196–200.

170. HHM, Salisbury Mss, A/112/74, Cromer to Salisbury, 31 Jan. 1900; BL, Lansdowne Mss, L(5)48, Lansdowne to Roberts, 23 Mar. 1900.

171. NWM, Egerton Mss, M1994/112/93, "Reminiscences of the 72nd Highlanders," 32.

172. BL, Lansdowne Mss, L(5)21, Maxwell to Cromer, 15 Jan. 1900; Cromer to Lansdowne, 29 Jan. 1900; SAD, 270/1/2, Wood to Wingate, 25 Jan. 1900; HHM, Salisbury Mss, A112/72, Cromer to Salisbury, 28 Jan. 1900.

173. Daly, *Sirdar*, 141–43.

174. Wessels, *Roberts and South Africa*, 45–48.

175. Gon, *Send Carrington!*, 99–100, 107–15, 119.

176. BL, Lansdowne Mss, L(5)48, Roberts to Lansdowne, 23 May and 13–17 Sept. 1900; NAM, Roberts Mss, 7101–23–188, Chamberlain to Lansdowne, 28 Aug. 1900.

177. NAM, Roberts Mss, 7101–23–188, Chamberlain to Lansdowne, 28 Aug. 1900; BL, Lansdowne Mss, L(5)48, Roberts to Lansdowne, 25 Oct. 1900.

178. HPL, Wolseley Autograph Collection, Baden-Powell to Wolseley, 14 Nov. 1900.

179. HPL, Wolseley Autograph Collection, Baden-Powell to Wolseley, 6 July and 8 Sept. 1901; Brodrick to Wolseley, 8 July 1901.

180. *HCCP* 1903 [C. 1790], 440–41, c. 10446.

181. NLS, Minto Mss, MS 12380, Pretyman to Minto, 1 July 1900.

182. NAM, Wilkinson Mss, OTP 13/23, Hamilton to Wilkinson, 8 Mar. 1900.

183. NAM, Roberts Mss, 7101–23–46, Hamilton to Roberts, 14 Mar. 1900.

184. LHCMA, Lyttelton Mss, 1st Accession/11, Stuart-Wortley to Margaret Talbot, 1 Apr. 1900.

185. Powell, *Buller*, 176.

186. Doolittle, *Soldier's Hero*, 230.

187. HHM, Salisbury Mss, A/101/130, Stewart to Barrington, Mar. 1900.

188. *HCCP* 1903 [C. 1790], 182, c. 4297–4301; BL, Lansdowne Mss, L(5)48, Roberts to Lansdowne, 21 Aug. 1900; *HCCP* 1903 [C. 1791], 446, c. 10520–21; James, *Roberts*, 380.

189. Winrow, "Stellenbosch or Courts Martial?," 6–10.

190. Winrow, "Prejudiced or Perceptive?," 8–12; Anglesey, *History of the British Cavalry*, 4:80.

191. BL, Lansdowne Mss, L(5)47, Roberts to Lansdowne, 30 Jan. 1900; L(5)48, Roberts to Lansdowne, 5–6 Feb. 1900; Pakenham, *Boer War*, 318.

192. Badsey, *Doctrine and Reform*, 100.

193. NAM, Roberts Mss, 7101-23-117-1, French to Roberts, 27 Feb. 1900.

194. LHCMA, Lyttelton Mss, 1st Accession/9, Miles to Lyttelton, 26 Mar. 1900.

195. NAM, Roberts Mss, 7101-23-117-1, Roberts to Lansdowne, 16 Mar. 1900; Winrow, "Bwab," 11–18.

196. Churchill, *My Early Life*, 333.

197. Atwood, *Life of Roberts*, 231; Atwood, "Sackings," 24–31, at 26.

198. Badsey, *Doctrine and Reform*, 101, 105, 118.

199. Harris, *Douglas Haig*, 36–37.

200. BL, Lansdowne Mss, L(5)48, Roberts to Lansdowne, 29 Apr. 1900.

201. BL, Lansdowne Mss, L(5)48, Roberts to Lansdowne, 1 Apr. 1900; NAM, Roberts Mss, 7101-23-188, Chamberlain to Lansdowne, 28 Aug. 1900.

202. Atwood, "Sackings," 26–27; Winrow, "First Cavalry Regiment to Pretoria," 8–13; Anglesey, *History of the British Cavalry*, 4:41–46.

203. BL, Lansdowne Mss, L(5)48, Lansdowne to Roberts, 14 July 1900.

204. BL, Lansdowne Mss, L(5)48, Lansdowne to Roberts, 23 Mar. 1900.

205. BL, Lansdowne Mss, L(5)48, Lansdowne to Roberts, 31 Mar. 1900.

206. Powell, *Buller*, 181.

207. Buller Family Mss, Buller to wife, 3 May 1900.

208. "Defender," *Warren and Spion Kop*, 203–8.

209. BL, Lansdowne Mss, L(5)49, Salisbury to Lansdowne, 12 Apr. 1900; Atwood, *Roberts and Kitchener*, 155; Surridge, "Lansdowne," in Gooch, *Boer War*, 36–37; Kerry, "Lansdowne at the War Office," 224–27.

210. Stephen Miller, "Redvers Buller," in Corvi and Beckett, *Victoria's Generals*, 51–73, at 67.

211. "Defender," *Warren and Spion Kop*, vii–xi, 217–18.

212. BL, Lansdowne Mss, L(5)48, Roberts to Lansdowne, 9 Feb., 16 Feb., and 5 July 1900; Lansdowne to Roberts, 20 July 1900; L(5)44, Bigge to Lansdowne, 6 July 1900.

213. Gleichen, *Guardsman's Memories*, 210–11, 214, 218–22.

214. Wessels, *Roberts and South Africa*, 148–49, 164–65.

215. Surridge, "Honour and Reputation," 12–14.

216. Atwood, *Life of Roberts*, 225–27.

217. Jeffrey Meriwether, "War Secretaries and Their Commanders-in-Chief: South Africa, Professional Rivalries, and the Politics of Reform," in Miller, *Soldiers and Settlers in Africa*, 171–94, at 187–90.

218. Midleton, *Records and Reactions*, 120.

219. CCRO, Pole-Carew Mss, CP/128, Diary of a Staff Officer, 24 Mar. 1900.

220. Macdiarmid, *Life of Grierson*, 153; Atwood, *Roberts and Kitchener*, 143.

221. BL, Lansdowne Mss, L(5)48, Lansdowne to Roberts, 1 June 1900.

222. BL, Lansdowne Mss, L(5)48, Roberts to Lansdowne, 19 and 28 June 1900.

223. BL, Lansdowne Mss, L(5)48, Roberts to Lansdowne, 13–17 Sept. 1900; HPL, Wolseley Mss, W/W.4/113, Wolseley to brother, 20 Dec. 1899.

224. Spies, *Methods of Barbarism?*, 168–69.

225. BL, Lansdowne Mss, L(5)48, Lansdowne to Roberts, 21 Sept. 1900.

226. BL, Lansdowne Mss, L(5)48, Roberts to Lansdowne, 9 Nov. 1900; Wessels, *Roberts and South Africa*, 160–62.

227. TNA, Kitchener Mss, PRO 30/57/14, Cromer to Kitchener, 19 Jan. 1899.

228. NAM, Rawlinson Mss, 5201-33-4, Diary, 14 Jan. 1898.

229. RA VIC/MAIN/W/15/19, Wolseley to Bigge, 10 Feb. 1899.

230. SAD, Wingate Mss, 233/5/17-20, Wingate to wife, 16 May 1898.

231. Keith Surridge, "Herbert Kitchener," in Corvi and Beckett, *Victoria's Generals*, 194–219, at 212–13.

232. Smith-Dorrien, *Memories*, 152.

233. Wessels, *Roberts and South Africa*, 154, 201; Wessels, *Kitchener and South Africa*, 165–68.

234. Birdwood, *Khaki and Gown*, 125.

235. NAM, Roberts Mss, 7101-23-122-2, Roberts to Kitchener, 19 Oct. 1901.

236. Wessels, *Roberts and South Africa*, 195–97.

237. Ibid., 229–35.

238. Wessels, *Kitchener and South Africa*, 58–60, 62–65, 67–69.

239. Arthur, *Life of Kitchener*, 2:78–80.

240. Wessels, *Roberts and South Africa*, 206–9, 211–15.

241. Wessels, *Kitchener and South Africa*, 88–91, 114–16, 148–50.

242. Surridge, *Managing the South African War*, 145.

243. Ibid., 144–48; Judd and Surridge, *Boer War*, 212–13.

244. Grenfell, *Memoirs*, 170.

Conclusion

1. Beckett, "Historiography of Small Wars," 276–98; Beckett, *Victorians at War*, 83–92.

2. NAM, Roberts Mss, 7101-23-122-2-146, Roberts to Brodrick, 11 oct. 1901.

3. Ian Beckett, "British Official History," in Wilcox, *Recording the South African War*, 33–42.

4. NAM, Roberts Mss, 7101-23-183, Roberts to Maurice, 16 Aug. 1907.

5. LHCMA, Maurice Mss, 3/2/101, Pole-Carew to Maurice, 4 Oct. 1906.

6. CCRO, Pole-Carew Mss, CO/F11/18/2, Pole-Carew to Buller, 6 Jan. 1902.

7. Bailes, "Technology and Imperialism," 84.

8. Ian Beckett, "'Selection by Disparagement': Lord Esher, the General Staff and the Politics of Command, 1904–14," in French and Holden Reid, *British General Staff*, 41–56.

9. NAM, MS Precedent Book, 2001-05-606-1.

10. Travers, "Hidden Army," 523–44.

11. Bowman and Connelly, *Edwardian Army*, 34–40.

12. Badsey, *Doctrine and Reform*, 203–6, 261–64.

13. Robins, *British Generalship*, 210–17.
14. David French, "'An Extensive Use of Weedkiller': Patterns of Promotion in the Senior Ranks of the British Army, 1919–39," in French and Holden Reid, *British General Staff*, 159–74; French, "Blimp and the British Army," 1182–1201.
15. Hew Strachan, "Introduction," in Strachan, *Big Wars and Small Wars*, 1–20, at 2.
16. Davison, *Challenges of Command*, 219–46.

Bibliography

Archives and Manuscript Collections

Australian Defence Forces Academy Library, Canberra.
    East, Gen. Sir Cecil James, Manuscripts.
Australian War Memorial, Canberra.
    Gellibrand, Maj. Gen. Sir John, Manuscripts.
Bodleian Library, Oxford.
    Alison, Gen. Sir Archibald, Manuscripts.
    Hughenden (Disraeli, Benjamin, Earl of Beaconsfield) Manuscripts.
    Kimberley, First Earl of, Manuscripts.
British Library, Euston Road, London [Asia, Pacific and Africa Collection (formerly Oriental and India Office Collection)].
    Baker, Lt. Gen. Sir Thomas, Manuscripts.
    Barrow, Gen. Sir George, Manuscripts.
    Bombay MS Letter-book
    Brackenbury, Gen. Sir Henry, Manuscripts.
    Browne, Gen. Sir Sam, Manuscripts.
    Burne, Sir Owen Tudor, Manuscripts.
    Cross, First Viscount, Manuscripts.
    Curzon, First Marquess, Manuscripts.
    Elgin, Ninth Earl of, Manuscripts.
    Hamilton, Lord George, Manuscripts.
    Lansdowne, Fifth Marquess of, Manuscripts.
    Luard, Hugh Bixby, Diary
    Lyall, Sir Alfred, Manuscripts.
    Lyttelton, Gen. Sir Neville, Letter-book
    Lytton, First Earl of, Manuscripts.
    Military Correspondence (India Office)
    Minto, Fourth Earl of, Manuscripts.
    Napier of Magdala, Field Marshal Lord, Manuscripts.
    Northbrook, First Earl of, Manuscripts.
    Northbrook-Ripon Correspondence
    White, Field Marshal Sir George, Manuscripts.
British Library, Euston Road, London [Manuscripts Collection].
    Airlie, Lt. Col. the Eleventh Earl of, Manuscripts.
    Campbell-Bannerman, Sir Henry, Manuscripts.
    Carnarvon, Fourth Earl of, Manuscripts.
    Colvile, Maj. Gen. Sir Henry Manuscripts.
    Cross, First Viscount, Manuscripts.
    Gladstone, William Ewart, Manuscripts.
    Hutton, Lt. Gen. Sir Edward, Manuscripts.
    Lansdowne, Fifth Marquess of, Manuscripts.

Spencer, Fifth Earl, (Althorp) Manuscripts.
Wolseley, Field Marshal Viscount, Letter Book
Cambridge University Library, Cambridge.
Cambridge, Field Marshal HRH George, Duke of, Manuscripts.
Childers, Hugh Culling Eardley, Manuscripts.
Campbell Collections, University of KwaZulu-Natal, Pietermaritzburg, S.A.
Wood, Field Marshal Sir Evelyn, Manuscripts.
Cornwall County Record Office, Truro.
Pole-Carew, Lt. Gen. Sir Reginald, Manuscripts.
Devon County Record Office, Exeter.
Buller, Gen. Sir Redvers, Manuscripts.
David M. Rubenstein Rare Books and Manuscript Library, Duke University, Durham, N.C.
Fleetwood-Wilson, Sir Guy, Manuscripts.
India Manuscripts.
Kitchener, Field Marshal Earl, Manuscripts.
Midleton, First Earl of, Manuscripts.
Pole-Carew, Lt. Gen. Sir Reginald, Manuscripts.
Roberts, Field Marshal Earl, Manuscripts.
Trafford, Maj. Lionel James, Manuscripts.
Wingate, Gen. Sir Francis Reginald, Manuscripts.
Wolseley, Field Marshal Viscount, Manuscripts.
Wood, Field Marshal Sir Evelyn, Manuscripts.
Gloucestershire Archives, Gloucester.
Hicks Beach, Sir Michael, Manuscripts.
Hatfield House Muniments, Hatfield.
Salisbury, Third Marquess of, Manuscripts.
Hove Public Library, Hove
Wolseley, Field Marshal Viscount, Manuscripts.
Imperial War Museum, Lambeth.
D'Oyly Snow, Lt. Gen. Sir Thomas, Manuscripts.
Smith-Dorrien, Gen. Sir Horace, Manuscripts.
Kent History and Library Centre, Maidstone.
Stanhope, Edward, Manuscripts.
KwaZulu-Natal Archives, Pietermaritzburg, S.A.
Wood, Field Marshal Sir Evelyn, Manuscripts.
Liddell Hart Centre for Military Archives, King's College, London.
Alison, Gen. Sir Archibald, Manuscripts.
Ferrier, Maj. Gen. James, Manuscripts.
Hamilton, Gen. Sir Ian, Manuscripts.
Lyttelton, Gen. Sir Neville, Manuscripts.
Maurice, Maj. Gen. Sir Frederick, Manuscripts.
Lincolnshire Archives, Lincoln.
Stanhope, Edward, Manuscripts.
Middle East Centre, St. Antony's College, Oxford.
Grenfell, Field Marshal Lord, Manuscripts.
National Archives, Kew.
Ardagh, Maj. Gen. Sir John, Manuscripts.
Buller, Gen. Sir Redvers, Manuscripts.

Cardwell, First Viscount, Manuscripts.
Carnarvon, Fourth Earl of, Manuscripts.
Childers, High Culling Eardley, Manuscripts.
Colonial Office Manuscripts.
Cromer, First Earl of, Manuscripts.
Hamilton, Lord George, Manuscripts.
Kitchener, Field Marshal Earl, Manuscripts.
Lansdowne, Fifth Marquess of, Manuscripts.
Midleton, First Earl of, (Brodrick) Manuscripts.
Napier, Maj. Gen. William, Manuscripts.
Simmons, Field Marshal Sir John Lintorn, Manuscripts.
War Office Manuscripts.
Wolseley, Field Marshal Viscount, Manuscripts.
National Army Museum, Chelsea.
Anstruther, Lt. Col. Philip, Manuscripts.
Badcock, Gen. Sir Alexander, Manuscripts.
Baker, Lt. Gen. Sir Thomas, Manuscripts.
Birdwood, Field Marshal Lord, Manuscripts.
Broadwood, Lt. Gen. Robert, Manuscripts.
Browne, Lt. Gen. Henry Ralph, Manuscripts.
Burn-Murdoch, Maj. Gen. Sir John, Manuscripts.
CinC's Selection Book
Chelmsford, Gen. Lord, Manuscripts.
Chelmsford-Pearson Correspondence.
Cooper Manuscripts.
Cowell, Maj. Gen. Sir John, Manuscripts.
Cunynghame, Gen. Sir Arthur, Manuscripts.
Fleetwood-Wilson, Sir Guy, Manuscripts.
Fox, Lt. Francis, Manuscripts.
Gough, Gen. Sir Charles John Stanley, Manuscripts.
Gough, Brig. Gen. Sir John Edmund, Manuscripts.
Haines, Field Marshal Sir Frederick Paul, Manuscripts.
Kempster, Brig. Gen. Francis, Manuscripts.
Kitchener-Wood Correspondence.
MS Precedent Books.
MS Private Letter Books.
Rawlinson, Gen. Lord, Manuscripts.
Richardson, Lt. Col. Arthur, Manuscripts.
Roberts, Field Marshal Earl, Manuscripts.
Spenser Wilkinson, Henry, Manuscripts.
Warre, Lt. Gen. Sir Henry James, Manuscripts.
Wolseley-Steele Correspondence.
National Library of Ireland, Dublin.
Kilmainham Manuscripts.
National Library of Scotland, Edinburgh.
Blackwood Publishers Manuscripts.
Haig, Field Marshal Earl, Manuscripts.
Haldane, Gen. Sir James Aylmer, Manuscripts.
Minto, Fourth Earl of, Manuscripts.

National Library of Wales, Aberystwyth.
    Hills-Johnes of Dolaucothi, Lt. Gen. Sir James, Manuscripts.
National Records of Scotland, Edinburgh.
    Dundonald, Lt. Gen. the Twelfth Earl of, Manuscripts.
    Spencer Ewart (Monro of Williamson), Lt. Gen. Sir John, Manuscripts.
National War Museum, Edinburgh.
    Egerton, Maj. Gen. Granville, Manuscripts.
Private Collections.
    Buller Family Manuscripts.
    Maude, Lt. Gen. Sir Frederick, Manuscripts.
    Primrose, Gen. James, Manuscripts.
Queen Mary University Library, London.
    Lyttelton, Gen. Sir Neville, Manuscripts.
Royal Archives, Windsor.
    Army Letters.
    Cambridge, Field Marshal HRH, George, Duke of, Manuscripts.
    Egypt Series.
    India Letters.
    Oriental Question Series.
    Ponsonby, Maj. Gen. Sir Henry Frederick, Manuscripts.
    South Africa Series.
Royal Artillery Museum, Larkhill.
    Brackenbury, Gen. Sir Henry, Manuscripts.
Royal Engineers Museum, Chatham.
    Durnford, Col. Anthony, Manuscripts.
South Lanarkshire Council Museum, Hamilton.
    Wolseley, Field Marshal Viscount, Diaries.
Sudan Archive, Durham University, Durham.
    Goodenough, Sir William Henry, Manuscripts.
    Hicks, Col. William, Manuscripts.
    Robertson, Sir James, Manuscripts.
    Wingate, Gen. Sir Francis Reginald, Manuscripts.
Suffolk Record Office, Ipswich.
    Cranbrook, First Earl of, Manuscripts.
University of Birmingham Cadbury Research Library Special Collections, Edgbaston.
    Chamberlain, Joseph, Manuscripts.
Warwickshire County Record Office, Warwick.
    Dormer of Grove Park, Lt. Gen. the Hon. Sir James Charlemagne, Manuscripts.
    Newdigate of Arbury, Lt. Gen. Sir Edward, Manuscripts.
Wellcome Library, Euston, London.
    Wolseley, Field Marshal Viscount, Manuscripts.
Wiltshire and Swindon Archives, Chippenham.
    Methuen, Field Marshal Lord, Manuscripts.

House of Commons Command Papers

1872 (78). Return of the Number of Officers of each Rank; on Full and Half Pay who have applied . . . for Permission to Retire from the Service by the Sale of their Commissions since 1st March 1871.

1872 (315). Return of the Number of English, Scotch, and Irish Commissioned Officers.

1873 (415). Return showing for each Military District or Command at Home and Abroad, since the Year 1850, the Periods during which such Commands have been held . . .

1874 [C.1018]. Report of the Commissioners appointed to enquire into Certain Memorials from Officers in the Army, in reference to the Abolition of Purchase.

1875 (457). Return showing the total number of Commissioned Officers of each substantive rank who were on Full Pay of the Army or on the Effective List of the Auxiliary Forces on 1 January 1870 and on 1 January 1875.

1876 [C. 1569]. Report of the Royal Commission on Army Promotion and Retirement.

1877 [C.1824]. Memorandum explanatory of the provisions of the proposed warrant for the Appointment, Promotion, and Retirement of Officers in the Combatant Ranks of the Army.

1877 [C.1851]. Royal Warrant for Appointment, Promotion and Retirement of Combatant Officers.

1877 [C. 1852]. Comparison of the Provisions of the Royal Warrant of the 13th August 1877, for the Promotion and Retirement of Combatant Officers, with those of previous Regulations.

1878–79 (15). Return of the Number of English, Scotch, and Irish Non-Commissioned Officers . . . and, similar Return of the Number of English, Scotch, and Irish Commissioned Officers.

1880 (197). Return of all Purchase Officers who were Killed in Action or otherwise met their Deaths in the recent South African and Afghanistan Campaigns . . .

1881 (167). Return showing, by Ranks and by Arms of the Service, the Number of Officers of the Army who have been Retired under Section VI of the Royal Warrant of 1877.

1881 (311). Return of all Rewards given since 1835, for Special Military Services.

1886 (166). Return of the Number of General Officers on the effective and retired lists on 1 April 1855, 1870, and 1885 respectively . . .

1896 [C.7987]. Memorandum showing the Duties of the Principal Officers and Departments of the War Office and Details of Office Procedure under the Order in Council dated 21st November 1895.

1899 (90). Return showing the Length of Service (from Date of First Commission) of Lieutenants promoted to Captains, Captains promoted to Majors, and Majors promoted to be Lieutenant-Colonels, in each Year respectively for 1892, 1893, 1894, 1895, 1890, 1897, and 1898 . . .

1902 [C. 982]. Report of the Committee Appointed to Consider the Education and Training of Officers of the Army.

1902 [C. 983]. Minutes of Evidence taken before the Committee Appointed to Consider the Education and Training of Officers of the Army.

1903 [C. 1421]. Report of the Committee . . . to enquire into the nature of the expenses incurred by Officers of the Army, and to suggest measures for bringing Commissions within reach of men of moderate means.

1903 [C. 1789]. Report to enquire into the Military Preparations and Other Matters connected with the War in South Africa.

1903 [C.1790]. Minutes of Evidence taken before the Royal Commission on the War in South Africa, vol. 1.

1903 [C.1791]. Minutes of Evidence taken before the Royal Commission on the War in South Africa, vol. 2.

1903 [C. 1792]. Appendices of the Minutes of Evidence taken before the Royal Commission on the War in South Africa.

Books, Articles, and Theses

Adye, Jr., Sir John. *Soldiers and Others I Have Known: A Volume of Reminiscences.* London: Herbert Jenkins, n.d. [1925].

Adye, Sr., Sir John. *Recollections of a Military Life.* London: Smith, Elder, 1895.

Alford, H. S. L., and W. D. Sword. *The Egyptian Soudan: Its Loss and Recovery.* London: Macmillan, 1898.

Amery, Leo. *My Political Life.* Vol. 1, *England before the Storm, 1896–1914.* London: Hutchinson, 1953.

———, ed. *The Times History of the War in South Africa, 1899–1902.* 7 vols. London: Sampson Low, Marston, 1900–1909.

Anderson, Dorothy. *Baker Pasha: Misconduct and Mischance.* Norwich, UK: Michael Russell, 1999.

Anderson, Olive. "The Growth of Christian Militarism in Mid-Victorian Britain." *English Historical Review* 86 (1971): 46–72.

Andreopoulos, George, and Harold Selesky, eds. *The Aftermath of Defeat: Societies, Armed Forces, and the Challenge of Recovery.* New Haven, Conn.: Yale University Press, 1994.

Anglesey, Marquess of. *A History of the British Cavalry, 1816–1919.* Vol. 3, *1872–98;* vol. 4, *1899–1913.* London: Leo Cooper at Secker & Warburg, 1982, 1986.

Anson, Major-General Sir Archibald. *About Others and Myself.* London: John Murray, 1920.

Appleyard, Major-General Frederick. *Addenda to Thirty-four Years' Army Service.* London: Knapp, Drewett & Sons, n.d. [1935].

———. *A Resumé of Thirty-four Years' Army Service.* London: Knapp, Drewett & Sons, n.d. [1904].

Arnstein, Walter. "The Warrior Queen: Reflections on Victoria and Her World." *Albion* 30 (1998): 1–28.

Arthur, Sir George. *General Sir John Maxwell.* London: John Murray, 1932.

———, ed. *The Letters of Lord and Lady Wolseley, 1870–1911.* London: William Heinemann, 1922.

———. *Life of Lord Kitchener.* 3 vols. London: Macmillan, 1920.

———. *Not Worth Reading.* London: Longmans, Green, 1938.

Atkins, John. *The Life of Sir William Howard Russell.* 2 vols. London: John Murray, 1911.

Atlay, J. B. *Lord Haliburton: A Memoir of his Public Service.* London: Smith, Elder, 1909.

Attridge, Steve. *Nationalism, Imperialism and Identity in Late Victorian Culture: Civil and Military Worlds.* Basingstoke, UK: Palgrave, 2003.

Atwood, Rodney. *The Life of Field Marshal Lord Roberts.* London: Bloomsbury, 2015.

———. *The March to Kandahar: Roberts in Afghanistan.* Barnsley, UK: Pen & Sword, 2008.

———. *Roberts and Kitchener in South Africa, 1900–02.* Barnsley, UK: Pen & Sword, 2011.

———. "Sackings in the South African War." *Soldiers of the Queen* 150 (2012): 24–32.

Badsey, Stephen. *Doctrine and Reform in the British Cavalry, 1880–1918.* Aldershot, UK: Ashgate, 2008.

———. "Mounted Cavalry in the Second Boer War." *Sandhurst Journal of Military Studies* 2 (1991): 11–28.

Bahlman, Dudley, ed. *The Diary of Sir Edward Walter Hamilton, 1880–85.* 2 vols. Oxford: Clarendon Press, 1972.

Bailes, Howard. "The Influence of Continental Examples and Colonial Warfare upon the Reform of the Late Victorian Army." Ph.D. thesis, University of London, 1980.

———. "Patterns of Thought in the Late Victorian Army." *Journal of Strategic Studies* 4 (1981): 29–45.

———. "Technology and Imperialism: A Case Study of the Victorian Army in Africa." *Victorian Studies* 24 (1980–81): 82–104.

Baker, Anne. *A Question of Honour: The Life of Lieutenant-General Valentine Baker Pasha.* London: Leo Cooper, 1996.

Balfour, Lady Betty. *Lord Lytton's Indian Administration, 1876–80.* London: Longmans, Green, 1899.

Ballard, Charles. *Smith-Dorrien.* London: Constable, 1931.

Barczewski, Stephanie. *Heroic Failure and the British.* New Haven, Conn.: Yale University Press, 2016.

Bartlett, Thomas, and Keith Jeffery, eds. *A Military History of Ireland.* Cambridge: Cambridge University Press, 1996.

Beattie, Hugh. *Imperial Frontier: Tribe and State in Waziristan.* Richmond, UK: Curzon, 2002.

Beaumont, Jacqueline. "The British Press and Censorship during the South African War." *South African Historical Journal* 41 (1999): 267–89.

Beaver, William. "The Development of the Intelligence Division and Its Role in Aspects of Imperial Policy-making, 1854–1901: The Military Mind of Imperialism." Ph.D. thesis, University of London, 1976.

———. *Under Every Leaf: How Britain Played the Greater Game from Afghanistan to Africa.* London: Biteback, 2012.

Beckett, Ian. *The Amateur Military Tradition, 1558–1945.* Manchester: Manchester University Press, 1991.

———. "The Annual Confidential Report and Promotion in the Late Victorian Army." *British Journal for Military History* 1 (2014): 12–28.

———. "Britain's Imperial War: A Question of Totality?" *Joernaal vir Eletydse Geskiedenis* 25 (2000): 1–22.

———. "Cavagnari's Coup de Main." *Soldiers of the Queen* 82 (1995): 24–28.

———, ed. *Citizen Soldiers and the British Empire, 1837–1902.* London: Pickering & Chatto, 2012.

———. "Daring a Wrong Like This: The War Office and the Jameson Raiders." *Soldiers of the Queen* 161 (2015): 3–9.

———. "Edward Stanhope at the War Office, 1887–92." *Journal of Strategic Studies* 5 (1982): 278–307.

———. "The Historiography of Small Wars: Early Historians and the South African War." *Small Wars and Insurgencies* 2 (1991): 276–98.

———. "The Indian Expeditionary Force on Malta and Cyprus, 1878." *Soldiers of the Queen* 76 (1994): 6–11.

———. *Isandlwana 1879.* London: Brassey's, 2003.

———. *Johnnie Gough VC: A Biography of Brigadier-General Sir John Edmond Gough VC.* London: Tom Donovan, 1989.

———, ed. *The Memoirs of Sir James Edmonds.* Brighton, UK: Tom Donovan, 2013.

———. "The Pen and the Sword: Reflections on Military Thought in the British Army, 1854–1914." *Soldiers of the Queen* 68 (1992): 3–7.

———. "Personality and the Victorian Army." *Soldiers of the Queen* 100 (2000): 3–5.

———. "The Road from Kandahar: The Politics of Retention and Withdrawal in Afghanistan, 1880–81." *Journal of Military History* 78 (2014): 1263–94.

———. "Soldiers, the Frontier and the Politics of Command in British India." *Small Wars and Insurgencies* 16 (2005): 280–92.

———. "The Stanhope Memorandum of 1888: A Re-interpretation." *Bulletin of the Institute for Historical Research* 57 (1984): 240–47.

———. "Such Generals as They Have Sent Out: Chelmsford's Major-Generals." *Soldiers of the Queen* 84 (1996): 16–19.

———. *The Victorians at War.* London: Hambledon, 2003.

———, ed. *Victorians at War: New Perspectives.* Society for Army Historical Research, Special Publication No. 16, 2007.

———. "Victorians at War: War, Technology and Change." *Journal of the Society for Army Historical Research* 81 (2003): 330–38.

———. "Wolseley and the Ring." *Soldiers of the Queen* 69 (1992): 14–25.

———. "Wolseley and Warren: A Case of Mistaken Identity?" *Soldiers of the Queen* 156 (2014): 10–14.

———, ed. *Wolseley in Ashanti: The Asante War Journal and Correspondence of Major-General Sir Garnet Wolseley, 1873–74.* Stroud, UK: History Press for the Army Records Society, 2009.

———. "Women and Patronage in the Late Victorian Army." *History* 85 (2000): 463–80.

Beckett, Ian, and John Gooch, eds. *Politicians and Defence: Studies in the Formulation of British Defence Policy, 1845–1970.* Manchester: Manchester University Press, 1981.

Bengough, Sir Harcourt. *Memories of a Soldier's Life.* London: Edward Arnold, 1913.

Bennett, Ernest. *The Downfall of the Dervishes: Being a Sketch of the Final Sudan Campaign of 1898.* London: Methuen, 1898.

Bennett, Ian. *A Rain of Lead: The Siege and Surrender of the British at Potchefstroom, 1880–81.* London: Greenhill Books, 2001.

Benyon, John. *Proconsuls and Paramountcy in South Africa.* Pietermaritzburg, S.A.: University of Natal Press, 1980.

Biddulph, Sir Robert. *Lord Cardwell at the War Office: A History of His Administration, 1868–74.* London: John Murray, 1904.

Birdwood, Lord. *Khaki and Gown: An Autobiography.* London: Ward, Lock, 1941.

Blood, Sir Bindon. *Four Score Years and Ten.* London: G. Bell & Sons, 1933.

Bond, Brian. "The Effect of the Cardwell Reforms in Army Organisation, 1874–1904." *Journal of the Royal United Service Institution* 105 (1960): 515–24.

———. "Prelude to the Cardwell Reforms, 1856–68." *Journal of the Royal United Service Institution* 106 (1961): 229–36.

———. "Recruiting the Victorian Army, 1870–92." *Victorian Studies* 5 (1962): 331–38.

———. "The Retirement of the Duke of Cambridge." *Journal of the Royal United Service Institution* 106 (1961): 544–53.

———. *The Victorian Army and the Staff College, 1854–1914.* London: Eyre Methuen, 1972.

———, ed. *Victorian Military Campaigns.* London: Hutchinson, 1967.

Bond, Brian, and Ian Roy, eds. *War and Society: A Yearbook of Military History.* London: Croom Helm, 1975.

Bourne, J. M. *Patronage and Society in Nineteenth-Century England.* London: Edward Arnold, 1986.

Bourne, Kenneth, and D. C. Watt, eds. *Studies in International History.* London: Longmans, 1967.

Bowman, Timothy, and Mark Connelly. *The Edwardian Army: Recruiting, Training and Deploying the British Army, 1902–14.* Oxford: Oxford University Press, 2012.

Boyden, Peter, Alan Guy, and Marion Harding, eds. *Ashes and Blood: The British Army in South Africa, 1795–1914.* London: National Army Museum, 1999.

Brackenbury, Henry. *The Ashanti War: A Narrative.* 2 vols. Edinburgh: William Blackwood & Sons, 1874.

———. *The River Column: A Narrative of the Advance of the River Column of the Nile Expeditionary Force, and Its Return Down the Rapids.* Edinburgh: William Blackwood & Son, 1885.

———. *Some Memories of My Spare Time.* Edinburgh: William Blackwood & Sons, 1909.

Bray, Jean. *The Mysterious Captain Brocklehurst: General Gordon's Unknown Aide.* Cheltenham, UK: Reardon, 2006.

Brice, Christopher, ed. *Forgotten Victorian Generals: Studies in the Exercise of Command and Control in the British Army, 1837–1901.* Solihull, UK: Helion, 2018.

———. *The Thinking Man's Soldier: The Life and Career of General Sir Henry Brackenbury, 1837–1914.* Solihull, UK: Helion, 2012.

A British Officer [William Elliot Cairnes]. *Social Life in the British Army.* New York: Harper & Brothers, 1899.

Brooke, Annie. *The Private Journal of Henry Brooke Late Brigadier-General Commanding 2nd Infantry Brigade, Kandahar Field Force, 1880.* Dublin: Henry Curwen, 1881.

Brown, Kenneth. "Modelling for War: Toy Soldiers in Late Victorian and Edwardian Britain." *Journal of Social History* 24 (1990): 237–54.

Bruce, Anthony. *The Purchase System in the British Army, 1660–1871.* London: Royal Historical Society, 1980.

Buckle, George, ed. *The Letters of Queen Victoria, 1862–85.* 2nd ser., 3 vols. London: John Murray, 1928.

Burleigh, Bennet. *Desert Warfare: Being the Chronicle of the Eastern Soudan Campaign.* London: Chapman & Hall, 1884.

———. *Sirdar and Khalifa: The Re-conquest of the Sudan, 1898.* London: Chapman & Hall, 1898.

Burn, W. L. *The Age of Equipoise.* London: George Allen & Unwin, 1964.

Burne, Sir Owen. *Memories.* London: Edward Arnold, 1907.

Burroughs, Peter. "Imperial Defence and the Victorian Army." *Journal of Imperial and Commonwealth History* 15 (1986): 55–72.

Butler, Elizabeth. *An Autobiography*. 1922. Reprint, Sevenoaks, UK: Fisher Press, 1993.

Butler, Sir William. *The Campaign of the Cataracts: Being a Personal Narrative of the Great Nile Expedition of 1884–85*. London; Sampson Low, Marston, Searle & Rivington, 1887.

———. *The Life of Sir George Pomeroy-Colley*. London: John Murray, 1899.

———. *Sir William Butler: An Autobiography*. New York: Charles Scribner's Sons, 1911.

Butterfield, Paul, ed. *War and Peace in South Africa, 1879–81: The Writings of Philip Anstruther and Edward Essex*. Melville, S.A.: Scripta Africana, n.d. [1986].

Callwell, Sir Charles, ed. *The Memoirs of Major-General Sir Hugh McCalmont*. London: Hutchinson, 1924.

———. *Service Yarns and Memories*. Edinburgh: William Blackwood & Sons, 1912.

———. *Small Wars: Their Principles and Practice*. 3rd ed. London: HMSO, 1906.

———. *Stray Recollections*. 2 vols. London: Edward Arnold, 1923.

Callwell, Sir Charles, and Sir John Headlam. *The History of the Royal Artillery: From the Indian Mutiny to the Great War*. 3 vols. Woolwich (London): Royal Artillery Institution, 1931–37.

Cantwell, Anthony, and David Moore. "The Victorian Army and Submarine Mining." *Fortress* 18 (1993): 32–47.

Castle, Ian, and Ian Knight. *Fearful Hard Times: The Siege and Relief of Eshowe, 1879*. London: Greenhill Books, 1994.

Cavendish, Anne, ed. *Cyprus 1878: The Journal of Sir Garnet Wolseley*. Nicosia: Cyprus Popular Bank Cultural Centre, 1991.

Cecil, Lord Edward. *The Leisure of an Egyptian Official*. London: Hodder & Stoughton, 1921.

Chamberlain, Muriel. "British Public Opinion and the Invasion of Egypt, 1882." *Trivium* 16 (1981): 5–28.

Chapman, Edward. "The March from Kabul to Kandahar in August and the Battle of the 1st of September 1880." *Journal of the Royal United Service Institution* 25 (1881): 282–315.

Chapman-Huston, Desmond, and Owen Rutter. *General Sir John Cowans: The Quartermaster-General of the Great War*. 2 vols. London: Hutchinson, 1924.

Chapple, John, and D. R. Wood. "Kabul to Kandahar, 1880: Extracts from the Diary of Lieutenant E. A. Travers, 2nd P. W. O. Goorkhas." *Journal of the Society for Army Historical Research* 59 (1981): 207–28; 60 (1982): 35–43.

Child, Daphne, ed. *The Zulu War Journal of Colonel Henry Harford*. Hamden, Conn.: Archon Books, 1980.

Childers, Spencer. *The Life and Correspondence of the Rt. Hon. Hugh Culling Eardley Childers*. 2 vols. London: John Murray, 1901.

Chilston, Viscount. *W. H. Smith*. London: Routledge & Kegan Paul, 1965.

Churchill, Randolph. *Winston S. Churchill Companion*. Vol. 1, *Part II, 1896–1900*. London: Heinemann, 1967.

Churchill, Winston S. *Lord Randolph Churchill*. 2 vols. London: Odhams, 1906.

———. *My Early Life: A Roving Commission*. London: Odhams, 1947.

———. *The River War*. 3rd ed. London: Eyre & Spottiswoode, 1933.

Clark, Samuel. *Distributing Status: The Evolution of State Honours in Western Europe*. Montreal: McGill-Queen's University Press, 2016.

Clarke, Sonia, ed. *Invasion of Zululand 1879: Anglo-Zulu War Experiences of Arthur Harness, John Jarvis 4th Viscount St. Vincent, and Henry Bulwer*. Johannesburg: Brenthurst Press, 1979.

———. *Zululand at War 1879: The Conduct of the Anglo-Zulu War.* Houghton, S.A.: Brenthurst Press, 1984.

Clements, W. H. *The Glamour and Tragedy of the Zulu War.* London: The Bodley Head, 1936.

Clifton, Gloria. *Professionalism, Patronage and Public Service in Victorian London: The Staff of the Metropolitan Board of Works, 1856–1889.* London: Athlone Press, 1992.

Collini, Stefan. "The Idea of 'Character' in Victorian Political Thought." *Transactions of the Royal Historical Society* 35 (1985): 29–50.

Collins, Bruce. "Defining Victory in Victorian Warfare, 1860–82." *Journal of Military History* 77 (2013): 895–929.

Collister, Peter. *Hellfire Jack VC: General Sir William Olpherts, 1822–1902.* London: British Association for Cemeteries in South Asia, 1989.

Colvile, Henry. *History of the Sudan Campaign.* 2 vols. London: HMSO, 1889.

———. *The Work of the Ninth Division.* London: Edward Arnold, 1901.

Cooke, A. B., and John Vincent. *The Governing Passion: Cabinet Government and Party Politics in Britain, 1885–86.* Brighton, UK: Harvester Press, 1974.

Corfield, Penelope. *Power and the Professions in Britain, 1700–1850.* London: Routledge, 1995.

Corvi, Steven, and Ian Beckett, eds. *Victoria's Generals.* Barnsley, UK: Pen & Sword, 2009.

Creagh, Sir O'Moore. *The Autobiography of General Sir O'Moore Creagh VC.* London: Hutchinson, n.d. [1925].

Crick, Timothy. *Ramparts of Empire: The Fortifications of Sir William Jervois, 1821–97.* Exeter: University of Exeter Press, 2012.

Cromer, Earl of. *Modern Egypt.* 2 vols. London: Macmillan, 1908.

Crook, M. J. *The Evolution of the Victoria Cross.* Tunbridge Wells, UK: Midas Books, 1975.

Cunningham, Hugh. "Jingoism in 1877–78." *Victorian Studies* 14 (1971): 429–53.

Cunynghame, Sir Arthur. *My Command in South Africa, 1874–78.* London: Macmillan, 1879.

Daly, Martin. "The Egyptian Army Mutiny at Omdurman, January–February 1900." *British Society for Middle Eastern Studies Bulletin* 8 (1981): 3–12.

———. *Empire on the Nile: The Anglo-Egyptian Sudan, 1899–1934.* Cambridge: Cambridge University Press, 1986.

———. *The Sirdar: Sir Reginald Wingate and the British Empire in the Middle East.* Philadelphia: American Philosophical Society, 1997.

Davison, Robert. *The Challenges of Command: The Royal Navy's Executive Branch Officers, 1880–1919.* Abingdon, UK: Ashgate, 2011.

Dawson, Sir Douglas. *A Soldier-Diplomat.* London: John Murray, 1927.

Dawson, Graham. *Soldier Heroes: British Adventure, Empire and the Imagining of Masculinities.* London: Routledge, 1994.

"Defender." *Sir Charles Warren and Spion Kop.* London: Smith, Elder, 1902.

De Groot, Gerrard. *Douglas Haig, 1861–1928.* London: Unwin Hyman, 1988.

Dennis, Peter, and Jeffrey Grey, eds. *The Boer War: Army, Nation and Empire.* Canberra: Army Historical Unit, 2000.

———, eds. *Raise, Train and Sustain: Delivering Land Combat Power.* Canberra: Australian Military History Publications, 2010.

Diamond, Michael. "The Victorian Army as Seen from the Music Hall." *Soldiers of the Queen* 92 (1998): 18–21.

Dighton, Adam. "Race, Masculinity and Imperialism: The British Officer and the Egyptian Army, 1882–99." *War and Society* 35 (2016): 1–18.

Dixon, Anthony. *The Army and Navy Club, 1837–2008*. London: Army & Navy Club, 2009.

Dominy, Graham. *Last Outpost on the Zulu Frontiers: Fort Napier and the British Imperial Garrison*. Urbana: University of Illinois Press, 2016.

Doolittle, Duncan. *A Soldier's Hero: General Sir Archibald Hunter*. Narragansett, R.I.: Anawan, 1991.

Doorn, Jacques van. *The Soldier and Social Change*. Beverly Hills, Calif.: Sage, 1975.

Douglas, Sir George. *The Life of Major-General Wauchope*. London: Hodder & Stoughton, 1905.

Dubow, Saul. "Colonial Nationalism, the Milner Kindergarten and the Rise of 'South Africanism,' 1902–10." *History Workshop Journal* 43 (1997): 53–85.

Duman, Daniel. "Pathways to Professionalism: The English Bar in the Eighteenth and Nineteenth Centuries." *Journal of Social History* 13 (1980): 615–28.

Duminy, Andrew, and Charles Ballard, eds. *The Anglo-Zulu War: New Perspectives*. Pietermaritzburg, S.A.: University of Natal Press, 1981.

Durand, Sir Mortimer. *The Life of Field Marshal Sir George White VC*. 2 vols. Edinburgh: William Blackwood & Sons, 1915.

Durey, Jill. "Ecclesiastical Patronage in Trollope's Novels and Victoria's England." *Churchman* 109 (1995): 250–70.

Durnford, Edward, ed. *A Soldier's Life and Work in South Africa, 1872 to 1879: A Memoir of the Late Col. A. W. Durnford, RE*. London: Sampson Low, Marston, Searle & Rivington, 1882.

Dyer, Gwynne. *War*. London: The Bodley Head, 1985.

Ehrman, John. *Cabinet Government and War, 1890–1940*. Cambridge: Cambridge University Press, 1958.

Eldridge, C. C. *England's Mission: The Imperial Idea in the Age of Gladstone and Disraeli, 1868–80*. London: Macmillan, 1973.

———. *Victorian Imperialism*. London: Hodder & Stoughton, 1978.

Elsmie, G. R. *Field Marshal Sir Donald Stewart*. London: John Murray, 1903.

Ewans, Martin. *Securing the Indian Frontier in Central Asia: Confrontation and Negotiation, 1865–95*. Abingdon, UK: Routledge, 2010.

Fargher, James. "In a Fit of Absent-Mindedness: The Suakin Expeditions and British Imperial Policy." *Soldiers of the Queen* 149 (2012): 24–32.

Farrar-Hockley, Anthony. *Goughie: The Life of General Sir Hubert Gough*. London: Hart-Davis, MacGibbon, 1975.

Farrell, Kevin. *The Military and the Monarchy: The Case and Career of the Duke of Cambridge in an Age of Reform*. Dahlonega: University Press of North Georgia, 2011.

Farwell, Byron. *Eminent Victorian Soldiers: Seekers of Glory*. New York: W. W. Norton, 1985.

———. *Mr. Kipling's Army*. New York: W. W. Norton, 1981.

———. *Queen Victoria's Little Wars*. New York: W. W. Norton, 1972.

Ferguson, Niall. *Empire*. London: Penguin, 2004.

Fergusson, T. G. *British Military Intelligence, 1870–1914*. London: Arms & Armour Press, 1984.

Finer, Samuel. *The Man on Horseback: The Role of the Military in Politics.* London: Pall Mall Press, 1962.

Fletcher Vane, Sir Francis. *Agin the Governments: Memories and Adventures.* London: Sampson Low, Marston, n.d. [1929].

Forbes, Archibald. *Memories and Studies of War and Peace.* London: Cassell, 1895.

———. *Souvenirs of Some Continents.* London: Macmillan, 1885.

Forrest, G. W. *Life of Field Marshal Sir Neville Chamberlain.* Edinburgh: William Blackwood & Sons, 1909.

Fortescue-Brickdale, Sir Charles, ed. *Major-General Sir Henry Hallam Parr: Recollections and Correspondence.* London: Fisher-Unwin, 1917.

Frankland, Noble. *Witness of a Century: The Life and Times of Prince Arthur, Duke of Connaught, 1850–1942.* London: Shepheard-Walwyn, 1993.

French, David. *The British Way in Warfare, 1688–2000.* London: Unwin Hyman, 1990.

———. "Colonel Blimp and the British Army: British Divisional Commanders in the War against Germany, 1939–45." *English Historical Review* 111 (1996): 1182–1201.

———. *Military Identities: The Regimental System, the British Army, and the British People, c. 1870–2000.* Oxford: Oxford University Press, 2005.

French, David, and Brian Holden Reid, eds. *The British General Staff: Reform and Innovation, 1890–1939.* London: Frank Cass, 2002.

French, Gerald. *Lord Chelmsford and the Zulu War.* London: The Bodley Head, 1939.

Gallagher, Thomas. "British Military Thinking and the Coming of the Franco-Prussian War." *Military Affairs* 39 (1975): 19–22.

———. "Cardwellian Mysteries: The Fate of the British Army Regulation Bill, 1871." *Historical Journal* 18 (1975): 327–48.

Gann, L. H., and Peter Duignan. *The Rulers of British Africa, 1870–1914.* London: Croom Helm, 1978.

Gatacre, Beatrix. *General Gatacre, 1843–1906.* London: John Murray, 1910.

Gibbs, Norman. *The Origins of Imperial Defence.* Oxford: Oxford University Press, 1955.

Glass, Stafford. *The Matabele War.* London: Longmans, 1968.

Gleichen, Lord Edward. *A Guardsman's Memories.* Edinburgh: William Blackwood & Sons, 1932.

Godwin-Austen, A. R. *The Staff and the Staff College.* London: Constable, 1927.

Goldsbrough, Richard. "Passed over for 'Strong Political Reasons': Sir Frederick Maude and the Politics of Appointment in the Second Afghan War." *Journal of the Society for Army Historical Research* 90 (2012): 151–66.

Gon, Philip. *The Road to Isandlwana: The Years of an Imperial Battalion.* Johannesburg: A. D. Donker, 1979.

———. *Send Carrington! The Story of an Imperial Frontiersman.* Craighall, S.A.: A. D. Donker, 1984.

Gooch, John, ed. *The Boer War: Direction, Experience and Image.* London: Frank Cass, 2000.

———. *The Plans of War: The General Staff and British Military Strategy, c. 1900–16.* London: Routledge & Kegan Paul, 1974.

———. *The Prospect of War: Studies in British Defence Policy, 1847–1942.* London: Frank Cass, 1981.

Gordon, Andrew. *The Rules of the Game: Jutland and British Naval Command.* 2nd ed. London: Penguin Books, 2005.

Gordon, Donald. *The Dominion Partnership in Imperial Defense, 1870–1914*. Baltimore: Johns Hopkins University Press, 1965.

Gordon, M. A. *Letters of General C. G. Gordon to His Sister*. London: Macmillan, 1890.

Gordon, Peter, ed. *The Political Diaries of the Fourth Earl of Carnarvon, 1857–90: Colonial Secretary and Lord Lieutenant of Ireland*. Cambridge: Cambridge University Press for Royal Historical Society, 2009.

Gosling, Edward. "Tommy Atkins, War Office Reform and the Social and Cultural Presence of the Late Victorian Army, c. 1868–99." Ph.D. thesis, University of Plymouth, 2016.

Gosse, Edmund. *Aspects and Impressions*. London: Cassell, 1922.

Gough, Sir Hubert. *Soldiering On*. London: Arthur Barker, 1954.

Gould, Robert Freke. *Military Lodges: The Apron and the Sword*. London: Gale & Polden, 1899.

Greaves, Adrian. "The Curious Case of Major-General C. E. Luard, RE." *Journal of the Anglo-Zulu War Historical Society* 36 (2014): 25–29.

———. *Isandlwana*. London: Cassell, 2001.

———, ed. *Redcoats and Zulus: Myths, Legend and Explanations of the Anglo-Zulu War, 1879*. Barnsley, UK: Pen & Sword, 2004.

———. *Rorke's Drift*. London: Cassell, 2002.

Greaves, Adrian, and Brian Best, eds. *The Curling Letters of the Zulu War: "There Was Awful Slaughter."* Barnsley, UK: Leo Cooper, 2001.

Greaves, Sir George. *Memoirs*. London: John Murray, 1924.

Grenfell, Lord. *Memoirs*. London: Hodder & Stoughton, n.d. [1925].

Gruber, Ira. *Books and the British Army in the Age of the American Revolution*. Chapel Hill: University of North Carolina Press, 2010.

Gupta, Partha Sarathi, and Anirudh Deshpande, eds. *The British Raj and Its Indian Armed Forces, 1857–1939*. New Delhi: Oxford University Press, 2002.

Guy, Alan J., and Peter B. Boyden, eds. *Soldiers of the Raj: The Indian Army, 1600–1947*. London: National Army Museum, 1997.

Hackett, Sir John. *The Profession of Arms*. London: Sidgwick & Jackson, 1983.

Haggard, Andrew. *Under Crescent and Star*. Edinburgh: William Blackwood & Sons, 1895.

Haig, Alan. *The Victorian Clergy*. London: Routledge, 1984.

Hake, A. Egmont, ed. *The Journals of Major-General C. G. Gordon at Kartoum*. London: Kegan Paul, Trench, 1885.

Haldane, Sir Aylmer. *A Soldier's Saga*. Edinburgh: William Blackwood & Sons, 1948.

Hamer, W. S. *The British Army: Civil-Military Relations, 1885–1905*. Oxford: Clarendon Press, 1970.

Hamilton, Ian B. M. *The Happy Warrior: A Life of General Sir Ian Hamilton*. London: Cassell, 1966.

Hamilton, Sir Ian. *Listening for the Drums*. London: Faber & Faber, 1944.

Hamilton-Browne, G. *A Lost Legionary in South Africa*. London: T. Werner Laurie, 1912.

Hamley, Sir Edward. "The Strategical Condition of Our Indian North-West Frontier." *Journal of the Royal United Service Institution* 22 (1878): 1027–46.

Hanna, Henry B. *Lord Roberts in War: A Study for the Day*. London: Simpkin, Marshall, 1895.

———. *The Second Afghan War, 1878–80.* 3 vols. Westminster: Archibald Constable, 1899–1910.

Hardie, Frank. *The Political Influence of Queen Victoria, 1861–1901.* 2nd ed. London: Frank Cass, 1938.

Harding, Marion, ed. *The Victorian Soldier: Studies in the History of the British Army, 1816–1914.* London: National Army Museum, 1993.

Harfield, Alan. *British and Indian Armies in the East Indies, 1685–1935.* Chippenham, UK: Picton, 1984.

———, ed. *The Life and Times of a Victorian Officer: Being the Journals and Letters of Colonel Benjamin Donisthorpe Donne.* Wincanton, UK: Wincanton Press, 1986.

Harries-Jenkins, Gwyn. *The Army in Victorian Society.* London: Routledge & Kegan Paul, 1977.

Harrington, Peter. *British Artists and War: The Face of Battle in Paintings and Prints, 1700–1914.* London: Greenhill Nooks, 1993.

Harris, J. Paul. *Douglas Haig and the First World War.* Cambridge: Cambridge University Press, 2008.

Harris, Stephen. *Canadian Brass: The Making of a Professional Army, 1860–1939.* Toronto: University of Toronto Press, 1988.

Harrison, Frederick. *Martial Law in Kabul.* London: Chapman & Hall, 1880.

Harrison, Sir Richard. *Recollections of a Life in the British Army.* London: Smith, Elder, 1908.

Harvie, Ian. "Gordon, Wolseley and the Road to Khartoum." *Soldiers of the Queen* 141 (2010): 11–21.

———. "The Wolseley Ring: A Case Study in the Exercise of Patronage in the Late Victorian Army." Master's thesis, University of Buckingham, 1993.

Havers, Michael, Edward Grayson, and Peter Shankland. *The Royal Baccarat Scandal.* London: William Kimber, 1977.

Hawkins, Angus, and John Powell, eds. *The Journal of John Wodehouse, First Earl of Kimberley for 1862–1902.* Camden 5th ser., vol. 9. London: Royal Historical Society, 1997.

Haycock, Ronald, and Keith Neilson, eds. *Men, Machines and War.* Waterloo, Ont.: Wilfrid Laurier Press, 1988.

Headrick, Donald. *The Invisible Weapon: Telecommunications and International Politics, 1851–1945.* New York: Oxford University Press, 1991.

———. *The Tentacles of Progress.* New York: Oxford University Press, 1988.

———. *The Tools of Empire.* New York: Oxford University Press, 1981.

———. "The Tools of Imperialism: Technology and the Expansion of European Colonial Empires in the Nineteenth Century." *Journal of Modern History* 51 (1979): 231–63.

Heathcote, T. A. *Balochistan, the British and the Great Game: The Struggle for the Bolan Pass, Gateway to India.* London: Hurst, 2015.

———. *The Indian Army: The Garrison of British Imperial India, 1822–1922.* Newton Abbot, UK: David & Charles, 1974.

———. *The Military in British India: The Development of British Land Forces in South Asia, 1600–1947.* Manchester: Manchester University Press, 1995.

Henderson, Diana. *Highland Soldier, 1820–1920.* Edinburgh: John Donald Publishers, 1989.

Henderson, G. F. R. *The Science of War: A Collection of Essays and Lectures, 1891–1903*. London: Longmans, Green, 1913.

Hevia, James. *The Imperial Security State: British Colonial Knowledge and Empire-Building in Asia*. Cambridge: Cambridge University Press, 2012.

Hichberger, J. W. M. *Images of the Army: The Military in British Art, 1815–1914*. Manchester: Manchester University Press, 1988.

Hicks, Jonathan. "A Solemn Mockery": *The Anglo-Zulu War of 1879—the Myth and the Reality*. Barry, UK: Fielding, 2006.

Hole, Hugh Marshall. *The Jameson Raid*. London: Philip Allan, 1930.

Holland, Bernard. *The Life of Spencer Compton, Eighth Duke of Devonshire*. 2 vols. London: Longmans, Green, 1911.

Holmes, David. "Who Wrote Chard's Reports? A Stylometric Analysis." *Journal of the Anglo-Zulu War Historical Society* 32 (2012): 50–62.

Holmes, David, and Elizabeth Johnson. "A Stylometric Foray into the Anglo-Zulu War of 1879." *English Studies* 93 (2012): 310–23.

Holmes, Richard. *The Little Field Marshal: Sir John French*. London: Cape, 1981.

Hopkins, A. G. "The Victorians and Africa: A Reconsideration of the Occupation of Egypt, 1882." *Journal of African History* 27 (1986): 363–91.

Hoskyns, C. "A Short Narrative of the Afghan Campaigns of 1879–80–81 from an Engineer's Point of View." *Journal of the Royal United Service Institution* 26 (1882): 431–55.

Howard, Sir Francis. *Reminiscences, 1848–90*. London: John Murray, 1924.

Huffer, Donald. "The Infantry Officers of the Line of the British Army, 1815–68." Ph.D. thesis, University of Birmingham, 1995.

Hummel, Chris, ed. *The Frontier War Journal of Major John Crealock, 1878*. Cape Town: Van Riebeeck Society, 1989.

Hunter, Archie. *Kitchener's Sword-arm: The Life and Campaigns of General Sir Archibald Hunter*. Staplehurst, UK: Spellmount, 1996.

Huntington, Samuel. *The Soldier and the State: The Theory and Politics of Civil-Military Relations*. New York: Belknap Press, 1957.

Hussey, John. "'A Very Substantial Grievance,' Said the Secretary of State: Douglas Haig's Examination Troubles, 1893." *Journal of the Society for Army Historical Research* 74 (1996): 169–80.

Hyam, Ronald. *Britain's Imperial Century, 1815–1914: A Study of Empire and Expansion*. London: Batsford, 1976.

Intelligence Branch, India. *Frontiers and Overseas Expeditions from India*. 6 vols. Kolkata: Superintendent of Government Printing, 1907–10.

Jackson, F. W. D. *Hill of the Sphinx: The Battle of Isandlwana*. London: Westerners Publications, 2002.

———. "Isandhlwana, 1879: The Sources Re-examined." *Journal of the Society for Army Historical Research* 43 (1965): 30–43, 113–32, 169–83.

Jackson, Sir Louis. *History of the United Service Club*. London: United Service Club, 1937.

James, Alan G. *The Master, the Modern Major-General and His Clever Wife: Henry James's Letters to Field Marshal Lord Wolseley and Lady Wolseley, 1878–1913*. Charlottesville: University of Virginia Press, 2012.

James, David. *The Life of Lord Roberts*. London: Hollis & Carter, 1954.

Janowitz, Morris. *The Professional Soldier: A Social and Political Portrait.* New York: Free Press, 1960.

Jeal, Tim. *Baden-Powell.* 2nd ed. New Haven, Conn.: Yale Nota Bene, 2001.

Jeffery, Keith. "The Eastern Arc of Empire: A Strategic View, 1850–1950." *Journal of Strategic Studies* 5 (1982): 531–45.

———. *Field Marshal Sir Henry Wilson: A Political Soldier.* Oxford: Oxford University Press, 2006.

Jenson, J. Vernon. "The X Club: Fraternity of Victorian Scientists." *British Journal for the History of Science* 5 (1970): 63–72.

Johnson, Douglas. "The Death of Gordon: A Victorian Myth." *Journal of Imperial and Commonwealth History* 10 (1982): 285–310.

Johnson, Franklyn. *Defence by Committee: The British Committee of Imperial Defence, 1885–1959.* London: Oxford University Press, 1960.

Johnson, Nancy E., ed. *The Diary of Gathorne Hardy, Later Lord Cranbrook, 1866–92: Political Selections.* Oxford: Clarendon Press, 1981.

Johnson, Robert. *The Afghan Way of War: Culture and Pragmatism—a Critical History.* London: Hurst, 2011.

———. "General Roberts, the Occupation of Kabul, and the Problems of Transition, 1879–80." *War in History* 20 (2013): 300–22.

———. "The Penjdeh Crisis and Its Impact on the Defence of India, 1885–97." Ph.D. thesis, University of Exeter, 1999.

———. "The Penjdeh Incident." *Archives* 24 (1999): 28–48.

———. "'The Russians at the Gates'? Planning the Defence of India, 1885–1900." *Journal of Military History* 67 (2003): 697–744.

———. *Spying for Empire: The Great Game in Central and South Asia, 1757–1947.* London: Greenhill Books, 2006.

Jones, Huw. *The Boiling Cauldron: Utrecht District and the Anglo-Zulu War, 1879.* Bisley, UK: Shermershill Press, 2006.

Jones, Spencer. *From Boer War to World War: Tactical Reform of the British Army, 1902–14.* Norman: University of Oklahoma Press, 2012.

Judd, Denis, and Keith Surridge. *The Boer War.* London: John Murray, 2002.

Keen, Caroline. *An Imperial Crisis in British India: The Manipur Uprising of 1891.* London: I. B. Tauris, 2015.

Kelly, Ian. *Echoes of Success: Identity and the Highland Regiments.* Leiden: Brill, 2015.

Kennedy, Greg, ed. *Imperial Defence: The Old World Order, 1856–1956.* Abingdon, UK: Routledge, 2008.

Keown-Boyd, Henry. *A Good Dusting: The Sudan Campaigns, 1883–99.* London: Leo Cooper with Secker & Warburg, 1986.

———. *Soldiers of the Nile: A Biographical History of the British Officers of the Egyptian Army, 1882–1925.* Thornbury, UK: Thornbury Publications, 1996.

Keppel-Jones, Arthur. *Rhodes and Rhodesia: The White Conquest of Zimbabwe, 1884–1902.* Kingston: McGill-Queen's University Press, 1983.

Kerry, Simon. "Lord Lansdowne at the War Office, 1895–1900." Ph.D. thesis, University of East Anglia, 2015.

Kiewiet, C. W. de, and F. H. Underhill, eds. *Dufferin-Carnarvon Correspondence, 1874–78.* Champlain Society No. 33. Toronto, 1995.

Knight, Ian. *Zulu: Isandlwana and Rorke's Drift, 22–23 January 1879.* London: Windrow & Greene, 1992.

———. *Zulu Rising*. London: Macmillan, 2010.

Kochanski, Halik. "Field Marshal Viscount Wolseley: A Reformer at the War Office, 1871–1900." Ph.D. thesis, University of London, 1996.

———. "Field Marshal Viscount Wolseley as Commander-in-Chief, 1895–1900: A Reassessment." *Journal of Strategic Studies* 20 (1997): 119–39.

———. *Sir Garnet Wolseley: Victorian Hero*. London: Hambledon Press, 1999.

Kourvetaris, Yorgos, and Betty Dobratz. *Social Origins and Political Orientation of Officer Corps in a World Perspective*. Denver, Colo.: University of Denver Press, 1973.

Laband, John, ed. *Companion to the Narrative of the Field Operations Connected with the Zulu War of 1879*. Constantia, S.A.: N & S Press, 1989.

———. "The Danger of Divided Command: British Civil and Military Disputes over the Conduct of the Zululand Campaigns of 1879 and 1888." *Journal of the Society for Army Historical Research* 81 (2003): 339–55.

———. *Kingdom in Crisis: The Zulu Response to the British Invasion of 1879*. Manchester: Manchester University Press, 1992.

———, ed. *Lord Chelmsford's Zululand Campaign, 1878–79*. Stroud, UK: Sutton Publishing for the Army Records Society, 1994.

———. *The Transvaal Rebellion: The First Boer War, 1880–81*. Harlow, UK: Pearson Education, 2005.

———. *Zulu Warriors: The Battle for the South African Frontier*. New Haven, Conn.: Yale University Press, 2014.

Laband, John, and Paul Thompson, eds. *Kingdom and Colony at War*. Pietermaritzburg, S.A.: University of Natal Press, 1990.

Lacey, Nicola. "The Way We Lived Then: The Legal Profession and the Nineteenth-Century Novel." *Sydney Law Review* 33 (2010): 599–621.

Lane-Poole, Stanley. *Watson Pasha: A Record of the Life-Work of Sir Charles Moore Watson*. London: John Murray, 1919.

Lankford, Nelson. "The Victorian Medical Profession and Military Practice: Army Doctors and National Origins." *Bulletin of the History of Medicine* 54 (1980): 511–28.

Larson, Magali Sarfatti. *The Rise of Professionalism: A Sociological Analysis*. Berkeley: University of California Press, 1977.

Leask, G. A. *Sir William Robertson*. London: Cassell, 1917.

Lee, Celia. *A Soldier's Wife: Jean, Lady Hamilton, 1861–1941*. London: Privately published, 2001.

Lee, John. *A Soldier's Life: General Sir Ian Hamilton, 1853–1947*. London: Macmillan, 2000.

Leeson, D. M. "Playing at War: The British Military Manoeuvres of 1898." *War in History* 15 (2008): 432–61.

Lehmann, Joseph. *All Sir Garnet: A Life of Field Marshal Lord Wolseley, 1833–1913*. London: Jonathan Cape, 1964.

———. *The First Boer War*. London: Jonathan Cape, 1972.

Lieven, Michael. "'Butchering the Brutes All over the Place': Total War and Massacre in Zululand, 1879." *History* 84 (1999): 614–32.

———. "Heroism, Heroics and the Making of Heroes: The Anglo-Zulu War of 1879." *Albion* 30 (1998): 419–38.

———. "A Victorian Genre: Military Memoirs and the Anglo-Zulu War." *Journal of the Society for Army Historical Research* 77 (1999): 106–21.

Lock, Ron. *Blood on the Painted Mountain: Zulu Victory and Defeat—Hlobane and Kambula, 1879*. London: Greenhill Books, 1995.

———. *Hill of Squandered Valour: The Battle for Spion Kop, 1900*. Newbury, UK: Casemate Publishers, 2011.

Lock, Ron, and Peter Quantrill. *Zulu Victory: The Epic of Isandlwana and the Cover-Up*. London: Greenhill Books, 2002.

Low, Charles Rathbone. *General Lord Wolseley of Cairo: A Memoir*. 2nd ed. London: Richard Bentley & Son, 1883.

Lowry, Donal, ed. *The South African War Reappraised*. Manchester: Manchester University Press, 2000.

Luvaas, Jay. *The Education of an Army: British Military Thought, 1815–1940*. Chicago: University of Chicago Press, 1964.

Lyttelton, Sir Neville. *Eighty Years: Soldiering, Politics, Games*. London: Hodder & Stoughton, n.d. [1927].

Macdiarmid, D. S. *The Life of Lieutenant-General Sir James Moncrieff Grierson*. London: Constable, 1923.

MacGregor, Lady Charlotte. *The Life and Opinions of Major-General Sir Charles Metcalfe MacGregor*. 2 vols. Edinburgh: William Blackwood & Sons, 1888.

Mackenzie, John, ed. *Imperialism and Popular Culture*. Manchester: Manchester University Press, 1986.

———, ed. *Popular Imperialism and the Military, 1850–1950*. Manchester: Manchester University Press, 1992.

———. *Propaganda and Empire: The Manipulation of British Public Opinion, 1880–1960*. Manchester: Manchester University Press, 1984.

Mackinnon, J. P., and S. H. Shadbolt. *The South African Campaign, 1879*. London: Sampson Low, Marston, Searle & Rivington, 1880.

Macleod Innes, J. *The Life and Times of General Sir James Browne, Buster Browne*. London: John Murray, 1905.

MacMunn, Sir George. *Behind the Scenes in Many Wars*. London: John Murray, 1930.

———. *The Romance of the Indian Frontiers*. London: Jonathan Cape, 1931.

———. *Vignettes from Indian Wars*. London: Sampson Low, Marston, n.d. [1932].

Macready, Sir Nevil. *Annals of an Active Life*. 2 vols. London: Hutchinson, 1924.

Magnus, Philip. *Kitchener: Portrait of an Imperialist*. 2nd ed. Harmondsworth, UK: Penguin, 1968.

Mahaffey, Corinne. "The Fighting Profession: The Professionalisation of the British Line Officer Corps, 1870–1902." Ph.D. thesis, University of Glasgow, 2004.

Mahajan, Sneh. *British Foreign Policy, 1874–1914: The Role of India*. London: Routledge, 2002.

———. "The Defence of India and the End of Isolation: A Study in the Foreign Policy of the Conservative Government, 1900–05." *Journal of Imperial and Commonwealth History* 10 (1982): 168–93.

Male, Rev. Arthur. *Scenes through the Battle Smoke*. London: Charles H. Kelly, 1901.

Malmesbury, Susan, Countess of. *The Life of Major-General Sir John Ardagh*. London: John Murray, 1909.

Manning, Stephen. *Evelyn Wood VC: Pillar of Empire*. Barnsley, UK: Pen & Sword, 2007.

———. "Foreign News Gathering and Reporting in the London and Devon Press—the Anglo-Zulu War, 1879: A Case Study." Ph.D. thesis, University of Exeter, 2005.

Mansel, Philip. *Pillars of Monarchy: An Outline of the Political and Social History of Royal Guards, 1400–1984*. London: Quartet Books, 1984.

Marder, Arthur. *From the Dreadnought to Scapa Flow: The Royal Navy in the Fisher Era, 1904–19*. 5 vols. Oxford: Oxford University Press, 1961–78.

Marling, Sir Percy. *Rifleman and Hussar: An Autobiography*. London: John Murray, 1931.

Matthew, H. C. G. *Gladstone, 1875–98*. Oxford: Clarendon Press, 1995.

Maurice, Sir Frederick. *The Life of General Lord Rawlinson of Trent*. London: Cassell, 1928.

———. *Sir Frederick Maurice: A Record of His Work and Opinions*. London: Edward Arnold, 1913.

Maurice, Sir Frederick, and Sir George Arthur. *The Life of Lord Wolseley*. London: William Heinemann, 1924.

Maurice, J. F. *Military History of the Campaign of 1882 in Egypt*. London: War Office, 1887.

Maurice, Sir J. F., and M. H. Grant. *History of the War in South Africa*. 4 vols. London: Hurst & Blackett, 1906–10.

Maxse, F. I. *Seymour Vandeleur: The Story of a British Officer*. London: William Heinemann, 1906.

Maxwell, Leigh. *My God—Maiwand! Operations of the South Afghanistan Field Force, 1878–80*. London: Leo Cooper, 1979.

May, Sir Edward. *Changes and Chances of a Soldier's Life*. London: Philip Allan, 1925.

McClintock, Mary Howard. *The Queen Thanks Sir Howard: The Life of Major-General Sir Howard Elphinstone*. London: John Murray, 1945.

McCourt, Edward. *Remember Butler: The Story of Sir William Butler*. London: Routledge & Kegan Paul, 1967.

McIntyre, W. David. "British Policy in West Africa: The Ashanti Expedition of 1873–74." *Historical Journal* 5 (1962): 19–46.

———. *The Imperial Frontier in the Tropics, 1865–75*. London: Macmillan, 1967.

Meadows, Jack. *The Victorian Scientist: The Growth of a Profession*. London: British Library, 2004.

Meinertzhagen, Richard. *Army Diary, 1899–1926*. Edinburgh: Oliver & Boyd, 1960.

Melville, C. H. *The Life of General the Rt. Hon. Sir Redvers Buller*. 2 vols. London: Edward Arnold, 1923.

Menzies, Mrs. Stuart. *Lord William Beresford VC: Some Memories*. New York: Brentano's, 1917.

Meriwether, Jeffrey. "The Intricacies of War Office Administration: Civilians, Soldiers and the Opening of the South African War, October–December 1899." *Archives* 28 (2003): 48–68.

———. "Procrastination or Pragmatism? British Defence Policy, War Office Administration and the South African War, 1898–1903." Ph.D. thesis, University of Exeter, 2001.

Midleton, Earl of. *Records and Reactions*. London: John Murray, 1939.

Miller, Stephen. *Lord Methuen and the British Army: Failure and Redemption in South Africa*. London: Frank Cass, 1999.

———, ed. *Soldiers and Settlers in Africa, 1850–1918.* Leiden: Brill, 2009.

Milne-Smith, Amy. "Club Talk: Gossip, Masculinity and Oral Communities in Late-Nineteenth-Century London." *Gender and History* 21 (2009): 86–106.

———. "A Flight to Domesticity? Making a Home in the Gentlemen's Clubs of London, 1880–1914." *Journal of British Studies* 45 (2006): 796–818.

Milton, John. *The Edges of War.* Cape Town: Juta, 1983.

Mingay, G. E., ed. *The Victorian Countryside.* 2 vols. London: Routledge & Kegan Paul, 1981.

Mitcham, John. *Race and Imperial Defence in the British World, 1870–1914.* Cambridge: Cambridge University Press, 2016.

Moncrieff, Sir George Scott. *Canals and Campaigns: An Engineer Officer in India, 1877–85.* London: British Association for Cemeteries in South Asia, 1987.

Moneypenny, William, and George Buckle, eds. *The Life of Benjamin Disraeli, Earl of Beaconsfield.* 6 vols. New York: Macmillan, 1920.

Moon, Howard. "The Invasion of the UK: Public Controversy and Official Planning, 1888–1918." Ph.D. thesis. 2 vols. University of London, 1968.

Moreman, Tim. *The Army in India and the Development of Frontier Warfare, 1849–1947.* Basingstoke, UK: Palgrave, 1996.

———. "The British and Indian Armies and North-West Frontier Warfare, 1849–1914." *Journal of Imperial and Commonwealth History* 20 (1991): 35–64.

Morgan, H. J. "The Social and Educational Background of Anglican Bishops: Continuities and Changes." *British Journal of Sociology* 20 (1969): 295–310.

Morgan, Kenneth. "The Boer War and the Media." *Twentieth Century British History* 13 (2002): 1–16.

Morton, Desmond. *Ministers and Generals: Politics and the Canadian Militia, 1868–1904.* Toronto: University of Toronto Press, 1970.

Muenger, Elizabeth. *The British Military Dilemma in Ireland: Occupation Politics, 1886–1914.* Lawrence: University Press of Kansas, 1991.

Napier, H. D. *Field Marshal Lord Napier of Magdala.* London: Edward Arnold, 1927.

———, ed. *Letters of Field Marshal Lord Napier of Magdala.* Norwich, UK: Jarrold & Sons, 1936.

Nasson, Bill. *The South African War, 1899–1902.* London: Arnold, 1999.

Nevill, H. L. *Campaigns on the North-West Frontier.* London: John Murray, 1912.

Nicoll, Fergus. *Gladstone, Gordon and the Sudan Wars: The Battle over Imperial Intervention in the Victorian Age.* Barnsley, UK: Pen & Sword, 2013.

———. *The Sword of the Prophet: The Mahdi of Sudan and the Death of General Gordon.* Stroud, UK: Sutton Publishing, 2004.

Omissi, David. *The Sepoy and the Raj: The Indian Army, 1860–1940.* Basingstoke, UK: Macmillan, 1994.

Omissi, David, and Andrew Thompson, eds. *The Impact of the South African War.* Basingstoke, UK: Palgrave, 2002.

Omond, John. *Parliament and the Army, 1642–1904.* Cambridge: Cambridge University Press, 1933.

Otley, C. B. "The Educational Background of British Army Officers." *Sociology* 7 (1973): 191–209.

———. "The Social Origins of British Army Officers." *Sociological Review* 18 (1970): 213–40.

Pakenham, Elizabeth. *Jameson's Raid*. London: Weidenfeld & Nicolson, 1960.

Pakenham, Thomas. *The Boer War*. London: Weidenfeld & Nicolson, 1979.

Paris, Michael. *Warrior Nation: Images of War in British Popular Culture, 1850–2000*. London: Reaktion Books, 2000.

Payne, David, Emma Payne, and Adrian Greaves, eds. *Harford: The Writings, Photographs and Sketches of Henry Harford, 1850–1937.* London: Ultimatum Tree, 2008.

Peck, John. *War, the Army and Victorian Literature*. Basingstoke, UK: Macmillan, 1998.

Pegram, Marjory. *The Wolseley Heritage: The Story of Frances, Viscountess Wolseley and Her Parents*. London: John Murray, 1939.

Perkin, Harold. *The Origins of Modern English Society, 1780–1880*. London: Routledge & Kegan Paul, 1969.

———. *The Rise of Professional Society: England since 1890*. London: Routledge, 1989.

Perlmutter, Amos. *The Military and Politics in Modern Times: On Professionals, Praetorians and Revolutionary Soldiers*. New Haven, Conn.: Yale University Press, 1977.

Perry, Nicholas. "The Irish Landed Class and the British Army, 1850–1950." *War in History* 18 (2011): 304–32.

Petersen, M. Jeanne. *The Medical Profession in Mid-Victorian London*. Berkeley: University of California Press, 1978.

Pionke, Albert. *The Ritual Culture of Victorian Professionals*. Farnham, UK: Ashgate, 2013.

Pollock, John. *Gordon: The Man behind the Legend*. 2nd ed. Oxford: Lion, 1995.

———. *Kitchener: The Road to Omdurman*. London: Constable, 1998.

Ponsonby, Arthur. *Henry Ponsonby: Queen Victoria's Private Secretary*. London: Macmillan, 1943.

Porter, Andrew. *The Origins of the South African War: Joseph Chamberlain and the Diplomacy of Imperialism, 1895–99*. Manchester: Manchester University Press, 1980.

———, ed. *The Oxford History of the British Empire*. Vol. 3, *The Nineteenth Century*. Oxford: Oxford University Press, 1999.

———. "Sir Alfred Milner and the Press, 1897–9." *Historical Journal* 16 (1973): 323–39.

Porter, Bernard. *The Absent-Minded Imperialists: Empire, Society, and Culture in Britain*. Oxford: Oxford University Press, 2005.

Porter, Dale. *The Thames Embankment: Environment, Technology and Society in Victorian London*. Akron, Ohio: University of Akron Press, 1998.

Porter, Dale H., and G. C. Clifton. "Patronage, Professional Values and Victorian Public Works: Engineering and Contracting the Thames Embankment." *Victorian Studies* 31 (1988): 319–49.

Potgeiter, T. D. "Nineteenth-Century Technological Development and Its Influence on the Anglo-Boer War, 1899–1902." *Joernal vir Eletydse Geskiedenis* 25 (2000): 116–35.

Powell, Geoffrey. *Buller: A Scapegoat? A Life of General Sir Redvers Buller VC, 1839–1908*. London: Leo Cooper, 1994.

Prest, Wilfrid, ed. *The Professions in Early Modern England*. London: Croom Helm, 1987.

Preston, Adrian. "British Military Policy and the Defence of India: A Study of British Military Policy, Plans and Preparations during the Russian Crisis, 1876–80." Ph.D. thesis, University of London, 1966.

————. "British Military Thought, 1856–90." *Army Quarterly* 88 (1964): 57–74.

————. "The Eastern Question in British Strategic Policy during the Franco-Prussian War." *Canadian Historical Association Historical Papers* (1972): 55–88.

————. "Frustrated Great Gamesmanship: Sir Garnet Wolseley's Plans for War against Russia, 1873–80." *International History Review* 2 (1980): 239–65.

————, ed. *In Relief of Gordon: Lord Wolseley's Campaign Journal of the Khartoum Relief Expedition, 1884–85.* London: Hutchinson, 1967.

————. "Sir Charles MacGregor and the Defence of India, 1857–87." *Historical Journal* 12 (1969): 58–77.

————. "Sir Garnet Wolseley and the Cyprus Expedition, 1878." *Journal of the Society for Army Historical Research* 45 (1967): 4–16.

————, ed. *Sir Garnet Wolseley's South African Diaries (Natal) 1875.* Cape Town: A. A. Balkema, 1971.

————, ed. *Sir Garnet Wolseley's South African Journal, 1879–80.* Cape Town: A. A. Balkema, 1973.

Preston, Adrian, and Peter Dennis, eds. *Swords and Covenants.* London: Croom Helm, 1976.

Preston, Richard. *Canada and Imperial Defence: A Study of the Origins of the British Commonwealth's Defence Organisation, 1867–1919.* Durham, N.C.: Duke University Press, 1967.

Prochaska, Frank. *Women and Philanthropy in Nineteenth-Century England.* Oxford: Oxford University Press, 1980.

Rait, Robert. *The Life of Field Marshal Sir Frederick Paul Haines.* London: Constable, 1911.

Razzell, P. E. "Social Origins of Officers in the Indian and British Home Armies, 1758–1962." *British Journal of Sociology* 14 (1963): 248–61.

Reader, W. J. *Professional Men: The Rise of the Professional Classes in Nineteenth-Century England.* London: Weidenfeld & Nicolson, 1966.

Repington, Charles. *Vestigia.* London: Constable, 1919.

Rettig, Tobias, and Karl Hack, eds. *Colonial Armies in Southeast Asia.* London: Routledge, 2009.

Riedl, Eliza. "Brains or Polo? Equestrian Sport, Army Reform and the Gentlemanly Officer Tradition, 1900–14." *Journal of the Society for Army Historical Research* 84 (2006): 236–53.

Roberts, Lord. *Forty-one Years in India.* 30th ed. London: Macmillan, 1898.

Robertson, Sir William. *From Private to Field Marshal.* London: Constable, 1921.

Robins, Simon. *British Generalship on the Western Front, 1914–18: Defeat into Victory.* London: Frank Cass, 2005.

Robinson, Charles. *Celebrities of the Army.* London: George Newnes, 1900.

Robinson, Ronald, John Gallagher, and Alice Denny. *Africa and the Victorians: The Official Mind of Imperialism.* 2nd ed. London: Macmillan, 1967.

Robson, Brian. "Buller at Suakin in 1884." *Soldiers of the Queen* 75 (1993): 1–7.

————. "The Eden Commission and the Reform of the Indian Army, 1879–95." *Journal of the Society for Army Historical Research* 60 (1982): 4–13.

————. *Fuzzy Wuzzy: The Campaigns in the Eastern Sudan, 1884–85.* Tunbridge Wells, UK: Spellmount, 1993.

————. "The Kandahar Letters of the Rev. Alfred Cane." *Journal of the Society for Army Historical Research* 69 (1991): 146–60, 206–20.

——. "Maiwand, 27 July 1880." *Journal of the Society for Army Historical Research* 51 (1973): 194–223.

——. "Mounting an Expedition: Sir Gerald Graham's 1885 Expedition to Suakin." *Small Wars and Insurgencies* 2 (1991): 232–39.

——. *The Road to Kabul: The Second Afghan War, 1878–81.* London: Arms and Armour Press, 1986.

——, ed. *Roberts in India: The Military Papers of Field Marshal Lord Roberts, 1876–93.* Stroud, UK: Sutton Publishing for the Army Records Society, 1993.

——. "The Strange Case of the Missing Official History." *Soldiers of the Queen* 76 (1984): 3–6.

Roper, Michael. *The Records of the War Office and Related Departments, 1660–1964.* Kew, UK: Public Record Office, 1998.

[Rothwell, J. S.] *Narrative of the Field Operations Connected with the Zulu War of 1879.* London: War Office Intelligence Branch, 1881.

Rowe, David, David Bearce, and Patrick McDonald. "Binding Prometheus: How the Nineteenth-Century Expansion of Trade Impeded Britain's Ability to Raise an Army." *International Studies Quarterly* 46 (2002): 551–78.

Roy, Kaushik, ed. *War and Society in Colonial India, 1807–1945.* New Delhi: Oxford University Press, 2006.

Royle, Trevor. *Fighting Mac: The Downfall of Major-General Sir Hector Macdonald.* 2nd ed. Edinburgh: Mainstream, 2003.

Rubin, G. R. "Parliament, Prerogative and Military Law: Who Had Legal Authority over the Army in the Late Nineteenth Century?" *Journal of Legal History* 18 (1997): 45–84.

Ryan, Martin. *William Francis Butler: A Life, 1838–1910.* Dublin: Lilliput Press, 2003.

St. Aubyn, Giles. *The Royal George: The Life of Prince George, Duke of Cambridge, 1819–1904.* London: Constable, 1963.

St. John, Ian. "Queen Victoria as a Politician." *Historian* 80 (2003): 24–31.

Satre, L. J. "St. John Brodrick and Army Reform, 1901–03." *Journal of British Studies* 15 (1976): 117–39.

Scott, Douglas, ed. *The Preparatory Prologue: Douglas Haig Diaries & Letters, 1861–1914.* Barnsley, UK: Pen & Sword, 2006.

Sebé, Berny. *Heroic Imperialists in Africa: The Promotion of British and French Colonial Heroes, 1870–1939.* Manchester: Manchester University Press, 2013.

Shadbolt, S. H. *The Afghan Campaigns of 1878–80.* 2 vols. London: Sampson Low, Marston, Searle & Rivington, 1882.

Shand, Alexander Innes. *The Life of General Sir Edward Bruce Hamley.* 2 vols. Edinburgh: William Blackwood & Sons, 1895.

Sheffield, Gary, ed. *Leadership and Command: The Anglo-American Military Experience since 1861.* London: Brassey's, 1997.

Shelley, Henry. *Colvile's Case: A Statement of Facts.* London: W. Tarrant, 1901.

Sherson, Erroll. *Townshend of Chitral and Kut.* London: William Heinemann, 1928.

Simon, Brian, and Ian Bradley, eds. *The Victorian Public School.* Dublin: Gill & Macmillan, 1975.

Sinclair, Hugh. *Camp and Society.* London: Chapman & Hall, 1926.

Skelley, Alan Ramsay. *The Victorian Army at Home: The Recruitment and Terms and Conditions of the British Regular, 1859–99.* London: Croom Helm, 1977.

Smith, Iain. *The Origins of the South African War, 1899–1902*. London: Longman, 1996.

Smith, Keith, ed. *Select Documents: A Zulu War Sourcebook*. Doncaster, UK: D. P. & G. Military Publishers, 2006.

———. *Studies in the Anglo-Zulu War*. Doncaster, UK: D. P. & G. Military Publishers, 2008.

———. *The Wedding Feast War: The Final Tragedy of the Xhosa People*. London: Frontline Books, 2012.

Smith, Martin. *General Sir William Lockhart: Soldier of the Queen Empress*. Privately published, 2011.

Smith, Melvin C. *Awarded for Valour: A History of the Victoria Cross and the Evolution of British Heroism*. Basingstoke, UK: Palgrave Macmillan, 2008.

Smith, Paul, ed. *Government and the Armed Forces in Britain, 1856–1990*. London: Hambledon Press, 1996.

Smith-Dorrien, Sir Horace. *Memories of Forty-eight Years' Service*. London: John Murray, 1925.

Smithers, A. J. *Honourable Conquests: An Account of the Enduring Work of the Royal Engineers throughout the Empire*. London: Leo Cooper, 1991.

Snook, Mike. *Beyond the Reach of Empire: Wolseley's Failed Campaign to Save Gordon and Khartoum*. London: Frontline Books, 2013.

———. *Go Strong into the Desert: The Mahdist Uprising in the Sudan, 1881–85*. Nottingham, UK: Perry Miniatures, 2010.

Spender, J. A. *Life of the Rt. Hon. Sir Henry Campbell-Bannerman*. 2 vols. London: Hodder & Stoughton, 1923.

Spiers, Edward. *The Army and Society, 1815–1914*. London: Longman, 1980.

———. *Engines for Empire: The Victorian Army and Its Use of Railways*. Manchester: Manchester University Press, 2015.

———. "Intelligence and Command in Britain's Small Colonial Wars of the 1890s." *Intelligence and National Security* 22 (2007): 661–81.

———. *The Late Victorian Army, 1868–1902*. Manchester: Manchester University Press, 1992.

———. "The Learning Curve in the South African War: Solders' Perspectives." *Historia* 55 (2010): 1–17.

———, ed. *Letters from Kimberley: Eyewitness Accounts from the South African War*. London: Frontline Books, 2013.

———, ed. *Letters from Ladysmith: Eyewitness Accounts from the South African War*. London: Frontline Books, 2010.

———. "Military Correspondence in the Late-Nineteenth-Century Press." *Archives* 32 (2007): 28–40.

———. *The Scottish Soldier and Empire, 1854–1902*. Edinburgh: Edinburgh University Press, 2006.

———, ed. *Sudan: The Reconquest Reappraised*. London: Frank Cass, 1998.

———. *The Victorian Soldier in Africa*. Manchester: Manchester University Press, 2004.

———. *Wars of Intervention: A Case Study—the Reconquest of the Sudan, 1896–99*. Occasional Papers 32. Shrivenham, UK: Strategic & Combat Studies Institute, 1998.

Spiers, Edward, Jeremy Crang, and Mathew Strickland, eds. *A Military History of Scotland*. Edinburgh: Edinburgh University Press, 2012.

Spies, S. B. *Methods of Barbarism? Roberts and Kitchener and Civilians in the Boer Republics, January 1900–May 1902.* Cape Town: Human & Rousseau, 1977.

Spottiswoode, Robert. *Reminiscences.* Edinburgh: Edinburgh Press, 1935.

Stacpoole-Ryding, Richard. *Maiwand: The Last Stand of the 66th (Berkshire) Regiment in Afghanistan, 1880.* Stroud, UK: History Press, 2008.

Stanley, Peter, ed. *But Little Glory: The New South Wales Contingent to the Sudan, 1885.* Canberra: Military Historical Society of Australia, 1985.

———. *White Mutiny: British Military Culture in India, 1825–75.* London: Hurst, 1998.

Stannus, H. J. *My Reasons for Leaving the British Army.* London: William Ridgway, 1881.

Stearn, Roger. "Archibald Forbes and the British Army." *Soldiers of the Queen* 61 (1990): 7–9.

———. "Bennett Burleigh: Victorian War Correspondent." *Soldiers of the Queen* 65 (1991): 5–10.

———. "The British Clausewitz? Spenser Wilkinson and His Message." *Soldiers of the Queen* 148 (2012): 3–9.

———. "Ernest Bennett and War." *Soldiers of the Queen* 105 (2001): 16–24.

———. "G. W. Steevens and the Message of Empire." *Journal of Imperial and Commonwealth History* 17 (1989): 210–31.

———. "War Images and Image Makers in the Victorian Era: Aspects of the British Visual and Written Portrayal of War, c. 1866–1906." Ph.D. thesis, University of London, 1987.

Steevens, G. W. *With Kitchener to Khartoum.* London: Thomas Nelson & Sons, n.d. [1898].

Stephenson, Sir Frederick. *At Home and on the Battlefield: Letters from the Crimea, China and Egypt, 1854–88.* Edited by Mrs. Frank Pownall. London: John Murray, 1915.

Stewart, A. T. Q. *The Pagoda War: Lord Dufferin and the Fall of the Kingdom of Ava, 1885–86.* London: Faber & Faber, 1972.

Stewart, Sir Norman. *My Service Days.* London: John Ouseley, 1908.

Stigger, Philip. "Promotion as a Campaigning Reward in the Victorian Army and an Unresolved Problem." *Journal of the Society for Army Historical Research* 76 (1998): 255–59.

Stockings, Craig. *Britannia's Shield: Lieutenant-General Sir Edward Hutton and Late-Victorian Imperial Defence.* Port Melbourne, Vic.: Cambridge University Press, 2015.

Stone, Jay, and Erwin Schmidl. *The Boer War and Military Reforms.* Lanham, Md.: University Press of America, 1988.

Strachan, Hew, ed. *Big Wars and Small Wars: The British Army and the Lessons of War in the Twentieth Century.* London: Routledge, 2006.

———. "The Early Victorian Army and the Nineteenth-Century Revolution in Government." *English Historical Review* 95 (1980): 782–809.

———. *The Politics of the British Army.* Oxford: Clarendon Press, 1997.

———. *Wellington's Legacy: The Reform of the British Army, 1830–54.* Manchester: Manchester University Press, 1984.

Street, Patrick, and John Tamplin. "War Correspondents in South Africa, 1899–1902." *Journal of the Orders and Medals Research Society* (Summer 1986): 96–102.

Streets, Heather. "Military Influence in Late Victorian and Edwardian Popular Media: The Case of Frederick Roberts." *Journal of Victorian Culture* 8 (2010): 231–56.

———. *Martial Races: The Military, Race and Masculinity in British Imperial Culture, 1857–1914.* Manchester: Manchester University Press, 2004.

Surridge, Keith. "'All You Soldiers Are What We Call Pro-Boer': The Military Critique of the South African War, 1899–1902." *History* 82 (1997): 582–600.

———. "The Ambiguous Amir: Britain, Afghanistan and the 1897 North-West Frontier Uprising." *Journal of Imperial and Commonwealth History* 36 (2008): 417–34.

———. "'The Honour and Reputation of the Army': Lord Roberts, the Government and the Fight at Nicholson's Nek." *Soldiers of the Queen* 93 (1998): 12–14.

———. "Lord Kitchener and the South African War, 1899–1902." *Soldiers of the Queen* 101 (2000): 19–25.

———. *Managing the South African War, 1899–1902: Politicians versus Generals.* Woodbridge, UK: Boydell Press for Royal Historical Society, 1998.

———. "More than a Great Poster: Lord Kitchener and the Image of the Military Hero." *Historical Research* 74 (2001): 298–313.

———. "Rebellion, Martial Law and British Civil-Military Relations: The War in Cape Colony, 1899–1902." *Small Wars and Insurgencies* 8 (1997): 35–60.

Sydenham, Lord. *My Working Life.* London: John Murray, 1927.

Symons, Julian. *Buller's Campaign.* London: Cresset Press, 1963.

———. *England's Pride: The Story of the Gordon Relief Expedition.* London: Hamish Hamilton, 1965.

Talbot Rice, Elizabeth, and Marion Harding, eds. *Butterflies and Bayonets: The Soldier as Collector.* London: National Army Museum, 1989.

Temple, Arthur. *Our Living Generals.* 3rd ed. London: Andrew Melrose, 1900.

Thomas, J. B. "Sir Redvers Buller in the Post-Cardwellian Army: A Study of the Rise and Fall of a Military Reputation." Ph.D. diss., Texas A & M University, 1993.

Thompson, Andrew. *Imperial Britain: The Empire in British Politics, c. 1880–1932.* Harlow, UK: Pearson Education, 2000.

Thornton, A. P. *For the File on Empire: Essays and Reviews.* London: Macmillan, 1968.

Toye, Richard. "'The Riddle of the Frontier': Winston Churchill, the Malakand Field Force and the Rhetoric of Imperial Expansion." *Historical Research* 84 (2011): 493–512.

Travers, Tim. "The Hidden Army: Structural Problems in the British Officer Corps, 1900–18." *Journal of Contemporary History* 17 (1982): 523–44.

———. *The Killing Ground: The British Army, the Western Front and the Emergence of Modern Warfare, 1900–18.* London: Allen & Unwin, 1987.

Tripodi, Christian. *Edge of Empire: The British Political Officer and Tribal Administration on the North-West Frontier, 1877–1947.* Farnham, UK: Ashgate, 2011.

———. "Grand Strategy and the Graveyard of Assumptions: Britain and Afghanistan, 1839–1919." *Journal of Strategic Studies* 33 (2010): 701–25.

Trousdale, William, ed. *War in Afghanistan: The Personal Diary of Major-General Sir Charles Metcalfe MacGregor.* Detroit, Mich.: Wayne State University Press, 1985.

Trustram, Myna. *Women of the Regiment: Marriage and the Victorian Army.* Cambridge: Cambridge University Press, 1984.

Tucker, Albert. "Army and Society in England, 1870–1900: A Reassessment of the Cardwell Reforms." *Journal of British Studies* 2 (1963): 110–41.

———. "The Issue of Army Reform in the Unionist Government, 1903–05." *Historical Journal* 9 (1966): 90–100.

Tulloch, Sir Alexander. *Recollections of Forty Years' Service.* Edinburgh: William Blackwood & Sons, 1903.

Turner, Sir Alfred. *Sixty Years of a Soldier's Life.* London: Methuen, 1912.

Usherwood, Paul, and Jenny Spencer-Smith. *Lady Butler, Battle Artist, 1846–1933.* Gloucester, UK: Sutton Publishing for National Army Museum, 1987.

Vandervort, Bruce. *Wars of Imperial Conquest in Africa, 1830–1914.* London: UCL Press, 1998.

Vaughan, Sir John Luther. *My Service in the Indian Army—and After.* Westminster: Archibald Constable, 1904.

Verner, Willoughby. *The Military Life of HRH George, Duke of Cambridge.* 2 vols. London: John Murray, 1905.

Vetch, R. H. *Life, Letters, and Diaries of Lieutenant-General Sir Gerald Graham VC.* Edinburgh: William Blackwood & Sons, 1901.

———. *Life of Lieutenant-General the Hon. Sir Andrew Clarke.* London: John Murray, 1905.

Vibart, Henry. *The Life of General Sir Harry Prendergast VC: The Happy Warrior.* London: Eveleigh Nash, 1914.

Villiers, Frederic. *Peaceful Personalities and Warriors Bold.* London: Harper & Brothers, 1907.

Vincent, John, ed. *A Selection from the Diaries of Edward Henry Stanley, 15th Earl of Derby, 1869–78.* Camden 5th ser., vol. 4. London: Royal Historical Society, 1994.

Walford, N. L. *Mr. Archibald Forbes and the Zulu War.* London: Tinsley, 1880.

Ward, S. G. P. "Majuba, 1881: The Diary of Colonel W. D. Bond, 58th Regiment." *Journal of the Society for Army Historical Research* 53 (1975): 87–97.

Ware, J. Redding, and R. K. Mann. *The Life and Times of Colonel Fred Burnaby.* London: Field & Tuer, n.d. [1885].

Warwick, Peter, ed. *The South African War: The Anglo-Boer War, 1899–1902.* London: Longman, 1980.

Waters, Wallscourt. *Secret and Confidential: The Experiences of a Military Attaché.* London: John Murray, 1926.

Watson, Sir Charles. *The Life of Major-General Sir Charles Wilson.* London: John Murray, 1909.

Welch, M. D. *Science and the British Officer: The Early Days of the Royal United Services Institute for Defence Studies, 1829–69.* London: RUSI Whitehall Paper No. 44, 1998.

———. *Science and the Pickelhaube: British Military Lesson Learning at the Royal United Services Institute, 1870–1900.* London: RUSI Whitehall Paper No. 47, 1999.

Wellesley, Frederick. *Recollections of a Soldier-Diplomat.* Edited by Sir Victor Wellesley. London: Hutchinson, n.d. [1947].

Wessels, André, ed. *Lord Kitchener and the War in South Africa, 1899–1902.* Stroud, UK: Sutton Publishing for the Army Records Society, 2006.

———, ed. *Lord Roberts and the War in South Africa, 1899–1902.* Stroud, UK: Sutton Publishing for the Army Records Society, 2000.

Western, Colonel J. S. E. *Reminiscences of an Indian Cavalry Officer.* London: George Allen & Unwin, 1922.

Whitaker, James, ed. *The Military Diary of Colonel W. W. C. Verner: An Account of the Nile Expeditions of 1885 and 1898.* Leeds, UK: Peregrine Books, 2003.

Whitehouse, Howard, ed. *"A Widow-Making War": The Life and Death of a British Officer in Zululand, 1879*. Nuneaton, UK: Paddy Griffith Associates, 1995.

Whybra, Julian, ed. *Studies in the Zulu War 1879*. 2 vols. Billericay, UK: Gift, 2012.

Wilcox, Craig, ed. *Recording the South African War: Journalism and Official History, 1899–1914*. London: Sir Robert Menzies Centre for Australian Studies, 1999.

———. *Red Coat Dreaming: How Colonial Australia Embraced the British Army*. Port Melbourne, Vic.: Cambridge University Press, 2009.

Wilkinson, Henry Spenser. *Thirty-five Years, 1874–1909*. London: Constable, 1930.

Wilkinson, Osborn, and Johnson Wilkinson. *The Memoirs of the Gemini Generals*. London: A. D. Innes, 1896.

Willcocks, Sir James. *From Kabul to Kumassi: Twenty-four Years of Soldiering and Sport*. London: John Murray, 1904.

———. *The Romance of Soldiering and Sport*. London: Cassell, 1925.

Williams, Rhodri. *Defending the Empire: The Conservative Party and British Defence Policy, 1899–1915*. New Haven, Conn.: Yale University Press, 1991.

Williams, W. Alister. *Commandant of the Transvaal: The Life and Career of General Sir Hugh Rowlands VC*. Wrexham, UK: Bridge Books, 2001.

Williams, Watkin. *The Life of General Sir Charles Warren*. Oxford: Basil Blackwell, 1941.

Wilson, Sir Guy Fleetwood. *Letters to Somebody: A Retrospect*. London: Cassell, 1922.

Wilson, Keith. "The Anglo-Japanese Alliance of August 1905 and the Defending of India." *Journal of Imperial and Commonwealth History* 21 (1993): 314–56.

Winrow, Andrew. "The British Regular Mounted Infantry, 1880–1913: Cavalry of Poverty or Victorian Paradigm?' D.Phil. thesis, University of Buckingham, 2014.

———. "'Bwab': A Portrait of Major-General John Palmer Brabazon." *Soldiers of the Queen* 164 (2016): 11–18.

———. "The First Cavalry Regiment to Pretoria: Lieutenant Colonel Möller and the 18th Hussars, 1899." *Soldiers of the Queen* 146 (2011): 8–13.

———. "Prejudiced or Perceptive? Lord Roberts's Relationship with the British Cavalry." *Soldiers of the Queen* 153 (2013): 8–12.

———. "Stellenbosch or Courts Martial? The Problem of Disciplining Senior Officers during the Anglo-Boer War." *Soldiers of the Queen* 158 (2014): 6–10.

———. "'The Two Do Not Go Together': The Victorian Cavalry Officer and the Turf." *Soldiers of the Queen* 136 (2009): 3–6.

Wolseley, Garnet. *The Soldier's Pocket Book*. London: Macmillan, 1886.

———. *The Story of a Soldier's Life*. 2 vols. Westminster: Archibald Constable, 1903.

Wood, Sir Elliott. *Life and Adventure in Peace and War*. London: Edward Arnold, 1924.

Wood, Sir Evelyn. *From Midshipman to Field Marshal*. 2 vols. London: Methuen, 1906.

———. *Winnowed Memories*. London: Cassell, 1918.

Wright, Thomas. *The Life of Colonel Fred Burnaby*. London: Everett, 1908.

Wright, William. *A British Lion in Zululand: Sir Garnet Wolseley in South Africa*. Stroud, UK: Amberley, 2017.

———. *A Tidy Little War: The British Invasion of Egypt, 1882*. Stroud, UK: Spellmount, 2009.

Yate, A. C. *Lieutenant Colonel John Haughton: A Hero of Tirah, a Memoir*. London: John Murray, 1900.

Yong, Tan Tai. *The Garrison State: The Military, Government and Society in Colonial Punjab, 1849–1947*. New Delhi: Sage Publications, 2005.

Younghusband, Sir George. *Forty Years a Soldier: A Volume of Recollections*. London: Herbert Jenkins, 1923.

———. *Indian Frontier Warfare*. London: Kegan, Paul, Trench, Trubner, 1898.

———. *A Soldier's Memories in Peace and War*. London: Herbert Jenkins, 1917.

Zetland, Marquess of, ed. *The Letters of Disraeli to Lady Chesterfield and Lady Bradford*. 2 vols. London: Ernest Benn, 1929.

Periodicals

Blackwood's Edinburgh Magazine
The Broad Arrow
Macmillan's Magazine
Minutes of the Proceedings of the Royal Artillery Institution
Naval and Military Gazette
The Nineteenth Century
United Service Magazine

Index

Page numbers in *italics* indicate illustrations.